BACK to the BOAT
and Beyond
True Stories from the Attic

Volume 1

By

Mary-Louise Alberta Kearney McComas

Years and years ago for many different reasons, our forefathers left their homes and countries of origin. Most of them came from England and Ireland on the paternal Kearney side of our family. My maternal Grassers came from Germany and France and on the McComas side they came from Scotland and Ireland as well as England. The families blended in the year 1962 when Charles Albert McComas, aged 24 years, married his young sweetheart, who was just a few weeks short of her 22nd birthday. She was Mary-Louise Alberta Kearney McComas, who is the writer of this book.

This is a story of the ancestry of our blended family, a family that is a blend of our many ancestral *families*. It is like a tree with many roots. Each ancestral family is a root. The story shows how and when they all came together. It tells of each of the many adversities they overcame, each of which helped to make our family the solid, firm oak tree that it now is, with many green branches that are the descendants for whom this book is written. It is a book that weaves our personal family into the social fabric of the times they lived in and how major forces like war, poverty, riches, and adventure all played an important part in forming our society of today and the family of which we are individually a part. It is my prayer that as you read these two volumes you will realize a little more about who you truly are and the family you came from. It has been an exciting adventure and journey to do the digging into the past as this process will preserve it for the future. Without this documentation it would truly be lost forever.

Dedication

I'd like to thank my husband, Charles Albert McComas, for his many years of being at my side as I started putting his side of the family history together and blending it into mine. Also, Charles, my immense gratitude I'd like to extend to you for your final proofreading of these entire two volumes. I had been working on my side for 10 years prior to his, as at the age of 12, I verbally bled my paternal Grandmother Alberta Atkinson Kearney and my paternal Great Aunt Cora Kearney Fraser for every factual bit of history of the family that they could remember. I'd like to thank them as well as both my parents, Albert Wintfield Kearney and Sylvia Mary Louise Grasser Kearney, and Charles Albert's parents, Charles McComas Jr. and Florence Elaine Holloman McComas, and his maternal grandparents, Albert Estus Holloman and Patty Brown Holloman. Thank you to all these parents and grandparents for the work they did in making this book become a reality and orchestrating it into what it is today.

Also, thank you, Aunt Dixie Nan McComas Chaney for the oral history you recorded for us, which is a legacy for the McComas family. I also want to thank my two maternal cousins Norman John Grasser and Allen Paul Grasser for their immense genealogical contribution to my maternal side of my family. Both Norman and Allen were genealogists and had a love for studying the family for years.

I'd also like to thank my five children: Anthony Joseph Bravo McComas, David Michael Bravo McComas, Selena Elizabeth McComas, Anne Mary-Louise McComas Front, and Albert Charles McComas for their patience with me and my genealogical hobby of getting all the facts down while trying to educate them "who is who" along the way! History of the past is so very important and crucial to all of us. Enjoy this read and please pass it on to future generations! My love I send to you all.

Mary-Louise Alberta Kearney McComas

November 2022

Graph Header Color CODE Guide

Blue   = **Born & Died in Europe**

Red   = **Immigrated to the United States or Canada**

Green   = **Left USA & Emigrated to Canada**

Turquoise   = **Born & Died in Canada**

Black   = **Born & Died or is Alive in United States**

Purple   = **Fought in a War & Served in the Military**

Table of Contents

A visual Guide to our Ancestral Families

Mary-Louise Kearney McComas

(Author)

Kearney & their Families = Volume 1

McComas & their Families = Volume 2

Volume 1

A. Kearney = Paternal **married S. Grasser =** Maternal

Paternal Line

J. Kearney married A. Atkinson –> Buchanan, Casey, Carson lines

G.W. Kearney married S. Smith of N.S. –> Bowser, Bell, Bird, Layton, Dungan, Yorke, Case, Vickery. Cunningham. Fones, Stanton, Hudson, Lord, Smith of R.I., Washington, Mead, Stafford, Soule of MA, Soule of N.B./N.S., West, Cooke, Latham, Walton, White, Holden, Hungerford, Eldridge, Nickerson, Phippen, Rieves, Sands lines

G. Kearney married C. Sherry line

Maternal Line

Syl. Grasser' s father was M. Grasser-> Dill lines

M. Grasser married W. Rades –> Neumann, Becker, Retzloff lines

Ste. Grasser married Fischbach –> Wagner lines

Paternal Line

Chapter 1: The Atkinsons

The Atkinson Family Line

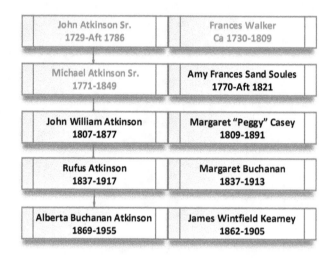

1. John Atkinson Sr. (Immigrant)

JOHN[1] ATKINSON SR.

- Born circa 1729 in Yorkshire, England.
- Married circa 1767 Frances Walker (1744-1809). They were married in Yorkshire, England.
- Arrival 1774 in Halifax, Nova Scotia aboard the ship the *Albion*.
- Died after 1785 in Southampton, Nova Scotia, Canada at the age of approx. 56.

Yorkshire is in the northern area of England. Life for John Atkinson and his wife Frances was extremely hard. John and his young family had been tenants on the Wentworth Estate, the area of the "Topcliffe Region" of Yorkshire, England. He and his wife Frances, who was pregnant and near full term with their fifth child, along with their four children (ages 1 yr. old, 3 yr. old, 4 yr. old and 6 yr. old) sailed from the port of Hull, Yorkshire, England aboard the vessel named the *Albion* in the spring of 1774. Their daughter Albion was born during the voyage and christened by the ship's captain. She was named for the ship they were aboard. They arrived in Halifax and later settled near River Hebert.

Eleven years later, at the opening of the community at Southampton, Nova Scotia, John Sr. and his wife Frances obtained a Land Grant in Cumberland County (year 1785). They were granted Lot #17 and moved to that area, where the family stayed for several generations.

Children of JOHN[1] ATKINSON and FRANCES WALKER were:

		i.	**CHARLES ATKINSON** (Immigrant) b. 1768 in Topcliffe, Yorkshire, England. It is unknown if he ever married and unknown if he had any children. Charles died in 1842 at the age of 74. Location at death is unknown.
		ii.	**MARTHA ATKINSON** (Immigrant) b. 1770 in Topcliffe, Yorkshire, England. It is unknown if she ever married and unknown if she had any children. Also unknown is where and when Martha died.

2.	iii.	**MICHAEL ATKINSON SR.** (Immigrant) b. 1771 in Topcliffe, Yorkshire, England. Michael married Amy Soule on 3 January 1797, in Southampton, Cumberland Co., Nova Scotia. Amy Soule was the daughter of Stephen & Rachael (Sand) Soule. Michael and Amy had 13 children during their marriage. Michael Atkinson died after 1849 in Southampton, Cumberland Co., Nova Scotia at the age of 78+.
	iv.	**JOHN ATKINSON JR.** (Immigrant) b. 1773 in Topcliffe, Yorkshire, England. John Jr. married Ann Brailey on May 3, 1815, in Southampton, Cumberland Co., Nova Scotia. It is unknown if they had any children during their marriage. Also unknown is when and where John Jr. died.
	v.	**ALBION ATKINSON** (Immigrant) b. 1774 born on the High Seas. It is unknown if she ever married and unknown if she had any children. Also, her death date and location are both unknown.
	vi.	**ANN ATKINSON** b. 1779 in River Hebert, Cumberland Co., Nova Scotia. It is unknown if she ever married and unknown if she had any children. Also, her death date and location are both unknown.
	vii.	**HANNAH ATKINSON** b. 1782 in River Hebert, Cumberland Co., Nova Scotia. It is unknown if she ever married and unknown if she had any children. Also, her death date and location are both unknown.
	viii.	**ELIZABETH ANN ATKINSON** b. 1783 in River Hebert, Cumberland Co., Nova Scotia. Elizabeth Ann died in 1822 at the age of 39. Location at death is unknown.
	ix.	**GEORGE ATKINSON** b. 1786 in Maccan, Southampton, Cumberland Co., Nova Scotia. George married Letitia Fulton on 23 February 1808 in Southampton, Cumberland Co., Nova Scotia. George died in 1866 at the age of 80.
	x.	**JOSEPH ATKINSON** b. 1788 in Maccan, Southampton, Cumberland Co., Nova Scotia. It is unknown if he ever married and unknown if he had any children. Also, his death date and location are both unknown.

2. Michael Atkinson Sr. (Immigrant)

MICHAEL[2] ATKINSON (*John*[1])

- Born in 1771 in Yorkshire, England.
- Arrival 1774 in Halifax, Nova Scotia aboard the ship the *Albion*.
- Married 3 January 1797 Amy Francis Sand Soule (1770-afrer 1821). They were married in Southampton, Cumberland Co., Nova Scotia. Amy was the daughter of Stephen Soule and Rachael Sand. Amy Soule b.1770 in River St. John, New Brunswick. Amy died after 1821 in Southampton, Cumberland County, Nova Scotia.
- Died 1849 in Southampton, Cumberland Co., Nova Scotia at the age of 78.

Michael Atkinson Sr. was only three years old when he, with his parents and siblings left the shores of northern England and sailed to Canada. Like his father, John Atkinson Sr., Michael later as a young man took up farming in this area of Southampton, Nova Scotia. It was here he met his beautiful bride, Amy Soule, who was the daughter of Stephen Soule and Rachael Sands. Amy was a descendant of George Soule, the Pilgrim Father. (NOTE: There is a double connection to this Pilgrim Father George Soule). For further information please see the "Kearney" and "Soules of Canada" chapters of this volume.

The Soule family is found on this Atkinson branch and on the Kearney branch as well, making Alberta Atkinson of the Atkinson line and her husband James Wintfield Kearney of the Kearney line

4

who married in 1898 connected. They are cousins! However, they did not realize this at the time of their marriage. They are the author's paternal grandparents.

Children of MICHAEL[2] ATKINSON SR. and AMY SOULE were:

	i.	**FRANCES ATKINSON** b. 3 July 1798 in Maccan, Southampton, Cumberland Co., Nova Scotia. Frances married William Cannon on 16 February 1816 in Southampton, Cumberland Co., Nova Scotia. It is unknown if they had any children. Frances died in 1857 in Southampton, Cumberland Co., Nova Scotia.
	ii.	**MARY "POLLY" ATKINSON** b. 12 April 1800 in Southampton, Cumberland Co., Nova Scotia. Mary "Polly" married twice. Husband #1 Patrick Quinn circa 1820 in Southampton, Cumberland Co., Nova Scotia. Husband #2 Thomas K. Watson. They were married circa 1830. It is unknown if she had any children during either marriage. Mary "Polly" died after 1881 at the age of approx. 81+ in Southampton, Cumberland Co., Nova Scotia.
	iii.	**DEBORAH ATKINSON** b. 1 January 1802 in Southampton, Cumberland Co., Nova Scotia. Deborah married William Roscoe circa 1820 in Southampton, Cumberland Co., Nova Scotia. Her sister Catherine married William's brother Josiah Roscoe. It is unknown if Deborah and William had any children during their marriage. Deborah died in 1871 at the age of 69 in Southampton, Cumberland Co., Nova Scotia.
	iv.	**CATHERINE ATKINSON** b. 31 October 1803 in Southampton, Cumberland Co., Nova Scotia. Catherine married Josiah Roscoe circa 1820 in Southampton, Cumberland Co., Nova Scotia. Catherine's sister Deborah married Josiah's brother, William Roscoe. It is unknown if Catherine and Josiah had any children during their marriage. Catherine died in 1871 at the age of 68 in Southampton, Cumberland Co., Nova Scotia.
	v.	**WILLIAM ATKINSON** b. 15 May 1805 in Southampton, Cumberland Co., Nova Scotia. William married Ann Smith circa 1825. It is unknown if William and Ann had any children during their marriage. William died on 1 June 1862 in Southampton, Cumberland Co., Nova Scotia, at age 57. He is buried in the Southampton Cemetery, Southampton, Cumberland Co., Nova Scotia.
3.	vi.	**JOHN WILLIAM ATKINSON** b. 24 July 1807 in Southampton, Cumberland Co., Nova Scotia. John William married Margaret Casey 19 December 1831 in Nappan, Cumberland Co., Nova Scotia. They had 11 children during their marriage. John William Atkinson died on 5 June 1877 in Westbrook, Southampton, Nova Scotia., Cumberland Co., Nova Scotia at the age of 80. He is buried in the Maccan United Baptist Church Cemetery in Maccan, Cumberland Co., Nova Scotia.
	vii.	**ELIZABETH ATKINSON** b. 31 January 1810 in Southampton, Cumberland Co., Nova Scotia. Elizabeth married Josiah Fulton on 5 July 1827 in Southampton, Cumberland Co., Nova Scotia. Elizabeth and Josiah had 7 children during their marriage. Elizabeth died after 1891 in Southampton, Cumberland Co., Nova Scotia at the age of approx. 81+.
	viii.	**AMY ATKINSON** b. 4 May 1812 in Southampton, Cumberland Co., Nova Scotia. Amy married Dennis McNamara circa 1835 in Southampton, Cumberland Co., Nova Scotia. It is unknown if they had any children during their marriage. Amy

		Atkinson McNamara died in 1874 at the age of 42 in Southampton, Cumberland Co., Nova Scotia.
	ix.	**ALBION ATKINSON** b. 26 August 1815 in Southampton, Cumberland Co., Nova Scotia. Albion married Hiram S. Brown circa 1830 in Southampton, Cumberland Co., Nova Scotia. Hiram S. Brown was the son of Elijah & Henrietta (Cannon) Brown. It is unknown if they had any children during their marriage. Albion Atkinson died on 27 May 1874 in Southampton, Cumberland Co., Nova Scotia at the age of 59.
	x.	**NAOMI ATKINSON** b. 25 August 1817 in Southampton, Cumberland Co., Nova Scotia. Naomi married John Casey who was the son of Jeremiah Casey and _____. They were married circa 1840 in Southampton, Cumberland Co., Nova Scotia. Naomi's brother Michael "John" Atkinson married Margaret Casey who was the sister of Naomi's husband John Casey. (See also the Casey chapter). Naomi Atkinson Casey died before 1861 in Southampton, Nova Scotia. Age approx. 44.
	xi.	**RUTH ATKINSON** b. 23 July 1819 in Southampton, Cumberland Co., Nova Scotia. Ruth married Oliver Blair circa 1840 in Southampton, Cumberland Co., Nova Scotia. It is unknown if Ruth and Oliver had any children during their marriage. Ruth died in 1850 in Maccan, Southampton, Nova Scotia at the age of 31.
	xii.	**NANCY ATKINSON** b. 1820 in Southampton, Cumberland Co., Nova Scotia. Nancy married Robert Fullerton on 9 Feb 1847 in Southampton, Cumberland Co., Nova Scotia. It is unknown if Nancy and Robert had any children during their marriage. Also, it is unknown as to when and where Nancy died.
	xiii.	**MICHAEL ATKINSON JR.** b. 28 September 1821 in Southampton, Cumberland Co., Nova Scotia Michael Jr. married Charlotte Taylor on 7 October 1845 in Southampton, Cumberland Co., Nova Scotia. It is unknown if Michael and Charlotte had any children. Michael Jr. died in 1894 in Maccan, Southampton, Nova Scotia at the age of 73.

3. John William Atkinson

JOHN WILLIAM [3] ATKINSON (Michael [2] *John*[1])

- Born 24 July 1807 in Southampton, Cumberland County, Nova Scotia, Canada.
- Military 10 May 1827.
- Married 19 December 1831 Margaret Casey (1809-1891). They were married in Nappan, Cumberland Co., Nova Scotia. Margaret was the daughter of Jeremiah Casey and his wife's name is unknown.
- Died 5 June 1877 in Maccan, Cumberland Co., Nova Scotia at age 80.
- Buried Maccan United Baptist Church Cemetery, Maccan, Cumberland Co., Nova Scotia.

Note: Some sources state his name was John William Atkinson, yet other sources state it was Michael "John" Atkinson. However, he went by his name of "John" Atkinson.

Tombstone of John William Atkinson
24 July 1807–5 June 1877
Maccan United Baptist Church Cemetery in Maccan, Cumberland Co., Nova Scotia.

Children of John William[3] Atkinson and Margaret Casey were:

	i.	**MARGARET ATKINSON** b. 1832 in Southampton, Cumberland Co., Nova Scotia. It is unknown if she ever married and unknown if any children were born to her. Also, unknown as to when and where she died.
	ii.	**TWIN: ELIZABETH ATKINSON** b. 1833 in Southampton, Cumberland Co., Nova Scotia. Elizabeth married Amos Atkinson (1824-1899) in 1854 in Southampton, Cumberland Co., Nova Scotia. Elizabeth Atkinson married her cousin Amos, who was the son of John Jr. and Ann Brailey Atkinson. Elizabeth and Amos had 7 children during their marriage. Elizabeth died on 25 March 1876 in Southampton, Cumberland Co., Nova Scotia at the age of 43.
	iii.	**TWIN: LYDIA ATKINSON** b. 1833 in Southampton, Cumberland Co., Nova Scotia. Lydia married Stephen Cannon circa 1850 in Southampton, Cumberland Co., Nova Scotia. Lydia Atkinson's father, Michael "John" Atkinson, was a brother to Stephen Cannon's mother, Frances (Atkinson) Cannon who was his sister. Frances Atkinson had married William Cannon. Therefore, Lydia and her husband, Stephen were first cousins. Lydia died in 1922 at the age of 89 in Southampton, Cumberland Co., Nova Scotia.
	iv.	**AMY AMELIA ATKINSON** b. 1835 in Southampton, Cumberland Co., Nova Scotia. Amy Amelia married James Alexander Fullerton. They were married circa 1850 in Southampton, Cumberland Co., Nova Scotia. It is unknown if Amy and James had any children. Amy Amelia died on 1 June 1913 at age 78. Her location at death is unknown.
4.	v.	**RUFUS S. ATKINSON** b. 8 November 1837 in Southampton, Cumberland Co., Nova Scotia. Rufus married Margaret Buchanan on 5 June 1865 in Hopewell, Albert Co., New Brunswick. Margaret Buchanan was the daughter of John Buchanan Sr. and Margaret Jane Carson. Rufus S. and Margaret had 10 children during their marriage. Rufus S. died on 14 September 1917 at the age of 79 in

		Westbrook, Southampton, Nova Scotia. He is buried in the Westbrook Memorial Gardens Cemetery in Westbrook Cumberland Co., Nova Scotia.
	vi.	**STEPHEN WALKER ATKINSON** b. 20 March 1841 in Clairmont, Cumberland Co., Nova Scotia. Stephen Walker married twice: 1st Wife Eunice Eleanor Mills (1850-1888). They married in 1869 and had 2 children. 2nd Wife Jennie Louise Knodell (1868-1940). They married in 1888 and had 6 children during their marriage. Stephen Walker died 27 March 1904 at the age of 63 in Springhill, Nova Scotia. He is buried in the Hillside Cemetery in Springhill, Cumberland Co., Nova Scotia.
	vii.	**TWIN: GEORGE ALFRED ATKINSON** b. 10 March 1843 in Southampton, Cumberland Co., Nova Scotia. George Alfred married Miriam Mills circa 1873. They had 4 children during their marriage. George Alfred died in 1904 at the age of 61. He is buried in the Oxford Pine Grove Cemetery in Oxford, Cumberland Co., Nova Scotia.
	viii.	**TWIN: FRANCIS M. ATKINSON** b. 10 March 1843 in Southampton, Cumberland Co., Nova Scotia. It is unknown if Francis M. ever married and had any children. Also unknown is when and where Francis died.
	ix.	**SARAH LAVENIA ATKINSON** b. 1845 in Southampton, Cumberland Co., Nova Scotia. Sarah Lavenia married James McAloney (1829-1909). They were married circa 1865 in Southampton, Cumberland Co., Nova Scotia. It is unknown how many children they had. Lavenia died 10 November 1942 at the age of 97.
	x.	**CATHERINE "KATEY" ATKINSON** b. circa 1850 in Southampton, Cumberland Co., Nova Scotia. Catherine married ____Roscoe circa 1870. It is unknown if they had any children. Also unknown is when and where Catherine died.
	xi.	**E. HUGH ATKINSON** b. 1856 in Southampton, Cumberland Co., Nova Scotia. E. Hugh died 1 February 1859 in Southampton, Cumberland Co., Nova Scotia at the age of 3 years.

4. Rufus S. Atkinson

Rufus S.[4] Atkinson (John[3], Michael[2], John[1])

- Born 8 November 1837 in Southampton, Cumberland Co., Nova Scotia.
- Married 5 June 1865 Margaret Buchanan in Hopewell, Albert Co., New Brunswick. Margaret was the daughter of John Buchanan Sr. and Margaret Carson.
- Died 1 September 1917 in Westbrook, Southampton, Cumberland Co., Nova Scotia, age 79 years.
- Buried: Westbrook Cemetery, Southampton, Cumberland Co., Nova Scotia.

Rufus Atkinson was a great farmer and had a large farm in Southampton, Nova Scotia. He and his wife Margaret took in their little granddaughter 2-year-old "Little Margaret" and raised her for several years. See the full story in the following pages described in the section on their daughter Alberta.

Children of Rufus[4] Atkinson and Margaret Buchanan were:

	i.	**MARY EMMA ATKINSON** b. 18 September 1866 in Westbrook, Southampton, Cumberland Co., Nova Scotia. Mary Emma died on 20 December 1876 in Westbrook, Southampton, Cumberland Co. Nova Scotia, at age 10. She is buried in the Westbrook Memorial Gardens Cemetery, Southampton, Cumberland Co., Nova Scotia.

	ii.	**EUGENE CARSON ATKINSON.** b. 27 June 1868 in Westbrook, Southampton, Cumberland Co., Nova Scotia. Eugene Carson married twice: Wife #1 Augretta Grace Harrington on 15 September 1913 in Westbrook, Southampton, Cumberland Co., Nova Scotia. They were divorced. Wife #2 Lorenda Porter Leary (1891-1988). They were married on 30 June 1926 in Parrsboro, Nova Scotia. It is unknown if Eugene had any children from either marriage. Eugene Carson died 27 October 1934 at the age of 66 in Westbrook, Southampton, Cumberland Co., Nova Scotia. He is buried in the Westbrook Memorial Gardens Cemetery, Southampton, Cumberland Co., Nova Scotia.
5.	iii.	**ALBERTA BUCHANAN ATKINSON** b. 27 November 1869 in Southampton, Cumberland Co., Nova Scotia. Alberta married James Wintfield Kearney. James Wintfield (1862-1905) was the son of George W. Kearney and his wife Salina Smith. Alberta and James were married on 28 December 1898 in Southampton, Nova Scotia, Alberta, and James had 4 children during their marriage. James died suddenly with pneumonia in April 1905, leaving Alberta with four small children (all under 6 years of age). It was a difficult time! (See her story later in this chapter.) Alberta Buchanan died on 16 November 1955 in Winchester, Massachusetts at the age of almost 86 years. She is buried in the Wildwood Cemetery in Winchester, Massachusetts in the United States.
	iv.	**ANNIE FLORENCE ATKINSON** b.17 February 1871 in Westbrook, Southampton, Cumberland Co., Nova Scotia. Anne Florence married twice: 1st Husband Cyrus Herbert Etter (1850-1915). Anne Florence and Cyrus Herbert were married on 25 April 1901. There were no children born during either of her two marriages. Anne's 2nd Husband was Herbert Lawrence Newcomb (1871-1949). Anne Florence and Herbert Lawrence were married in 1921 in Massachusetts. Anne Florence died 22 August 1954 in Cambridge, Middlesex Co., Massachusetts at age 83. She is buried in the South Wellfleet Cemetery Route #6, Wellfleet, Barnstable Co., Massachusetts alongside her second husband Herbert Lawrence Newcomb.
	v.	**WILLIAM ERNEST ATKINSON** b. 19 July 1873 in Westbrook, Southampton, Cumberland Co., Nova Scotia. He never married or had any children. William Ernest died on 17 March 1909 at age 35 in Boston, Suffolk Co., Massachusetts. His remains were shipped back to Nova Scotia. He is buried in the Westbrook Cemetery, Southampton, Cumberland Co., Nova Scotia.*
	vi.	**AINSLEY ROBERT ATKINSON** b. 25 May 1874 in Westbrook, Southampton, Cumberland Co., Nova Scotia. Ainsley married Alfreda Jane Whalen (1880-1953). They were married on 8 October 1898. Ainsley and Alfreda had 4 children during their marriage. Robert Ainsley died in 1948 in Dorchester, Suffolk Co., Massachusetts at the age of 74. He is buried in the Mount Auburn Cemetery in Cambridge, Middlesex Co., Massachusetts.
	vii.	**EUDELLA JANE "Jennie" ATKINSON** b.12 May 1875 in Westbrook, Southampton, Cumberland Co., Nova Scotia. Eudella Jane married George Alexander Gray on 11 June 1913. After Eudella Jane's mother and Eudella Jane's sister both died, Eudella Jane returned to Parrsboro and to her family of origin for the funeral. With her sister Alberta Atkinson Kearney's permission, she took Alberta's daughter Margaret Kearney back to Los Angles, California and raised her as her own daughter. Eudella Jane and her husband George also had 2 children shortly thereafter, a son named Russell Gray (1914-2005) and several years later a daughter Lucille Gray (1916-1935). Eudella Jane died 21 December 1933 at the age of 58 in Norwalk, Los Angeles

		Co., California. She is buried in the Woodlawn Cemetery in Santa Monica, Los Angeles, California.
	viii.	**MAUDE MARGARET ATKINSON** b. 7 April 1878 in Westbrook, Southampton, Cumberland Co., Nova Scotia. Maude Margaret married Daniel Webster McAloney (1878-1962). They were married on 15 September 1913 in Westbrook, Southampton, Cumberland Co., Nova Scotia. Maude Margaret died during a miscarriage on 10 November 1913 in Westbrook, Cumberland Co., Nova Scotia, at age 35. She is buried along with the miscarriage (small baby) in the Westbrook Memorial Gardens Cemetery in Southampton, Cumberland Co., Nova Scotia.
	ix.	**JOHN CRAIG ATKINSON** b. 21 July 1881 in Westbrook, Southampton, Cumberland Co., Nova Scotia. John Craig went missing (circa 1900) when he went on a lumber camping trip in northern Canada. He was missing for many years. Then later he showed up! It is unknown if he ever married or if he had any children. He died on 29 June 1954 aged 72 in Prince Rupert, Skeena-Queen Charlotte Reginal District, British Columbia, Canada. He is buried in the Fairview Cemetery in Prince Rupert, British Columbia, Canada.
	x.	**FREDERICK Rufus ATKINSON** b. 6 December 1882 in Westbrook, Southampton, Cumberland Co., Nova Scotia. Frederick Rufus married Maybelle Claire Brockway Deters (1884-1970). They were married in 1920. It is unknown if they had any children during their marriage. Fred died 22 December 1940 at the age of 58 in Proviso Township, Cook Co., Illinois. He is buried in the Evergreen Cemetery and Mausoleum in the (Chicago area), Everton Park, Cook Co., Illinois.

*Truro Daily Newspaper (Truro, Massachusetts - Cape Cod) March 30, 1909
Page 2 included the following Obituary:

DEATH OF WILLIAM ATKINSON OF SOUTHAMPTON, CUMB. CO.

The death occurred recently in Boston, Mass., of William Atkinson, second son of Rufus Atkinson, of Southampton, Cumb. Co. Mr. Atkinson has been in failing health for some time and gradually grew worse till finally he was removed to the hospital, where his death took place a week later. Deceased he was in the thirty-sixth year of his age and was highly respected by all who knew him. Besides a father and mother, he leaves to mourn four brothers and four sisters. The brothers are Ainsley, of Cambridge, Mass., John of British Columbia, and E. C. Atkinson, of Southampton. One sister, Mrs. Etter, resides in Roxbury, Mass. The others are Mrs. Alberta *Marney*, (my italics see below) * of Parrsboro, Miss Jennie, teacher at Halfway River, and Miss Maud at home.

The remains were brought to Southampton for burial, where funeral services were conducted from his home by Rev. Mr. McLaren. Interment took place in the Westbrook Cemetery.

Please note:
- Marney – This is a newspaper printed mistake and should read "Kearney."
- It says four brothers, but only lists three (missing Frederick). He had six sisters; two died early. By elimination I get Mrs. Etter as Annie Florence Etter, later by 2nd marriage Annie Newcomb.

5. Alberta Buchanan Atkinson

Alberta Buchanan[5] Atkinson (Rufus[4], John[3], Michael[2], John[1])

- Born 27 November 1869 in Southampton, Cumberland Co., Nova Scotia.
- Married 28 December 1898 James Wintfield Kearney in Southampton, Cumberland Co., Nova Scotia. James Wintfield (1862-1905) was the son of George W. Kearney and Salina Smith.
- Died 16 November 1955 in Winchester, Middlesex Co., Massachusetts, at age 85.
- Buried Wildwood Cemetery, Winchester, Middlesex Co., Massachusetts.

Alberta was a seamstress and a fabulous knitter! She was my paternal grandmother and I feel she was a hero of our family! She not only was a survivor of her times, but she sustained and brought her family through a difficult period of their lives. Alberta was 8 weeks pregnant with her fourth child when suddenly her world was absolutely turned upside down! Her husband James Wintfield Kearney, was a professional painter who not only painted the outsides of houses but also did amazing work on their interiors and was especially known throughout Parrsboro and beyond for his beautiful and creative scroll work in ceiling paintings. But one cold windy day, in late March 1905, he came home with a bad cold and went to bed. Despite Alberta's care and the love of his dear young family — Albert aged 6 years, Anne age 4 years, Margaret age 2 years and his unborn daughter later known as Freda —James never arose from his sick bed. His cold developed into pneumonia.

Penicillin and other antibiotics had not yet been invented. James died just a week later 5 April 1905. They were not wealthy but had saved up a little money and Alberta spent it on a tombstone where she sadly buried her dear husband in the Four Corners Cemetery in Parrsboro, Nova Scotia. Now the only things she had were her deep abiding faith, her little family, and a gift of knowledge of how to sew and how to knit. She used these skills along with her faith to provide for her family during these hard difficult years.

Overwhelmed at times, with two babies plus two school-age children, she made an extremely hard decision. Her mother and dad, who lived 10 miles down the road, offered to take her two-year-old "Little Margaret," who was still in diapers, and they kindly offered to care for her and raise her. Alberta struggled hard with this decision but in the long run she felt it was better for "Little Margaret" to have a better life with her grandmother and grandfather who lived on a big farm. Life would be more exciting for "Little Margaret" she rationalized, but it was an extremely hard, hard decision!

"Little Margaret" enjoyed the farm life with animals and her grandparents' attention, but they were getting older. Her Aunt Maude (Margaret Maude), living also at home on the farm, helped care for "Little Margaret." Suddenly, there was much excitement in the family as Aunt Maude was getting married! Also, Maude found out that she was going to have a baby! Well, excitement and delight in the household turned into a volcanic disaster! "Little Margaret's" grandmother, Margaret, died in July. In September Aunt Maude got married. Then in November Aunt Maude had a miscarriage and she and the baby both died. Grandpa Rufus was getting old and could now no longer manage the farm and raising "Little Margaret." Her mother Alberta was still trying to make ends meet and was in overwhelm!

Meanwhile Alberta's father-in-law, George W. Kearney (a widower), who had moved into her home a few years earlier, now also died. He died in Alberta's home. Now that Alberta's mother had died as well as her sister Maude, Alberta could not take in her own little daughter. A difficult time. Let us look at what happened in that very difficult year, 1913.

11

11 June 1913 – Eudella Jane "Aunt Jennie" (Alberta's sister) married George Gray a wealthy man in California. Aunt Jennie became pregnant shortly after her wedding.

30 July 1913 – Margaret Buchannan Atkinson (Alberta's mother) died (suicide) at age 76 years!

25 August 1913 – George W. Kearney (Alberta's elderly father-in-law who had been living with Alberta and her children), died at the age of 76 years in Alberta's home.

15 September 1913 – Margaret "Maude" Atkinson (Alberta's sister) married Daniel McAloney.

15 September 1913 – Eugene Carson Atkinson (Alberta's brother) married Augretta Grace Harrington.

10 November 1913 – Margaret "Maude" Atkinson McAloney (recently married) had a miscarriage (2 months pregnant) and also had "Brain Fever." She and the baby both died! "Maude" had been taking care of "Little Margaret" after Margaret Grandmother's 's death just a few months earlier.

15 November 1913 – Eudella Jane Atkinson Gray (Aunt Jennie) arrived in Southampton, Nova Scotia for her sister Mabel's funeral and the decision was made for Little Margaret to go with Aunt Jennie to California to live on a peach farm in Los Angles where Aunt Jennie and Uncle George Gray lived. There was really no one able to take care of little Margaret now!

Alberta's sister Aunt Eudella Jane (Aunt Jennie) had been a schoolteacher in western Canada. She had married a very wealthy man in California, a George Gray who owned a peach farm in the Los Angeles area of California. "Aunt Jennie came home for her sister's funeral and saw that "Little Margaret," who was then 11 years old, was in in need of a home. Grandmother Margaret had been raising Little Margaret but when she died, Mabel took over Little Margaret's care. Now Maude had died, and Alberta (Little Margaret's mother) was completely overwhelmed. Rufus (Little Margaret's grandfather) was also in overwhelm! Their home was in complete discord! Aunt Jennie took Little Margaret back home with her to Los Angeles, California. There, Little Margaret grew up and only saw her biological mother Alberta again just a few times in her life, due to the distance across the country, World War II going on, and Alberta's difficult financial situation. Little Margaret was definitely traumatized and kept her feelings inside for years and was securely guarded!

Alberta continued to struggle; she wanted a good education and good jobs for her children. She decided in 1918 to leave her country, Canada, and head for the United States as her sister Annie and her three brothers Fred, Ainsley and William had done years before her. She took her daughters Anne and Freda with her and left her son Albert to "tie up loose ends" in Canada for a year and then he too followed in 1919 their path to Boston. Alberta rented a rooming house at 53 Oxford Street, Cambridge, Massachusetts and there took in boarders to raise income. She ran the boarding house for twenty years, 1918–1938. When Albert followed and left Nova Scotia in 1919, he lived with his mother in the boarding house in Cambridge until he married in 1938. (See more on Albert's story in the Kearney chapter.)

Both Alberta's daughters, Anne and Freda, had now left their mother's boarding house. Anne had married Dr. Sandford Hiram Moses, and Freda, who was single, moved in with Anne and Sandford. Albert was now married in 1938, and this left Alberta all alone She decided to give up the boarding house. It was decided that she would move in with Albert and his new bride, Sylvia.

Two years later. when Albert and Sylvia started a family of their own, they had two children. Alberta again was helpful to her family as she cared for my sister Diane and me (Mary-Louise) while our mother Sylvia was our dad Albert's right hand at his work. Our Grandmother Alberta ("Grandma

Bertie") made lunches and cared for us, deeply loving us as we grew up. She was very patient with us. I had a desire to be a nurse when I grew up (which I later did). At the young age of 7, I asked Santa for a nurses' kit and he graciously delivered my desired package. I was so excited! My patient each day was Grandma Bertie. I would check her heart every day with my new stethoscope. When I felt she needed a pill, I would put a "Rice Krispies" cereal kernel in a cup and serve her this medicine. Another memory I have is she and I playing "Store" together. She would always be my customer and I was always the store clerk. We used paper money and imitation coins. To gather the goods, she had marked on her list, I would climb up on a chair and get them down from my mother's pantry cupboard. Then I would add them up using my toy cash register to store Grandma Bertie's imitation money.

Another memory: one cold wintery day, I remember I came home for lunch and was crying because I had lost one of my mittens which Grandma Bertie had made. She wiped away my tears and sent me back to school after feeding me a delicious lunch and telling me not to worry. When I returned home from school that very day, three hours later, waiting for me was a matching mitten which she had knitted while I was back at school. That was my Grandma Bertie! She took really good care of Diane and me as we grew up despite a difficult and challenging role to play so as to not collide with her daughter-in-law Sylvia in the kitchen over issues of helping to raise Sylvia and Albert's two daughters. Yet Grandma Bertie always handled things pretty well.

I remember every Friday she would bake homemade rolls using yeast, placing the bread dough containing the yeast over the radiator to make the bread rise! Coming home from school on Fridays was a special treat to enter the house to the smell of freshly baked rolls.

Grandma Bertie would go over to Winchester to her daughter Anne's home where she visited with her other grandchildren Libbie and Hiram. As she grew older, Alberta shared her role of taking care of Diane and myself with her sister, our Aunt Annie, who needed a home after her husband Uncle Herbert had died.

Aunt Annie and Uncle Herbert lived in Wellfleet, Massachusetts on Cape Cod. Diane and I would spend two weeks with them each summer. I remember the hill I would sit on in their front yard in Wellfleet Center and with pencil and paper I would keep track of all the different license plates I saw go by. I had a dream in my mind of visiting each of the states which those license plates represented. That was the beginning of my yearning for travel! Uncle Herbert managed a jelly store in the barn behind their home. He had many customers from all over the country. People loved his Cape Cod Jelly! When Uncle Herbert died of prostate cancer, Aunt Annie was devastated! She tried living by herself for a while but became too lonely, so it was decided that she would move in with us and Grandma Bertie would move to Winchester to be with her daughters Anne, Freda, and Anne's husband Uncle Dr. Sanford.

Aunt Annie died at our home in 1954 via suicide (just like her mother had years ago)! I was 14 years old when this happened. Grandma Bertie died one year later of a major heart attack, in 1955. Grandma Bertie died at the age of 85 years old, a few weeks short of turning 86. I was 15 years old. I was so privileged to have known Grandma Bertie intimately and loved her dearly! She has verbally given me much family genealogical information and answered so many questions about our family, which I kept asking! However, she hated seeing pictures of herself and of her loved ones who had died. It was just too painful for her! Their memories were too hard to bear so burning the pictures was like putting them in a permanent past! However, Alberta had an extraordinarily strong faith and was a model Christian. She was active in her faith and attended the Harvard Epworth Methodist Church where Charles Albert and I were later married. I remember Grandma Bertie sewing bandages for the wounded soldiers of WWII. She led a faithful Christian servanthood life for me to follow, not only to trust our Lord Jesus but also to walk and act in her Christian faith.

Children of ALBERTA BUCHANAN[5] ATKINSON and JAMES WINTFIELD KEARNEY are documented in the Kearney chapter.

Source Citations for this Chapter

Verbal family knowledge from Cora Kearney Fraser and Albert Wintfield Kearney.

Loose papers & Letters from Genealogist Marion Kyle of Parrsboro, Nova Scotia Canada.

History of West Brook and Halfway River written for the Women's' Institute, 1960.

Loose papers of Odelite Juvelis of Swampscott, Massachusetts, 1989.

The Chignecto Project: Birth Records of Cumberland Co., Nova Scotia, Canada.

Marriage Records of Cumberland Co., Nova Scotia, Canada.

Cemetery Records of Cumberland Co. Nova Scotia, Canada.

Roots Web: Immigrant Ships, Transcribers Guild, 2002.

Census Records of Cumberland Co., Nova Scotia, Canada, 1871, 1881, 1901.

Ottawa House By-the-Sea Genealogical Museum, Parrsboro, Nova Scotia, Canada.

Research work of Elizabeth Moses Merrow of Bloomfield, Connecticut.

Ancestry.com Research Records.

Familysearch.com Records of the Latter-Day Saints.

Massachusetts Death Index and Findagrave.com

Obituary - Truro Daily Newspaper (Truro, Massachusetts - Cape Cod) March 30, 1909.

https://www.findagrave.com

Chapter 2: The Bells

The Bell Family Line

Thomas Bell Sr. Ca 1617-1655		Ann Culver 1620-Aft. 1656	
Deborah Bell **1650-Aft 1694**		**James Yorke II** **1648-1676**	

1. Thomas Bell Sr. (Immigrant)

THOMAS[1] BELL SR.

- Born circa 1617 in England.
- Married circa 1637 Ann Culver (1620-after 1656). Thomas Sr. and Ann were married in Boston, Suffolk Co., Massachusetts.
- Died 7 June 1655 in Boston, Suffolk Co., Massachusetts.

Thomas Bell Sr. (Immigrant) came to the colonies circa 1630. He married Ann Culver who was born in 1620 in Dedham, Essex, England and came to the Bay State colonies with her parents when she was about 10 years old. Ann (Culver) Bell was the daughter of Edward Culver (Immigrant). Edward was born circa 1600 in Dedham, Essex, England. He immigrated to the Bay State colonies with his wife Alis (Luicone) Culver and their 10-year-old daughter, Ann Culver (later Bell). Ann's mother Alis (Luicone) Culver was born in 1603 in Dedham, Essex, England. Alis died in 1638 in Dedham, Norfolk Co., Massachusetts. Ann's father Edward Culver (Immigrant) died in Mystic, New London, Connecticut on 19 September 1685.

Thomas Bell Sr. (Immigrant) and his wife Ann (Culver) Bell had nine children. They were all born in Boston, Suffolk Co., Massachusetts. The oldest three children all died at birth including a set of twins (their firstborn). The fourth child lived to be 13 years old. Their next to the youngest was a daughter who they named Moremercy Bell and nicknamed her "Mercy." She was born in the cold winter month of January and only lived three days. Their youngest child, a son, only lived one month in November of 1653. Their youngest daughter Deborah (our direct ancestor) was only 4 years old when her father, Thomas, died in 1655. Out of the 9 children, only three survived to adulthood. Deborah's mother Ann (Culver) Bell, after her first husband Thomas Bell Sr. (who gave her nine children) had died, went on and remarried but had no further children. The following year, after Thomas Sr. died in 1656, she married William Mullins Jr. (b.1596-1672) in 1657. Ann (Culver) Bell Mullins died after 1696. Her second husband William Mullins JR. had died in 1672. William Mullins Jr. had been the son of William Mullins Sr., who had been a passenger on the 1620 *Mayflower* ship.

Thomas Bell Sr. had been the Executioner for Boston in the early years of 1637-1653. He was granted land for carrying out his duties and obtained a lot of land in payment. It was noted that he was granted a "great lott at the mount" which later proved to be at Mt. Wollaston in Braintree, Massachusetts. He "obtained this land for three heads." (Author's comment: Gruesome to think about!) Thomas Bell Sr.'s main house lot was on the south side of Summer Street in Boston, Massachusetts, close to its modern intersection of Hawley Street and near Wheeler's Pond a short distance further to the south. Wheeler's Pond was the watering place which no longer exists. He was a neighbor of the famous Mary Dyer of Boston. Mary was executed in Boston in 1660, a period of 5 years after Thomas Bell Sr. had died.

Children of THOMAS[1] BELL SR. and ANN CULVER were:

	i.	**TWIN: THOMAS HODGSON I BELL** b. 24 JunE 1638 in Boston, Suffolk Co., Massachusetts. Thomas Hodgson, I died at birth on 24 June 1638 in Boston, Suffolk, Co., Massachusetts.
	ii.	**TWIN: JOHN BELL** b. 24 June 1638 in Boston, Suffolk Co., Massachusetts. John died at birth on 24 June 1638 in Boston, Suffolk Co., Massachusetts.
	iii.	**JOAN Bell** b. 4 March 1640 in Boston, Suffolk Co., Massachusetts. Joan died at birth on 4 March 1640 in Boston, Suffolk Co., Massachusetts.
	iv.	**TABITHA Bell** b. 24 March 1641 in Boston, Suffolk Co., Massachusetts. She died at the age of 13 years old on 29 February 1654.
	v.	**THOMAS HODGSON II BELL** b. 3 August 1642 in Boston, Suffolk Co., Massachusetts. It is unknown if he ever married and if he had any children. He died in 1695 at the age of 53 in Stonington, New London Co., Connecticut. **
	vi.	**HOPESTILL BELL** b. July 1644 in Boston, Suffolk Co., Massachusetts. She married Samuel Austins in 1669 in Andover, Essex Co., Massachusetts. It is unknown if they had any children during this marriage. Hopestill died on 28 November 1669 at the age of 25.
	vii.	**MOREMERCY BELL** b. 14 January 1647 in Boston, Suffolk Co., Massachusetts died at age 3 days old on 17 January 1647 in Boston, Suffolk Co., Massachusetts.
2.	viii.	**DEBORAH BELL** b. 29 November 1650 in Boston, Suffolk Co., Massachusetts. She married Husband #1 James Yorke II on 19 January 1669. Deborah and James II had 4 children during their marriage. Husband #2 Henry Eliot Sr. Deborah and Henry were married on 12 March 1679. Deborah and Henry Sr. had 8 children during their marriage. Deborah died after 1720 in Stonington, New London Co., Connecticut at approx. age 70.
	ix.	**JOSEPH BELL** b. 1 November 1653 in Boston, Suffolk Co, Massachusetts. Joseph died at on 29 November 1653 in Boston, Suffolk Co., Massachusetts at age of less than 1 month old.

** It was noted in a diary of Thomas Minor that on 22 August 1674 this Thomas Bell of Stonington was a "Taylor" (tailor), and it took him 3 days to make a "Wasket" (Waistcoat) for Thomas Minor.

2. Deborah Bell

DEBORAH^2 BELL (*Thomas^1*)

- Born 29 November 1650 in Boston, Suffolk Co., Massachusetts.
- Married 19 January 1669 Husband #1 James Yorke II, son of James Yorke I and Johannah ____, in Stonington, New London Co., Connecticut.
- Married 12 March 1679 Husband #2 Henry Eliot Sr. in Stonington, New London Co., Connecticut.
- Died after 1720 in Stonington, New London Co., Connecticut at the age of at least 70 years.

Deborah and her father, Thomas Bell Sr. **(Immigrant)** and their families, as well as Deborah's first husband James York II and their children, all knew well and interacted with the famous Indian Interpreter Thomas Stanton who also lived in Stonington, Connecticut around the same time. It is noted in the history of Stonington, Connecticut that Deborah and her husband James York II and later second husband William Mullins Jr., with her family, all lived on Summer Street in that town. It is also noted that her mother, Anne (Culver) Bell Mullins also lived on Summer Street in Stonington, Connecticut. They all owned parcels of land on that street. For further details and information on the Stanton family see the Stanton chapter.

Deborah's brother Thomas Bell and his brother-in-law, James York II, had become "Freemen of Stonington." They were among the eight men presented on 17 May 1673 the honor of being made "Freemen of Stonington". According to the Merriam-Webster's Dictionary, "freemen" are men who are enjoying civil and political liberty. They have the full rights of being a citizen. This term "freemen" used in the 1600's is not to be confused with the later term used in the Masonic Lodge Order, which did not form until the 1700s. Deborah remarried after her first husband James Yorke II died 26 October 1676 at the age of 28. Deborah and James Yorke II had 4 children from their marriage, three sons and a daughter.

Children of DEBORAH^2 BELL and JAMES YORKE II are documented in the Yorke chapter.

Deborah's second marriage was 12 March 1679 when she married Henry Eliot Sr. They had 8 children by this marriage. Deborah Bell Eliot died after 1720 in Stonington, New London Co., Connecticut at the age of 70.

Children of DEBORAH^2 BELL and HENRY ELIOT SR. were:

	i.	**DEBORAH ELIOT** b. 11 April 1680 in Stonington, New London Co., Connecticut.
	ii.	**ANNA ELIOT** b. 28 November 1681 in Stonington, New London Co., Connecticut.
	iii.	**HOPESTILL ELIOT** b. 16 August 1684 in Stonington, New London Co., Connecticut.
	iv.	**MARY ELIOT** b. 22 May 1687 in Stonington, New London Co., Connecticut. Mary married William Bentley circa 1707 in Stonington, New London Co., Connecticut.
	v.	**DOROTHY ELIOT** b. 15 April 1688 in Stonington, New London Co., Connecticut.
	vi.	**ELIZABETH ELIOT** b. 3 August 1690 in Stonington, New London Co., Connecticut.

	vii.	**HENRY ELIOT JR.** b. 16 April 1693 in Stonington, New London Co., Connecticut.
	viii.	**JOSEPH ELIOT** b. 21 October 1694 in Stonington, New London Co., Connecticut.

Source Citations for this Chapter

Thomas Bell, Boston Executioner and his son Thomas Bell of Stonington, Connecticut by Gale Ion Harris, FASG.

Diary of Thomas Minor (date 22 August 1674), page 124, Stonington, Connecticut Library.

The New England Historical and Genealogical Register, 1847-2011, Volume 9 (1855).

Stonington, New London Co., Connecticut Vital Records from Barbour, 1668-1852.

Chapter 3: The Birds

The Bird Family Line

Robert Bird Ca 1555-Aft 1588	Amy ____ Ca 1555- ____
Dorothy Bird 1588-1675	Thomas Lord Sr. 1585-1645

1. Robert Bird

ROBERT[1] BIRD

- Born circa 1555 in Towcester, Northton Co. England.
- Married circa 1585 Amy ____ in Towcester, Northton Co. England.
- Died date unknown at this time.

Children of ROBERT[1] BIRD and AMY____ were:

2.	i.	**DOROTHY BIRD** (Immigrant) b. 25 May 1588 in St. Laurence Church, Towcester, Northton Co., England. Dorothy married Thomas Lord Sr. (1585-1644). They were married on 23 February 1610 near Towcester, Peterborough, Northton Co., England. Thomas Lord Sr. was the son of Richard Thomas Lord Sr. and Joan (surname unknown) of Towcester, England. Dorothy Bird and Thomas Lord Sr. had 18 children during their marriage. They immigrated to America and arrived in Boston, Massachusetts Bay Colony in 1636. Dorothy died in 1675 in Hartford, Hartford Co. Connecticut at the age of 87.

2. Dorothy Bird (Immigrant)

DOROTHY[2] BIRD (*Robert*[1])

- Born 1588 in Towcester, Northton Co., England baptized 25 May 1588 in St. Laurence Church, Towcester, Northton Co., England.
- Married 23 February 1610 Thomas Lord Sr., son of Richard Lord and Joan _____ (near Towcester), Peterborough, Northton Co, England.
- Arrival 1636 in Boston, Massachusetts Bay Colony.
- Died 1675 in Hartford, Hartford Co., Connecticut at the age of 87.
- Buried the Old Center Cemetery in Hartford, Hartford Co., Connecticut.

In 1990, for my 50th birthday, my husband and I took a trip to England. We visited the church where Dorothy (Bird) Lord had been baptized years earlier. What an honor that was to see the very baptismal font where that sacred event had happened. Dorothy Bird was baptized 25 May 1588 in St. Laurence Church, Towcester, Northton Co., England.

Baptismal Font – St. Lawrence Church in Towcester, England

St. Lawrence Church - Towcester, England

<u>An Amazing Woman</u>

Dorothy Bird was an amazing woman! She grew up in the small town of Towcester in England and met and married her charming husband, Thomas Lord. Together over the years they bore and raised 18 children. They crossed the Atlantic in search of a new home in the colonies. On arriving in Boston in 1636, they settled in what is now Cambridge, Massachusetts. They joined a group of pioneers who, with the leadership of Rev. Thomas Hooker, were asked by the colony to search out some land on the Connecticut River.

They gathered all their possessions and walked through the wooded forests to what is now known as Hartford, Connecticut. It took this little group of pioneers two weeks to walk from Newtown (known now as Cambridge), Massachusetts to Hartford. They carried all that they owned, their cooking utensils and their beds along with their Bibles. They also assisted Rev. Hooker's wife, who was dying; she was carried on a homemade litter (now known as a stretcher). A sturdy bunch of folks this was!

Once they reached their destination, they parcelled out the new land and started the little Hartford community. The year was 1636/37. They were not spring chickens! Thomas was 50 years old and Dorothy 46 years old when they left England for the journey via ship to Cambridge and then by foot on to Hartford, Connecticut carrying with them all their earthly possessions! They had deep abiding faith. Note the name of their firstborn child. She was called Thank Ye and their last name was Lord.

Dorothy's husband Thomas Lord Sr. reached Hartford but died on 17 May 1644 at age 59, long before Dorothy, who died at the age of 88. She wrote her Last Will and Testament on 12 May 1675 and her will is on display at the courthouse in Hartford, Connecticut. It is fascinating to read and see all her earthly possessions spelled out with detail and to whom she was passing them on. Pictured here is the tombstone of Dorothy Bird and her husband Thomas Lord Sr. It is not clear if they are both buried here, as Thomas Sr. died much earlier and there is another marker in the "Ancient Cemetery" in Hartford, Connecticut which is thought to be where Thomas Lord Sr. is possibly buried.

This tombstone is in the
First Church of Hartford Burying Ground
to the rear of the church in Hartford, Connecticut

Children of DOROTHY BIRD and THOMAS LORD SR. are documented in the Lord chapter.

Source Citations for this Chapter

Towcester. Northamptonshire. England British History Online

St. Lawrence Church Towcester, Northamptonshire England History and Church Records

Ancestry Records Bird and Lord families https://ancestry.com

Records of the Church of Latter-Day Saints familysearch.org

Records of Early History of Hartford, Connecticut

Chapter 4: The Bowsers

The Bowser Family Line

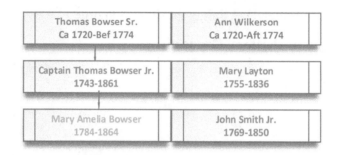

1. Thomas Bowser Sr.

THOMAS[1] BOWSER SR.

- Born circa 1720 in Acklam, Yorkshire, England.
- Married 13 November 1739 Ann Wilkinson in Acklam, Yorkshire, England.
- Died before 1774 in Acklam, Yorkshire, England at age approx. 44.

All of Thomas Bowser Sr. and his wife Ann Wilkinson Bowser's adult children left England and headed to the Canadian frontier. They, the parents, did NOT join them. They both stayed in England and died there. However, they did raise very courageous and adventuresome young adult children.

Children of THOMAS[1] BOWSER SR. and ANN WILKINSON were:

2A.	i.	**"THE PIONEER" THOMAS[2] Bowser JR.** (IMMIGRANT) b. October 1743 in Acklam, Yorkshire England. Thomas Jr. (The Pioneer married Mary Layton on 13 January 1773 in Acklam, Yorkshire, England. Thomas and Mary had 12 children during their marriage. "The Pioneer" Thomas Bowser died on 6 October 1816 Sackville, Westmoreland Co., New Brunswick at age 73.
	ii.	**RICHARD Bowser** (Immigrant) b. May 1744 in Acklam, Yorkshire, England. Richard married Elizabeth Harris on 5 May 1785 in Windsor, Hants Co., Nova Scotia. Richard died after 1788 Windsor, Hants Co., Nova Scotia age approx. 44.
	iii	**ANN Bowser** (Immigrant) b. June 1747 in Acklam, Yorkshire, England. Ann married John Hutchinson on 7 November 1775 in Musquodoboit Valley, Halifax Co., Nova Scotia. Ann died after 1788 in Musquodoboit Valley, Halifax Co., Nova Scotia at age approx. 41+.
2B.	iv.	**MARY Bowser** (Immigrant) b. July 1750 in Acklam, Yorkshire, England. Mary married Rev. John Smith Sr. on 29 September 1772 in Yorkshire, England. Rev. John was the son of William Smith and ___ unknown name. Mary and Rev. John had 9 children in this marriage. Mary died after 1783 at approx. 33+.

2A. Captain Thomas Bowser Jr. "THE PIONEER" (Immigrant)

CAPTAIN THOMAS[2] BOWSER JR. "THE PIONEER" and a SEA CAPTAIN (Thomas Sr.[1])

- Born October 1743 in Acklam, Yorkshire, England.
- Married 13 January 1773 Mary Layton, daughter of John Layton and Ann Boynton, in Acklam, Yorkshire, England.
- Arrival: 1774 – Ship named *the Duke of York*. Captain Thomas Bowser Jr. sailed from England to St. John, New Brunswick, Canada with his wife Mary (Layton) Bowser and their newborn son Thomas Bowser III.
- Occupation: Mariner (Sea Captain).
- Died 1816 in Sackville, Westmorland Co., New Brunswick, Canada at age 73.

Captain Thomas Jr. was known as "The Pioneer." He was also a "Planter" and a sea captain.

Planters were not farmers who planted a crop for farming. The word "Planters" was an Elizabethan term for Colonists of the now east coast of the United States. They were men who saw the "handwriting on the wall" about an upcoming war – The Revolutionary War. They led a contingent of people moving up to Nova Scotia and New Brunswick where there was good land and peace from war!

There were two huge contingents of people at this period: one coming from Massachusetts, Connecticut, and Rhode Island, and the other contingent from England. They did have to work with the Indians of this area, but trading was the peaceful manner of doing business for the early years. There was a large garrison built at Fort Cumberland from 1755 to 1768, which meant that there were vessels sailing to and from this region. There was an upcoming danger of the French and Indians going to war, but this did not seem to deter the Planters.

In 1759 a Grant of Cumberland Township was made to several incoming families. The book "Planter and Pioneer" lists "Thomas Bowser Pioneer" in Sackville and his wife Mary (Layton) Bowser with their newborn son Thomas Bowser III in 1774 arriving on the vessel the *Duke of York*. Around the same time, his brother Richard Bowser, 28 years old, a farmer, along with two of his sisters, one married to John Smith Jr., the other sister Ann, who was single on the journey but later married John Hutchinson in Halifax, Nova Scotia, Canada, all made the trip across the water coming on the vessel *Two Friends*.

Thomas Bowser Jr. stayed in Sackville, New Brunswick but the John Smith Jr. family eventually moved on to Diligent River and then later to Parrsboro, Nova Scotia.

Children of "THE PIONEER" THOMAS[2] BOWSER JR. and MARY LAYTON were:

	i.	**THOMAS BOWSER III** (Immigrant) b. 1774 in Acklam, Yorkshire, England. Thomas III was the small baby who made the journey across the Atlantic with his parents. He grew up in the new Canadian settlement. He married Frances King circa 1795 in New Brunswick. It is not known how many children they had. Thomas III died in 1860 in Coles Island, New Brunswick.
	ii.	**EBENEZER BOWSER** b. 1776 in Sackville, Westmorland Co., New Brunswick. Ebenezer married Lydia Ward circa 1796 in Sackville, Westmorland Co., New Brunswick. It is not known how many children they had during their marriage. Also unknown is Ebenezer's death date and his location at death.
	iii.	**ELIZABETH BOWSER** b. 13 January 1778 in Sackville, Westmorland Co., New Brunswick, Elizabeth married ____ Boyd circa 1798 in Sackville, Westmorland Co.,

		New Brunswick. It is not known how many children they had during their marriage. Also unknown is Elizabeth's death date and her location at death.
	iv.	**RICHARD SHEPHERD BOWSER** b.1781 in Sackville, Westmorland Co., New Brunswick. Richard married Sara Atkinson circa 1800. It is not known how many children they had during their marriage. Richard died in 1851 in New Brunswick at age 70.
3.	v.	**MARY AMELIA BOWSER** b. 22 May 1784 in Sackville, New Brunswick. Mary Amelia married John Smith Jr. on 14 March 1806 in Sackville, New Brunswick. They had 9 children during their marriage. Mary Amelia died 5 March 1864 at Diligent River, Cumberland Co., Nova Scotia at the age of 79.
	vi.	**GEORGE BOWSER** b. 1785 in Sackville, Westmorland Co., New Brunswick. It is unknown if George ever married and if he had any children. George died in 1845 in New Brunswick at age 60.
	vii.	**WILLIAM H. BOWSER** b. 1788 in Sackville, Westmorland Co., New Brunswick. William H. married Rebecca Burnham circa 1820 in Sackville, Westmorland Co, New Brunswick. It is not known how many children they had during their marriage. Also unknown is William H's death date and his location at death.
	viii.	**JOSEPH BOWSER** b. 1791 in Sackville, Westmorland Co., New Brunswick. Joseph married twice. Wife #1 Ann Bulmer. Joseph and Ann married circa 1820 in Sackville, Westmorland Co., New Brunswick. Wife #2 Lucy Ann Bent. Joseph and Lucy Ann married circa. 1867 in Sackville, Westmorland Co., New Brunswick. Joseph died in 1869 at age 78. It is unknown how many children Joseph had in both marriages.
	ix.	**BENJAMIN BOWSER** b. 1793 in Sackville, Westmorland Co., New Brunswick. Benjamin married Mary Ann Richardson on 21 Apr 1821 in Sackville, Westmorland Co., New Brunswick. It is not known how many children they had during their marriage. Benjamin died in 1862 in Dorchester, Westmorland Co., New Brunswick at the age of 69.
	x.	**LAYTON BOWSER** b. 1797 in Sackville, Westmorland Co., New Brunswick. Layton married Ann ___. They were married circa 1820 in Sackville, Westmorland Co., New Brunswick. It is not known how many children they had during their marriage. Also unknown is Layton's death date and his location at death.
	xi.	**JOHN BOWSER** b. 1799 in Sackville, Westmorland Co., New Brunswick. John married Mary E. Scotson on 2 August 1825 in Sackville, Westmorland Co., New Brunswick. It is not known how many children they had during their marriage. John died in 1879 in Sackville, Westmorland Co., New Brunswick at the age of 80.
	xii.	**ANN BOWSER** b. 1800 in Sackville, Westmorland Co., New Brunswick. Ann married Christopher Humphrey on 21 June 1821 in Sackville, Westmorland Co., New Brunswick. It is not known how many children they had during their marriage. Ann's death date and her location at death are unknown.

2B. Mary Bowser* (Immigrant)

MARY^2 BOWSER (*Thomas^1*)

- Born July 1750 in Acklam, Yorkshire, England.
- Married 29 September 1772 Rev. John Smith Sr., in Yorkshire, England. Rev. John Smith was the son of William Smith and ____. This was Rev. John Smith's second marriage. His first marriage was to Jane Appleby, who bore him two sons: John Smith Jr. and George Smith. For details see The Smiths of Nova Scotia chapter.
- Died after 1783 in Nova Scotia, Canada at age 33+.

Note: *John Smith Jr.'s stepmother was Mary Bowser. Mary Bowser was the sister of Captain Thomas Bowser Jr. "The Pioneer."

Captain Thomas Bowser Jr. "The Pioneer" was the father of Mary Amelia Bowser, who married John Smith Jr. John Smith Jr.'s wife was Mary Amelia Bowser.

Therefore, John Smith Jr.'s wife (Mary Amelia Bowser) was his stepmother's niece!

Children of MARY^2 BOWSER and REV. JOHN SMITH SR are documented in the Smith Family of Nova Scotia chapter.

3. Mary Amelia Bowser

MARY AMELIA^3 BOWSER (Captain Thomas Jr. "The Pioneer,"^{2} Thomas Sr.^{1})

- Born 22 May 1784 in Sackville, New Brunswick Co., Canada.
- Married 14 March 1806 John Smith Jr., in Sackville, New Brunswick. John Smith Jr. was the son of Rev. John Smith Sr. and Jane Appleby, via John Smith Sr.'s first marriage.
- Died 5 March 1864 at Diligent River, Cumberland Co., Nova Scotia, Canada at age 79.

Children of MARY AMELIA^3 BOWSER and JOHN SMITH JR. are documented in the Smith Family of the Nova Scotia chapter.

Source Citations for this Chapter

Planters, Paupers and Pioneers: English Settlers in Atlantic Canada by Lucille H. Campey.

Reginal Burton Bowser of Moncton, New Brunswick Canada, Letter explaining the family connection.

Genealogy of the Bowser family of Yorkshire.

The Chignecto Isthmus by Howard Trueman.

Chignecto Isthmus and Its First Settlers by Howard Trueman.

A Genealogical Review of the Bowser Family by Reginald Burton Bowser.

Irish Emigration and Canadian Settlement (Patterns, Links and Letters) by Cecil J. Houston & William J. Smyth, University of Toronto Press, 1990.

Women's' Institute of Halfway River and Westbrook: Verbal information on Bowser family.

Chapter 5: The Buchanans

The Buchanan Family Line

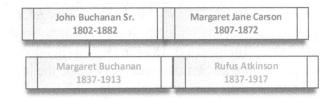

John Buchanan Sr.
1802-1882

Margaret Jane Carson
1807-1872

Margaret Buchanan
1837-1913

Rufus Atkinson
1837-1917

1. John Buchanan Sr. (Immigrant)

JOHN[1] BUCHANAN SR.

- Born 1802 in Scotland.
- Married circa 1830 Margaret Jane Carson in Donegal, Ireland.
- **Arrival 1834 Passengers on the ship *Britania*.**
- Died 15 May 1882 in Hopewell, Alberta Co, New Brunswick. at age 80.
- Buried in the Albert Pioneer Cemetery #02, Hopewell, Albert Co., New Brunswick.

The Original Buchanan Homestead

John Buchanan Sr. was a carpenter and house builder. John and his wife Margaret Jane Carson immigrated directly from Donegal, Ireland to New Brunswick together in 1834 following their marriage in Ireland. They crossed the Atlantic and were passengers on the ship *Britania*. They settled in Hopewell, Alberta County, New Brunswick, Canada.

In 1990 my sister Diane, cousins Libbie and Joyce, and a friend, Barbara, were all gathered in St. John, New Brunswick. We drove through New Brunswick, and into Nova Scotia. Fantastic trip! A highlight for me was discovering the *inside* of John Buchanan Sr.'s home in Hopewell, New Brunswick. We were driving through Hopewell. I was the driver when all this occurred! I drove by a street called Buchanan Street. Screech went the brakes! There were three old homes on this short street.

I hopped out of the car and went up to one of them and knocked on the door. I asked the man who opened the door if the builder of this home had been John Buchanan, and the man answered, "He sure did!" He added, "He did a marvellous job!" The man then invited me in to look at the inside of his home. I waved in the other passengers of the car with the man's permission, and they reluctantly came in and joined me for the tour inside. The man who answered the door said his mother was having surgery the next morning and was extremely nervous about the upcoming surgery. She suddenly appeared and served us tea and crumpets. She was delighted with our spontaneous visit. She was 90 years old. She said it was the best medicine to have company just "drop in" and she was so excited that we were related to the builder of her home. She was ecstatic and no longer concerned about her upcoming surgery. When we left, the man was so gracious and grateful for our visit. We were delighted to see the inside of the home, with the wide stairway leading up to the second floor. I felt the walls were speaking to us. A delightful, memorable afternoon which was truly a serendipity moment in time!

Children of JOHN[1] BUCHANAN SR. and MARGARET JANE CARSON were:

	i.	**Susannah Buchanan** (Immigrant) b. 8 September 1828 in Donegal, Ireland. Susannah married Chandler Dowling in 1850 in New Brunswick. Susannah and Chandler had 10 children during their marriage. Susannah died 28 October 1905 in Hillsborough, Albert Co., New Brunswick at the age of 77.
	ii.	**Thomas Buchanan** (Immigrant) b. 1831 in Donegal, Ireland. It is not known if Thomas ever married and had any children. It is also unknown the date he died and his location.
	iii.	**Samuel "John" Buchanan** b. 1834 in Hopewell, Albert Co., New Brunswick. Margaret Jane was pregnant with Samuel when they made the journey across the Atlantic. It is not known if Samuel ever married and had any children. It is also unknown the date he died and his location.
	iv.	**Triplet: Mary I Buchanan** b. 1836 in Hopewell, Albert Co., New Brunswick. Mary I died in 1836, possibly at birth.
	v.	**Triplet: Mary II Buchanan** b. 1836 in Hopewell, Albert Co., New Brunswick. Mary II married ____ McFeters. It is unknown if they had any children. Mary II died on 18 December 1880 in Hopewell, Albert Co., New Brunswick at the age of 44.
	vi.	**Triplet: John Buchanan Jr**. b. 1836 in Hopewell, Albert Co., New Brunswick. John Jr. married Elizabeth Boutiher in 1886, They had 9 children during their marriage. It is believed John Jr. died in Nova Scotia but the date is not known.
2.	vii.	**Margaret Buchanan** b. 28 June 1837 in Hopewell, Albert Co., New Brunswick. Margaret married Rufus Atkinson on 5 June 1865 in Hopewell, Albert Co., New Brunswick. Rufus was a son of Michael "John" Atkinson and Margaret "Peggy" Casey. Margaret and Rufus had 10 children during their marriage. Margaret Buchanan Atkinson died on 30 July 1913 in Southampton, Cumberland Co., Nova Scotia at age 76.
	viii.	**William M. Buchanan** b. 1839 in Hopewell, Albert Co., New Brunswick. It is not known if William M. ever married and had any children. William M. died on 23 December 1919 in Boston, Suffolk Co, Massachusetts at the age of 80.
	ix.	**Jane Buchanan** b. 1842 in Hopewell, Albert Co., New Brunswick. It is not known if Jane ever married and had any children. It is unknown the date she died and the location.
	x..	**Floanna Buchanan** b. 1846 in Hopewell, Albert Co., New Brunswick. It is not known if she ever married and had any children. She died after 1851, but the exact date of death and her location are unknown.
	xi.	**Twin: Joseph Buchanan** b. 1848 in Hopewell, Albert Co., New Brunswick Joseph died 22 May 1861 in Hopewell, Albert Co., New Brunswick at the age of 13. (He died the same month as his younger 10-year-old sister, Arminda, had also died).
	xii.	**Twin: Robert Carson Buchanan** b. 22 April 1848 in Hopewell, Albert Co., New Brunswick. It is not known if Robert Carson ever married and had any children. Robert Carson Buchanan died 22 November 1935 in Bathurst, Gloucester Co., New Brunswick at the age of 87. He is buried in the Bathurst Cemetery in Bathurst, New Brunswick.

	xiii.	**Arminda Buchanan** b. 1851 in Hopewell, Albert Co., New Brunswick. Arminda died at the age of 10 (the same month and same year that her older brother Joseph died). Both are buried in the Riverside-Albert Cemetery in Hopewell, New Brunswick.

Children of MARGARET JANE CARSON and John Buchanan are documented above.

However, let me share a few notes about their large family. Margaret Jane Carson and John Buchanan gave birth to 13 children. In this large family they had one set of triplets and one set of twins.

Birth Order Numbered as follows:
1. Susannah Buchanan b. 8 September 1828 in Donegal, Ireland.
2. Thomas Buchanan b. 1831 in Donegal, Ireland.
   All their other children were born in Hopewell, Alberta Co., New Brunswick, Canada.

Triplets:
4. Mary Buchanan #1 b. 1836 Hopewell, New Brunswick died at birth.
5. Mary Buchanan #2 b. 1836 Hopewell, New Brunswick died 18 December 1880 age 44.
6. John Buchanan Jr. b. 1836 Hopewell, New Brunswick died unknown date.

Twins:
*11. Joseph Buchanan b. 1848 Hopewell, New Brunswick died 22 May 1861 at age 13.
 12. Robert Carson Buchanan b. 1848 Hopewell, New Brunswick died 22 November 1935 at age 87.

Sad Loss!
Joseph Buchanan died the same month as his sister Arminda Buchanan.
*11. Joseph Buchanan b. 1848 Hopewell, New Brunswick died 22 May 1861 at age 13.
13. Arminda Buchanan b. 1851 Hopewell, New Brunswick died 7 May 1861 at age 10.

What a tragic blow, the loss of two children within a few weeks of each other. Wonder how they died – a tragic accident or a horrible illness? Both are devastating! Both children are buried in the same cemetery where their parents would be buried years later. It is the Riverside-Albert Cemetery in Hopewell, Albert Co., New Brunswick.

The children's tombstone.

2. Margaret Buchanan

MARGARET[2] BUCHANAN (John[1] Sr.)

- Born 28 June 1837 in Hopewell, Albert Co., New Brunswick.
- Married 5 June 1865 Rufus Atkinson, son of Michael "John" Atkinson and Margaret Casey. Margaret and Rufus married in Hopewell, Albert Co., New Brunswick.
- Died 30 July 1913 in West Brook, Southampton, Cumberland Co., Nova Scotia, at age 76.
- Buried Westbrook Cemetery, Southampton, Cumberland Co., Nova Scotia.

Margaret and Rufus were wonderful grandparents and helped their daughter Alberta during a family crisis. They raised their granddaughter Margaret (Alberta's 2-year-old daughter) when Alberta was in total overwhelm. For the full story about this event, please see the Alberta (Atkinson) Kearney section in the Alberta Atkinson portion of the Atkinson chapter.

Here is a picture of Margaret (Buchanan) and her husband Rufus Atkinson. The picture is hanging in the hallway of the author's home. The Bible in the picture is intact and is actually not only in the picture but is inside the black box which is sitting on the white lace on top of the bookcase. The bookcase containing the Bible is very near my study. Inside the black box pictured here is that very Bible with handwritten dates of births, marriages, and deaths of family members as well as the Holy Word. It is a true treasure!

Children of MARGARET[2] BUCHANAN and RUFUS ATKINSON are documented in the Atkinson chapter.

Source Citations for this Chapter

Verbal personal history from my paternal Grandmother Alberta Buchanan Atkinson Kearney.

Find a Grave.com.

Ancestry.com.

Public Archives of Canada 1851, 1861, 1871,1881 Census of Canada.

Personal visit to the Original Buchanan Homestead.

Cemeteries of Albert Co. New Brunswick (Name Indexed – Buchanan Name is Listed).

Riverside-Albert Cemetery in Hopewell, Albert Co. New Brunswick.

Handwritten note from Charles Buchanan (a descendant of John Buchanan Sr.).

Marriage Register (1846-1887) Albert Co., New Brunswick.

Albert Co., New Brunswick Court Records.

Passenger List of the ship *Britania* of 1834.

Real Estate Tax Lists 1874 and 1877.

Probate of Last Will and Testament of John Buchanan 1882.

Chapter 6: The Carsons

The Carson Family Line

____ Carson **Circa 1780-____**	Barbara ____ 1781-aft 1852
Margaret Jane Carson 1808-1872	John Buchanan Sr. 1802-1882

1A. Husband _____ Carson

_____ FIRST NAME UNKNOWN.
- Born circa 1780 in Scotland or Ireland.
- Married circa 1780 Barbara ____ in Donegal, Ireland.
- Died after 1809 in Donegal, Ireland.

1B. Wife Barbara _____ Carson - Pearson (Immigrant)

BARBARA CARSON-PEARSON[1]
- Born 1781 in Donegal, Ireland.
- Married circa 1807 Husband #1 _____ Carson in Donegal, Ireland.
- Married circa 1825 Husband #2 _____ Pearson.
- Arrival 1834 Passengers on the ship *Britania* in New Brunswick, Canada.
- Died after 1852 in Hopewell, Albert Co., New Brunswick at the age of 71.
- Buried in the Albert Pioneer Cemetery, Riverside Albert, Albert Co., New Brunswick.

1st Marriage

Barbara ____Surname unknown married twice. Husband #1 ____ Carson. They had 1 child, a daughter named Margaret Carson, born in 1808 Donegal, Ireland.

2nd Marriage

Barbara remarried. Husband #2 was ____ Pearson. It is not known what became of this husband, but it is believed that in 1834, Barbara travelled to New Brunswick, Canada aboard the vessel the *Britania* with her daughter Margaret Carson, son-in-law John Buchanan, and their two small children. The two children were: Susannah Buchanan b. 1828 and Thomas Buchanan b. 1831. Both children had been born in Donegal, Ireland.

Last Heard of:

Barbara Carson Pearson is noted to be in the 1851 New Brunswick Census as living in Hopewell, Albert Co., New Brunswick. She is also noted to be residing there in 1852. She was then 71 years old and is presumed to be living with her daughter Margaret, son-in-law John Buchanan and their large family.

Child of ____[1] CARSON and BARBARA ____ was:

2.	i.	**MARGARET JANE CARSON** (IMMIGRANT) b. 1808 in Donegal, Ireland. Margaret Jane married John Buchanan Sr. circa 1827 in Donegal, Ireland. Margaret Jane and John had 13 children during their marriage. *She arrived in 1834 as a passenger with her family on the ship Britania in New Brunswick, Canada.* Margaret Jane died 11 April 1872 in Hopewell, Albert Co, New Brunswick. She and her husband are both buried in the Riverside-Albert Pioneer Cemetery in Hopewell, New Brunswick.

2. Margaret Jane Carson (Immigrant)

MARGARET JANE[2] CARSON (first name unknown[1])

- Born 1808 in Donegal, Ireland.
- Married circa 1827 John Buchanan Sr. in Donegal, Ireland.
- *Arrival 1834 Passengers on the ship Britania in New Brunswick, Canada.*
- Died 11 April 1872 in Hopewell, Albert Co., New Brunswick at the age of 64.
- Buried in the Albert Pioneer Cemetery, Riverside Albert, Albert Co., New Brunswick.

Children of MARGARET JANE [2] CARSON and John Buchanan are documented in the Buchanan chapter.

Source Citations for this Chapter

New Brunswick, Canada Census of 1851.

Passenger List of the ship *Britania* of 1834.

Ancestry.com.

Chapter 7: The Cases

The Case Family Line

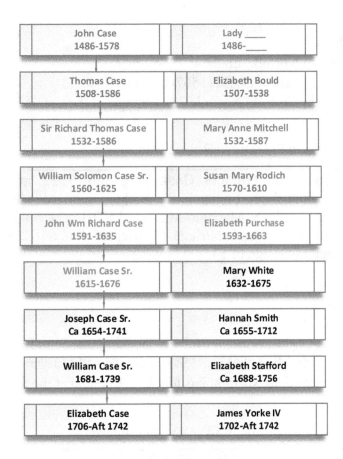

The Family Name

CASE

In ancient days the family name "Case" stood as an occupational term. It was used for the family makers of boxes and chests. It was a trade passed down from generation to generation.

1. John Case

JOHN[1] Case

- Born 1486 Chesham, Bois, Chiltern, Buckinghamshire, England.
- Married circa 1507 Lady _____ (circa 1486-__) in England.
- Died 1578 Chesham, Bois, Chiltern, Buckinghamshire, England at age 86.

Child of JOHN[1] CASE and LADY _____ was:

2.	i.	**THOMAS CASE** b. 22 April 1508. Thomas married Elizabeth Bould (1507-1545). They were married in England circa 1530. They had 1 child during their marriage.

2. Thomas Case

THOMAS[2] Case. (John[1])

- Born 22 April 1508 in Norfolk, England.
- Married circa 1530 Elizabeth Bould (1507-1545) in England.
- Died 29 June 1586, in Norfolk, Norfolk Co., England at the age of 78.

Child of THOMAS[2] CASE and ELIZABETH BOULD was:

3.	i.	**SIR RICHARD THOMAS CASE** b. 1 July 1532 in Chesham, Bois, Chiltern, Buckinghamshire, England. Sir Richard married Maryann Mitchel in 1558 in Norfolk, England. Maryann Mitchel (1532-1587). Sir Richard and Maryann had 7 children during their marriage. Sir Richard died on 12 November 1586 in Norfolk, England at the age of 54.

3. Sir Richard Case

SIR RICHARD[3] CASE (Thomas[2], John[1])

- Born 1 July 1532 in Chesham, Bois, Chiltern, Buckinghamshire, England.
- Married 1558 Maryann Mitchel (1532-1587). Richard and Maryann married in Norfolk, England.
- Died 12 November 1586, in Norfolk, Norfolk Co., England at the age of 54.

Children of SIR RICHARD[3] CASE and MARYANN MITCHEL were:

	i.	**THOMAS CASE** b. 1558 in Norfolk, England. It is unknown if he ever married and had any children. Also, his death date and location at death is unknown.
4.	ii.	**WILLIAM SOLOMON CASE SR.** b. 26 October 1560 in Norfolk, England. William Solomon married Susan Mary Rodich circa 1592. Susan Mary Rodich (1570-1610). They had 2 children during their marriage. William Solomon died on 8 September 1625 in Norfolk, England.
	iii.	**ROBERT CASE** b. 1563 in Norfolk, England. It is unknown if he ever married and had any children. Also, his death date and location at death is unknown.
	iv	**Twin Richard Case Jr.** b. 1565 in Norfolk, England. It is unknown if he ever married and had any children. Also, death date and location at death is unknown.
	v..	**Twin William Case** b. 1565 in Norfolk, England. It is unknown if he ever married and had any children. Also, death date and location at death is unknown.
	vi.	**EDWARD CASE** b. 1567 in Norfolk, England. It is unknown if he ever married and had any children. Also, death date and location at death is unknown.
	vii.	**HENRY CASE** b. 1571 in Norfolk, England. It is unknown if he ever married and had any children. Also, death date and location at death is unknown.

4. William Solomon Case Sr.

WILLIAM[4] Solomon Case Sr. (Sir Richard Thomas[3], Thomas[2], John[1])

- Born 26 October 1560 in Norfolk, England.
- Married circa 1613 Susan Mary Rodich (157-1610). They were married in England.
- Died 8 September 1625 in Norfolk, England age 65.

Children of WILLIAM[4] CASE and MARY RODICH were:

	i.	**WILLIAM SOLOMON CASE JR.** b. circa 1614 Aylesham, Gravesend, Kent, England. William Solomon Jr. died 20 August 1635 at sea aboard the ship *Dorset* en route to Boston, Massachusetts in America.
5.	ii.	**JOHN WILLIAM "RICHARD" CASE** (Immigrant) b. 1615 Aylesham, Gravesend, Kent, England. John married Elizabeth Purchase circa 1611 in England. Elizabeth Purchase (1593-1663) was the daughter of John Purchase and Mary ____. John William and Elizabeth had 1 child, a son named William Case Sr. They immigrated as a family of three to America between the years of 1645-1649 and settled in Rhode Island. John William "Richard" died on 18 October 1676 in Little Compton, Newport Co., Rhode Island. He is buried there in Little Compton, Rhode Island.

5. John William "Richard" Case (Immigrant)

JOHN WILLIAM RICHARD[5] CASE (Wm Solomon[4], Sir Richard Thomas[3], Thomas[2], John[1])

- Born September 1615 in Aylesham, Gravesend. Kent, England.
- Arrival circa 1650 Bay State American Colonies.
- Married circa 1635 *Elizabeth Purchase in England. Elizabeth Purchase (Immigrant)
- (1593-1663). She was the daughter of John Purchase and Mary ____. John Purchas, (Elizabeth's father) was one of the first settlers of Hartford, Connecticut.
- Died 18 October 1676, Little Compton, Newport Co., Rhode Island at age 61.

*Elizabeth Purchase's father was John Purchase (b. 1570 – d. October 1645). John Purchase came to the colonies circa 1630 and he and the Lord family were the first settlers of Hartford, Connecticut. John Purchase (Immigrant) was the son of Oliver Purchase (1545-1605) and Margaret Kreables (1542-1585), both of Gravesend, Kent, England. Their son, John Purchase (Immigrant), had four wives who are as follows:

John Purchase's Four Wives

1) Mary _____ (1569-1637) mother of Elizabeth Purchase (1593-1663).
2) Charlotte Jane _____ (1614-1683).
3) Fl (Florence) Jane Palmer (1614-1653).
4) Joan Parkis (1578- 1683). After John Purchas' death, Joan remarried to Nicholas Palmer 29 October 1646 in Hartford, Connecticut.

John Purchase was in Hartford by 1639 and received a land grant "by the courtesies of the town". He was an early member of the First Church in Hartford. His home lot was on the west side of the road which led to the Cow Pasture, near the pond. He served in the Pequot War, He is noted to have owned land in the Soldier's Field of Hartford, Connecticut in 1639.

The Pequot War

The war broke out in 1637 after an English tradesman was murdered by one of the Pequot Indian tribe. Conflict simmered between the English and the Pequot people. The Dutch of New York and the Pequot Indians had maintained a trading relationship in which they exchanged European goods (European cloth, metal tools and firearms) in exchange for wampum and furs. ("Wampum" is small beads made by the Native American people from seashells, strung together and used for decoration or necklaces and was used for money.) On 29 August 1636 Massachusetts Bay launched a punitive explosion against the inhabitants of Block Island regarding the murder of the tradesman on Block Island. After several hours of failed negotiations with the Pequot Sachem, Sassacus, at the Pequot River, the English forces then attacked and destroyed villages on both sides of the river. This act sparked the start of the Pequot War. It raged on for eleven long months and extended from Connecticut and Rhode Island to New York. On 5 August 1637, evidence of Sassacus' death was brought to Boston. Sassacus and his bodyguards had been attacked and killed in late July 1637 near the present-day Dover Plain, New York. At that point, the Pequot Indians were subdued, and the war was over.

The Tripartite Treaty - also known as "The Hartford Treaty" 21 September 1638

Narragansett and Mohegan leadership and the English gathered at Hartford to negotiate the Tripartite Treaty, known also as the Hartford Treaty. This treaty attempted to establish the English on the Connecticut River as the new sachems of the region who would mediate and settle native disputes. It assigned the Pequot captives to the Mohegan and the Narraganset tribes.

Child of JOHN WILLIAM "RICHARD"[5] CASE and ELIZABETH PURCHASE was:

6.	i.	WILLIAM CASE SR. (IMMIGRANT) b. September 1615 Aylesham, Gravesend, Kent, England. William Sr. married Mary White (1632-1675) in 1649 in Watertown, Massachusetts. Mary White (1632-1675) was the daughter of Emanuel White (1602-1684) and his wife Katherine Benfield 91607-1682). Emmanuel White and his wife Katherine also immigrated to America. There does not appear to be any connection known with our other studied White family in this book. Mary White was born in Newport, Rhode Island. William and Mary had 3 children during their marriage. William Sr. died 18 October 1676 at age 61 in Little Compton, Newport Co., Rhode Island. His wife Mary White died one year earlier in 1675 at age 43. Both are buried together in Little Compton, Rhode Island.

6. William Case Sr. (Immigrant)

WILLIAM[6] CASE SR (John Wm Richard[5], Wm Solomon[4], Sir Richard Thomas[3], Thomas[2], John[1])

- Born September 1615 in Aylesham, Gravesend, Kent, England.
- **Arrival circa 1645-1649 Bay State American Colonies.**
- Married 1649 *Mary White. She was the daughter of Emmanuel White & Katherine Benfield.
- Died 18 October 1676, Little Compton, Newport Co., Rhode Island, age 61.

*Mary White (1632-1675) was the wife of William Case Sr. She was the daughter of Emmanuel White (1604-1634) and his wife Katherine Benfield (1607-1682). Emmanuel and Katherine (Mary White's parents) also immigrated from England, and both died in Newport, Rhode Island. Mary White was born in 1632 in Newport, Newport Co., Rhode Island. She married William Case Sr. in Newport in 1649. They had 3 sons. Mary White Case died 12 July 1675 in Little Compton, Newport Co., Rhode Island at the age of 43.

Mary's mother Katherine Benfield was also born in England in 1607. She died in Newport, Newport Co., Rhode Island in 1682 at the age of 75. Mary White was born in 1632 in Newport, Newport Co., Rhode Island. She married William Case Sr in Newport in 1649. They had 3 sons. Mary died 12 July 1675 in Little Compton, Newport Co., Rhode Island at the age of 47.

William Case Sr. immigrated from Aylesham, Gravesend, Kent, England and arrived in Newport, Rhode Island between 1645-1649. It was here that he met his bride-to-be Mary White, who was born in Newport. They were married in Newport in 1649. Mary was age 17 and William was age 34. They raised three sons in Rhode Island.

On 22 May 1655 it was announced by the Moderator at the General Court of Elections held at Providence, Rhode Island that William Case Sr. was received as a Freeman of the Colony. William Case Sr.'s name also appears in the List of Freemen of Newport, Rhode Island in 1655.

Children of WILLIAM[6] CASE and MARY ___ were:

	i.	**WILLIAM CASE JR.** b. circa 1652 in Newport, Newport Co., Rhode Island. William Jr. married twice. Wife #1 ___ circa 1670. Wife #2 Abigail ___ 1680. William Jr. died in 1718 in East Greenwich, Rhode Island.
7.	ii.	**JOSEPH CASE SR.** b. 1654 in Portsmouth, Rhode Island. Joseph married Hannah Smith circa 1677 in Kings Town, Rhode Island. Hannah Smith (1655-1712) was the daughter of John Smith Sr. and Margaret ____. Hannah was born in Prudence Island, Rhode Island. Joseph and Hannah had 7 children during their marriage. Joseph Sr. died in 1741 in South Kingston, Rhode Island at the age of 87.
	iii.	**JAMES CASE** b. circa 1656 in Portsmouth, Rhode Island. James married Anna ___ circa 1670. It is unknown if he ever had any children. James died circa 1718 in Little Compton, Rhode Island.

7. Joseph Case Sr. (Fought in King Philip's War)

JOSEPH[7] CASE SR (William[6] Sr., John Wm Richard[5], Wm Solomon[4], Sir Richard Thomas[3], Thomas[2], John[1])

- Born circa 1654 in Portsmouth, Rhode Island.
- **1675 Fought in King Philip's War in the Rhode Island area.**
- Married circa 1677 Hannah Smith of Rhode Island in Kings Town, Rhode Island. Hannah Smith (ca 1655-1712) was the daughter of John Smith Sr. and Margaret _____.
- Died 1741 in South Kingston, Rhode Island at the age of 87.

Started 20 June 1675 - Ended 12 April 1676

What started King Philip's War?

Following the death of Ousamequin in 1662, his son and heir Metacom (known as King Philip by the English colonists) believed the alliance forged by his father was no longer being honored by the colonists. At this same time, the colonies were expanding into Wampanoag land all the time and relations soured between the two groups. This situation came to a head following the death of Ousamequin some 40 years after the *Mayflower* had landed. The colonists demanded the Peace Agreement should mean the Wampanoag people hand over all their guns and they hung three men of the Indian tribe for the murder in 1675 of Christian native John Sossamon, who had told the Plymouth Colony of the Indians' plan to attack the English settlements. Metacom (King Philip) refused the peace agreement and led an uprising of the Wampanoag, Nipmuck, Pawcatuck and Narragansett tribes. The colonist army burned villages as they went, killing native Indian women and children. The war decimated the Narragansett, Wampanoag and many other smaller tribes, and paved the way for additional English settlements. Thousand were killed, wounded, and captured and sold into slavery or indentured servitude. After these welcoming Indian tribes had helped the colonists settle in this new land, the colonists turned on them and tried to eliminate the Indian race! Now, 55 years later, these Indians were enslaved to the very people whom they had helped and had welcomed into their land two generations earlier. What an injustice! After many months of horrific fighting, the Narragansett tribe was defeated and their chief was killed, while the Wampanoag and other tribes were gradually subdued by the colonist army. After King Philip's wife and son were captured, Metacom (King Philip) fled to his secret headquarters at Mount Hope in Rhode Island, but the colonists searched for him and found him in August 1676. The war had already ended in April 1676. The colonists hung King Philip and beheaded him, while his body was drawn and quartered. They placed his head on a spike and then displayed that for two decades at the Plymouth Colony.

Metacom, who was King Philip (Son of Ousamequin)

Following the horrific war, in Kingstown, Rhode Island, town papers state that on 12 July 1703, Joseph Case Sr. and other men of Kingstown were appointed to lay out the highways and roads in the Kingstown area of Rhode Island.

Joseph Case Sr. Last Will & Testament (1741)

Joseph Case Sr. wrote his will on 21 February 1734, and it was carried out in 1741. His wife Hannah (Smith) Case had already died in 1712. Their oldest son Joseph Jr. also had died two years earlier in 1739. Here is what the will reads: To his oldest grandson, William Case Sr.'s eldest son of William Case Sr., deceased, he left one quarter of his whole farm which he had bought from Ezekiel Bull, and the remainder of his farm he left to his other children. He directed that his burying place be three rods square where his wife Hannah is buried and the burial area to be fenced in and maintained by his grandsons, for which he paid them a specific designated amount from his Last Will and Testament.

Children of JOSEPH[7] CASE SR. and HANNAH SMITH were:

	i.	**JOSEPH CASE JR.** b. 16 July 1678 in Kings Town, Rhode Island. Joseph Jr. married Elizabeth Mitchell circa 1703 in South Kingston, Rhode Island. It is unknown if they ever had any children. Joseph Jr. died on 13 January 1739 in South Kingston Rhode Island, at the age of 60.
8.	ii.	**WILLIAM CASE** b. 27 May 1681 in Kings Town, Rhode Island. (Originally Kings Town, the settlement's name later changed to Kingstown, and still later to Kingston, which name remains today.) William married Elizabeth Stafford circa 1704 in South Kingstown, Rhode Island. Elizabeth Stafford (circa 1688-1756) was the daughter of Joseph Stafford Sr. and Sarah Holden. William and Elizabeth had 7 children during their marriage. William died 1739 in South Kingstown, Rhode Island at age 58. He is buried in South Kingstown, Rhode Island.
	iii.	**MARY CASE** b. 2 December 1682 in Kings Town, Rhode Island. Mary married Henry Knowles circa 1702 in South Kingston, Rhode Island. It is unknown if they ever had any children. Mary died 16 November 1709 at age 26 in Rhode Island.
	iv.	**HANNAH CASE** b. 6 July 1687 in Kings Town, Rhode Island. Hannah married ____ Brooks circa 1700. It is unknown if the couple had any children. Also, Hannah's death date and location at her death are both unknown.

	v.	**MARGARET CASE** b. 20 August 1690 in Kings Town, Rhode Island. Margaret married Abraham Perkins on 29 June 1718 in South Kingston, Rhode Island. It is unknown if they had any children during their marriage. Margaret died in 1752 at the age of 62.
	vi.	**JOHN CASE** b. 20 November 1692 in Kings Town, Rhode Island. John married Elizabeth Sunderland circa 1720 in West Greenwich, Rhode Island. It is unknown if they ever had any children during their marriage. John died 1763 at the age of 71.
	vii.	**EMANUEL CASE B.** b. 2 November 1699 in Kings Town, Rhode Island. Emanuel married Hannah circa 1723 in South Kingston, Rhode Island. Emanuel died in 1770 at age 71.

8. William Case Sr.

WILLIAM[8] CASE SR. (Joseph[7] Sr., William[6] Sr., John Wm Richard[5], Wm Solomon[4], Sir Richard Thomas[3], Thomas[2], John[1])

- Born 27 May 1681 in Kings Town, Rhode Island.
- Married circa 1704 Elizabeth Stafford, (circa 1688-1756). They were married in South Kingstown, Rhode Island. Elizabeth Stafford was the daughter of Joseph Stafford Sr. and Sarah Holden.
- Died 1739 in South Kingston, Rhode Island at the age of 58 years.

Children of WILLIAM[8] CASE Sr. and ELIZABETH STAFFORD were:

	i.	**WILLIAM CASE JR.** b. 8 September 1705 in South Kingston, Rhode Island. (He is mentioned in his grandfather Joseph Case, Sr.'s Last Will and Testament. It is unknown if he ever married and had any children. Death date and location at death are unknown.
9.	ii.	**ELIZABETH CASE** b. 7 December 1706 in South Kingston, Washington Co., Rhode Island. Elizabeth married James Yorke IV on 11 June 1727 in South Kingston, Washington Co., Rhode Island. James Yorke IV (1702-after 1742) was the son of James Yorke III and Hannah Stanton. They had 6 children during their marriage. Elizabeth died after 1742 in South Kingston, Washington Co., Rhode Island at approx. 36 years.
	iii.	**EDWARD CASE** b. 17 February 1708 in South Kingston, Rhode Island. It is unknown if he ever married and had any children. Death date and location at death are unknown.
	iv.	**HANNAH CASE** b. 6 November 1713 in South Kingston, Rhode Island. It is unknown if she ever married and had any children. Death date and location at death are unknown.
	v.	**SARAH CASE** b. May 1715 in South Kingston, Rhode Island. It is unknown if she ever married and had any children. Death date and location at death are unknown.
	vi.	**MARY CASE** b. 5 January 1718 in South Kingston, Rhode Island. It is unknown if she ever married and had any children. Her death date and location at death are unknown.

	vii.	**MARGARET CASE** b. 19 December 1721 in South Kingston, Rhode Island. It is unknown if she ever married and had any children. Death date and location are unknown.

9. Elizabeth Case

ELIZABETH^9 CASE (William^8, Joseph^7 Sr., William^6 Sr., John Wm Richard^5, Wm Solomon^4, Sir Richard Thomas^3, Thomas^2, John^1)

- Born 7 December 1706 in South Kingston, Washington Co., Rhode Island.
- Married 11 June 1727 James Yorke IV in South Kingston, Washington Co., Rhode Island. James Yorke IV (1702-after 1743) was the son of James Yorke III and Hannah Stanton.
- Died after 1742 in South Kingston, Washington Co., Rhode Island at approx. age 36 years.

Children of ELIZABETH^9 CASE and JAMES YORKE IV are documented in the Yorke chapter.

Source Citations for this Chapter

https://ancestors.family.search.org/en/G7LJ-Z1P/thomas-case-1508-1586.

The Genealogy Dictionary of Rhode Island by John Osborne Austin, NEHGS Library, Boston, Massachusetts.

Genealogies of Rhode Island Families Volume I, Baltimore Genealogical Publishing Company, 1983.

Ancestry.com Research.

https://www.findagrave.com/memorial/120596569/william-case.

Battlefields of the Pequot War information from the Mashantucket Pequot Museum & Research Center, 10 Pequot Trail, Ledyard, CT 06338.

Early Pioneer Families of Hartford Connecticut (The John Purchase Family).

Vital Records —Births, Marriages and Deaths of Rode Island, Providence, Rhode Island.

North America Family Histories (1500-2000).

Chapter 8: The Caseys

The Casey Family Line

Jeremiah Casey Ca 1780-____	Name Unknown Ca 1780-____
Margaret "Peggy" Casey 1809-1891	John William Atkinson 1807-1877

1. Jeremiah Casey Sr. (Immigrant)

JEREMIAH[1] CASEY SR.

- Born circa 1780 in Northern Ireland.
- Married circa 1800 ____.
- Died after 1881 in Nappan, Nova Scotia at the age of approx. 101+.

There are many land records in the Amherst area, Cumberland Co., Nova Scotia. stating that both Jeremiah Casey Sr. and his son, Jeremiah Casey Jr. owned land in Amherst, Nova Scotia.

Children of JEREMIAH[1] CASEY SR. and _____ were:

	i.	JEREMIAH CASEY JR. b. 1804 in Amherst, Cumberland Co., Nova Scotia, Jeremiah Jr. like his father was a farmer and owned a large amount of land in Amherst. It is unknown who he married and unknown if they had any children. Jeremiah Jr. died in 1871 at the age of approx. 67 in the Nappan area, Nova Scotia.
2.	ii.	MARGARET "PEGGY" CASEY b. 1809 in Amherst, Cumberland Co., Nova Scotia. Margaret married John William Atkinson (1807-1877). They were married on 19 December 1831 in Nappan, Cumberland Co., Nova Scotia. He was the son of Michael Atkinson Sr. and his wife Amy Frances Sand Soules. Both Margaret "Peggy" and her brother John Casey married Atkinson siblings. Naomi Atkinson, who was John Atkinson's sister, married Peggy's brother John Casey. Margaret "Peggy" and John had 11 children during their marriage. There is a beautiful poem written about her entitled "Aunt Peggy" which was written for her by her niece and was read at her funeral. It is enclosed below. Margaret "Peggy," a widow in later years, died in 1891 at the age of 82 in Maccan, Southampton, Cumberland Co., Nova Scotia. She is buried in the Maccan United Baptist Cemetery in Maccan, Cumberland Co., Nova Scotia alongside her husband John William Atkinson.
	iii.	JOHN CASEY b. 1810 in Nappan, Cumberland Co., Nova Scotia. John married Naomi Atkinson circa 1840 in Southampton, Cumberland Co., Nova Scotia. Naomi was the daughter of Michael Atkinson Sr. and Amy Soules and a sister of Naomi's brother Michael "John" Atkinson, who married Margaret "Peggy" Casey. It is unknown as to how many children John and Naomi had during their marriage. Also unknown is when and where they died. It was most likely in the Nappan area of Nova Scotia according to verbal information from family.

	iv.	**ELIZABETH CASEY** b. 1816 in Nappan, Cumberland Co., Nova Scotia. Elizabeth married unknown first name Pullen. It is also unknown if they had any children. Elizabeth's death date and location at time of her death are also unknown.

2. Margaret "Peggy" Casey

MARGARET[2] "Peggy" CASEY (Jeremiah Sr.[1])

- Born 1809 in Amherst, Cumberland Co., Nova Scotia, Canada.
- Married 19 December 1831 John William Atkinson (1807-1877). They were married in Nappan, Cumberland Co., Nova Scotia. John William was the son of Michael Atkinson Sr. and Amy Soules.
- Died 1891 in Maccan, Cumberland Co., Nova Scotia at the age of 82.
- Buried in the Maccan United Baptist Cemetery, Maccan, Cumberland Co., Nova Scotia.

Margaret Casey's brother John Casey married Naomi Atkinson, who was Margaret's husband John William's sister.

A niece of Margaret "Peggy" Casey Atkinson wrote a beautiful poem about her Aunt Peggy in memory of her. Here is that poem:

"AUNT PEGGY"

To new land form in forest wide,
Her partner led her forth a bride.
A log-built cot her residence,
The leafy fields her sure defense.
Her home lit up by tallow dips.
Or lacking those, by pitch pine chips
A yawning fireplace all aglow,
Where pots and kettles simmered slow,
An iron oven for the bread,
With red hot cinders o'er it spread,
Suspended from a crane by hooks,
Each furnished with two S like crooks.
Beside a baker made of tin,
To bake the buns and biscuits in –
The mode in early solitude,
The hero settlers cooked their food.
Aunt Peggy's doughnuts, stews, and pies,
The memory of them never dies!
Her husband felled the maple trees,
And soon bread grain fields met the breeze.
He labored in "sweat of brow."
And forest fled from axe and plough.
Together they the harvests bound,
Sang and rejoiced to till the ground:
Alone the distaff well she drew –

Woolens and linens rose to view –
In those were rosy children dressed,
With which the rural home was blest –
Wove tablecloths and toweling,
As white as snow drifts on the wing:
She saved the poultry from the hawks.
And herded bears from out the flocks –
The song of wheel the hours beguile,
And crickets played their harps awhile.
Her life was strong and toils to meet.
Her hopes serene, her sleep was sweet.
No matches then struck lurid light.
The coals were neatly raked at night.
And if by chance the light went out,
"Aunt Peggy" could by strokes quite stout,
Knock fire from cold, blue steel and flint,
Or when the catching spunk outran,
Could flash it from the musket pan –
She did her part, a noble part –
With cheerful face and kindly heart
A living from the wilds to win.
And let God's blessed sunlight in; --
No church within the forest dim,
The hoot of owl her grandest hymn.
No school to train the family young,
They learned sweet lore from Nature's tongue.
Of health and competence possessed.
They now "arise and call her blest."
There came a change, the vigil light,
Burned in her cottage home at night.
He was hers for "better, worse,"
Fell sick – she proved a perfect nurse:
The head of home now called to be,
Support and sunshine both was she.
She saw her partner go before,
Then stood alone on stormy shore!
But bore the stroke upheld by grace,
And kept the sunlight in her face.
And many hopeful years did live,
And many words of cheer did give.
The neighbors love to see her come.
She left a blessing in their home,
Her sparkling wit, and soulful cheer,
Won her "Aunt Peggy," far and near, --
But she is gone to peaceful rest.
Her memory fragrant, cheers, blest!
All honor to the early dead.
From whom the wilderness has fled!
They cleared the way for churches, schools,

50

For mental light and moral rules:
Made forest wilds their wreaths disclose,
The desert blossom as the rose.
We reap the fruits in later years,
Sown by those whole souled pioneers.
Good institutions we possess.
Were molded in the wilderness.
We took our now fertile lands.
From early toiling settlers' hands.
Of honest and industrious fames,
With reverence let us speak their names.

Written by S.O.F (niece of Margaret "Peggy" Casey)

Note: Written and spelled exactly as S.O.F. wrote this poem.

In Memory of Margaret Casey Atkinson ("Aunt Peggy")

Children of Margaret[2] Casey and John William Atkinson are documented in the Atkinson chapter. They had eleven children.

Source Citations for this Chapter

Poem (handwritten) by Margaret "Peggy" Casey Atkinson's niece "S.O.F" in Author's file.

1861 and 1881 Cumberland Co., Nova Scotia, Canada National Census.

1827, 1838 Nova Scotia, Canada Census and Assessment + Poll Tax Records.

Ancestry.com.

Findagrave.com.

Chapter 9: The Cookes

The Cooke Family Line

John Cooke Ca 1480-____	Alice Saunders Ca 1483-____
Sir Anthony Cooke 1504-1576	Lady Ann Fitzwilliam 1504-1588
Richard Cooke 1521-1567	Lady Alice Anne Caunton 1526-1618
Rev. William Cooke 1562-1615	Martha Susan White 1575-1648
Elizabeth Cooke 1605-1674	Rev. William Walton 1605-1658

1. John Cooke

JOHN[1] COOKE

- Born circa 1480 in London, England.
- Married circa 1503 Alice Saunders (1483-__).
- Died date unknown in England at age unknown.

Child of JOHN[1] COOKE and ALICE SAUNDERS was:

2.	i.	SIR ANTHONY COOKE b. 1504 London, England. Sir Anthony married circa 1520 Lady Ann Fitzwilliam (1504-1588). They were married in Colchester, Essex, England. They had one child during their marriage. Sir Anthony died 10 June 1576 in London, Middlesex, England at the age of 72.

2. Sir Anthony Cooke

SIR ANTHONY[2] COOKE (John [1])

- Born March 1504 in London, England.
- Married circa 1520 Lady Ann Fitzwilliam (1504-1588). They were married in Colchester, Essex, England.
- Died 10 June 1576 London, Middlesex, England at the age of 72.

Child of Sir Anthony [2] Cooke and LADY ANN FITZWILLIAM was:

3.	i.	Richard Cooke b. 1521 in London, Middlesex, England. Richard married Lady Alice Anne Caunton (1526-1618). They were married in 1539 in London, England. Richard and Lady Alice Anne had 2 children during their marriage. Richard died 3 October 1579 in London, Middlesex, England at the age of 46.

3. Richard Cooke

RICHARD COOKE (Sir Anthony[2], John [1])

- Born 1521 London, England.
- Married 1539 Lady Alice Anne Caunton (1526-1618).
- Died 3 October 1567 in London, England at age 46.

Children of Richard[3] Cooke and LADY ALICE ANNE CAUNTON were:

	i.	SIR WILLIAM COOKE b. 1542 London, England. It is unknown if he ever married and had any children. Sir William died 1572 in London, Middlesex, England at age 30.
4.	ii.	REV. WILLIAM COOKE (ANGLICAN VICAR) b. 1562 Stratton, Dorsetshire, England. Rev. William married Martha Susan White (1575-1648). They were married on 27 April 1597 in Stockton, Wiltshire, England. Rev. William and Martha Susan had 11 children during their marriage. Rev. William Cooke died on 26 June 1615 in Crediton, Devonshire, England at the age of 53.

4. Rev. William Cooke (Anglican Vicar)

REV. WILLIAM [4] COOKE, VICAR. (Richard[3], Sir Anthony[2], John[1])

- Born 1562 Stratton, Dorsetshire, England.
- Married 27 April 1597 Martha Susan White (1575-1648) at Stockton, Wiltshire, England.
- Died 26 June 1615 in Crediton, Devonshire, England at age 40.

Reverend William Cook was born circa 1562 in Stratton, Devonshire, England. He grew up in that area and attended the Magdalen University College at Oxford, England. He graduated in 1567 with a master's degree. He was a Nonconformist. Reverend Cooke displeased the Queen of England. She wrote a letter to the Fellowes of Magdalen, commanding them to elect Nicholas Bond as President. Twelve of the Fellowes including Rev. Cooke petitioned the Archbishop of Canterbury on behalf of the Nonconformist candidate, Ralph Smith, who was elected. This displeased the Queen, and the election was overturned in 1589. Rev. Cooke was a Lecturer at Magdalen, and he was given a year's leave to preach in Wales.

Nine years later in 1598, Rev. Cooke resigned from the college and became the Second Vicar of Crediton in Devonshire. He had been the Vicar Preacher two years before that. He married (a year earlier) on 27 April 1597 at Stockton, Wiltshire, Martha White, who was the daughter of the Gentleman John White. The rector of Stockton was John Terry, who was the husband of Martha's sister Mary.

As Vicar of Crediton, Rev. William became one of the twelve governors of Crediton. William and Martha had seven children. All their children were born there in Crediton. Rev. William died 26 June 1615 and was buried in the churchyard of the Holy Cross Church Cemetery in Crediton, Devonshire, England. One of his children, Elizabeth, married the Reverend William Walton Jr. They married in England. They sailed to the new colonies in 1636 and settled in Marblehead, Massachusetts. For further information please see the Walton chapter.

Children of REV. WILLIAM [4] COOKE (ANGLICAN VICAR) and ELIZABETH COOKE were:

	i.	**MARTHA COOKE** b. 1598 in Crediton, Devonshire, England. Baby Martha died 1598 as a stillborn.
	ii.	**NATHANIEL COOKE** b. 1603 in Crediton, Devonshire, England. Nathaniel died 1603 as a stillborn.
5.	iii.	**(TWIN) ELIZABETH COOKE** (Immigrant) b. 1605 in Crediton, Devonshire, England. Elizabeth married Rev. William Walton Jr. (Immigrant) on 10 April 1627 in Matravers, Dorset, England. Elizabeth and Rev. William Walton Jr had 9 children during their marriage. They immigrated to America and arrived in the Bay State Colony of New England in 1636. Elizabeth died 29 September 1674 in Marblehead, Essex Co., Massachusetts at the age of 69.
	iv.	**(TWIN) ROGER COOKE** b. 1605 in Crediton, Devonshire, England. It is unknown if he ever married and unknown if he had any children. Roger's death date and his location at death are also unknown.
	v.	**SAMUEL COOKE** b. 1606 in Crediton, Devonshire, England. Samuel died 1606 as a stillborn.
	vi.	**SUSANNAH #1 COOKE** (Immigrant) b. 1607 in Crediton, Devonshire, England. Susannah #1 died 1637 at the age of 30. She died shortly after arrival in the Bay State.
	vii.	**(TRIPLET) NATHANIEL COOKE** (Immigrant) b. 1609 in Crediton, Devonshire, England. It is unknown if he ever married and unknown if he had any children. Nathaniel died in 1695 at the age of 86. (Location in America as to where he died is unknown.)
	viii.	**(TRIPLET) SUSANNAH #2 COOKE** (Immigrant) b.1609 in Crediton, Devonshire, England. It is unknown if she ever married and unknown if she had any children. Susannah #2 died 1695 at the age of 86. (Location in American as to where she died is unknown.)
	ix.	**(TRIPLET) WILLIAM COOKE** (Immigrant) b. 1609 in Crediton, Devonshire, England. It is unknown if he ever married and unknown if he had any children. William died 1638 at the age of 29 in the Bay State Colony.
	x.	**MARY COOKE** (Immigrant) b. 1613 in Crediton, Devonshire, England. It is unknown if she ever married and unknown if she had any children. Mary died 1674 at the age of 61. (Location in America is unknown as to where she died.)
	xi.	**MARTHA COOKE** (Immigrant) b. 1614 in Crediton, Devonshire, England. It is unknown if she ever married and unknown if she had any children. Martha died in 1695 at the age of 81. (Location in America is unknown as to where she died).

5. Elizabeth Cooke (Immigrant)

ELIZABETH COOKE (Rev. William [4] Anglican Vicar, Richard [3], Sir Anthony [2], John [1])

- Born 1605 in Crediton, Devonshire, England.
- Married 10 April 1627 Rev. William Walton Jr. (1605-1658) (Immigrant). Elizabeth and Rev. William Jr. were married in Matravers, Dorset, England.
- Died 29 September 1674 Marblehead, Essex, Massachusetts at age 72.

Children of Elizabeth Cooke and REV. WILLIAM WALTON, JR. are listed in the Walton chapter.

Source Citations for this Chapter

Findagrave.com.

https://www.wikitree.com/wiki/Cooke896.

Ancestry.com.

"The Hennessee Family Genealogical Pages."

England, Select Dorset Church of England Parish Registers, 1538-1999.

Gloucestershire, England, Church of England Baptisms, Marriage, and Burials, 1538-1813.

Wiltshire, England, Extracted Church of England Parish Records.

Chapter 10: The Cunninghams

The Cunningham Family Line

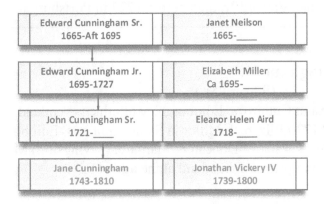

Edward Cunningham Sr. 1665-Aft 1695	Janet Neilson 1665-____
Edward Cunningham Jr. 1695-1727	Elizabeth Miller Ca 1695-____
John Cunningham Sr. 1721-____	Eleanor Helen Aird 1718-____
Jane Cunningham 1743-1810	Jonathan Vickery IV 1739-1800

Cunningham Surname
"Konigham"
Teutonic 12th century
is derived from
"regium domicillum"
The King's House

1. Edward Cunningham Sr.

EDWARD CUNNINGHAM SR.

- Born 1665 in Saint Cuthberts, Edinburgh, Midlothian, Scotland.
- Married 1694 Janet Neilson (1665-____). They were married in Saint Cuthberts, Edinburgh, Midlothian, Scotland.
- Died after 1695 in Saint Cuthberts, Edinburgh, Midlothian, Scotland at age approx. 30+.

Child of EDWARD[1] CUNNINGHAM SR. and JANET NEILSON was:

2.	i.	**EDWARD CUNNINGHAM JR.** b. 1695 in Saint Cuthberts, Edinburgh, Midlothian, Scotland. Edward Jr. married Elizabeth Miller on 24 April 1720 in Saint Cuthberts, Edinburgh, Midlothian, Scotland. Elizabeth (1699-____) was the daughter of Duncan and Margaret (Livingston) Miller. Edward and Elizabeth had one child during their marriage. Edward Jr. died before 1727 in Portsburg, Scotland at age of 32+.

2. Edward Cunningham Jr.

EDWARD[2] CUNNINGHAM JR. (Edward[1] Sr.)

- Born 1695 in in Saint Cuthberts, Edinburgh, Midlothian, Scotland.
- Married 24 April 1720 Elizabeth Miller in Saint Cuthberts, Edinburgh, Midlothian, Scotland. Elizabeth was the daughter of Duncan & Margaret (Livingston) Miller.
- Died before 1727 in Portsburg, Scotland at the age of 32+.

Child of EDWARDS[2] CUNNINGHAM JR. and ELIZABETH MILLER was:

3.	i.	**JOHN CUNNINGHAM SR.** b. 6 March 1721 in Saint Cuthberts, Edinburgh, Midlothian, Scotland. John Sr. married Eleanor Helen Aird on 1 July 1742 in St Cuthberts, Edinburgh, Midlothian, Scotland. Eleanor (1718-___). Eleanor Helen was the daughter of John & Helen (Brown) Aird. John and Eleanor had 6 children during their marriage. Eleanor's death date and place are both unknown. John Sr. died circa 1760 at age 39+ place unknown.

3. John Cunningham Sr.

JOHN CUNNINGHAM (John[3] Sr, Edward[2] Jr., Edward[1] Sr.)

- Born 6 March 1721 in Saint Cuthberts, Edinburgh, Midlothian, Scotland.
- Married 1 July 1742 Eleanor (Helen) Aird (21 October 1718–unknown date). John and Eleanor were married in Saint Cuthberts, Edinburgh, Midlothian, Scotland. Eleanor was the daughter of John & Helen (Brown) Aird.
- Died circa 1760 in an unknown place at the age of 39 +.

Many Scots migrated to Ireland in the 17th and 18th centuries. The migration was first encouraged by King James I of Great Britain to strengthen the Protestant presence and its domination in Northern Ireland. This may well have been why the Cunningham family ancestors emigrated first to Limerick, Ireland and then on to Roscommon, where there were many scattered Scottish settlers.

John Cunningham and his wife moved from Edinburgh, Scotland to Limerick, Ireland where their first child, Jane Cunningham, was born. They did not stay there long but moved on to Roscommon, Ireland where their other five children were born. However, failed crops in Ireland and the British Crown's influence further encouraged emigration of the Scotch Irish settlers to Nova Scotia or to the colonies in America. The Scots Irish settlers were also called "The Irish Presbyterians."

So, they moved again from Rosemond, Ireland with plans to settle in the new colony in Pennsylvania in America. It is unclear if only the children went with other older relatives or whether their parents made the trip with them, but their parents did not survive the journey.

By the 1760s Jane and her siblings had all emigrated to North America. The children were all together in one large ship but there is no mention of their parents (John and Eleanor). Either they never made the dangerous trip across the water, or they were killed in the horrific accident that occurred on the journey. The six Cunningham children were 17 years, 15 years, 12 years. 10 years, 6 years, and the youngest 4 years old at the time of their crossing the Atlantic to the new world. They were headed to their family in Pennsylvania and were aiming for either the ports of Boston, Massachusetts, or New York.

The journey was very difficult and awfully long. Towards the end of this long, difficult journey, suddenly rough waters rose, and a storm surprised them all. Unfortunately, it took the vessel off its course. They were navigating for Pennsylvania but the horrible weather conditions at sea took them in a straight northerly direction. Unknown to them, they were headed for a treacherous sandbar called Sable Island off the coast of Halifax, Nova Scotia. Suddenly without warning they hit a sandbar and became shipwrecked. They were abandoned on the sandbar for a long, long time. Their ship sank. Their food supplies were reduced to zero as the food was all destroyed in the ship's accident. They were facing starvation. They found a stray dog on the sandbar and killed it for food. Long after the storm had passed another shipping vessel was sighted passing by. They managed to catch the captain's attention and the rescuing boat took them all aboard. The rescuing ship took them safely into the Halifax's Harbor and left the boys there at the boys' request. However, the girls wanted to go further along to the Boston Harbor, which is what they did. This shipwreck accident occurred in 1760.

Sable Island – where their vessel was shipwrecked in 1760

Sable Island, a 44-kilometer-long sandbar about 300 kilometers east southeast of Halifax, Nova Scotia, is renowned for its wild horses. For sailors, it was the "graveyard of the Atlantic," an island hidden by waves, storms and fog that meant only death and destruction. Since 1583 there have been over 350 recorded shipwrecks on Sable Island. Truly little now remains of the ships that were wrecked on the island: a shoe buckle, a few coins, ship name boards, timbers buried and later found in the sand.

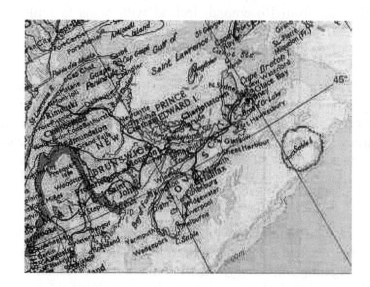

There were many passengers besides the Cunningham children on the wrecked ship and it is not known how many drowned in the stormy shipwreck accident but what is known is that the three brothers, John, Richard, and Michael, all survived. Jane was found later, having made it to Boston, Massachusetts (see section below). Mary, her sister, made it to Massachusetts also and later married a man named ____ Mercer. Also, Magdalene made it safely to Massachusetts but where she went afterwards is still unknown. More is known about the three boys as Richard's grandson, Leonard Cunningham, compiled a family history based on verbal information from the older relatives. This book is called *The Cunningham Family of Antigonish, Nova Scotia* by Leonard Cunningham. Much of this family information mentioned here is derived from that book.

John Cunningham Jr. —not much is known of him. He went off to an area near St. John's River, in New Brunswick. It is believed by the family that he became the Superintendent of Indian Affairs in that area. No further information is recorded.

Richard Cunningham received an important position at the Royal Dockyard by working his way up. It was with that connection that he met and later married Elizabeth Day. She was the granddaughter of Dr. George Day who was the Surgeon of the Royal Artillery. When Dr. Day came to this area in 1756, he brought with him several thousand settlers and he received several large grants of land, one of which is now the Township of Newport, Hants Co., Nova Scotia, right next to the land grants at Falmouth in Hants Co, Nova Scotia which is where Jane, Richard's sister, ended up. (For more on Jane's story see further in this chapter). Small world. Dr. George Day helped Richard Cunningham and his wife, Elizabeth Day (Dr. Day's granddaughter) obtain land grants in Antigonish, Nova Scotia. Richard obtained a land grant of 1,000 acres and his wife Elizabeth obtained a land grant of 700 acres, all in Antigonish. Richard went on to become quite a politician. He was a farmer but also became involved with political affairs. He was elected to represent the Yarmouth township in the Legislative Assembly of Nova Scotia. He was also a Justice of the Peace. At home he had worship services three time every day (on rising, at dinnertime and at 9:00 p.m.). He required all members of the household to attend. He lived to a good old age of 75 years. His wife Elizabeth had a respiratory illness and died much earlier at the age of 48. They had 5 children.

Michael Cunningham was quite young (4 years old) at the time of the shipwreck accident in traveling to America. He had a difficult start to life and life itself was not very easy for him at all.

As a young man working at the dockside in Halifax with his brother Richard, he was kidnapped by a bunch of thugs from a French privateer vessel and taken aboard and sent to France. He was imprisoned in France for two years. While in prison he managed to learn the French language and was an avid reader of French books. When he broke free of imprisonment, he made the trip from Paris to New York City in America. There he met a young woman. They fell in love and became engaged. However, she died suddenly, and Michel remained a bachelor for the rest of his life! He made it from New York City to his Cunningham family in Antigonish, Nova Scotia bringing with him several French books. Michael remained there in Antigonish for the remainder of his life. He, like Richard, was very spiritual and he fasted and prayed specifically once a year in gratitude for God's faithful watch over his life. Michael died 30 July 1815 at the age of 59. There is a family burial cemetery near the very first orchards in Antigonish which the Cunningham family had planted years earlier. Michael is buried there.

Children of JOHN[3] CUNNINGHAM SR. (Immigrant) and ELEANOR HELEN AIRD were:

4.	i.	**JANE CUNNINGHAM** (Immigrant) b. 8 November 1743 in Limerick, Ireland. Jane married Jonathan Vickery IV (1739-1800). They were married on 17 April 1764. They had 8 children during their marriage. Jane died in 1810 in Parrsboro, Nova Scotia at the age of 67.
	ii.	**JOHN CUNNINGHAM JR.** (Immigrant) b. September 1745 in Roscommon, Ireland. It is unknown if he ever married and had any children. John died in St. John, New Brunswick. His death date is unknown.
	iii.	**RICHARD CUNNINGHAM** (Immigrant) b. 14 September 1748 in Roscommon, Ireland. It is unknown if he ever married and had any children. Richard died in St. John, New Brunswick. His death date is unknown.
	iv.	**MARY CUNNINGHAM** (Immigrant) b. 1750 in Roscommon, Ireland. Mary married ____ Mercer. It is unknown if they ever had any children. It is believed that Mary died in Massachusetts but date is unknown.
	v.	**MAGDALENE CUNNINGHAM** b. 1752 in Roscommon, Ireland. She died before 1760 and never made the trip across the ocean. She died in Ireland, but date is unknown.
	vi.	**MICHAEL CUNNINGHAM** (Immigrant) b. 1756 in Roscommon, Ireland Michael never married. He died on 30 July 1815 in Antigonish, Nova Scotia.

4. Jane Cunningham (Immigrant)

JANE[4] CUNNINGHAM. (John[3] Sr, Edward[2] Jr. Edward[1] Sr.)
- Born 8 November 1743 in Limerick, Ireland.
- Married 17 April 1764 Jonathan Vickery IV (1739-1800) in Falmouth, Nova Scotia.
- Died 1810 in Parrsboro, Cumberland Co., Nova Scotia at the age of 67.

Jane also was in the horrific shipwreck accident in the attempt to reach America. She got separated from her three brothers when the rescue boat took her and her sister Mary on to Boston, Massachusetts. The ship had left her brothers, John, Richard and Michael in Halifax, Nova Scotia.

However, Boston was where Jane wanted to go and where, a few years later, she ended up meeting her future husband, Jonathan Vickery IV. Still months later, Jane and Jonathan traveled up to the new promising land of Falmouth, Nova Scotia where they received a land grant. They were married there in Falmouth, Hants Co., Nova Scotia on 17 April 1764. This was four years after Jane had been in the horrific shipwreck in her travels to America. There in Nova Scotia they raised eight children during their marriage. Years later, they moved to Parrsboro, Cumberland Co., Nova Scotia where they obtained further land grants. Jane and her husband Jonathan Vickery IV are both buried in unmarked graves in Parrsboro, Cumberland Co., Nova Scotia.

Children of Jane[4] Cunningham and Jonathan Vickery IV were all born in Falmouth, Hants Co., Nova Scotia, and are documented in the Vickery chapter.

Source Citations for this Chapter

Leonard Cunningham compiled a family history based on verbal information from the older relatives. This book is called: *The Cunningham Family of Antigonish, Nova Scotia* by Leonard Cunningham.

Much of this family information in this Cunningham chapter is derived from this book.

Scotland, Extracted Parish Records, 1571-1997.

Ireland. Select Birth and Baptisms, 1620-1911.

Ancestry Family Trees.

www.myheritage.com.

Chapter 11: The Dungans

The Dungan Family Line

Sir Patrick O'Donnagain Sr. 1485-1528	Mary de Glynn Farrelly 1508-1528
Chaplain Patrick Dungan Jr. 1528-1564	Lady Ann Wogan 1532-1563
Sir John Patrick Donegan 1554-1592	Margaret Mary Forester 1555-1597
Sir Thomas Dungan Sr. 1584-1626	Mary Elizabeth Barnwell 1582-1626
William Dungan Sr. 1611-1636	Frances Latham Weston 1610-1677
Frances Dungan 1630-1697	Capt. Randall Holden Sr. 1612-1692

**The Dungannon Castle
(later called the O'Neill Castle)
Located in Tyrone in Northern Ireland**

Family Name Changes

It is interesting to note how many times the last name of **Dunagan** has changed over the years. In the 1400s, it was spelled as it sounded, **O'Donnagain**. Later it was changed to **Dongan,** then changed to **Donegan,** and then later still changed to **Dungan**. The Old Castle spells it yet another way, **Dungannon**!

1. Sir Patrick O'Donnagain Sr.

SIR PATRICK[1] O'DONNAGAIN SR.

- Born 1485 in Castleton, Kildare, Ireland.
- Married 1527 Mary de Glynn Farrelly (1508-1528).
- Died 1528 in Castleton, Kildare, Ireland at the age of 43.

Child of SIR PATRICK[1] O'DONNAGAIN SR. and MARY DE GLYNN FARRELLY O'DONNAGAIN was:

2.	i.	**CHAPLAIN SIR PATRICK JR. O'DONNAGAIN** b. 2 July 1528 in Castleton, Kilfrought (Kildare), Ireland. Married 1553 Lady Ann "Missy" Wogan (1532-1563). Chaplain Patrick and "Missy" had 5 children in their marriage. Chaplain Patrick died in 1564 in Dublin, Ireland at the age of 36.

2. Chaplain Sir Patrick Dongan Jr.

CHAPLAIN SIR PATRICK[2] JR. (Sir Patrick[1])

- Born 25 July 1528 in Castleton, Kildrought, (later known as Kildare, Ireland).
- Married 1552 Lady Ann (called "Missy") Wogan (1532-1563) in Castleton, Kildrought, (Kildare), Ireland.
- Died 1564 Dublin, Dublin Co., Ireland at the age of 36.

Children of CHAPLAIN SIR PATRICK[2] DONGAN JR. and LADY ANN "MISSY" WOGAN were:

	i.	**WILLIAM DONGAN** b. 1552 in Castleton, Kildrought (Kildare) Ireland. William died in 1554 at the age of 2.
3.	ii.	**SIR JOHN DONEGAN** b.1554 in Castleton, Kildrought (Kildare), Ireland; married in 1553 Lady Ann Forester (called "Missy") Wogan in Castleton, Kildrought (Kildare), Ireland. Lady Ann "Missy" Forester (1532-1563) was the daughter of Walter Forester and Margaret Netterville. Missy's last name Wogan was her last name from her recently first deceased husband. Sir John and Margaret had 7 children in their marriage. Sir John Patrick Donegan died 8 August 1592 Dublin, Ireland at age 38.
	iii.	**RICHARD DONEGAN** b. 1556 in Castleton, Kildrought (Kildare), Ireland. It is unknown if he ever married and had children. Death date and place of death are unknown.
	iv.	**THOMAS DONGAN** b. 1559 in Castleton, Kildrought (Kildare), Ireland. It is unknown if he ever married and had children. Death date and place of death are unknown.
	v..	**WALTER DONEGAN** b. 1560 in Castleton, Kildrought (Kildare), Ireland. It is unknown if he ever married and had children. Death date and place of death are unknown.

3. Sir John Donegan 2nd Remembrance of the Exchequery & The Earl of Dungannon

SIR JOHN[3] DONEGAN (Chaplain Sir Patrick[2], Sir Patrick[1])

- Born 1554 in Castleton, Kildare, Ireland.
- Married 1578 Lady Margaret Mary Forester in Castleton, Kildrought (Kilgore) Ireland. Margaret Mary Forester (1555-1597) was the daughter of Walter Forester and Margaret Netterville.
- Died 8 August 1592 in Dublin, Dublin Co., and Ireland.

Children of SIR JOHN[3] DONEGAN and LADY MARGARET MARY FORESTER were:

	i.	**GENTLEMAN THOMAS JON DONEGAN I** b. 1574 in Castleton. Kildrought (Kildare), Ireland. It is unknown if he ever married and had children. Place of death is unknown. Thomas Jon died in 1626 at the age of 52.
	ii.	**EDWARD DONEGAN I** b. 1577 in Castleton. Kildrought (Kildare), Ireland. It is unknown if he ever married and had children. Place of death is unknown. Edward died in 1622 at the age of 45.
	iii.	**SIR WALTER DONEGAN** b. 1579 in Castleton. Kildrought (Kildare), Ireland. It is unknown if he ever married and had children. Place of death is unknown. Sir Walter died in 1526 at the age of 49.
	iv.	**EDWARD DONEGAN II** b. 1582 in Castleton. Kildrought (Kildare), Ireland. It is unknown if he ever married and had children. Place of death is unknown. Edward II died in 1639 at the age of 57.
4.	v.	**SIR THOMAS DUNGAN SR. I** b. 1584 in Castleton. Kildrought (Kildare), Ireland. Sir Thomas was married twice: Wife #1 Jane Rockfort (1581-1604). They were married in 1600. There were no children during this marriage. Wife #2 Mary Elizabeth Barnwell (1582-1626). They were married in 1605. Mary Elizabeth was the daughter of Johannes Barnwell. Sir Thomas I and Mary Elizabeth had 7 children during this marriage. Sir Thomas Sr. died in 1626 in Castleton, Kildrought, (Kildare), Ireland.
	vi.	**WILLIAM DONEGAN** b. 1589 in Castleton. Kildrought (Kildare), Ireland. It is unknown if he ever married and had children. Place of death is unknown. William died in 1622 at the age of 33.
	vii.	**THOMAS DONEGAN II** b. 1589 in Castleton. Kildrought (Kildare), Ireland. It is unknown if he ever married and had children. Place of death is unknown. Thomas II died in 1663 at the age of 74.

Leinster Province in Ireland
Kildare and Dublin are both in this Province
Castleton is in Kildare

4. Sir Thomas Dungan Sr.

SIR THOMAS[4] DUNGAN SR. (Sir John[3], Chaplain Sir Patrick[2], Sir Patrick[1])

- Born 1584 in Castleton, Kildrought (Kildare), Ireland.
- Married 1600 Wife #1 Jane Rockfort (1581-1604). They were married in Celbridge, Kildare, Ireland. No children resulted from this marriage.
- Married 1605 Wife #2 Mary Elizabeth Barnwell (1582-1626). They were married in Celbridge, Kildare, Ireland.
- Died 21 December 1626 Hurch, Dublin, Ireland at age 42.
- Buried in Celbridge, Kildrought (Kildare), Ireland.

Sir Thomas Dungan Sr. married twice. His first marriage was to Jane Rockfort in 1600 at Tom's young age of 16 years old. That marriage produced no children and Jane died four years later. "Tom" again married the following year in 1605. He was now 21 years old. He married Mary Elizabeth Barnwell in 1605 and they had seven children by this marriage. The first three children were all born in Celbridge, Kildrought, (Kildare), Ireland. Then the family moved to Dublin, Ireland, probably because of Thomas' work. The remaining four children were all born in Dublin, Ireland.

Tom died in Hurch, Dublin, Ireland on 18 September 1626. His body was taken back to his hometown of Celbridge, Kildare, for burial. His wife Mary Elizabeth Barnwell Dungan died 21 December 1626 (same year), just several months after her husband died. Both husband and wife are buried together in Celbridge. Their children, now left without parents, were ages 6 years, 9 years, 11 years, 13 years, 16 years, 19 years, and 21 years. The older ones took care of the younger ones with family support in the area. Hard times!

Children of THOMAS[4] DUNGAN SR. and MARY ELIZABETH BARNWELL were:

	i.	THOMAS DUNGAN JR. b. 1605 in Celbridge, Kildrought (Kildare) Ireland. It is unknown if he ever married and had any children. Place of death is unknown. Thomas died in 1663 at the age of 74.
5.	ii.	WILLIAM DUNGAN SR. b. 1607 in Celbridge, Kildrought (Kildare), Ireland. William Sr. married Frances Latham Weston (1610-1677). Frances was born 15 February 1610

		in Kempston, Bedfordshire, England. They were married on 27 August 1629 in the Westminster Cathedral in London, England. William Sr. and Frances had 4 children during their marriage. William Sr. died on 18 September 1636 in St. Martins Field, London, England at age 29. His widow Frances immigrated to America and settled in Rhode Island. She remarried twice more in Rhode Island. (See the Latham chapter.)
	iii.	**Elinor Dungan**. b. 1610 in Celbridge, Kildrought (Kildare), Ireland. It is unknown if she ever married and had any children. Place of death is unknown. Elinor died in 1663 at the age of 74.
	iv.	**Gerald Dungan** b. 1613 Dublin, Dublin Co., Ireland. It is unknown if he ever married and had any children. Date of death and place of death are unknown.
	v.	**Oliver Dungan** b. 1615 Dublin, Dublin Co., Ireland. It is unknown if he ever married and had any children. His date of death and place of death are unknown.
	vi.	**Luke Dungan** b. 1617 Dublin, Dublin Co., Ireland. It is unknown if he ever married and had any children. Date of death and place of death are unknown.
	vii.	**Jane Dungan** b. 1620 Dublin, Dublin Co., Ireland. It is unknown if she ever married and had any children. Date of death and place of death is unknown.

Interesting Note

Castleton is in Kildare County. It is in an area of Celbridge. At one time, a long time ago, there was a castle known as "The Castle of Kildrought." It stood in the northern end of the town of Celbridge. The castle burned down years ago, but the area was referred to as Castleton. Today where the old castle stood, there is a large building called "The Castleton House." This area in the town of Celbridge is still today referred to as Castleton.

5. William Dungan Sr.

WILLIAM[5] DUNGAN SR. (Sir Thomas[4], Sir John[3], Chaplain Sir Patrick[2], Sir Patrick[1]).

- Born circa 1611 in St. Martin in the Field, London, Middlesex Co., England.
- Married 27 August 1629 Frances Latham Weston in the Westminster Cathedral in London, Middlesex Co., England. Frances was a widow of Lord West, of London, England. Frances Latham Weston (1610-1677) was the daughter of Lewis Latham (the famous Falconer of King Charles I) and Lewis' wife Elizabeth.
- Died September 1636 in London, Middlesex Co., England at the age of 25.
- Buried 20 September 1636 London, Middlesex Co., England.

William Dungan Sr. was 16 years old when he married. This marriage produced four children. William Dungan was a "Perfumer" and sold different perfumes which were a necessity during that period as people only bathed very infrequently. The months of May and June were popular months to be married as the brides would bathe in the rivers and lakes during the springtime when the weather was warmer. Ordinarily, people would use perfume to cover their body odor.

William set up his perfume-selling business in London, England. He was a merchant in the business area of London. It was there where he met his bride of the future. She was Frances Latham, daughter of Lewis Lathan (the famous Falconer of King Charles I) and his wife Elizabeth. Frances had been a very recent widow of Lord Weston. There were no children in that marriage. William and Frances were married 27 August 1629 in the Westminster Cathedral in London, England.

William and Frances had 4 children during their marriage. Unfortunately, William Sr. died at an early age of 25 on 18 September 1636, leaving Frances a young widow (a second time) at 26 years old. She now had four small children to care for: ages 8 years, 7 years, 6 years, and 4 years. William Dungan Sr. was buried in the St. Martins of the Fields Cemetery in London, Middlesex, England. His widow Frances Lathan Weston Dungan remarried circa 1635 and she with her 3rd husband Jeremiah Clarke took her four children, left England, and crossed the Atlantic. Frances married again a 4th time in America. (See the Latham chapter for more about her life).

Children of WILLIAM[5] DUNGAN SR. and FRANCES LATHAM WESTON were:

	i.	**Barbara Dungan** (Immigrant) b. 1628 in London, Middlesex Co; England. Barbara married James Baker in Rhode Island in 1644. It is unknown how many children they had during their marriage. Barbara died in 1702 in Rhode Island at the age of 74.
	ii.	**William Dungan Jr.** (Immigrant) b.1629 in London, Middlesex Co; England. It is unknown if he ever married and had any children. His death date and place of death are unknown.
6.	iii.	**Frances Dungan** (Immigrant) b. circa 1630 in London, Middlesex Co., England. She married Captain Randall Holden Jr. in 1648 in Warwick, Rhode Island. Captain Randall Holden Jr. (1612-1692) was the son of Randall Holden Sr. and Margaret Gale. Frances and Captain Randall Jr. had 11 children during their marriage. Frances died in 1692 in Warwick, Rhode Island at the age of 62.

	iv.	**Rev. Thomas Dungan** (Immigrant) b. 1632 in London, Middlesex Co; England. Rev. Thomas married Elizabeth Weaver in 1650 Newport, Rhode Island. He and his wife moved to Pennsylvania. It is unknown how many children they had during their marriage. He was the first minister in that area where they settled. Rev. Thomas established a Baptist Church there in Cold Spring, Pennsylvania and was their first minister. Rev. Thomas died in 1688 at the age of 56 in Old Cold Spring, Bucks Co., Pennsylvania.

6. Frances Dungan (Immigrant)

FRANCES[6] DUNGAN (William[5], Sir Thomas[4], Sir John[3], Chaplain Sir Patrick[2], Sir Patrick[1])

- Born circa 1630 in London, Middlesex Co., England.
- Married 1648 Captain Randall Holden Jr. in Warwick, Kent Co., Rhode Island. Captain Randall Holden Jr. (1612-1692) was the son of Randall Holden Sr. and Margaret Gale.
- Died 1697 in Warwick, Kent Co., Rhode Island.

Children of FRANCES[6] DUNGAN and CAPTAIN RANDALL HOLDEN are documented in the Holden chapter.

Source Citations for this Chapter

Direct Ancestors and Direct Descendants of Old World Dungans Article found on ancestry.com.

History of the Sir Dungan Castle (1554-1592) Web Source History of Dalkey.

Dungan Genealogy found on ancestry.com collections Provo, Utah.

One Hundred and Sixty Allied Families by John Psborne Austin, Salem Press, 1893, Salem, Massachusetts.

Ancestry of Jeremy Clarke of Rhode Island and Dungan Genealogy by Alfred Rudolph Justice, 1922.

https://ancestors.familysearch.org (Dungan Family research).

https://myheritage.com/names/dongan_dungan (Dungan Family).

https://freepages.genealogy.rootsweb.com-mylines/dungan02.htm (Dungan Family).

Ancestry of Thirty-Three Rhode Islanders (born in the 18th Century) by J.O. Austin 1889.

The Genealogical Dictionary of Rhode Island Comprising Three Generations of Settlers who Came Before 1900 by John Osborne Austin 1889.

Chapter 12: The Eldridges

The Eldridge Family Line

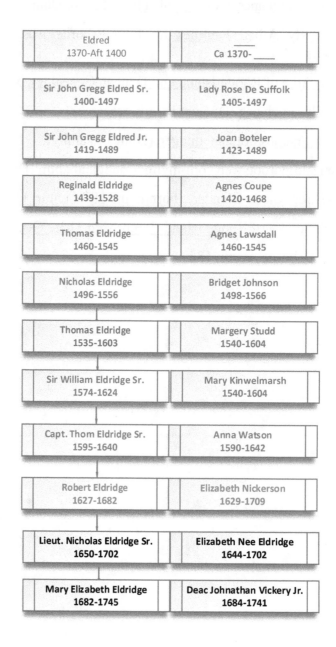

Eldred 1370-Aft 1400	____ Ca 1370- ____
Sir John Gregg Eldred Sr. 1400-1497	Lady Rose De Suffolk 1405-1497
Sir John Gregg Eldred Jr. 1419-1489	Joan Boteler 1423-1489
Reginald Eldridge 1439-1528	Agnes Coupe 1420-1468
Thomas Eldridge 1460-1545	Agnes Lawsdall 1460-1545
Nicholas Eldridge 1496-1556	Bridget Johnson 1498-1566
Thomas Eldridge 1535-1603	Margery Studd 1540-1604
Sir William Eldridge Sr. 1574-1624	Mary Kinwelmarsh 1540-1604
Capt. Thom Eldridge Sr. 1595-1640	Anna Watson 1590-1642
Robert Eldridge 1627-1682	Elizabeth Nickerson 1629-1709
Lieut. Nicholas Eldridge Sr. **1650-1702**	**Elizabeth Nee Eldridge** **1644-1702**
Mary Elizabeth Eldridge **1682-1745**	**Deac Johnathan Vickery Jr.** **1684-1741**

1. Eldred

ELDRED[1]

- Born 1370 in England.
- Married circa 1400 ____ unknown name.
- Died after 1400 Lincolnshire, England age 30+.

Child of ELDRED [1] and _____ was:

2.	i.	**SIR JOHN GRIGG ELDRED SR.** b. 1400 in Corby, Lincolnshire, England. He married Lady Rose De Suffolk (1405-1497). They were married in 1419 and had one child during their marriage. Sir John Gregg Sr. died in 1497 at the age of 97 in Grantham, Lincolnshire, England.

2. Sir John Gregg Eldred Sr.

SIR JOHN GREGG[2] ELDRED SR. (Eldred[1])

- Born 1400 in Corby, Lincolnshire, England.
- Married 1419 Lady Rose De Suffolk (1405-1497). They were married in Corby, Lincolnshire, England.
- Died 1497 in Grantham, Lincolnshire, England at the age of 97.

Children of SIR JOHN GREGG[2] ELDRED SR. SR. and LADY ROSE DE SUFFOLK were:

3.	i.	**SIR JOHN GREGG ELDRED JR.** b. 1419 in Corby, Lincolnshire, England. He married Joan Boteler (1423-1489). They were married in Corby, Lincolnshire, England, and they had 7 children during their marriage. Sir John Gregg Jr. of Corby died in 1497 in Knettishall, Suffolk, England at the age of 70.
	ii.	**JOHN BASS ELDRED** b. 1420 in Corby, Lincolnshire, England. It is unknown if he ever married and had any children. His death date and place of death are unknown.

3. Sir John Gregg Eldred Jr.

SIR JOHN GREGG[3] ELDRED JR. (John Gregg Sr[2], Eldred[1])

- Born 1419 in Corby, Lincolnshire, England.
- Married 1439 Joan Boteler (1423-1489). They were married in Corby, Lincolnshire, England.
- Died 9 April 1489 in Knettishall, Suffolk, England age 70.

Children of SIR JOHN GREGG[3] ELDRED JR. and JOAN BOTELER were:

4.	i.	**Reginald Eldred** b. 1439 in Corby, Lincolnshire, England. He married Agnes Coupe (1420-1468). They were married in 1457. They had 5 children during their marriage. Reginald Eldred died on 8 March 1528 in Knettishall, Suffolk, England at age 89.
	ii.	**Nicholas Eldred I** b. 1440 in Corby, Lincolnshire, England. It is unknown if he ever married and had any children. His death date and place of death are unknown.
	iii.	**John Eldred** b. 1448 in Corby, Lincolnshire, England. It is unknown if he ever married and had any children. His death date and place of death are unknown.
	iv.	**Martha Eldred** b. 1449 in Corby, Lincolnshire, England. It is unknown if she ever married and had any children. Her death date and place of death are unknown.
	v.	**Robert Eldred** b. 1451 in Corby, Lincolnshire, England. It is unknown if he ever married and had any children. Robert died 1528. Location is unknown. His age at death was 67.

	vi..	**Ann Eldred** b. 1453 in Corby, Lincolnshire, England. It is unknown if she ever married and had any children. Her death date and place of death are unknown.
	vii.	**Nicholas Eldred II** b. 1454 in Corby, Lincolnshire, England. It is unknown if he ever married and had any children. Nicholas Eldred II died in 1513. Location is unknown. His age at death was 59.

4. Reginald Eldridge (Eldred changed to Eldridge)

REGINALD[4] ELDRIDGE (John Gregg Jr [3], John Gregg Sr[2], Eldred[1])

- Born 1439 in Corby, Lincolnshire, England.
- Married 1457 Agnes Coupe (1420-1468) in Corby, Lincolnshire, England.
- Died 8 March 1528 in Knettishall, Suffolk, England age 89.

The Name Changed! Why, Might You Ask?

The Eldred family was a family of nobility and unfortunately, they had a history of warring against each other. The simple answer to the question of why the name changed is this author does not factually know.

However, putting the puzzle pieces of ancient history together, one might surmise this situation. Over years and years, the family of nobility may have intermarried with commoners and this sector of the family may have lived on the ridge of land nearby. In order to distinguish themselves from the other family members of nobility, they could have changed their name based on their location to The Eldreds of the Ridge which became The Eldredges.

Children of REGINALD [4] ELDRIDGE and AGNES COUPE were:

	i.	**TWIN: MARY ELDRIDGE.** b. 1460 in Knettishall, Suffolk, England. It is unknown if she ever married and had any children. Her death date and place of death are unknown.
5.	ii.	**Twin: Thomas Eldridge** b. 1460 in Knettishall, Suffolk, England. Thomas married Agnes Lawsdall (1460-1545). Thomas and Agnes married in 1495. They had 5 children during their marriage. Thomas died in 1545 at age 85 in Knettishall, Suffolk, England.
	iii.	**Agnes Eldridge** b. 1462 n Knettishall, Suffolk, England. It is unknown if she ever married and had any children. Her death date and place of death are unknown.
	iv.	**Henrie Eldridge** b. 1466 n Knettishall, Suffolk, England. It is unknown if he ever married and had any children. Henrie died in 1483. Location at death is unknown.
	v.	**John Eldridge** b. 1468 n Knettishall, Suffolk, England. It is unknown if he ever married and had any children. His death date and place of death are unknown.

5. Thomas Eldridge

THOMAS [5] ELDRIDGE (Reginald[4], John Gregg Jr [3], John Gregg Sr[2], Eldred[1])

- Born 1460 in Knettishall, Suffolk, England.
- Married 1495 Agnes Lawsdall (1460-1545). They were married in Knettishall, Suffolk, England.
- Died 1545 in Knettishall, Suffolk, England at the age of 85.

Children of THOMAS⁵ ELDRIDGE. and AGNES LAWSDALL were:

	i.	**ANN ELDRIDGE** b. in Knettishall, Suffolk, England. It is unknown if she ever married and had any children. Her death date and place of death are unknown.
6.	ii.	**NICHOLAS "THE YEOMAN" ELDREDGE** b. 1496 in Knettishall, Suffolk, England. He married Bridget Johnson (1498-1566). Nicholas and Bridget were married in 1518. They had 6 children during their marriage include two sets of twins. Nicholas died on 6 October 1556 in Knettishall, Suffolk, England.
	iii.	**Robert Eldridge** b. 1498 in Knettishall, Suffolk, England. It is unknown if he ever married and had any children. His death date and place of death are unknown.
	iv.	**Symon** Eldridge b. 1501 in Knettishall, Suffolk, England. It is unknown if he ever married and had any children. His death date and place of death are unknown.
	v.	**Jane Eldridge** b. 1507 in Knettishall, Suffolk, England. It is unknown if she ever married and had any children. Her death date and place of death are unknown.

6. Nicholas "The Yeoman" Eldridge

NICHOLAS⁶ ELDRIDGE "THE YEOMAN" (Thomas⁵, Reginald⁴, John Gregg Jr ³, John Gregg Sr², Eldred¹)

- Born 1496 in Knettishall, Suffolk, England.
- Married 1518 Bridget Johnson (1498-1566) in Knettishall, Suffolk, England.
- Died 8 October 1556 Knettishall, Suffolk, England age 60.

Many described Nicholas Eldridge as "The Yeoman." This meant that he was a tough man and an extremely hard worker. He was a fisherman.

Children of NICHOLAS⁶ ELDRIDGE "THE YEOMAN" and BRIDGET JOHNSON were:

	i.	**TWIN: JOHN ELDRIDGE** b. 1529 in Knettishall, Suffolk, England. It is unknown if he ever married and had any children. His death date and place of death are unknown.
	ii.	**TWIN: RICHARD** b. 1529 in Knettishall, Suffolk, England. It is unknown if he ever married and had any children. His death date and place of death are unknown.
	iii.	**TWIN: WILLIAM ELDRIDGE**; b. 1531 in Knettishall, Suffolk, England. It is unknown if he ever married and had any children. William died in 1603 at the age of 72. His location at his death is unknown.
	iv.	**TWIN: EDMUND ELDRIDGE** b. 1531 in Knettishall, Suffolk, England. It is unknown if he ever married and had any children. Edmund died in 1559 at the age of 28. His location at his death is unknown.
	v.	**ALYCE ELDRIDGE** b. 1534 in Knettishall, Suffolk, England. It is unknown if she ever married and had any children. Alyce died in 1617 at the age of 83. Her location at her death is unknown.

7.	vi.	**THOMAS ELDRIDGE "THE MARINER"** b. 1535 in Ipswich, Suffolk, England. Thomas married Margery Studd in 1558. They were married in Ipswich, Suffolk, England. They had 14 children during their marriage. His greatest accomplishment was his seafaring trip around the world with the famous Sir Thomas Cavendish, an English navigator and explorer. Thomas died in October 1603 in Ipswich, Suffolk, England. He is buried in the St. Clements Cemetery in Ipswich, Suffolk, England. He died at the age of 68.

7. Thomas Eldridge Sr. "The Mariner"

THOMAS[7] ELDRIDGE SR. "THE MARINER" (Nicholas[6], Thomas[5], Reginald[4], John Gregg Jr [3], John Gregg Sr[2], Eldred[1])

- Born 1535 in Ipswich, Suffolk, England.
- Married 1558 Margery Studd (1540-1604) in Ipswich, Suffolk, England.
- 1586-1588 His seafaring round-the-world trip.
- Died October 1603 in Ipswich, Suffolk, England.
- Buried in St. Clements Cemetery in Ipswich, Suffolk, England at the age of 68.

Thomas Eldridge Sr. was referred to most frequently as "The Mariner." However, he was also a merchant selling merchandise of seafaring supplies in Ipswich, England most of his life. His greatest accomplishment was his seafaring trip around the world with the famous Sir Thomas Cavendish, an English navigator and explorer. It was the third and final trip of Sir Thomas Cavendish. To make this remarkable journey, Thomas Eldridge Sr. left a successful business and left behind his wife Margery Studd Eldridge and his children. The ships left Plymouth, England on 2 July 1586 and sailed around the world, a voyage taking them to many different parts of the world. They started out with 123 men aboard three different ships: **the *Desire*, the *Content*** and **the *Hugh Galant***. They voyagers returned to Plymouth, England two years later

On 9 September 1588, **the *Desire*** returned home. It was the only ship that survived the journey. Of the 123 men who went with them when they left, only 50 men returned, surviving the trip!

Sir Thomas Cavendish (1556-1592)
Famous Navigator & Explorer
Circumnavigated the globe three times

Thomas Eldridge Sr., known as "The Mariner" b. in 1535 in Ipswich, England 1535

Summary and Timeline of his Life

He took a two-year trip circumnavigating the globe	1586-1588
Left his successful business to take the global sea voyage	
Left his wife Margery Studds Eldridge	
Left their 13 children (youngest was only 7 yrs. old)	
Went with Cavendish (Navigator & Explorer) who died 1592	1592
On his return home had another child with Margery b.1595	1595
(which was their 14th child)	
Thomas Eldridge "The Mariner" dies 1603 at age 68 years	1603
His wife Margery Studd Eldridge dies 1603 at age 63 years	1603

Both Thomas and his wife Margery died the same year. leaving 14 children, the youngest being 8 years old, and the oldest was 44 years old.

Children of THOMAS [7] ELDRIDGE SR. and MARGERY STUDD were:

	i.	**RICHARD ELDRIDGE** b. 1559 in Ipswich, Suffolk, England. It is unknown if he ever married and had any children. Richard died in 1624, age 65. Location at death unknown.
	ii.	**THOMAS ELDRIDGE** b. 1561 in Ipswich, Suffolk, England. It is unknown if he ever married and had any children. Thomas died in 1624, age 53. Location at death unknown.
	iii.	**CHRISTIAN ELDRIDGE I** b. 1563 in Ipswich, Suffolk, England. Christian I died in 1563 at birth – a stillborn in Ipswich, Suffolk, England.

	iv.	**CHRISTIAN ELDRIDGE II** b. 1564 in Ipswich, Suffolk, England. It is unknown if he ever married and had any children. Christian II died in 1664 at age 100. His location at death is unknown.
	v.	**JOHN Eldridge** b. 1565 in Ipswich, Suffolk, England. It is unknown if he ever married and had any children. John died in 1646 at the age of 81. His location at death is unknown.
	vi.	**MARY ELDRIDGE** b. 1566 in Ipswich, Suffolk, England. It is unknown if she ever married and had any children. Mary died in 1646 at the age of 80. Her location at death unknown.
	vii.	**MARGERY ELDRIDGE** b. 1568 in Ipswich, Suffolk, England. It is unknown if she ever married and had any children. Her death date and place of death ae unknown.
	viii.	**JANE ELDRIDGE** b. 1569 in Ipswich, Suffolk, England. It is unknown if she ever married and had any children. Her death date and place of death are unknown.
	ix.	**SUSAN ELDRIDGE** b. 1571 in Ipswich Suffolk, England. It is unknown if she ever married and had any children. Susan died in 1646 at the age of 75. Her location at death is unknown.
	x.	**PHILIP ELDRIDGE** b. 1573 in Ipswich, Suffolk, England. It is unknown if he ever married and had any children. Philip died in 1629 at the age of 56. His location at death unknown.
8.	xi.	**SIR WILLIAM ELDRIDGE of Bury Sr.** b. December 1574 in Ipswich, Suffolk, England. He married Mary Kinwelmarsh (1576-1630). They were married on 4 October 1596. They had 5 children during their marriage. Sir William died 23 June 1624 in Ipswich, Suffolk, England at the age of 50.
	xii.	**ANNE ELDRIDGE** b. 1575 in Ipswich, Suffolk, England. It is unknown if she ever married and had any children. Her death date and place of death are unknown.
	xiii.	**EDWARD ELDRIDGE** b. 1579 in Ipswich, Suffolk, England. It is unknown if he ever married and had any children. His death date and place of death are unknown.
	xiv.	**THOMAS A. ELDRIDGE** b. 1595 in Ipswich, Suffolk, England. Thomas A. died in 1640 at the age of 45. Location at death is unknown.

8. Sir William Eldridge of Bury Sr.

SIR WILLIAM[8] ELDRIDGE SR. of BURY (William[7], Thomas[6], Nicolas[5], Reginald[4], John Gregg Jr[3], John Gregg Sr[2], Eldred[1])

- Born December 1574 in Ipswich, Suffolk, England.
- Married 4 October 1596 Mary Kinwelmarsh (1540-1604) in Ipswich, Suffolk, England.
- Died 23 June 1624 in Ipswich, Suffolk, England at the age of 50.

Children of SIR WILLIAM [8] ELDRIDGE OF BURY, SR. and MARY KINWELMARSH were:

	i.	**JOHN THOMAS ELDRIDGE** b. 1593 in Ipswich, Suffolk, England. It is unknown if he ever married and had any children. John Thomas died in 1624 at the age of 31. His location at death is unknown.

	ii.	**WILLIAM** Eldridge b. 1594 in Ipswich, Suffolk, England. It is unknown if he ever married and had any children. William died in 1624 at the age of 30. His location at death is unknown.
9.	iii.	**CAPTAIN THOMAS JOHN ELDRIDGE** b. 1595 in Ipswich, Suffolk, England. He married Anna Watson (1590-1642). They were married in 1617 in Ipswich, Suffolk, England. They had 7 children during their marriage. Captain Thomas John died on 4 December 1640 in Ipswich, Suffolk, England at the age of 45.
	iv.	**MARY ANN ELDRIDGE** b. 1598 in Ipswich, Suffolk, England. It is unknown if she ever married and had any children. Mary Ann died in 1679 at the age of 61. Location at her death is unknown.
	v.	**ROBERT** Eldridge b. 1607 in Ipswich, Suffolk, England. It is unknown if he ever married and had any children. Robert died in 1627 at the age of 20. His location at death is unknown.

9. Captain Thomas John Eldridge Sr.

CAPTAIN THOMAS JOHN[9] ELDRIDGE SR. (Thomas[8], William[7], Thomas[6], Nicolas[5], Reginald[4], John Gregg Jr[3], John Gregg Sr[2], Eldred[1])

- Born 1595 in Ipswich, Suffolk, England.
- Married 1617 Anna Watson (1590-1642) in Ipswich, Suffolk, England. Anna Watson died 27 December 1642 in St. Christopher Le Stocks, London, England at the age of 52.
- Died 4 December 1640 in Ipswich, Suffolk, England age 45.

Their children all immigrated to America, but Captain Thomas John Eldridge Sr. and his wife Anna Watson stayed in England and died there.

Children of Captain THOMAS JOHN[9] ELDRIDGE SR. and ANNA WATSON were:

	i.	**TWIN: JOHN ELDRIDGE** (IMMIGRANT) b. 1619 in Ipswich, Suffolk, England. It is unknown if he ever married and had any children. His death date and place of death are unknown.
	ii.	**TWIN: CHARLES ELDRIDGE** (IMMIGRANT) b. 1619 in Ipswich, Suffolk, England. It is unknown if he ever married and had any children. His death date and place of death are unknown.
	iii.	**SAMUEL ELDRIDGE** (IMMIGRANT) b. 27 November 1620 in Ipswich, Suffolk, England. Samuel married twice: Wife #1 Elizabeth ____circa 1638. Wife #2 Elizabeth Miller. She and Samuel were married on 25 November 1640 in St. Mary of the Quay, Ipswich, Suffolk, England. It is unknown if they had any children during their marriage. Samuel died on 13 April 1697 Yarmouth, Barnstable Co., Massachusetts at the age of 77.
	iv.	**THOMAS ELDRIDGE JR.** (IMMIGRANT) b. 1622 in Ipswich, Suffolk, England. It is unknown if he ever married and had any children. Unknown death date and place.
	v.	**MARY Eldridge** (IMMIGRANT) b. 23 July 1626 in Ipswich, Suffolk, England. It is unknown if she ever married and had any children. Mary died elderly after year 1700.

	vi.	**TWIN: WILLIAM ELDRIDGE** (IMMIGRANT) b. 4 September 1627 in Ipswich, Suffolk, England. He married Anne Lumpkin on 3 March 1645 in Yarmouth, Barnstable Co., Massachusetts. It is unknown if they had any children during their marriage. William died 16 November 1676 in Yarmouth, Barnstable Co., and Massachusetts at age 49.
10.	vii.	**TWIN: ROBERT ELDRIDGE** (IMMIGRANT) b. 4 September 1627 in Ipswich, Suffolk, England. Robert married Elizabeth Nickerson (1629-17006). They arrived in 1635 in the Bay Colony and were married in October 1649 in New England. They had 14 children during their marriage. Robert Sr. died on 18 January 1682 in Chatham, Barnstable Co., Massachusetts at the age of 55.

10. Robert Eldridge Sr.

ROBERT[10] ELDRIDGE SR. (John[9], Thoma[8], William[7], Thomas[6], Nicolas[5], Reginald[4], John Gregg Jr [3], John Gregg Sr[2], Eldred[1])

- Born 1627 in Ipswich, Suffolk, England.
- Arrival 1635 in the Bay Colony aboard the ship the *Rose*.
- Married October 1649 Elizabeth Nickerson (1629-1709) in New England.
- Died 18 January 1682 in Chatham, Barnstable Co., Massachusetts at the age of 55.

Robert Eldridge Sr. came over to America, arriving in the Bay Colony in 1635 aboard the *Rose*, which had come from Yarmouth, England.

Children of ROBERT[10] ELDRIDGE. SR. and ELIZABETH NICKERSON were:

	i.	**SAMUEL ELDRIDGE** b. 28 October 1644 in Cambridge, Middlesex Co., Massachusetts. It is unknown if he ever married and had any children. Samuel died in 1720 at the age of 76 in Kingston, Washington Co., Rhode Island.
	ii.	**TRIPLET: JAMES ELDRIDGE** b. 1648 in Yarmouth, Barnstable Co., Massachusetts. He died in 1649 at the age of 1 year in Yarmouth, Barnstable Co., Massachusetts.
	iii.	**TRIPLET: ELIZABETH ELDRIDGE** b. 1648 in Yarmouth, Barnstable Co., Massachusetts. She died in 1649 at the age of 1 year in Yarmouth, Barnstable Co., Massachusetts.
	iv.	**TRIPLET: DESIRE ELDRIDGE** b. 1648 in Yarmouth, Barnstable Co., Massachusetts. She died in 1649 at the age of 1 year in Yarmouth, Barnstable Co., Massachusetts.
	v.	**MERCY ELDRIDGE** b. 1649 in Yarmouth, Barnstable Co., Massachusetts. It is unknown if she ever married and had any children. It is also unknown when and where she died.
11.	vi.	**LIEUTENANT NICHOLAS ELDRIDGE** b. 18 August 1650 in Yarmouth, Barnstable Co., Massachusetts. He married Elizabeth Howe (1644-1702). They were married in 1679 in Barnstable, Barnstable Co., Massachusetts. They had 6 children during their marriage. Lieutenant Nicholas died 30 April 1702 in a drowning accident in Chatham, Barnstable Co., Massachusetts at the age of 52.

	vii.	**ROBERT ELDRIDGE JR.** b. 1652 in Yarmouth, Barnstable Co., Massachusetts. It is unknown if he ever married and unknown if he had children. Robert died 5 October 1732 in Smyrna, Kent Co., Delaware at the age of 76.
	viii.	**TRIPLET: WILLIAM ELDRIDGE** b. 1656 in Yarmouth, Barnstable Co., Massachusetts. It is unknown if he ever married and had any children. William died 27 April 1749 in Chatham, Barnstable Co., Massachusetts at the age of 93.
	ix.	**TRIPLET: MARY ELDRIDGE** b. 1656 in Yarmouth, Barnstable Co., Massachusetts. It is unknown if MARY ever married and had any children. Mary died 3 May 1706 in Chatham, Barnstable Co., Massachusetts at the age of 50. It was the same day her sibling (triplet) Hannah also died.
	x.	**TRIPLET: HANNAH ELDRIDGE** b. 1656 in Yarmouth, Barnstable Co., Massachusetts It is unknown if she ever married and had any children. Hannah died 3 May 1706 in Chatham, Barnstable Co., Massachusetts at the age of 50. It was the same day her sibling (triplet) Mary also died.
	xi.	**MARTHA Eldridge** b. 1658 in Yarmouth, Barnstable Co., Massachusetts. It is unknown if she ever married and had any children. Martha died 6 May 1706 in Chatham, Barnstable Co., Massachusetts at the age of 48. She died 3 days after both her siblings Mary and Hannah had also died.
	xii.	**ISAAC ELDRIDGE** b. 1659 in Chatham, Barnstable Co., Massachusetts. It is unknown if he ever married and had any children. It is also unknown when and where he died.
	xii.	**JOSEPH ELDREDGE** b. 1662 in Sandwich, Barnstable Co., Massachusetts. It is unknown if he ever married and had any children. Joseph died 24 September 1735 in Boston, Suffolk Co., Massachusetts at the age of 73.
	xiv.	**BRIDGET ELDRIDGE** b. 1664 in Yarmouth, Barnstable Co., Massachusetts. It is unknown if she ever married and had any children. Bridget died in 1735 in Harwich, Barnstable Co, Massachusetts at the age of 71.

11. Lieutenant Nicholas Eldridge Sr.

LIEUTENANT NICHOLAS[11] ELDRIDGE SR. (Robert[10], John[9], Thoma[8], William[7], Thomas[6], Nicolas[5], Reginald[4], John Gregg Jr[3], John Gregg Sr[2], Eldred[1])

- Born 18 August 1650 in Yarmouth, Barnstable Co., Massachusetts.
- Married 1679 Elizabeth nee Eldridge (1644-1702). They were married in Barnstable, Barnstable Co., Massachusetts.
- Died 30 April 1702 in Chatham, Barnstable Co., Massachusetts (drowning accident) at age 52.

Children of LIEUTENANT NICHOLAS[11] ELDRIDGE and ELIZABETH HAWES were:

	i.	**JOHN ELDRIDGE** b. 1680 in Chatham, Barnstable Co., Massachusetts. It is unknown if he ever married and had any children. John died on 20 February 1723 in Wells, York Co., Maine at the age of 43.

	ii.	**Nicholas Eldridge Jr**. b. 1682 in Chatham, Barnstable Co., Massachusetts. It is unknown if he ever married and had any children. Nicholas Jr. died in 1727 at the age of 45. Location where he died is unknown.
12.	iii.	**MARY ELIZABETH ELDRIDGE** b. 1682 in Chatham, Barnstable Co., Massachusetts. She married Deacon Johnathan Vickery II Jr. (1683-1741). They married in 1706 in Barnstable Co., Massachusetts. They had 3 children during their marriage. Mary Elizabeth died 13 November 1745 in Truro, Barnstable Co., Massachusetts at the age of 63. She is buried in the Old North Cemetery in Truro. Barnstable Co., Massachusetts.
	iv.	**JAMES ELDRIDGE Sr.** b. 1689 in Chatham, Barnstable Co., Massachusetts. James married Ruth Huggins (1700-1764). They were married in 1728 in Chatham, Barnstable Co., Massachusetts. They had 1 child during their marriage. James Sr. died on 19 July 1757 in Chatham, Barnstable Co., Massachusetts at the age of 68.
	v.	**MARTHA Eldridge** b. 1692 in Chatham, Barnstable Co., Massachusetts. It is unknown if she ever married and had any children. Martha died in 1740 at the age of 48 in Eastham, Barnstable Co., Massachusetts.
	vi.	**DESIRE Eldridge** b. 1698 in Chatham, Barnstable Co., Massachusetts. It is unknown if Desire ever married and had children. She died in 1745 at the age of 77. Her location at her death is unknown.

12. Mary Elizabeth Eldridge

MARY ELIZABETH [12] ELDRIDGE (Nicholas[11], Robert[10], John[9], Thoma[8], William[7], Thomas[6], Nicolas[5], Reginald[4], John Gregg Jr [3], John Gregg Sr[2], Eldred[1])

- Born 1682 in Chatham, Barnstable Co., Massachusetts (1684-1604).
- Married 1706 Deacon Johnathan Vickery II Jr. (1684-1741) Barnstable Co, Massachusetts.
- Died 13 November 1745 in Truro, Barnstable Co., Massachusetts age 63.

It was a difficult day, 30 April 1702! Mary Elizabeth Eldridge lost both her father and her father-in-law that day due to a drowning accident. Her husband Deacon Jonathan Vickery Jr. lost his father in the same drowning accident. Both fathers were in the boat together fishing when an unexpected storm came up and capsized their fishing vessel. The two other men in that boat with them who perished that day. Such a tragic day for Mary Elizabeth, Jonathan, and their friends' families as well as their entire church family, for Rev. Johnathan Vickery Sr. was the pastor of their church!

Children of MAY ELIZAETH[12] ELDRIDGE R. and DEACON JONATHAN VICKERY II JR. are documented in the Vickery chapter.

83

The story of Captain Asa Eldridge
Yarmouth, Barnstable Co.,
Massachusetts

CAPT. ASA ELDRIDGE.
BORN 1809 - DIED 1856.

This author has done the research on the family of Asa Eldridge and has traced them back to Ipswich, Suffolk, England, so Asa is one of our cousins!

Captain Asa Eldridge was born 25 July 1809 in Yarmouth, Barnstable Co., Massachusetts. He loved the sea and became a sea captain. In 1854 at the age of 45, he raced the famous clipper ship the *Red Jacket* from New York City to Liverpool, England and won the race in 13 days, 1 hour and 25 minutes. A book was written about his life and his career as a ship captain entitled: *The Lost Hero of Cape Cod: Asa Eldridge and the Maritime Trade that Shaped America* by Vincent Miles. Two years after the famous *Red Jacket* clipper ship race, in 1856 he was the captain of the steamship the SS *Pacific* which completely disappeared on its journey, on a routine voyage from Liverpool to New York City. It is presumed that the ship hit an iceberg in the northern waters. Captain Asa and his ship was never found and presumed lost at sea.

The Famous *Red Jacket* Clipper Ship
Fastest record in history of Clipper Ship Races
Captain Asa Eldridge
New York City to Liverpool, England
13 days 1 hour & 25 minutes, 1854

Source Citations for this Chapter

https://www.ancestry.com

https://www.familysearch.org

https://www.geni.com

https://findagrave.com

https://en.wikipedia.org

Edmund West, comp. *Family Data Collection - Individual Records* [database on-line]. Provo, Utah, USA: Ancestry.com Operations Inc, 2000.

The Lost Hero of Cape Cod Asa Eldridge and the Maritime Trade that Shaped America by Vincent Miles.

A History of the Ancestors in America of Marion Bassett Luitweller (that include the Eldridge family) Tuttle, Morehouse & Taylor Publishers, New Haven, Connecticut, 1930.

The Oxford Dictionary of National Biography by J.M. Blatchly (Eldred, Thomas (1561-1624), 1st publication 2004, on-line edition 2008.

The Massachusetts Birth, Marriages and Death Index, Boston, Massachusetts.

Chapter 13: The Foneses

The Fones Family Line

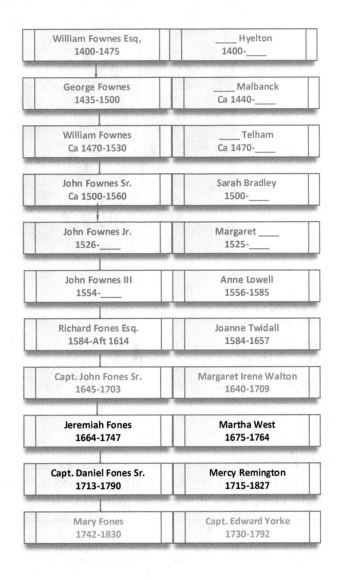

William Fownes Esq, 1400-1475	____ Hyelton 1400-____
George Fownes 1435-1500	____ Malbanck Ca 1440-____
William Fownes Ca 1470-1530	____ Telham Ca 1470-____
John Fownes Sr. Ca 1500-1560	Sarah Bradley 1500-____
John Fownes Jr. 1526-____	Margaret ____ 1525-____
John Fownes III 1554-____	Anne Lowell 1556-1585
Richard Fones Esq. 1584-Aft 1614	Joanne Twidall 1584-1657
Capt. John Fones Sr. 1645-1703	Margaret Irene Walton 1640-1709
Jeremiah Fones 1664-1747	**Martha West 1675-1764**
Capt. Daniel Fones Sr. 1713-1790	**Mercy Remington 1715-1827**
Mary Fones 1742-1830	Capt. Edward Yorke 1730-1792

1. William Fownes, Esq.

WILLIAM [1] FOWNES ESQUIRE

- Born 1400 in Saxby, Devonshire, England.
- Married circa 1434 ____Hyelton (1400-__). They were married in England.
- Died 1475 at Saxby, Devonshire, England at the age of 75.

Child of WILLIAM [1] FOWNES and ____HYELTON was:

2.	i.	**GEORGE FOWNES** b. 1435 in Saxby, Devonshire, England. George married ____ Malbanck (1430-__) They were married in 1469 in Saxby, Devonshire, England. They had 1 child, a son, during their marriage. George Fownes died in 1500 at age 65.

The Shires of England

(Examples: Devonshire, Worcestershire, Bedfordshire)

Shiring: An Anglo-Saxon achievement. The process of shiring has been described as the defining of territories expressed in different land areas or provinces to provide for defense and upkeep of the burhs. The area of western Mercia, which was organized into tenth-century shires, was from c. 700. The territory of discrete peoples: those of Original Mercia, the Hwicce, Wreocensaete and Magonsaete, whose obligations to the state were expressed in their respective hidage allocations. The development of a scheme of political organization, taxation, and governance over the succeeding three-hundred-year period—from one allocating tribute owed by peoples to one aligning communities to the hinterlands of defended settlements—represents the development of a farsighted and sophisticated statecraft.

2. George Fownes

GEORGE[2] FOWNES (William[1])

- Born circa 1435 in Saxony, Devonshire, England.
- Married circa 1469 ____ Malbanck in Saxby, Devonshire, England.
- Died 500 at Saxby, Devonshire, England at the age of 65.

Child of GEORGE[2] FOWNES SR and __ MALBANCK was:

3.	i.	**WILLIAM [2] FOWNES** b.1470 in Saxony, Devonshire, England. William married ____ Telham (1470-___). They were married circa in 1499 in Saxony, Devonshire, England. They had 1 child, a son, during their marriage. William died 1530 in Saxby, Worcester, England.

3. William Fownes

WILLIAM[3] FOWNES (George[2], William[1])

- Born circa 1470 in Saxony, Devonshire, England.
- Married circa 1499 ____ Telham in Saxony, Devonshire, England.
- Died 1530 at Saxby, Worcester, England.

Child of WILLIAM[3] FOWNES SR. and ___ TELHAM was:

4.	i.	**JOHN FOWNES SR.** b. 1500 in Saxby, Worcestershire, England. John Sr. married Sarah Bradley (1500-___) in 1525. They were married in Saxby, Worcestershire, England. John and Sarah had 1 child, a son, during their marriage. John Sr. died in 1560 in Worcestershire, England.

4. John Fownes Sr.

JOHN[4] FOWNES SR. (William[3], George[2], William[1])

- JOHN FOWNES SR.
- Born circa 1500 in Saxby, Worcestershire, England.
- Married circa 1525 Sarah Bradley (1500 - __). John Sr. and Sarah married in Saxby, Worcestershire, England.
- Died 1560 in Worcestershire, England at the age of 60.

Child of JOHN[4] FOWNES SR. and SARAH BRADLEY was:

5.	i.	**JOHN FOWNES JR.** b.1526 in Worcestershire, England. John Jr. married Margaret ___ (1525- ___). They were married in 1553. John Jr. and Margaret had 1 child, a son, during their marriage. John Jr. died unknown date in England.

5. John Fownes Jr.

John⁵ Fownes JR (John I⁴, William³, George², William¹)
- Born 1526 in Worcestershire, England.
- Married 1553 Margaret ___ (1525 - ___).
- Died unknown date in England.

Child of John⁵ Fones JR .and Margaret ___ was:

6.	i.	**JOHN FOWNES III** b. 1554 Bedford Parish of Bromsgrove, Worcestershire, England. John III married Ann Lewell (circa 1556-1585). They were married circa 1572 in England. John III and Anne had 6 children during their marriage. John III died date unknown in Suffolk, England.

6. John Fownes III

John III⁶ Fownes (John II⁵, John I⁴, William³, George², William¹)
- Born circa 1554 in Bedford, Parish of Bromsgrove, Worcestershire, England.
- Married circa 1572 Anne Lewell (1556-1585). They were married in England.
- Died date unknown in Suffolk, England.

Bromsgrove, Worcestershire Co., England

In the 16th century the Worcestershire clothing industry gave employment to 8,000 people. The clothing industry declined in the 17th century, but silk manufacture later replaced it at Kidderminster and Blockley.

King Henry VIII confined cloth making to Bromsgrove, Kidderminster, Droitwich, Evesham, and Worcester. Rural production of cloth had been spurred by rural poverty and the need to supplement incomes. Trade in Worcester and the cloth trade in Kidderminster was still controlled by guilds. Fulling (new cleaning cloth) around Worcestershire and dyeing in the Teme valley were major employers. Rope making was prominent around Bromsgrove. However, tanning was the largest single industry across the county, concentrated near rivers and streams in the north and west of the county.

Children of John⁶ III Fownes Sr. and Ann Lewell were:

7A Gov	i.	**THOMAS FONES II** b. 24 March 1573 London, Middlesex, England. Thomas married twice: Wife #1: Ann Agnes Browne (b. circa 1575 & died 20 May 1618), It is unknown if they had any children during their marriage. Wife #2 Priscilla ____ (circa 1575-___). They had one son during their marriage. This son was John Fones III. Further information later in this chapter but for now please note, Anne Winthrop (b.16 January 1585 – d.16 May 1618) was married on 25 February 1605 in London, England to Thomas Fones II who was a son of John Fones III. Anne Wynthropp (Winthrop) was a sister of John Winthrop who became the Governor of the Massachusetts Bay Colony in the early 1600s. Thomas II died 15 April 1629 in Groton, Suffolk, England at age 56.
	ii.	**NICHOLAS FONES** b. circa 1575 Bedford, Worcestershire, England. It is unknown who he married and also unknown if they had any children during their marriage. Also unknown is when and where he died.

	iii.	**ROBERT FONES** b. circa 1577 Bedford, Worcestershire, England. It is unknown who he married and unknown if they had any children during their marriage. Also unknown is when and where he died.
	iv.	**WILLIAM FONES** b. 1580 b Bedford, Worcestershire, England. It is unknown who he married and unknown if they had any children during their marriage. Also unknown is when and where he died.
	v.	**HUMPHREY FONES** b. circa 1582 Bedford, Worcestershire, England. It is unknown who he married and unknown if they had any children during their marriage. Also unknown is when and where he died.
7B	vi.	**RICHARD FONES ESQUIRE OF BRISTOL** b. 1584 Bristol, Gloucestershire, England. Richard of Bristol married Joan Twidall (1584-1676). They were married circa 1572 in Bristol, Gloucestershire, England. They had 4 children during their marriage. Richard died after 1614 in Bristol, Gloucestershire, England at the age of approx. 30.

7A. (See the Governor John Winthrop Connection Section ahead)
7B. Richard Fones Esquire of Bristol

RICHARDS[7] FONES ESQUIRE OF BRISTOL (John III[6], John II[5], John I[4], William[3], George[2], William[1])

- Born 1584 in Bristol, Gloucestershire, England.
- Married 25 February 1605 Joanne Twidall (1584-1657). They married in Bristol, England.
- Died after 1614 in Bristol, England, near London at age approx. 30.

Children of RICHARD[1] FONES of Bristol and JOANE TWIDALL___ were:

8B.	i.	**THOMAS FONES** b. 1587 Devon, England. Thomas married Joane Heale (1590-1670). They were married circa 1625 in Devon England. They had 3 children (all sons), during their marriage. Thomas died in 1637 in England at the age of 50.
	ii.	**GEORGE FONES** b. 1612 Devon, England. It is unknown if he ever married and had any children. His death date and location at death are both unknown.
	iii.	**RICHARD FONES** (IMMIGRANT) b. 1614 Bristol, England. Richard married ____ Greene in Kings Towne, Washington Co., Rhode Island. It is unknown if they had any children. Also unknown is where and when Richard Fones died.

8B. Thomas Fones of Bristol

THOMAS[7] FONES of BRISTOL (John 111[6], John II[5], John I[4], William[3], George[2], William[1])

- Born 1587 in Bristol, Gloucestershire, England.
- Married circa 1625 Joane Heale (1590-1670). Thomas and Joan were married in Bristol, England.
- Died in 1637 in Bristol, England at the age of 50.

Children of THOMAS [8B] FONES. of BRISTOL and JOANE HEALE were:

	i.	**SUSANNA FONES** b. 1614 Devon, England. It is unknown if she married and had any children. She died in 1648 at the age of 34 but her location at death is unknown.
	ii.	**ELIZABETH FONES** b. 1629 Devon, England. It is unknown if she ever married and had any children. Her death date and location at death are also both unknown.
	iii.	**JOHN FONES** b. 1630 Devon, England. He died as a small child circa 1634 in Devon, England at the age of approx. 4 years.
	iv.	**SAMPSON FONES** b. 1633 Devon, England. It is unknown if he ever married and had any children. His death date and location at death are also both unknown.
9B.	v.	**HONORABLE CAPTAIN JOHN FONES SR. (IMMIGRANT)** b. 1635 Devon, England. Captain John Sr. married Margaret Irene Walton. They were married in 1660 in Warwick, Kent Co., Rhode Island. They had 6 children during their marriage. Captain John Sr. died 20 December 1703 in Kingston, Washington Co., Rhode Island age 68.
	vi.	**TWIN: WILLIAM FONES** b. 1636 Devon, England. It is unknown if he ever married and had any children. His death date and location at death are also both unknown.
	vii.	**Twin: Thomas Fones** b. 1636 Devon, England. It is unknown if he married and had any children. His death date and location at death are also both unknown.
	viii.	**SAMPSON FONES** b. 1637 Devon, England. Sampson was born the year that his father died. It is unknown if he ever married and had any children. His death date and location at death are also both unknown.

8B. Captain Honorable John Fones Sr. (Immigrant)

CAPTAIN HONORABLE JOHN[8] FONES SR. (Richard[7], John III[6], John Jr.[5], John Sr.[4], William[3], George[2], William[1])

- Born 1635 in Devon, England.
- Married 1660 Margaret Irene Walton (1640-1709) in Warwick, Kent, Rhode Island.
- Died 20 December 1703 Kingston, Washington Co., Rhode Island at the age of 68.

Children of CAPTAIN HONORABLE JOHN[8] FONES SR. and MARGARET IRENE WALTON were:

	i.	**SAMUEL FONES** b. 1662 Jamestown, Newport Co., Rhode Island. It is unknown if he ever married and unknown if he had any children. Samuel died in 1751 in Jamestown, Newport Co., Rhode Island at the age of 89.
	ii.	**JOHN FONES JR.** b. 1662 Jamestown, Newport Co., Rhode Island. It is unknown if he ever married and unknown if he had any children. John Jr. died 1738 in Jamestown, Newport Co., Rhode Island at the age of 76.
9B.	iii.	**JEREMIAH FONES** b. 1663 Jamestown, Newport Co., Rhode Island. Jeremiah married Martha West (1676-1764). (Martha was the granddaughter of "The Pilgrim," George Soule). Jeremiah and Martha had 7 children during their marriage. Jeremiah died 29 April 1747 at the age of 84 in North Kingstown, Washington Co.,

		Rhode Island. He is buried in the Chestnut Hill Cemetery in Exeter, Washington Co., Rhode Island.
	iv.	**MARY FONES** b. 1668 Jamestown, Newport Co., Rhode Island. It is unknown if she ever married and unknown if she had any children. Mary died in 1722 in Jamestown, Newport Co., Rhode Island at the age of 54.
	v.	**JAMES FONES** b. 1670 Jamestown, Newport Co., Rhode Island. It is unknown if he ever married and unknown if he had any children. James died in 1764 in Jamestown, Newport Co., Rhode Island at the age of 94.
	vi.	**DANIEL FONES** b. 1672 Jamestown, Newport Co., Rhode Island. It is unknown if he ever married and unknown if he had any children. Daniel died in 1703 in Jamestown, Newport Co., Rhode Island at the age of 31.

9B. Jeremiah Fones

JEREMIAH[9] FONES (Captain Honorable John[8], Richard[7], John III[6], John Jr.[5], John Sr.[4], William[3], George[2], William[1])

- Born 1664 Jamestown, Newport, Rhode Island.
- Married 30 March 1694 Wife #1 Elizabeth Havens in Jamestown, Newport, Rhode Island.
- Married 9 November 1710 Wife #2 Martha West (1675-1764) (Granddaughter of Pilgrim George Soule). Jeremiah and Martha married in Jamestown, Rhode Island.
- Died 29 April 1747 North Kingston, Washington Co., Rhode Island at the age of 83.
- Buried 1747 Chestnut Hill Cemetery, Exeter, Kingstown, Rhode Island.
  There were no children of the marriage of JEREMIAH[9] FONES SR and ELIZABETH HAVENS.

Children of JEREMIAH[9] FONES SR and MARTHA WEST were:

	i.	**DINAH FONES** b. 1710 Jamestown, Newport Co., Rhode Island. Dinah died in 1711 at the age of 1 year old.
	ii.	**MARY FONES** b. 20 September 1711 in Jamestown, Newport Co., Rhode Island. She married ___ Hill. They married circa 1730 in North Kingston, Washington Co., Rhode Island. Her married name of Mary Hill was mentioned in her brother Samuel Fones's will. Mary's death date and location at death are both unknown.
10B	iii.	**CAPTAIN DANIEL FONES SR.**, b.9 March 1713 in Jamestown, Newport Co., Rhode Island. He married Mercy Remington circa 1740 in North Kingstown, Washington Co., Rhode Island. Captain Daniel and Mercy had 5 children during their marriage. Captain Daniel died 1790 at the age of 77.
	iv	**SAMUEL FONES** b. 10 March 1714 in North Kingston, Washington Co., Rhode Island. Samuel died before 19 November 1739 in North Kingston, Washington Co., Rhode Island at age approx. 25.
	v.	**SQUCIE/SCUSIE FONES** b. 23 February 1718 in North Kingston, Washington Co., Rhode Island. She married twice: Husband #1 Samuel Place. They were married circa 1726 in North Kingston, Washington Co., Rhode Island. Husband. Squcie and Samuel had 4 children during this marriage. Husband #2 Benjamin Cole. They were married circa 1747 in North Kingston, Washington Co., Rhode Island.

		Squcie and Benjamin had 6 children during their marriage. Squcie died circa 1774 in North Kingston, Washington Co., Rhode Island. Squcie was known as "Daughter of Fones."
	vi..	**THOMAS FONES** b. 23 January 1726 in North Kingston, Washington Co., Rhode Island. Thomas died in 1727 at the age of 1 year old in North Kingston, Washington Co., Rhode Island.
	vii.	**JOSEPH FONES** b. circa 1728 Jamestown, Newport Co., Rhode Island. It is unknown if he ever married and unknown if he had any children. Joseph's date of death and location at death are also both unknown.

10B. Captain Daniel Fones Sr. (Revolutionary War)

CAPTAIN DANIEL[10] FONES SR. (Jeremiah[9], Captain Honorable John[8], Richard[7].John III[6], John Jr.[5], John Sr.[4], William[3], George[2], William[1])

- Born 9 March 1713 in Jamestown, Newport Co., Rhode Island.
- Married 1740 Mercy Remington (1715-1827). They were married in North Kingston, Washington Co., Rhode Island.
- Died 9 August 1790 in North Kingston, Washington Co., Rhode Island at the age of 77.

Captain Daniel Fones Sr. (1713-1790) served in the Revolutionary War.

He was a captain and served with the Newport Rhode Island Company, He went on an expedition against Cape Breton and was captain of the colony sloop *Tartar*, 14 guns, 12 swivels with 90 men aboard.

The *Tartar*
The armed sloop of the Colony of Rhode Island
The naval militia of King George's War
(also known as The Revolutionary War).
Daniel Fones was the captain of the *Tartar*.
The year was 1775.

Children of CAPTAIN DANIEL[10] FONES SR. and MERCY REMINGTON were as follows:

11B	i.	MARY FONES b. 1742 North Kingston, Washington Co., Rhode Island. She married Captain Edward Yorke. Mary and Captain Edward had 9 children during their marriage. Mary died 1830 in Falmouth, Hants Co., Nova Scotia at the age of 88.
	ii.	DANIEL FONES JR. b. 09 December 1744 in North Kingston, Washington Co., Rhode Island. Daniel Jr. died 1790 in North Kingston, Washington Co., Rhode Island age 56.
	iii.	MARTHA FONES b. 1746 North Kingston, Washington Co., Rhode Island. Martha married Michael Spencer on 3 August 1767 in North Kingston, Washington Co., Rhode Island. It is unknown how many children she had. When and where she died are unknown.
	iv.	ELIZABETH FONES b. 1749. North Kingston, Washington Co., Rhode Island. It is unknown if she ever married and if she had any children. Also, unknown is when and where she died.
	v.	FONES (FEMALE) FONES b. 1750 North Kingston, Washington Co., Rhode Island. She died at birth as a stillborn.

11B. Mary Fones (Emigrated to Nova Scotia Canada)

MARY[11] FONES (Captain Daniel,[10] Jeremiah[9], Captain Honorable John[8], Richard[7].John III[6], John Jr.[5], John Sr.[4], William[3], George[2], William[1])

- Born 1742 in North Kingston, Washington Co., Rhode Island.
- Married 23 January 1755 Captain Edward Yorke, son of James Yorke IV and Elizabeth Case in North Kingston, Washington Co., Rhode Island.
- Died 1830 in Falmouth, Hants Co., Nova Scotia, Canada at age 88.

Children of MARY[4] FONES and CAPTAIN EDWARD YORKE are documented in the Yorke chapter.

Governor John Winthrop Connection

Gov. Winthrop's Line	= Thomas Fones II (1573-1629)
Author (MLM) Line	= Richard Fones Esq. of Bristol (1584-after 1614)

Thomas II Fones and Richard Fones were brothers.

Their father was John Fones III (1584-1582).

The following is a short history of Governor John Winthrop's ancestral family.

Governor of the Massachusetts Bay State Colony
Governor John Winthrop
1586-1649

Through the Fones family line, we find that Governor John Winthrop is our close relative by marriage. How we are connected is explained as follows. <u>Our Line is **7B** and Gov. Winthrop's line is 7A</u>. The two lines converged. Gov. Winthrop's ancestor is Thomas II Fones, and our line is through Richard Fones. Good to remember: Thomas Fones II and Richard Fones are brothers; both are John Fones III's sons.

7A. Thomas Fones II

(Line of the Governor John Winthrop of the Bay State)

THOMAS[7] FONES II

- Born 24 March 1573 London, Middlesex, England.
- Married 25 February 1605 Wife #1 Anne **Winthrop** London, England (**sister of Gov. John Winthrop**). Anne Winthrop (b. 16 January 1585-16 May 1618).
- Married circa 1618 Wife #2 Priscila ____ Sherman (circa 1555-1662) in London, England.
- Died 15 April 1629 in London, England age 56.

Anne Winthrop (b.16 January 1585-d.16 May 1618) was married on 25 February 1605 in London, England to Thomas Fones II, who was a son of John Fones III. <u>Anne Wynthropp (Winthrop) was a sister of John Winthrop, who became the Governor of the Massachusetts Bay Colony in the early 1600s.</u>

In 1595, Thomas Fones II (Anne's husband) was an apprentice at a "grocery shoppe" in London, England. After Anne (Winthrop) and Thomas Fones II were married on 25 February 1604, Thomas decided to leave the grocery store apprenticeship and he opened his own apothecary shop there at the sign of the Three Fawns on Old Bailey Street in London. They had six children during this marriage (four girls and two boys). Thomas and his family lived in very cramped conditions above the "Pharmacy Shoppe" on Old Bailey Street. There were 2 parents, 6 children and 2 servants. Thomas' wife Anne died 1n 1618 when their daughter Elizabeth (known as Bess) was 12 years old. Bess was one of the older children who was helping her father with the apothecary business. It was during this period that Bess learned the art of being a pharmacist.

Following Anne death, Thomas remarried, to a woman named Priscilla ___ Sherman, who was a widow of Bezalel Sherman. In addition to Thomas' pharmaceutical responsibilities, Thomas offered general medical advice along with a range of services such as surgical procedures and midwifery. He also operated a retail shop selling ingredients for medicines, tobacco, and patented medicines. By the 15th century his profession had gained the status of skilled practitioners. Such work marked the beginnings of chemistry and pharmacology.

It was probably because Thomas and his family were strong Puritans that he refused the knighthood from the King of England. Thomas was well educated and quite prosperous. It was very unfortunate, that Thomas became a sickly man in his mid-life, and he died 15 April 1529 at the age of 56. Thomas wrote his Will two days prior to his death. After Thomas' death, Priscilla ___ Sherman Fones remarried again. There were no children born of Thomas II Fones and Priscilla's marriage.

Children of THOMAS II[7] FONES. and ANNE WINTHROP were:

	i.	**Dorothy Fones** b. 1608 London, England. It is unknown if she ever married and had any children. Dorothy died in 1673 at age 65. Location at her death is unknown.
	ii.	**(TWIN) JOHN FONES** b. 1610 London, England. It is unknown if he ever married and had any children. It is unknown when and where he died.
	iii.	**(TWIN) ELIZABETH FONES WINTHROP FAKE HALLET** b. 1610 London, England. It is unknown if she ever married and had any children. Elizabeth died in 1673 at age 63. Her location at death is unknown.
	iv.	**Martha Fones Winthrop** b, 1611 London, England. It is unknown if she ever married and had any children. Martha died in 1634 at age 23. Her location at her death is unknown.
	v.	**ANNE FONES** b **1612** London, England. It is unknown if she ever married and had any children. Anne died in 1673 at age 61. Her location at death is unknown.
	vi.	**SAMUEL FONES** b. 1616 London, England. It is unknown if he ever married and had any children. It is unknown as to when and where Samuel died.

Parents of Governor John Winthrop and Anne Winthrop Fones were:

Father was ADAM WINTHROP III:
- Born 10 August 1548 Bishop Gate, City of London, England.
- Married 25 February 1604 Anne Browne. They were married in Groton, Suffolk, England.
- Died 28 March 1623 Groton, Bamberg District, Suffolk, England at the age of 75.
- Buried St. Bartholomew's Churchyard, Groton, Bamberg District, Suffolk, England.

Mother was ANNE AGNES BROWNE:

- Born 13 January 1549 the Burroughs, London, Middlesex, England.
- She was a daughter of Henry Browne and his wife Agnes ____ Browne.
- Married 25 February 1604 Adam Winthrop III in Groton, Suffolk, England.
- Died 19 April 1629 Groton, Suffolk, England at the age of 80.
- Buried St. Bartholomew's Churchyard, Groton, Bamberg District, Suffolk, England.

Children of ADAM WINTHROP III and ANNE AGNES BROWNE were:

	i.	**Sarah Winthrop** b. 1579 in Groton, Suffolk, England. She married John Frost Sr. It is unknown if they ever had any children. Sarah died but date is unknown. She died in Suffolk, England.
	ii.	**Anne Winthrop I** b. 5 January 1580 in Groton, Suffolk, England. Anne I was only 15 days old when she died. She died on 20 January 1580 in Groton, England.
Sis.	iii.	**Anne Winthrop II** b. 16 January 1585 in Groton, Suffolk, England. Anne married Thomas Fones Jr. on 25 February 1604. Ann and Thomas Jr. had 6 children. She died on 16 May 1618 at the age of 33 in England.
Gov	iv.	**Governor John Winthrop** b. 12 January 1587 in Groton, Suffolk, England. He married 4 times. Wife #1 Mary Forth. Wife #2 Thomasine Cloptoin. Wife #3 Margaret Tyndal. Wife #4 Martha Rainsborough. He had many children from all four wives. The following children survived to adulthood: John the Younger (1606-1676), Henry (1608-1630), Mary (1611-1643), Stephen (1619-1658), Deane (1623-1704), Samuel (1627-1674). He had many other children, but the others all died as stillborn or as small children. John Winthrop was a strict Puritan like his mother. He crossed the ocean and became the first Governor of the Massachusetts Bay Colony of New England. Gov. John Winthrop died on 26 March 1649 at the age of 62. He is buried in downtown Boston, Massachusetts in the King's Chapel Church Burying Ground. His son John Jr. later became Governor of the new colony in Connecticut. Another son, Samuel, became Governor of Antigua.
	v.	**Jane Winthrop** b. 17 June 1592 in Groton, Suffolk, England. Jane married Thomas Gosling on 5 January 1612. It is unknown if they ever had any children during their marriage. It is unknown as to when and where Jane died.
	vi.	**Lucy Winthrop** b. 9 January 1600 in Groton, Suffolk, England. Lucy married Emmanuel Downing on 10 April 1622. It is unknown if they had any children during their marriage. Lucy died in 1679 at the age of 79.

Review of the Fones – Winthrop Connection

6. John Fownes III

JOHN[6] III FOWNES

- Born circa 1554 in Bedford, Parish of Bromsgrove, Worcestershire, England.
- Married 1572 Anne Lewell (1556-1585).
- Died date unknown in Suffolk, England (unknown death age).

Children of JOHN[6] III FOWNES SR. and ANN WINTHROP ___ were:

7A Gov	i.	**Thomas Fones Jr.** b. 24 March 1573 London, Middlesex, England. Thomas Jr. married twice: Wife #1 Anne Winthrop (b.16 January 1585- 16 May 1618). Anne was the sister of Gov. John Winthrop of Massachusetts. Thomas and Anne were married at the Groton Manor in Suffolk, England on 25 February 1605. They had 6 children during their marriage. Following Anne's death Thomas Jr. remarried, Wife #2 Priscilla ___ Sherman. They were married circa 1618 in London England. There were no children born in the marriage of Thomas Jr. and Priscilla. Thomas Jr. died on 15 April 1629 at the age 56 in Groton, Suffolk, England.
	ii.	**Nicholas Fones** b. circa 1575 Bedford, Worcestershire, England. It is unknown if he ever married and had any children. Death date and location are both unknown.
	iii.	**Robert Fones** b. circa 1577 Bedford, Worcestershire, England. It is unknown if he ever married and had any children. Death date and location are both unknown.
	iv.	**William Fones** b. 1580 b Bedford, Worcestershire, England. It is unknown if he ever married and had any children. Death date and location are both unknown.
	v.	**Humphrey Fones** b. circa 1582 Bedford, Worcestershire, England. It is unknown if he ever married and had any children. Death date and location are both unknown.
7B	vi.	**Richard Fones of Bristol** b. 1584 Bristol, Gloucestershire, England. Richard married on 25 February 1605 Joan Twidall (1584-1676). They had 4 children. Richard died after 1614 in Bristol, Gloucestershire, England at approx. 30.

A.

7A. Thomas Fones Jr. (Governor Winthrop Connection)

THOMAS[7] FONES JR. (JohnIII[6], John Jr.[5], John Sr.[4], William[3], George[2], William[1])

- Born 24 March 1573 in London, Middlesex, England.
- Married 25 February 1605 Wife #1 Anne **Winthrop** London, England (**sister of Gov. John Winthrop**) married at Groton Manor, Suffolk, England Anne Winthrop (born 16 January 1585- died 16 May 1618).
- Married circa 1618 Wife #2 Priscila ____ Sherman (circa 1755-1662) in London, England.
- Died 15 April 1629 in London, England at the age of 56.

Children of THOMAS II[7] FONES and ANNE WINTHROP were:

	i.	**Dorothy Fones** b.1608 London, England. It is unknown if she ever married and had any children. Dorothy died 1673 in England.
	ii.	**(Twin) John Fones** b. 1610 London, England. It is unknown if he ever married and had any children. Death date and location are both unknown.
	iii.	**(Twin) Elizabeth Fones Winthrop Fake Hallet** b. 1610 London, England. It is unknown if she ever married and had any children. Elizabeth died 1673 in England.
	iv.	**Martha Fones Winthrop** b, 1611 London, England. It is unknown if she ever married and had any children. Martha died in 1634 in England.
	v.	**Anne Fones** b. 1612 London, England. It is unknown if she ever married and had any children. Death date and location are both unknown.
	vi.	**Samuel Fones** b.1616 London, England. It is unknown if he ever married and he had any children. Death date and location are both unknown.

B.

7B. Richard Fones Esquire of Bristol (Brother of Thomas Fones Jr.) (Author's Connection)

RICHARD[7] FONES ESQUIRE OF BRISTOL (John III[6], John Jr.[5], John Sr.[4], William[3], George[2], William[1])

- Born 1540 in Bristol, Gloucestershire, England.
- Married 25 February 1605 Joanne Twidall (1584-1657). Richard and Joanne married in Bristol, England.
- Died after 1614 in Bristol, England at age approx. 30.

Children of RICHARD[7] FONES. OF BRISTOL and JOANNE TWIDALL were:

8B	i.	THOMAS FONES b. 1587 in Plymouth, Devon, England. Thomas married Joane Heal (1590-1670). Thomas and Joane were married in 1613. They had 7 children. Thomas died in 1637 in England at the age of 50.
	ii.	JOHN FONES b. 1610 Plymouth, Devon, England. It is unknown if he ever married and if he had any children. His death date and location at death ae both unknown.
	iii.	GEORGE FONES b.1612 Plymouth, Devon, England. It is unknown if he ever married and if he had any children. His death date and location at death ae both unknown.
	iv.	RICHARD FONES b. 1614 Plymouth, Devon, England. It is unknown if he ever married and if he had any children. His death date and location at death are both unknown.

8B. Thomas Fones Sr.   (Author's Connection)

THOMAS FONES Sr. (John III[6], John Jr.[5], John Sr.[4], William[3], George[2], William[1])

- Born 1587 in Plymouth, Devon, England.
- Married 1613 Joane Heal (1590-1670). Thomas and Joane married in Bristol, England.
- Died 1637 in England at the age of 50.

Children of THOMAS[7] FONES. and JOANE HEAL were:

	i.	**SUSANNA FONES** b. 1614 Bristol, England. It is unknown if she ever married and had any children. Susanna died in 1648 at the age of 34.	
	ii.	**ELIZABETH FONES** b. 1629 Bristol, England. It is unknown if she ever married and had any children. Her death date and location are both unknown.	
	iii.	**JOHN FONES** b.1630 Bristol, England. It is unknown if he ever married and had any children. His death date and location are both unknown.	
	iv.	**SAMPSON FONES** b.1633 Bristol, England. He died in 1635 in Bristol, England at age 2.	
9B.	v.	**TWIN: CAPTAIN HONORABLE JOHN FONES JR.** (IMMIGRANT) b. 1635 Bristol, England. Captain John Jr. married Margaret Irene Walton. They were married in 1660 in Walton Warwick, Kent, Rhode Island. Captain John died on 20 December 1703 in Kingston, Washington Co., Rhode Island at the age of 68.	
	vi.	**TWIN: WILLIAM FONES** b.1635 Bristol, England. It is unknown if he ever married and had any children. His death date and location are both unknown.	
	vii	**THOMAS FONES** Jr. b. 1637 Bristol, England. It is unknown if he ever married and had any children. Thomas died in 1703 at the age of 66 in England.	

Source Citations for this Chapter

Genealogical Dictionary of Rhode Island by John Osborne Austin, 1969. The person (Daughter of Fones) is the same as #177 (Squcie/Scusie Fones) in The George Soule Book, Published by the General Society of the Mayflower Descendants, Plymouth, Massachusetts, page 95.

Mayflower Families (through Five Generations) Volume Three (George Soule the Pilgrim) Published by the General Society of the Mayflower Descendants, Plymouth, Massachusetts, 1980.

Vital Records of Jamestown Marriages in Rhode Island. Page 8.

Fones Records on Microfilm Archives of Nova Scotia, T.B. Smith Collections MG1/Vol.8 #31

New England Marriages Prior to 1700 page 273.

Genealogies of Rhode Island Families Volume II, 1989 Inscriptions in Family Burial Grounds at North Kingston. Rhode Island, Fones Burial Ground at Newcomb's Station page 575.

http://freepages.genealogy.rootsweb.com/-dav4is/ODTs/FONES.shtml The Fones Family 1470-1795.

https://www.ancestry.com

https://www.geni.people/John-Fones

https://www.familysearch.org/person/details/KHKR-87G

https://findagrave.com/memorial/67847126/jeremiah-fones

http:/www.google.com/search Governor John Winthrop

http: www.kindredkonnections.com

Chapter 14: The Holdens

The Holden Family Line

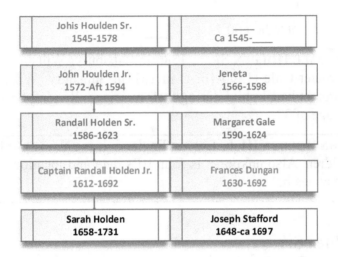

Johis Houlden Sr. 1545-1578	____ Ca 1545-____
John Houlden Jr. 1572-Aft 1594	Jeneta ____ 1566-1598
Randall Holden Sr. 1586-1623	Margaret Gale 1590-1624
Captain Randall Holden Jr. 1612-1692	Frances Dungan 1630-1692
Sarah Holden 1658-1731	Joseph Stafford 1648-ca 1697

1. Johis Houlden Sr.

JOHIS HOULDEN SR.

- Born 1545 in Walsall, Staffordshire, England.
- Married circa 1570 _____.
- Died after 1578 in Walley, Lancashire, England, age approx. 33.

The Holden name started out as did so many families with the spelling of the last name as it sounded Houlden. Staffordshire is the seat of where the name is originally found. As the family grew, they moved to Lancashire, and later, then to the new colony across the water.

Children of JOHIS[1] HOULDEN Sr. and _____ were:

	I.	**ELYANNE HOULDEN** b. 1571 in Whalley, Lancashire, England. It is unknown if she ever married and unknown if any children. Also unknown is date and location at time of her death and her age at death.
2.	ii.	**JOHN HOULDEN JR.** b. May 1572 in Whalley, Lancashire, England. John Jr. married Jeneta ___ (1566-1598) in 1585 in England. John Jr. and Jeneta had 2 children during their marriage. John Jr. died after 1594 in England age approx. 22+.
	iii.	**WILL HOULDEN** b. 1576 in Whalley, Lancashire, England. It is unknown if he ever married or had any children. Also unknown is his date and location at time of his death and his age at death.
	iv.	**FELICIA HOULDEN** b. 1578 in Whalley, Lancashire, England. It is unknown if she ever married or had any children. Also unknown is date and location at time of her death and her age at death.

2. John Houlden Jr.

JOHN[1] HOULDEN JR. (John[1])

- Born May 1572 in Whalley, Lancashire, England.
- Married 1585 Jeneta ____ (1566-1598). John Jr. and Jeneta were married in England.
- Died after 1594 in England at the age of approx. 22+.

Children of JOHN HOULDEN JR. and JENETA ____ were:

3.	I.	**RANDALL HOLDEN SR.** b. 1586 in Salisbury, Wiltshire, England. Randall married Margaret Gale (1590-1624) in 1611 in Salisbury, Wilshire, England. Randall and Margaret had 1 child during their marriage. Randall Sr. died 23 November 1623 at the age of 37.
	ii.	**JOHN HOLDEN III** b. 1594 in England. It is unknown if he ever married or had any children. Also unknown is John III's date and location at time of his death and his age at death.

3. Randall Holden Sr.

RANDALLL[3] HOLDEN SR. (John[2], John[1])

- Born May 1572 in Whalley, Lancashire, England.
- Married 1648 Margaret Gale (1590-1624). Randall Sr. and Margaret were married in Salisbury, Wiltshire, England.
- Died 23 November 1623 in Lancashire, England at the age of 37.

Children of RANDALL[3] HOLDEN AND MARGARET GALE were:

4.	i.	**CAPTAIN RANDALL JR.** (Immigrant) b. 12 March 1612 in Salisbury, Wiltshire, England. He immigrated to the American colonies and arrived in Bay Path Colony approx. 1635. In 1648 he married Frances Dungan in 1648 in Warwick, Kent Co., Rhode Island. Frances was the daughter of William Dungan Sr. and Frances Latham. Captain Randall and Frances had 11 children during their marriage. Randall Jr. died 23 August 1692 in Rhode Island at the age of 80.

4. Captain Randall Holden Jr. (Immigrant)
Co-Founder of Warwick, Rhode Island

CAPTAIN RANDALL[4] HOLDEN JR. (Randall[3], John[2], John[1])

- Born 1612 in Salisbury, England.
- Arrival in Bay Path Colony approx. 1635.
- Married 1648 Frances Dungan. Captain Randall Jr. and Frances were married in Warwick, Kent Co., Rhode Island. Frances was the daughter of William Dungan Sr. and Frances Latham.
- Died 23 August 1692 in Warwick, Kent Co., Rhode Island at the age of 80.

1635:

The Stormy Trip:

Randall Holden Jr. left Plymouth, England around 1635. He was single and travelled with 101 other passengers, all of whom were complete strangers to him. They set sail together for the new colonies across the water. Only 40 of these passengers survived the trip! They were at sea for two stormy months being tossed to and fro in such bad, horrible weather. The survivors described themselves as "Saints" who had survived the trip. Half of the group who had survived the trip then died during their first winter in the new colony due to malnutrition and the harsh New England winter that presented itself to these weary survivors.

In **1637**, Randall Holden and Roger Williams were witnesses to the Deed of Aquidneck and other islands in the bay except Prudence Island. For more about Prudence Island, see the chapter on John Smith of Rhode Island. This same Roger Williams was the founder of Rhode Island. Randall Holden and Roger Williams witnessed the deed from Canonicus and Miantonomi to William Coddington for 40 fathoms of white beads. Miantonomi was to give 10 coats and 20 hoes to present inhabitants who were to move before winter.

1638:

One year later in 1638, Randall Holden became one of the nineteen signers of a compact at Portsmouth, Rhode Island, which read as follows:

The Portsmouth, Rhode Island Contract

"We whose names are underwritten, do here solemnly in the presence of Jehovah, incorporate ourselves into a Bodie Politick and as he shall help, will submit our persons, lives and estates unto our Lord Jesus Christ, the King of Kings and Lord of Lords, and to all those perfect and most absolute laws of his given us in his holy word of truth to be guided and judged thereby."

The same year (1638), Randall Holden was appointed Marshall for a year, of Aquidneck (later known as Rhode Island) and he was elected as Corporal as well. He was granted 5 acres on the north side of Aquidneck.

Samuel Gorton (1593-1677) and several of his contemporaries **including our Captain Randall Holder Jr.** were out of step with many of the complex political and religious viewpoints of their times upon their arrival in the Bay State Colony. (Gorton arrived in Boston in 1636 just after the banishment of Roger Williams to today's Rhode Island.)

From the time **Randall Holder Jr.** arrived, when he was single and a man of about 23 years of age **(circa 1635)** up to the time of the Commonwealth Charter in 1644, there was friction! These years were fraught with difficulty. Gorton and his followers showed a resistance to the Puritan hierarchy but each one of these followers had an ardent love of liberty. These men were Samuel Gorton (the leader) and followers **Randall Holden Jr.**, John Greene, Francis Weston, and John Wickees. After leaving Boston they went to Providence where they became involved in more problems. They left there and settled in Papaquinapaug, a section of the northern side of Pawtuxet. That all occurred before 1648. In the year of 1648, **Randall Holden Jr.** married Frances Dungan in Warwick, Rhode Island, and he and their first daughter, named Frances, was born in Warwick a year later in September 1649.

1643:

Despite all this, the Gorton group decided to stay there and began clearing the land, building their home, and planting corn. This was now the spring of 1643. By that autumn in 1643 the General Court of Massachusetts sent a letter addressed to Samuel Gorton, John Wickes, **Randall Holden**, Robert Potter, Francis Weston, Richards Carder, John Warner, and William Waddle. (Note that others had joined the group by now.) This letter informed them of complains of Fonham and Socononoco stating that the Gorton group had wronged these sachems. The messenger who had delivered the letter was given a verbal reply to carry back to the Court of Massachusetts in which Gorton's group challenged the jurisdiction of the Massachusetts court and stated that they (the Gortonists) were only subject to the Crown. Soon afterwards Gorton sent a very sarcastic letter which both he and **Randall Holden Jr.** signed, in which they denounced the conduct of Fonhema and forbade his return to Shawomet. The following week three commissioners and forty soldiers set out for Shawomet.

SHAWOMET

Shawomet was a large tract of land which Randall Holden and Samuel Gorton, along with the group they belonged to, had purchased from the Narragansett Chief in January 1643 for 144 fathoms of wampum (seashell beads). They initially named the settlement Shawomet, the Narragansett name for the site, but they later changed the name to Warwick. Later that year, he, and others of Shawomet were summoned to appear in court in Boston to answer a complaint from two Indian sachems concerning some unjust and injurious dealing towards them. The Shawomet men refused the summons claiming that they were loyal subjects of the King of England and beyond the jurisdiction of Massachusetts Bay Colony. The Boston Court sent soldiers who confiscated the men's writings, then carried the men to Boston for trial. The official charges against them had nothing to do with any transactions with the Indians, but instead were about their writings and their beliefs. The men were charged with heresy and sedition, sentenced to confinement, and threatened with death should they break jail or preach their heresies or speak against church or state. Randall Holden was imprisoned in Salem in November 1643 but was released from prison in March 1644 and banished from both Massachusetts and Shawomet (which had been claimed by the Massachusetts Bay Colony). Both Randall Holden and John Greene boarded a ship in New Amsterdam (later known as New York) and sailed back to England to seek redress for the wrongs committed against them and they did not return to New England for two years, returning in September 1646.

The Massachusetts Bay Colony's intent was to talk with the Gortonists' group but if they failed to comply, they would face death. Meanwhile the Gortonists sent their women and children into the woods and others into boats to gain protection from neighboring plantations. Before the assault took place, a conference was held for conciliatory purposes. The Commissioners stated the charges, which were in essence that the Shawomet group had wronged subjects of Massachusetts, Arnold and the sachems and unless they repented, they must be conducted to Boston for a trial or be slaughtered where they dwelt. Gorton's group declined to accept their terms and suggested that they be allowed to make an appeal to England. This request was refused, and they then suggested that the case be settled by arbitration. A temporary truce was made while a messenger was dispatched to give a message to Governor Winthrop. The governor in turn sent back a message which was not favorable toward the Gortonists. All hope of conference and arbitration was at a complete end and the small group prepared to defend itself against four times their number! The siege lasted several days during which the cattle of Shawomet were driven off and several homes were pillaged. Miraculously, no one on either side was killed. However, the captors pierced the heart of the settlement's economy by taking away the cattle. The Gortonists surrendered and were marched back to Boston with firm orders that if they spoke a word or caused the commissioners any discontent, their captors would harm them.

Gorton, in his Simplicities of Defense, described the number of cattle taken. There he stated:

"The number of cattle they took from us was four score head or thereabouts, besides Swine and Goats which they and the Indians lived upon during the time of the siege, also breaking violently into our house, taking away our corn with other provisions for our families to live upon."

1643

On Friday October 13, 1643, the victorious army entered Boston with their captured men and booty. They were told they were to attend church services that Sunday for the good of their souls. They had said they would only attend if Gorton could preach after the service. Records report that the sermon was directed at the Gortonists but was paradoxically answered by Gorton, who considered himself a match for any preacher in the Bay Colony. (The church where this occurred was most likely King's Chapel on the present-day Tremont Street in Boston.)

On Tuesday October 17, 1643, the small group was brought to trial and charges of heresy and sedition were filed against them. It is interesting to note what the charge read:

"Upon much examination and serious condition of your writings, with your answers about them, we do charge you to be a blasphemous enemy of the true religion of our Lord Jesus Christ and his holy ordinances, and also of all civil authority among the people of God, and particularly in this jurisdiction."

The above emphasis was placed on heresy rather than on the illegal occupation of lands that were considered by Massachusetts as part of her jurisdiction. No mention was made at all about Fonham.

The accused were asked theological questions rather than jurisdictional ones during the trial. Gorton was asked the following three questions to which he gave written replies:

Questions:

1) Whether the fathers who died before Christ was born of the Virgin Mary, were justified, and saved only by the blood which he shed, and the death which he suffered after his incarnation?

2) Whether the only price of our redemption, were not the death of Christ upon the cross, with the rest of his sufferings and obedience in the time of his life here, after he was born of the Virgin Mary?

3) Who is that God who thinks we serve?

Gorton made written replies to these questions and displeased most of the judges. Here the trial ended, the case was closed, and the verdict was rendered. Colonial law dictated that heresy was punishable with prison or banishment (blasphemy by death). All the magistrates but three condemned Gorton to die for blasphemy. However, the sentences of the deputies, the representatives of the people, refused their assent to the death penalty.

The sentence was changed to read that Gorton and six of his followers were to be confined in irons during the pleasure of the court. Also, they were to be set to work, and if they should break jail, or proclaim any heresy or reproach the church or state, they would suffer death. They were split up and sent to different towns (to prevent their unifying together). This is how they were split up:

Gorton was sent to Charlestown.
John Wickes was sent to Ipswich.
Randall Holden was sent to Salem.
Richard Carder was sent to Roxbury.
Francis Weston was sent to Dorchester.
Robert Potter was sent to Rowley.

Three others were treated mildly:
William Waddell was allowed to reside in Watertown.
Robert Richard Waterman was dismissed with a fine.
Nicholas Power disclaimed signing the bold
letter to Massachusetts. He was discharged with a reprimand.
Greene was fortunate enough to flee during the siege.

The duration of their confinement in these towns was throughout the winter. The following March 1644, an act was passed by the General Court releasing them from prison and banishing them from the jurisdiction of Massachusetts including Providence and the lands of the subject Indians. They were further ordered if they were discovered within the above limits within fourteen days, they were risking their lives. However, they gave them only two hours to move on out and threatened to kill them if they did not! The Gortonists returned to Shawomet.

1644:

In the spring of 1644, the Narragansetts swore allegiance to England and entrusted Samuel Gorton, John Wilkes, **Randall Holden,** and John Warner to act as their commissioners in trust for the conveyance of their submission to England. The Indians took this action in resentment toward Massachusetts and because they believed the Gortonists were politically powerful enough to be able to withstand condemnation by Massachusetts. Soon Gorton, **Holden** and Greene set sail for England to make known the allegiance of the Narragansetts and procure the necessary protection from Massachusetts for their settlement at Shawomet. They went to England via New York. In Fuller's writing he states: "Samuel Gorton and **Randall Holden** accompanied by John Greene sailed to England from New York in the same year (1644)."

1645
June 2nd, 1645:

"Randall Houlding of Portsmouth ...in the Nanhigansett bay ... doe sell unto Anthony Paine of the sane Towne one percell of Land containing e one hundred Acres ... butting to the North upon the Mill Swamp neer unto Portsmouth, bordering to the south upon the Lands of Ralph Earll – and the Lands of John Roome close adjoyninge to the East of the afore-said hundred acres bordering to the West upon the Lands of William Freeborne ... Wit Randall Houldon"

1646:

Randall Holden Jr. returned home, landing in Boston September 13, 1646. He brought with him the order of the English commissioners and delivered it to the Massachusetts authorities. After some hesitation he was allowed to land and to pass through the state to his home at Shawomet. The trip of the group was successful, and Massachusetts was ordered to hold the situation in abeyance and allow the settlers to live at Shawomet in peace.

1647:

In this year we find **Captain Randall** had registered for military service in 1647. Soon after Gorton and his followers settled within Pawtucket [pre-1648], there was more unrest as the four prominent settlers of Pawtucket (William Arnold, Benedict Arnold, Robert Cole, and William Carpenter) petitioned Massachusetts to take Pawtuxet under its jurisdiction. This act prompted Sam Gorton and his associates to remove themselves from Pawtuxet to the area of Shawmut, just south of Occupasspawtuxet. There they purchased land from the Indians and settled.

The Gortonists thought themselves free from existing governments, but troubles were immediate for these men of independent views and strong convictions. A plot was in the making involving the four dissenting settlers of Pawtuxet who had sworn allegiance to Massachusetts. William Arnold and Benedict Arnold were made local officers of the peace at Pawtuxet, by order of Massachusetts and the local Indian sachems, Socononoco of Pawtuxet and Fonham of Shawomet. They had given titles of their lands to the Bay Colony. To make matters worse, Socononoco and Fonham denied that they had ever sold Shawomet to the Gorton group. This extraordinary act of the sachems put Gorton and his associates in a very precarious position, because these settlers supposed they were outside the jurisdiction of Providence and Pawtuxet. Now Massachusetts Bay, which had previously exiled them and threatened the lives of the Shawomet purchasers, laid claim to the new settlement.

In 1647 **Randall Holden Jr**. was a member of the Town Council of Warwick and was frequently a moderator of the town meetings. He was also treasurer of the town. In 1652 he was the Commissioner from Warwick. In 1655 he was on the Roll of Freemen of Warwick (there were 38 of them in all).

1648:
And that is what happened. Two years later **Randall Holden** married Frances Dungan. The couple married in 1648 in Warwick, Kent Co., Rhode Island. Frances was the daughter of William Dungan Sr. and Frances Latham. **Randall** and Francis went on in their lives and had eleven children and made their home in Warwick in a section called Shawomet. The years that followed still found this man active and involved with the heart and soul of the Rhode Island settlers.

1658

In 1658 **Randall Holden Jr**. became a Captain.

1659

23rd of March 1659:
"... **Randall Howldon** of Warwick ... have received of Benedict Arnold of Newport and Mr. Brenton of the same ... one hundred fifty five pound in peage & for the two Sachems Wequaganuett and Kaskatape and sixty pounds for Quissuckquansh the Chief Sachem ... for ... Quononaqutt and the Island called Dutch Island ... also... have Received for all mt ... Troubles ... about the premises made to ... other Indians as House and the rest ... one hundred Thirty and six pounds Eighteen Shillings and Eleven pence ... at the rate of peage "Six a penny ...".

1661

In 1661 **Captain Randall Holden Jr**. was appointed to receive contributions for the expenses of the colony's agents in England (Rodger Williams and John Clarke) who were seeking a charter for Rhode Island.

1666

Captain Randall Holden Jr. became a Deputy.

1669

June 1669: "**Captain Randall Houldon** of Warwick ... aged 57 years ... the Purchassers gave that little Island Called Dyres Island to Mr. Willian Dyre sent that was then one of us ... 24th day of June 1669."

1671

In 1671, **Captain Randall Holden Jr.** was authorized, with others to make assessments on respective towns for arrears of taxes due the colony.

1676

In 1676, during the period of King Philip's War, the **Captain Randall Holden Jr.** was on a committee on matters concerning Narragansett.

1679

In 1679, **Captain Randall Holden Jr.** was in England and wrote a letter with John Greene about Mount Hope to the Right Honorable Lords Commissioners for Trade and Plantations.

1683

1683 found **Captain Randall Jr.** on another committee drafting a letter to the King.

1688

In 1688 the, **Captain Randall Jr.** was Justice of the Court of Common Pleas. This was just a few years before his death in 1692.

1688 at the age of 76 years **Captain Randall Holden Jr.**'s occupation is listed as Justice of the Court of Common Pleas in Rhode Island.

1692

Captain Randall Holden Jr. died 23 August 1692 in Warwick, Kent Co., Rhode Island at age 80.

Children of CAPTAIN RANDALL[4] HOLDEN JR. and FRANCES DUNGAN were:

I.	**FRANCES HOLDEN** b. 29 September 1649 in Rhode Island. Frances married John Holmes on 1 December 1871 in Warwick, Kent Co., Rhode Island. It is unknown if Frances and John had any children. Frances died in 1679 in Rhode Island at the age of 30.
ii.	**ELIZABETH HOLDEN** b. August 1652 in Rhode Island. Elizabeth married John Rice on 16 July 1674 in Warwick, Kent Co., Rhode Island. It is unknown if Elizabeth and John had any children. Elizabeth's death date and location at death are unknown as well as her age at death.
iii.	**MARY HOLDEN** b. August 1654 in Rhode Island. Mary married John Carder on 1 December 1671 in Warwick, Kent Co., Rhode Island. It is unknown if Mary and John had any children. Mary's death date and location at death are unknown as well as her age at death.
iv.	**JOHN HOLDEN** b. January 1656 in Rhode Island. It is unknown if he ever married and had any children. Also unknown is death date and location at death as well as age at death.

5.	v.	**SARAH HOLDEN** b. February 1658 in Rhode Island. Sarah married Joseph Stafford Sr (1648-1697). Sarah and Joseph had 9 children during their marriage. Sarah died in 1731 in Rhode Island at the age of 73.
	vi.	**RANDAL HOLDEN III** b. April 1660 in Rhode Island. Randall III married Bethiah Waterman on 27 January 1687 in Warwick, Kent Co., Rhode Island. It is unknown if they had any children during their marriage. Randall III died 13 September 1726 at the age of 66.
	vii.	**MARGARET HOLDEN** b. January 1663 in Rhode Island. Margaret married John Eldred circa 1683 in Warwick, Kent Co., Rhode Island. It is unknown if Margaret and John had any children during their marriage. Margaret died 1740 at the age of 77.
	viii.	**LIEUTENANT CHARLES HOLDEN** b. 22 March 1666 in Rhode Island. Lieut. Charles married Catharine Greene circa 1686 in Warwick, Kent Co., Rhode Island. It is unknown if Lieut. Charles and Catharine had any children during their marriage. Lieut. Charles died 21 July 1717 at the age of 51.
	ix.	**BARBARA HOLDEN** b. 2 July 1668 in Rhode Island. Barbara married Samuel Wickham on 4 June 1691 in Warwick, Kent Co., Rhode Island. It is unknown if Barbara and Samuel had any children during their marriage. Barbara died in 1707 at the age of 39.
	x.	**SUSANNAH HOLDEN** b. 8 December 1670 in Rhode Island. Susannah married Benjamin Greene on 21 January 1689 in Warwick, Kent Rhode Island. It is unknown if Susannah and Benjamin had any children during their marriage. Susannah died on 11 April 1734 at the age of 63.
	xi.	**ANTHONY HOLDEN** b. 16 October 1673 in Rhode Island. It is unknown if he ever married or had any children. Also unknown is his death date and location at death as well as his age at death.

5. Sarah Holden

SARAH[5] HOLDEN (Randall[4], Randall[3], John[2], John[1])

- Born February 1658 in Warwick, Kent Co., Rhode Island.
- Married circa 1678 Joseph Stafford Sr. Sarah and Joseph Sr. were married in Warwick, Kent Co., Rhode Island. Joseph Sr. was the son of Thomas Stafford Sr. and Elizabeth _____.
- Died 1731 in Warwick, Kent Co., Rhode Island. At the age of 73.

Children of SARAH HOLDEN, and JOSEPH STAFFORD SR. are documented in the Stafford chapter.

AN ADDITIONAL SIDE NOTE:
The TOWN
Of
HOLDEN, MASSACHUSETTS

In driving through Holden, Massachusetts, I was intrigued with the thought of one of my ancestors coming to the colonies and having an entire town named after him. So, I started to explore this thought and made this discovery! The small little quaint town of Holden, Massachusetts was founded by

Samuel Holden
(1675-1740)

Samuel Holden was the son of Joseph Holden. Samuel became a successful merchant in London, England and was made the director of the Bank of England (1720-1727) and its Deputy Governor (1727-1729) and its Governor (1730-1731). Samuel Holden never came to the colonies. He was a merchant, politician, and a Nonconformist activist! As a dissenter, Samuel Holden chaired a committee for the repeal of the Corporation Act and other Test Acts. He entered Parliament in 1735 trying to introduce legislation in that area. When he died in 1740, he left 160,000 pounds, a lot of money, and he granted part of it to Harvard College in Cambridge, Massachusetts, a considerable sum during the time of their construction of a chapel. Today you will see in Harvard Yard, the Holden Chapel named for Samuel. Likewise, during his lifetime he saw the struggling colonists trying to set up a form of government in the wooded lands across the water. The colonists were trying to construct a little house in the wilderness, a house that was used for a meeting house and for a church. Although Samuel Holden never crossed the Atlantic to the new frontier, his money did! He supplied the struggling colonists with a large sum of money to start their little town. For that blessing, the townspeople incorporated the town and in Samuel Holden's honor, they named the town, HOLDEN, after him the year after he died in 1741.

Colonial Aquidneck (Rhode Island) and the surrounding Bay State Colony

Source Citations for this Chapter

Foreword by Paul Campbell, Librarian of the Rhode Island Historical Society and Indexed by Carol Lee Ford, <u>Genealogies of Rhode Island Families, from Rhode Island Periodicals, Volume I,</u> Genealogical Publishing Co., Inc, Baltimore, Maryland, 1983, pages 472-477.

<u>Selected Aspects of Warwick History for Social Studies Teachers in Warwick, Rhode Island</u> (A Thesis presented to the Faculty of the Graduate School, Rhode Island College of Education), by Paul A. Clancy, June 1958, Private Printing, pages 23 -36.

Fuller, Oliver Payson BA, <u>History of Warwick, Rhode Island, Settlement in 1642 to the Present Time</u>, Angell, Burlingame Co., Printers, 1875, page 25.

Albert Kleeberg, <u>Rhode Island Land Evidence Volume I, 1648-1696 Abstracts, Rhode Island Historic Society</u>, Genealogical Publishing Company, Baltimore, Maryland, 1970, page 38 & page 69.

<u>Holden, Massachusetts Town History</u>: www.google.com.

Chapter 15: The Hudsons

The Hudson Family Line

Rudulphus Herdson Sr. 1475-1530	Mary Elizabeth Pyle 1478-1545
Rudulphus Hudson Jr. 1498-1555	Lady Barbara Watson 1504-1568
Sir Christopher Hudson 1540-1598	Ann Richardson 1541-____
William Hudson Sr. 1559-1613	Lady Ann Tankard 1573-1615
John Hudson 1613-1688	Ann Rogers 1634-1712
Elizabeth Hudson 1658-1706	**Rev. Jonathan Vickery 1648-1706**

Author's Note:

This was an exceedingly difficult chapter to write. The overall historic content of this chapter is accurate but matching the dates and the relationships was a challenge! I cannot in all honesty, guarantee their accuracy. However, I hope you will enjoy reading this chapter. However, it is tragically sad as one of its endings is, but hopefully you will find it still worth your time and interest.

To start with the family name **HUDSON** did not occur until the early 1500s when Rudulphus Hutchinson Herdson and his son Gentleman Henry Sr. I[st] changed their name from Herdson to HUDSON. From the year 1180, when William Hutchinson was born until the early 1500s, the Hudson family was the Hutchinson family. Then the name changed to Herdson. Why they changed the name is unknown. Rudulphus Rudolph's family was originally from Normandy and his father was Anthony Hutchinson (1454-1494). The wife of Anthony was Judith Crossland (1558-**1483**). They were Rudolph's parents. Rudolph also had a brother named William Hutchinson. The ancestry of the Hutchinson family goes back to 1180 but I will concentrate here in this chapter on what happened to the Hudson family starting with the name change to Hudson in the early 1500s onward into the early days of the American colony in the 1600s.

1. Rudulphus "Rudolph" Herdson Hudson Sr.

RUDULPHUS HERDSON HUDSON SR.

- Born 1475 in Tamworth, Staffordshire, England.
- Married 1496 Wife #1 Elizabeth Pyle (1478-1545) in Tamworth, Staffordshire, England.
- Married circa 1514 Wife #2 Lady Jane Elizabeth Rawmarsh (1472-1545) in London, Middlesex, England.
- Died 27 June 1530 in London, Middlesex, England at the age of 55.
- Buried in a tomb in the Christ Church, Grey Friars Burial Grounds, Newgate Street, London, England.

The symbolism of the lions rearing signifies with strength, courage, and loyalty as character traits. The boars' heads suggest allegiance to King Richard III, a member of the House of York. The Hudson family originated in Yorkshire, England so their family members were supportive of King Richard III. The Hudson family was connected to the aristocracy. King Richard III died in 1485. Both Rudolph and his son Henry I designed this coat of arms for the Hudson family.

Rudulphus Rudolph Hudson moved away from Yorkshire and moved to London at some point. He became an Alderman (member of the British Council), and he was quite wealthy. He married twice and had eight sons and three daughters by his first wife Elizabeth Pyle. All their names are not known. The ones that are known are listed below. All their places of birth and death dates are also unknown.

There are two lines in this Chapter. The A line in the Author's ancestors' line. The B line is the line of the famous explorer Henry Hudson who found the Henry Hudson River in New York. The famous river is named for him. The two lines are connected, as the two lines are related. They are cousins!

Children of RUDULPH[1] HERDSON HUDSON SR. and MARY ELIZABETH PYLE were:

2A.	i.	**Randolph Rudolph Hudson Jr.** (Author's Line) b. 1498 in Tamworth, Staffordshire, England. Randolph Rudolph married Lady Barbara Watson (1504-1568) in 1520 in Staffordshire, England. They were the parents of 12 sons and 3 daughters. Randolph Jr died in 1555 at age 53. He is buried in Saint Dustan & All Saints Church Graveyard in Stephney, Middlesex, England.
2B.	ii.	**Gentleman Henry Sr.** (Famous Explorer's Line) b. 1500 in Tamworth, Staffordshire, England. Henry Sr. married Lady Barbara Watson (1504-1568) in Tamworth, Staffordshire, England. They were married in 1520. Henry Hudson Sr. died 20 December 1555 in Tamworth, Staffordshire, England at age 55.
	iii.	**Edward Hudson** b. 1502. It is not known if he married and had children. Death date and location at death are also unknown.
	iv.	**John Hudson** b. 1504. It is not known if he married and had children. Death date and location at death are also unknown.
	v.	**Thomas Hudson** b.1506. It is not known if he married and had children. Death date and location at death are also unknown.
	vi.	**Daughter Hudson** b. date unknown. It is not known if she married and had children. Death date and location at death are also unknown.
	vii.	**Daughter Hudson** b. date unknown. It is not known if she married and had children. Death date and location at death are also unknown.
	viii.	**Christopher Hudson Sr.** b 1511 in Normandy, Yorkshire, England. It is not known if he ever married and had any children. Death date is also unknown. Christopher died in Yorkshire, England.
	ix.	**Son Hudson** b. date unknown. It is not known if he married and had children. Death date and location at death are also unknown.
	x.	**Daughter Hudson** b. date unknown. It is not known if married and had children. Also, death date and location at death are also unknown.
	xi.	**Son Hudson** b. date unknown. It is not known if he married and had children. Death date and location at death are also unknown.
	xii.	**Son Hudson** b. date unknown. It is not known if he married and had children. Death date and location at death are also unknown.

Children of RUDOLPH[1] HERDSON HUDSON and LADY JANE ELIZABETH RAWMARSH were:

	xiii.	**Richard Hudson** b. 1515. It is not known if he married and had children. Death date and location at death are also unknown.
	xiv.	**Robert Hudson** b. 1518. It is not known if he married and had children. Death date and location at death are also unknown.

2A. Randolph Rudolph Hudson Jr.

RANDOLPH RUDOLPH [2] HUDSON JR. (Rudolph[1] Sr.)

- Born 1498 in Normandy, Yorkshire, England.
- Married 1520 Lady Barbara Watson (1504-1568), daughter of Sir Edward Watson and Lady Isabelle Emma Smith.
- Died 22 December 1555 in London, England.
- Buried in Saint Dunstan & All Saints Church, Stepney, Middlesex, England.

Children of RANDOLPH RUDOLPH[2] HUDSON JR. and BARBARA WATSON were:

	i.	**Thomas Hudson** b. 1522 in Tamsworth, Staffordshire, England. It is not known if he married and had children. Death date and location at death are also unknown.
	ii.	**John Hudson** b. 1525 in Tamsworth, Staffordshire, England. It is not known if he married and had children. Death date and location at death are also unknown.
	iii.	**Abigail Hudson** b. 1525 in Tamsworth, Staffordshire, England. It is not known if she married and had children. Death date and location at death are also unknown.
	iv.	**William Hudson** b. 1528 in Tamsworth, Staffordshire, England. It is not known if he married and had children. Death date and location at death are also unknown.
	v.	**Edmund Hudson** b. 1529 in Tamsworth, Staffordshire, England. It is not known if he married and had children. Death date and location at death are also unknown.
	vi.	**Edward Hudson** b. 1530 in Tamsworth, Staffordshire, England. It is not known if he married and had children. Death date and location at death are also unknown.
	vii.	**Alice Hudson** b. 1532 in Tamsworth, Staffordshire, England. It is not known if she married and had children. Death date and location at death are also unknown.
	viii.	**George Hudson** b. 1534 in Tamsworth, Staffordshire, England. It is not known if he married and had children. Death date and location at death are also unknown.
	ix.	**Twin: Thomas Hudson** b. 1537 in Tamsworth, Staffordshire, England. It is not known if he married and had children. Also, death date and location at death are also unknown.
	x.	**Twin: Anne Hudson** b. 1537 in Tamsworth, Staffordshire, England. It is not known if married and had children. Death date and location at death are also unknown.

3A.	xi.	**Sir Christopher Hudson** b. 1540 in Tamsworth, Staffordshire, England. He married Ann Richardson in 1558. Ann was born in 1541. They were married in 1558 in Gisborough, Yorkshire, England. Sir Christopher and Ann had 1 child, a son. Sir Christopher became a Knight. He died 6 April 1598 at the age of 58 in Birstall, Yorkshire, England.
	xii.	**Henry Hudson** b. 1541 in Tamsworth, Staffordshire, England. It is not known if he married and had children. Death date and location at death are also unknown.
	xiii.	**James Hudson** b. 1543 in Tamsworth, Staffordshire, England. It is not known if he married and had children. Death date and location at death are also unknown.

3A. Sir Knight Christopher Hudson

SIR KNIGHT CHRISTOPHER[3] HUDSON (Rudolph[2]Jr. Rudolph[1] Sr)

- Born 1540 in Yorksdale, Yorkshire, England.
- Married 1558 Ann Richardson b.1541 in Gisborough, Yorkshire, England.
- Died 6 April 1598 in Birstall, Yorkshire, England at age 58.

Child of SIR KNIGHT CHRISTOPHER[3] HUDSON and ANN RICHARDSON was:

4 A.	i.	**William Hudson Sr.** b. 1559 in Yorkshire, England. William married twice. Wife #1 Alice Turner (1560-1630) married 1583 in Epping, Essex, England. (there were no children born of this marriage. Wife #2 Lady Ann Tankard (1573-1615) married 1584 in Epping, Essex, England. William Sr. and Lady Ann had 7 children during their marriage. Lady Ann died in 1615 at the age of 42 in Epping, Essex, England. William Hudson Sr. died on 24 May 1613 at the age of 54 in Epping, Essex, England.

4A. William Hudson Sr.

William[4] Hudson Sr. (Christopher[3], Rudolph[2] Jr., Rudolph[1] Sr)

- Born circa 1559 in Epping, Essex, England.
- Married wife #1 Alice Turner (1560-1630) married 1583 Epping, Essex, England.
- Married wife #2 Lady Ann Tankard (1573-1615) married 1584 Epping, Essex, England. Lady Ann died in 1615 in Epping, Essex, England at the age of 42.
- Died 24 May 1613 in Epping, Essex, England at the age of 54.

There were no children born to WILLIAM HUDSON SR. and ALICE TURNER

Children of WILLIAM[4] HUDSON SR. and LADY ANN TANKARD were:

	i.	**HANNAH HUDSON** b. circa 1584 Upon Hill, Yorkshire, England It is unknown if she married and had any children. Death date and location at death are unknown.
	ii.	**ANNA JOSSELYNE HUDSON** b. 1585 Upon Hill, Yorkshire, England. Anna died 1615 at the age of 30. She died in England.
	iii.	**DANIEL HUDSON** b. circa 1595 Upon Hill, Yorkshire, England. It is unknown if he married and had any children. Death date and location at death are unknown.

	iv.	**ANNA HUDSON** b. 1588 Upon Hill, Yorkshire, England. It is unknown if she married and had any children. Death date and location at death are unknown.
	v.	**WILLIAM HUDSON JR.** b. 1590 Upon Hill, Yorkshire, England. It is unknown if he married and had any children. William Jr. died in 1656 at the age of 66. Location at death is unknown.
5A.	vi.	**RALPH HUDSON** b. 1593 Upon Hill, Yorkshire, England. **(Immigrant)** Ralph Hudson and Marie Watts were married in 1621 in London, England. They arrived in Boston, Bay Colony of America in 1636 and travelled aboard the ship the *Susan and Ellen*. Ralph and Marie had 3 children during their marriage. Two of their children were born in England and immigrated to America with them. The third child was born on American soil. Ralph died in 1651 at the age of 58 in Boston, Suffolk Co., Massachusetts. Ralph and his wife Marie are buried in the King's Chapel Burying Ground, which is the oldest graveyard in Boston.
5B.	vii.	**JOHN HUDSON** b. 1613 Upon Hill, Yorkshire, England. **(Immigrant).** John arrived in Boston, Bay Colony of America in 1636 travelling aboard the ship *Susan and Ellen*. John was single and was 23 years old when he travelled to the American shores. John married Ann Rogers in the Bay Colony of America. John and Ann had 5 children during their marriage. John died in 1688 Duxbury, Plymouth Co., Massachusetts.

- Note: **5B.** John Hudson was **5A.** Ralph's younger brother. John and his older brother Ralph spent much of the time together when they were growing up. Ralph and John's father, William Hudson Sr., had died the year John was born in 1613. Their mother died when John was 2 years old in 1615. Ralph was like his protective older brother, and they were close in birth order, Ralph the older being #6 in birth order and John the younger being #7. It is understandable that Ralph brought his close brother John, now 23 years old, along with himself (Ralph) and his wife Marie Watts and their two small daughters Hannah and Elizabeth. They also had 5 servants with them when they made the journey across the Atlantic to their new home in the Bay Colony of Massachusetts. They all arrival in 1635 in Boston, Bay Colony aboard the ship the *Susan & Ellen*. John married after they arrived in the Bay Colony and he settled in the Plymouth, Massachusetts. John's 5 children all were born in Hull, Massachusetts and are much younger than his older brother Ralph's 3 children.

5A. Ralph Hudson (Immigrant)

RALPH HUDSON (William[4] Sr., Christopher[3], Rudolph[2] Jr., Rudolph[1] Sr)

- Born 1593 in Upon Hill, Yorkshire England.
- Married 1620 Marie Watts (1593-1651) in London, Middlesex, England.
- Arrival 1635 in Boston, Bay Colony aboard the ship the *Susan & Ellen*.
- Died 26 September 1651 Boston, Suffolk Co, Massachusetts.
- Buried King's Chapel Burying Ground in Boston, Massachusetts.

Ralph and John were close brothers. Once they arrived in the Bay State Colony however, they and their families settled in different areas. Ralph stayed in Boston, Massachusetts and he died there.

John moved to the Plymouth area of Massachusetts and raised his family there.

Note: Both children of Ralph's (Hannah age 14 yrs. and her sister Elizabeth age 5 yrs.) were aboard the *Susan & Ellen* that sailed across the Atlantic in 1636 but Nathaniel Hudson (their brother) was born after the trip on Massachusetts soil. He was born the year that they landed in the Bay Colony of Massachusetts.

Children of RALPH HUDSON and MARIE WATTS were:

		i.	**HANNAH HUDSON** b. 1621 in London, Middlesex, England. (Immigrant). She and her family arrived in Boston, Suffolk Co., Massachusetts in 1635 when she was 14 years old Hannah died in 1643 in Massachusetts at the age of 22.
		ii.	**ELIZABETH HUDSON** b. 1630 in London, Middlesex, England. (Immigrant). She and her family arrived in Boston, Suffolk Co., Massachusetts in 1635 when she was 5 years old. Elizabeth died in 1643 in Massachusetts at the age of 13.
		iii.	**NATHANIEL HUDSON** b. 1635 in Boston, Suffolk Co., Massachusetts. He was born the very year that his family arrived in Boston, Suffolk Co., and Massachusetts. It is unknown if he married and had any children. Nathaniel died in 1701 in Massachusetts at age 66.

5B. John Hudson (Brother of Ralph Hudson) (Immigrant)

Note: This is the Author's Line.

JOHN[5] HUDSON (William[4] Sr., Christopher[3], Rudolph[2] Jr., Rudolph Sr.)

- Born 1613 in Upon Hill, Yorkshire, England.
- Arrival 1635 in Boston, Suffolk Co., Massachusetts aboard the ship named the *Susan & Ellen*. John was age 22 years old at time of the journey.
- Married 1654 Ann Rogers (1634-1712) in the Massachusetts, Bay State (Boston, Massachusetts).
- Died 1688 in Duxbury, Plymouth Co., Massachusetts.
- Buried in Burial Hill, Plymouth, Plymouth Co., Massachusetts.

Elizabeth Hudson b. 1658, whose father was John Hudson and had crossed the Atlantic when he was 22 years old with his close older brother Ralph who was 33 years old at the time of their journey. (See story above under #4A about their close relationship.) John and Ralph were close brothers. Ralph's daughter was also an Elizabeth Hudson. However, she was born 1630. Both these Elizabeth Hudson's were first cousins. However, John's daughter Elizabeth was born in 1658 and his brother Ralph' daughter Elizabeth had already died in 1643 at the age of 13. They were cousins but due to the early death of Ralph's daughter, the two cousins, both named Elizabeth, sadly never met.

Children of JOHN[5] HUDSON and ANN ROGERS were:

	i.	**MARY HUDSON** b. 1654 Boston, Suffolk Co., Massachusetts. She married James Bishop. Unknown are the date of marriage and whether they had any children during their marriage. Mary died 1740. Her location at death is also unknown.

	ii.	**RHODA HUDSON** b. 1656 in Marshfield, Plymouth Co., Massachusetts. Rhoda married ___ Palmer in Marshfield, Plymouth Co., and Massachusetts. The date of their marriage is unknown as is whether they had any children during their marriage. Rhoda's death date and her location at death are also unknown.
6 A.	iii.	**ELIZABETH HUDSON** b. 1658 in Marshfield, Plymouth Co., Massachusetts. Elizabeth married Rev. Johnathan Vickery (1648-1706). They were married in 1678 in Hull, Suffolk Co., and Massachusetts. Rev. Johnathan was the son of George and Rebecca Phippen. They had 7 children during their marriage, all born in Hull, Suffolk Co., Massachusetts. Elizabeth Hudson died 1706 in Monomoit (Chatham), Barnstable Co., Massachusetts at the age of 48.
	iv.	**ABIGAIL HUDSON** b. 1660 in Marshfield, Plymouth Co., Massachusetts. Abigail married John Stetson. They were married in 1676 but it is unknown if they had any children during their marriage. Abigail died 1727 at the age of 67. Her location at death is unknown.
	v.	**HANNAH HUDSON** b. 1662 in Marshfield, Plymouth Co., Massachusetts. Hannah married Japheth Turner. The date of their marriage and whether they had any children during their marriage are unknown. Hannah's death date and the location at her death are also unknown.

6A. Elizabeth Hudson

ELIZABETH[6] HUDSON (John[5], William[4] Sr., Christopher[3], Rudolph[2] Jr., Rudolph[1] Sr)

- Born 1658 in Marshfield, Plymouth Co., Massachusetts.
- Married 1678 Rev. Johnathan Vickery (1648-1706) in Hull, Suffolk Co., Massachusetts. Johnathan was the son of George and Rebecca Phippen.
- Died 1706 in Monomoit (Chatham), Barnstable Co., Massachusetts.

Children of ELIZABETH[6] HUDSON and REV. JOHNATHAN VICKERY are documented in the Vickery chapter.

XXXXXXXXXXXXXXXXXXXXXXXXXXXXXXXXXXXXXXXXXXXXXX

The Other Major Line of This Hudson Family (The B) Line

This is the Henry Hudson Famous Explorer's Line

Children of RUDOLPH HERDSON HUDSON and MARY ELIZABETH PYLE were:

2A.	i.	**Randolph Rudolph Hudson Jr.** (Author's Line) b. 1498 in Tamworth, Staffordshire, England. Randolph Rudolph Jr. married Lady Barbara Watson (1504-1568) in 1520 in Staffordshire, England. They were the parents of 12 sons and 3 daughters. Randolph Jr died 1555 at the age of 57 and is buried in Saint Dustan & All Saints Church Graveyard in Stephney, Middlesex, England.

2B.	ii.	**Gentleman Henry Hudson Sr.** (Famous Explorer's Line) b.1500 in Tamworth, Staffordshire, England. Henry Sr. married Lady Barbara Watson (1504-1568) in Tamworth, Staffordshire, England. They were married in 1520. Henry Hudson Sr. died 20 December 1555 in Tamworth, Staffordshire, England at age 55.
	iii.	**Edward Hudson** b. 1502. It is not known if he married and had any children. Death date and location at death are both unknown.
	iv.	**John Hudson** b.1504. It is not known if married and not known if any children. Also, death date and location at death also both unknown.
	v.	**Thomas Hudson** b. 1506. It is not known if he married and had any children. Death date and location at death are both unknown.
	vi.	**Daughter Hudson** b. date unknown. It is not known if she married and had any children. Death date and location at death are both unknown.
	vii.	**Daughter Hudson** b. date unknown. It is not known if she married and had any children. Death date and location at death are both unknown.
	viii.	**Christopher Hudson Sr.** b 1511 in Normandy, Yorkshire, England. It is unknown if Christopher ever married and if he had any children. Christopher died in Yorkshire, England. However, his death date is unknown.
	ix.	**Son Hudson** b. date unknown. It is not known if he married and had any children. Death date and location at death are both unknown.
	x.	**Daughter Hudson** b. date unknown. It is not known if she married and had any children. Death date and location at death are both unknown.
	xi.	**Son Hudson** b. date unknown. It is not known if he married and had any children. Death date and location at death are both unknown.

2B. Gentleman Sir Henry Herdson Hudson Sr.

GENTLEMAN SIR HENRY HERDSON HUDSON SR.

- Born 1500 in Tamworth, Staffordshire, England.
- Married 1520 Lady Barbara Watson (1504-1568 in Tamworth, Staffordshire, England.
- Died 20 December 1555 in Tamworth, Staffordshire, England at age 55.

Gentleman Sir Henry Sr. was extremely wealthy and had close relations with the Crown and nobility. Henry I was named in Queen Mary's Charter 6 February 1555 as one of the founders of the Muscovy Company. Henry I was an Alderman in the City of London, England, and a Director of the Russian Fur Company. He was also associated with the Dutch East India Company. Henry's official title was Gentleman, Alderman of London, Lord of Manors. He had gathered considerable wealth in trade and was lord over many manors, some of which were given to him by King Henry VIII for service to the Crown. He was obviously of aristocracy, demonstrated by his collection of titles and the ownership of a coat of arms that identified his family. Henry, I had land in Lincolnshire and Sussex. He purchased the manors of Bertram's, Newington, Belhouse of Walton, Folkston, Ackhanger, Terlingham and Skelting. He was named as Lord of the Manor of Sweeton in Devon, the heart of Dartmoor, which is now a 5-star resort, coming in at number #2 in all the United Kingdom.

The inscription on Henry Hudson Sr.'s tombstone was in the St. Dunstan's Cemetery where he is buried. Sadly, the area was bombed in WW II. The City of London chose not to reconstruct the church and the surrounding area, Instead, they turned it into a lovely city garden among the ruins of this medieval church. Here is what the inscription said:

"Here lyres Henry Hudson's corps, Within the Tombe of Stone: His soul, through faith in Christ's death, To GOD in Heaven is gone. Whiles that he lived an Alderman And skinner was his state: To Verture bare hee all his love, To Vice bare he, his hate. He had to wife one Barbara Which made this tombe you see By whom he had of issue store, Eight sonnes and daughters three."
Obit 22 December An. Dom., 1555

Children of SIR HENRY HERDSON HUDSON SR. and LADY BARBARA WATSON were:

	i.	**Captain Thomas Hudson** b. 1520 in Tamworth, Staffordshire, England. It is unknown if he ever married and had any children. Captain Thomas died in 1570 in Tamworth, Staffordshire, England at the age of 50.
	ii.	**John Hudson** b. 1521 in Tamworth, Staffordshire, England. John married Eugenia Boswell (1530-___). It is unknown if they had any children. John died in 1583 at the age of 62. His location at his death is unknown.
	iii.	** **William" Hudson Sr.** b.1523 in Tamworth, Staffordshire, England. William married Alice Turner. (1575-1611). They married in 1542 and they had 5 children, including at least two sons, Nicolas and Richard. Richard sailed to Virginia in 1635 and is the progenitor of the Hudson name in America. It is unknown when and where William died.
	iv.	**Edward Hudson** b. 1525 in Tamworth, Staffordshire, England. It is unknown if he ever married and had any children. Death date and location at death are unknown.
	v.	**Annie Hudson** b. 1527 in Tamworth, Staffordshire, England. It is unknown if she ever married and had any children. Death date and location at death are unknown.
3B.	vi.	** **Henry Hudson Jr.** b. 1528 in Tamworth, Staffordshire, England. Henry Jr. married twice: Wife #1 Barbara Alderman. They had many children, but their names and dates are unknown. Wife #2 Katherine Elkington (1541-1622). They married in 1560 in the city of London, England. They had 10 children during their marriage. Henry Hudson Jr. died on 7 March 1621 in London, England at the age of 93.
	vii.	**Sir Christopher Hudson** b. 1531in Tamworth, Staffordshire, England. It is unknown if he ever married and had any children. Death date and location at death are unknown.
	viii.	**Rudolph ("Ralph") Hudson** b.1533 in Tamworth, Staffordshire, England. It is unknown if he ever married and had any children. Death date and location at death are unknown.

	ix.	**George Hudson** b. 1535 in Tamworth, Staffordshire, England. It is unknown if he ever married and had any children. Death date and location at death are unknown.
	x.	**Abigail Hudson** b. 1537 in Tamworth, Staffordshire, England. It is unknown if she ever married and had any children. Death date and location at death are unknown.
	xi.	**Alice Hudson** b. 1539 in Tamworth, Staffordshire, England. It is unknown if she ever married and had any children. Death date and location at death are unknown.

** Two of Henry Hudson Sr.'s grandchildren are <u>Richard Hudson Sr.</u> and <u>Henry Hudson III</u>.

Henry Hudson Sr.'s sons were William Hudson Sr. and Henry Hudson Jr.

- William Hudson Sr's. son, **Richard Hudson Sr.** sailed aboard the ship called *Safety* to Virginia in 1635, and he is the progenitor of the Hudson family line in the United States. **Richard Hudson Sr.** is known as "The Immigrant."
- Henry Hudson Jr.'s son, **Henry Hudson III** is the famous explorer who discovered the Hudson River and the Hudson Bay in New York in 1611 (both were eventually named after him).

3B. Henry Hudson Jr.

HENRY[3B] HUDSON JR.

- Born 1528 in Tamworth, Staffordshire, England.
- Married ___ Wife #1 Barbara Alderman (1540-1610). Many children, names unknown.
- Married 1559 Wife #2 Katherine Elkinton (1542-1622). Ten children during this marriage.
- Died 7 March 1621 in London, England.

Children of HENRY[3B] HUDSON JR. and BARBARA ALDERMAN are many but are unknown.
Names of children and marriage dates are unknown. Research did say they were married but the information was extremely unclear as to the dates and names of any children born of this marriage.

Children of HENRY HUDSON JR. and KATHERINE ELKINTON were:

	i.	**William Hudson** b. 1559 in Tamworth, Tamworth Borough, England. It is unknown if he ever married and had any children. Death date and location at death are unknown.
	ii.	**Captain Thomas Hudson I** b. 1564 in Tamworth, Tamworth Borough, England. It is unknown if he ever married and had any children. Captain Thomas died 1570. His location at death is unknown.
	iii.	**Richard Hudson** b. 1565 in Tamworth, Tamworth Borough, England. It is unknown if he ever married and had any children. Also unknown are death date and location at death.
	iv.	**Mary Ann Hudson** b. 1567 in Tamworth, Tamworth Borough, England**.** It is unknown if she ever married and had any children. Also unknown are death date and location at death.
	v.	**EDWARD HUDSON** b. 1572 in Tamworth, Tamworth Borough, England. It is unknown if he ever married and had any children. Also unknown are death date and location at death.

4B.	vi.	**HENRY HUDSON III** (Immigrant) (Famous EXPLORER) b. 1570 in Tamworth, Tamworth Borough, England. He married Katherine _____ (1572-1624). They were married in 1590 in London, Middlesex, England. They had 4 children during their marriage. Henry Hudson III was the famous explorer who discovered the Hudson River in New York state which was named after him. Henry Hudson III died 23 June 1611. He was abandoned at sea along with his 20-year-old son, John Hudson, as well as seven loyal crewmen after a mutiny by the crew in the Hudson River Bay region (currently the upstate New York and Quebec, Canada area).
	vii.	**WILLIAM HUDSON I** b. 30 September 1575 in Tamworth, Tamworth Borough, England. He married Alice ____. It is unknown if they had any children during their marriage. William died on 9 April 1630 in Northampton, Virginia at the age of 55. He is buried in the St. Editha Graveyard, Tamworth, England.
	viii.	**John Hudson** b. 1578 in Tamworth, Tamworth Borough, England. It is unknown if he ever married and had any children. Also unknown are death date and location at death.
	ix.	**Christopher Hudson** b. 1592 in Tamworth, Tamworth Borough, England. It is unknown if he ever married and had any children. Death date and location at death are unknown.
	x.	**Oliver Hudson b. 1597** in Tamworth, Tamworth Borough, England. It is unknown if he ever married and had any children. Also unknown are death date and location at death.

4B. Henry Hudson III (The Famous Explorer) (Immigrant)

HENRY[4B] HUDSON III (THE FAMOUS EXPLORER)

- Born 12 September 1570 in Castleton, Kildare, Ireland.
- Married 1590 Katherine ___ (1572-1624). They were married in London, Middlesex, England.
- Died 23 June 1611. Abandoned at sea with his 20-year-old son John Hudson (who also died) as well as seven men in the Hudson River Bay region (today upstate New York and the region into Quebec, Canada). Henry Hudson III died at the age of 41.

Henry Hudson III
1570-1611

125

The Hudson River in New York was named for this explorer, Henry Hudson III. He started his career as a "cabin boy" and worked his way up to be captain. The Muscovy Company hired him to find a new passage to China. On 1 May 1607, he set sail on the *Hopewell*, traveling as far as the Svalbard Archipelago, north of Norway. He discovered what is now known as the Jen Mayen Island before he was stopped by ice! His 2nd expedition for the Muscovy Company was in April 1608. He reached as far as Novaya Zemlya in the Arctic Ocean and was again thwarted by ice! He was then dropped by the Muscovy Company but in 1609 he was hired by the Dutch East India Company to lead an expedition in finding as easterly passage to Asia. He set sail in the ship *Half Moon* and sailed northeasterly but again was blocked by ice!

In a fourth attempt he changed direction and headed southward to what is known now as Virginia in search for a southwest passage. He sailed up the Chesapeake and the Delaware Bay before deciding that they would not lead to the Pacific Ocean. They then sailed north into what is now New York Harbor and proceeded up to what is today the Hudson River before the river narrowed and halted their progress. Henry was the first European to explore the river and his voyage established Dutch claims to this region and a fur trade with the local tribes. In 1610, again working with the English, under the auspices of their East India Company, Henry set sail in the ship *Discovery* on 17 April 1610. By June he had sailed into what is now called the Hudson Strait, between the present-day Baffin Island and Quebec, Canada. He followed it into the bay which is now named for him.

He attempted to find a passage through but as winter approached, he headed south. The *Discovery* was hauled close to shore and by 10 November 1610, they were trapped in ice in the St. James Bay. By spring, rations were in short supply and the decision was made by the crew to head back to England. Henry divided the food and gave each man equal portions, but some men ate their portion immediately and then falsely accused Captain Hudson of hoarding food and playing favorites. The crew then mutinied on 21 June 1611. The captain, his 20-year-old son John Hudson and seven crew members who were loyal to the captain were set adrift in a small open boat with no food, no water, and no weapons. The remainder of the crew took the *Discovery* and sailed back to England. The abandoned Henry Hudson III, his son John, and the seven men who were loyal to Henry were never heard of again!

Back in England, some suggested that Henry III, his son John, and the seven men had been murdered as there was blood found on the *Discovery*. Henry's wife Katherine demanded a rescue party be sent out to find her husband, son and the seven other men. A search party then went out, but they returned without having found them. Henry Hudson III's discoveries led to the development of the Dutch colonies in that region, and he is seen now as a significant early explorer of the New World. He did not actually live in America, but he apparently died here, so I consider him an Immigrant.

Children of HENRY[4B] HUDSON III (Immigrant) (Famous EXPLORER) and KATHERINE ___ were:

| | i. | **John Hudson** (Immigrant) (Son of Famous EXPLORER) b. 1591 in London, Middlesex, England. John went on the exploration trip with his father at age 20 yrs. Unfortunately, he died with his father on that famous trip. They were abandoned at sea (along with seven other men) in America/Canada after discovering the famous river which was named after Henry Hudson III in the Hudson River Bay region (currently in New York and into Canada). John tragically died on 23 June 1611 at age 20, somewhere in the northern New York/Canadian wilderness in North America. |
| | ii. | **David Hudson** b. 1594 in London, Middlesex, England. It is unknown if he ever married and had any children. Also unknown are death date and location at death. |

	iii.	**HENRY Hudson IV** b. 1596 in London, Middlesex, England. It is unknown if he ever married and had any children. Also unknown are death date and location at death.
	iv.	**Oliver Hudson b.** 1600 in London, Middlesex, England. It is unknown if he ever married and had any children. Also unknown are death date and location at death.

Source Citations for this Chapter

https://www.wikitree.com/wiki/Hudson-749

https://www.findagrave.com/memorial/6621707.henry-hudson

https://www.ancestry.com/family-
tree/pt/PersonMatch.aspx?tid=6229385&pid=172232821731&_phsrc=jJ09768&_phstart=defa
ult&usePUBJs=true&c...

https://findagrave.com/memorial/87638498/william-hudson

https://www.familysearch.org/tree/person/details/9ZZL-F1K

https://www.wikitree.com/wiki/Hudson-5143

https://www.findagrave.com/memorial/103541441/ralph-hudson

https://www.geni.com/people/Katherine-
Hudson/6000000002126335338?through=6000000005922029177

Chapter 16: The Hungerfords

The Hungerford Family Line

Salisbury Cathedral – Salisbury England

Pictured on the page after the chart is Lord Robert Hungerford, 2nd Baron (1409-1459). He was a landowner and a Great to the 6th Power Grandson of our oldest researched ancestor:

Walter Hungerford Sr., 1st Baron
born 1110 AD
Wiltshire, England
Died 1200 AD at age 90
Heytesbury, Wiltshire, England

Chart below shows the different generations.

10 Generation

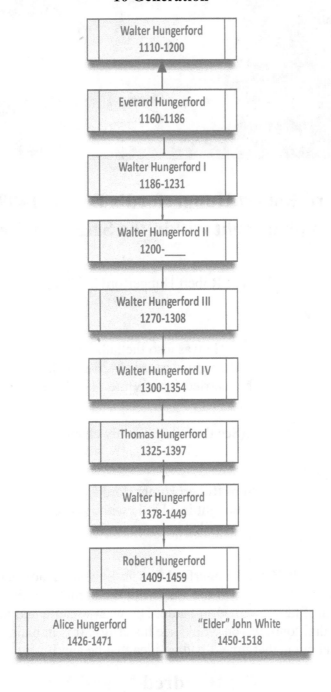

Walter Hungerford
1110-1200

Everard Hungerford
1160-1186

Walter Hungerford I
1186-1231

Walter Hungerford II
1200-___

Walter Hungerford III
1270-1308

Walter Hungerford IV
1300-1354

Thomas Hungerford
1325-1397

Walter Hungerford
1378-1449

Robert Hungerford
1409-1459

Alice Hungerford
1426-1471

"Elder" John White
1450-1518

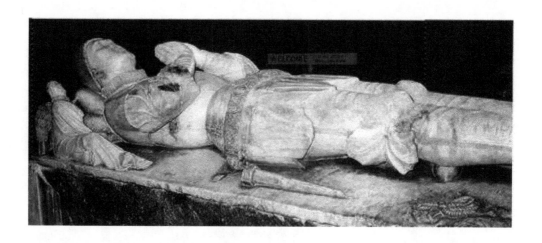

Lord Robert Hungerford's Effigy (1409-1459)
lies in plain sight within the Salisbury Cathedral.

Lord Robert Hungerford 2nd Baron
(1409-1459)

He was also the father of
Alice Hungerford (1426-1471),
who married John White "The Elder"

(See the White Family chapter)

Lord Robert Hungerford 2nd Baron
Fought in a battle with France
He was killed in battle on 14 May 1459

Robert Hungerford 2nd Baron Hungerford was an English landowner. He was married and had a family. He was called to serve in one of the wars with the French. In his will he asked to be buried in the Salisbury Cathedral if he was killed in battle. His wish was granted and if you happened to be in this magnificent cathedral touring, you would see his effigy. It is in plain sight. I saw him when I was visiting in the cathedral but at that time, I had no idea that he and I were related.

The Hundred Years' War

1337-1453

The Hundred Years' War was between England and France. It had major social and economic effects on both countries. It was a long, stressful conflict between the two nations and their people. The Hungerford family was surely affected by this war. A few battles continued, even after the war had ended. Our Robert Hungerford was caught up in one of these battles, six years after the war had ended. He was killed in battle fighting the French on 14 May 1459.

A long conflict inevitably ensued, in which the French kings steadily reduced and weakened the Angevin empire. This struggle, which could well be termed the "First Hundred Years' War," was ended by the Treaty of Paris between Henry III of England and Louis IX of France, which was finally ratified in December 1259. By this treaty Henry III was to retain the duchy of Guyenne (a much-reduced vestige of Aquitaine with Gascony), doing homage for it to the French king, but had to resign his claim to Normandy, Anjou, Poitou, and most of the other lands of Henry II's original empire, which the English had, in any case, already lost. In return, Louis pledged himself to hand over to the English in due course certain territory which protected the border of Guyenne: lower Saintonge, Agenais, and some lands in Quercy. This treaty stood a fair chance of being respected by two rulers such as Henry and Louis, who admired each other and were closely related (they had married sisters), but it posed many problems for the future. It had been agreed, for instance, that the lands in Saintonge, Agenais, and Quercy, which were held at the time of the treaty by Louis IX's brother Alphonse, Count of Poitiers and Toulouse, should go to the English at his death if he had no heir. When Alphonse died without issue in 1271, the new king of France now was English!

Source Citations for this Chapter

https://www.wikitree.com/wikiHungerford-6

https://en.wikipedia.org/wiki/Robert_Hungerford._2nd_Baron_Hungerford

https://www.amazon.com/Hundred-Years-War-c-1300-c-1450-Cambridge-ebook/dp/BOOE3UR020

Author's personal visit to Salisbury Cathedral, Salisbury, England.

Chapter 17: The Kearneys

The Kearney Family Line

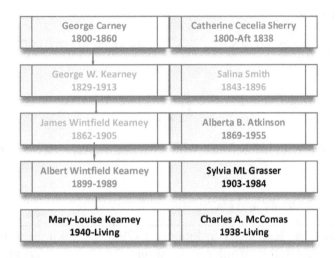

George Carney 1800-1860	Catherine Cecelia Sherry 1800-Aft 1838
George W. Kearney 1829-1913	Salina Smith 1843-1896
James Wintfield Kearney 1862-1905	Alberta B. Atkinson 1869-1955
Albert Wintfield Kearney 1899-1989	**Sylvia ML Grasser 1903-1984**
Mary-Louise Kearney 1940-Living	**Charles A. McComas 1938-Living**

1. George Carney

GEORGE[1] KEARNEY

- Born circa 1800 in Clondahorky, Parish, Donegal, Ireland.
- Married 22 August 1825 Catherine Cecelia Sherry in St. John, St. John Co., New Brunswick, Canada. Catharine Cecelia Sherry (1800-1837) was born in Ireland. She was the daughter of John Sherry (1 January 1772-8 March 1840) and his wife Elizabeth Clarke (15 April 1779-1838) both born and died in Devon, England. It is unknown if Catherine had any siblings. It is also unknown how she got to Canada.
- Died circa 1860 in Apple River, Cumberland Co., Nova Scotia, Canada.

George Carney came by himself to St. John, New Brunswick, Canada aboard the *Margaret Hill* or *Marcus Hill* ship in April 1818. This information was obtained from this Land Grant document below:

(I obtained this document from his granddaughter, the author's Great Aunt Cora Kearney Fraser, who had obtained it from her father, George W. Kearney who was the author's Great Grandfather.)

Application for Land Grant Deed of George Kearney April 1818

[This document has unreadable portions; I have left a blank where they are.]

To the Excellency Major General George Stacy Smyth, Lieutenant Governor and Commander in Chief of the Province of New Brunswick, Canada.

The humble petition of George Carney Herewith "says" that he is a Native of Ireland, born in the parish of Clondahorky, County of Donegal and was a British Subject. He came in the ship M____ Hill and landed in St. John in the month of April Eighteen Hundred and Eighteen. His present place of residence is in the Grand Lakes Parish of Westborough, Queens County where he has resided since he comes to the province and has always resided in his native Country before his immigration and that he is a Single Man and have ____ no land from the Crown. And having received encouragement of ____ have humbly proclaimed to ask that he may have a lot of land given to him which land has not been taken by any person and is in its natural ____ state, lying on the Cumberland Creek at the Head of the Grand Lake and joining land occupied by the ____ ____ ___, he begs. May be given to him. Your ____ Likewise ____ That is his intention and that he has the ability forth with to Cultivate and Improve by himself, his servants, or associates for the Land for which he applies according to the____ Instructions and that he has not directly nor indirectly bargained or agreed for the Lake or Transfer of such land to any person or persons like _____.

If his Excellency of his worried Clemency should grant his petition you _ as in ____ bound will for ___ Prayers

Signed X George Carney

His handwritten X MARK

Note: He signed this with his X Mark which means he was unable to read or write.

Children of GEORGE[1] KEARNEY and CATHERINE SHERRY were:

2.	i.	GEORGE W. KEARNEY b. January 1829 in St. John, St. John Co., New Brunswick. He married Salina Smith on 12 January 1858 at the West Brook Methodist Church, West Brook, Cumberland Co., Nova Scotia. Salina (1843-1896) was the daughter of William Smith and Amelia Yorke. George W. was a carpenter and built a beautiful home for himself and his wife at Diligent River, Nova Scotia. He also helped build a home for his son James W. and James' bride Alberta Atkinson on Western Avenue in Parrsboro, Nova Scotia. George W. and Salina had 12 children during their marriage. George W. died 25 August 1913 at the age of 84 in Parrsboro, Nova Scotia at the home of his daughter-in-law, Alberta Atkinson Kearney. He is buried in an unmarked grave in the Four Corners Methodist Cemetery in Parrsboro, Nova Scotia. His wife Salina Smith Kearney (1843-1896) died at age 53 and is buried in the Warton Cemetery in Wharton, Cumberland Co., Nova Scotia.
	ii.	JAMES KEARNEY b. 1833 in St. John, St. John Co., New Brunswick married Mary Ann Cameron on 31 December 1850 in Simonds Parish, St. John, New Brunswick. Mary Ann was the daughter of Anthony Cameron and Margaret Reed Boyd. They lived in St. John, New Brunswick and had 4 children in their marriage. James died 28 April 1901 on Broad Street in St. John, New Brunswick. See Burial Application below.
	iii.	MARGARET MARJORIE "MARGERY" KEARNEY b. 17 December 1837 in St. John, St. John Co., New Brunswick. She married Robert Dickey Field on 11 December 1853 in Parrsboro, Nova Scotia. She always signed her name "Margery." Robert Dickey (1832-1905) was the son of William Field and Mary Ann Burgess of Hants Co., Nova Scotia. Margery and Robert Dickey lived in Apple River, Nova Scotia. They had 9 children during their marriage. Margery died 4 May 1917 in Apple River, Cumberland Co., Nova Scotia at the age of 79. See picture below.
	iv.	RICHARD MICHAEL KEARNEY (IMMIGRANT) b. 1838 in Nova Scotia. He married Anna Marie Morgan (1838-1877). They left Nova Scotia and immigrated to Northern California. They had 7 children in their marriage. Richard Michael died 14 January 1906 in Napa Co., California at the age of 68.

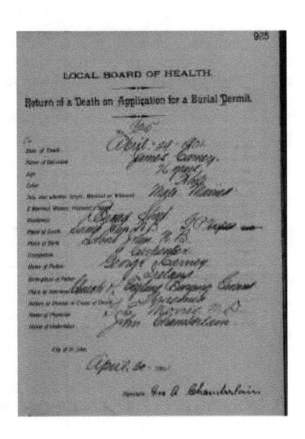

James Kearney (Application for Burial April 1902)

Marjorie "Margery" Kearney

with her husband

Robert Dickey Field

2. George W. Kearney

GEORGE W [2] KEARNEY (George [1])

- Born January 1829 in St. John, St. John Co., New Brunswick.
- Married 12 January 1858 Salina Smith, daughter of William Smith and Amelia Yorke in West Brook Methodist Church, West Brook, Cumberland Co., Nova Scotia.
- Died 25 August 1913 in Parrsboro, Cumberland Co., Nova Scotia, at age 84.
- Buried in an unmarked grave at the Four Corners Cemetery in Parrsboro, Nova Scotia.

George W. was a carpenter and built a beautiful home for himself and his wife Salina Smith at Diligent River, Nova Scotia. He also helped build a home for his son James W. and James' bride Alberta Atkinson on Western Avenue in Parrsboro, Nova Scotia. George W., a widower himself, went to live with his daughter-in-law Alberta Atkinson Kearney to help after his son James Wintfield died prematurely, leaving Alberta widowed with four small children. George W. died 8 years later at Alberta's home in Parrsboro.

Children of GEORGE W.[2] KEARNEY and SALINA SMITH were:

	i.	**WILLIAM KEARNEY** b. 6 October 1858 in Diligent River, Cumberland Co., Nova Scotia. It is not known if he ever married and had any children. William died on 19 January 1895 at the age of 36.
3.	ii.	**JAMES WINTFIELD KEARNEY** b. 26 November 1862 in Diligent River, Cumberland Co., Nova Scotia. He married Alberta Buchanan Atkinson on 28 December 1898 in Southampton, Cumberland Co., Nova Scotia. Alberta Buchanan Atkinson (1869-1955) was the daughter of Rufus Atkinson and Margaret Buchanan. James Wintfield and Alberta had 4 children during their marriage. Their marriage was cut short when James died suddenly with pneumonia on 5 April 1905 at the age of 43. His wife Alberta was 8 weeks pregnant with their 4th child when he died. James died at home on Weston Avenue in Parrsboro. He is buried in Four Corners Methodist Cemetery in Parrsboro, Nova Scotia.
	iii.	**HELENA LILLIAN KEARNEY** b. 21 January 1864 in Diligent River, Cumberland Co., Nova Scotia. She married Thomas Fulton Sr (23 July 1848 – 6 March 1911). Helena and Thomas were married on 27 June 1884 in Parrsboro, Cumberland Co., Nova Scotia. Thomas Fulton was the son of Josiah McKinley Fulton (1803-1866) and Elizabeth Atkinson (31 January 1810 – died after 1891). Josiah and Elizabeth lived in Southampton, Nova Scotia. Helena Lillian Kearney and Thomas Fulton had 5 children during their marriage. Helena died in 1901 in Parrsboro, Cumberland Co., Nova Scotia at the age of 37. From this line came the Fulton boys (many of whom immigrated to Marblehead, Essex Co., Massachusetts, and many of them lived very long lives. They are our Fulton Marblehead Cousins!).
	iv.	**CAPTAIN JOHN ALLISON "JACK" KEARNEY** b. 1866 in Four Corners, Parrsboro, Cumberland Co., Nova Scotia. Captain Jack died in 1900 at sea, off Nantucket Island, Nantucket Co., Massachusetts in a ship accident during a horrific storm at the age of 34.
	v.	**TWIN: LORNA E. KEARNEY** b. 1868 at Diligent River, Cumberland Co., Nova Scotia. It is unknown if she ever married and had children or had died young. Her death date and location at death are both unknown.
	vi.	**TWIN: LAURA KEARNEY** b. 1868 at Diligent River, Cumberland Co., Nova Scotia Laura died circa 1903 at Diligent River, Cumberland Co., Nova Scotia at the age of 35.
	vii.	**GEORGE HUBERT KEARNEY** b. 30 November 1870 at Diligent River, Cumberland Co., Nova Scotia. George Hubert died very young 30 January 1871 in Diligent River, Cumberland Co., Nova Scotia at the age of 2 months.

	viii.	**TWIN: MINA KEARNEY** b. 1873 at Diligent River, Cumberland Co., Nova Scotia. Mina died in 1881 at the age of 8 in her home at Diligent River, Nova Scotia.
	ix.	**TWIN: MABEL KEARNEY** b. 1873 at Diligent River, Cumberland Co., Nova Scotia. Mabel died 23 February 1904 in Windsor, Hants Co., Nova Scotia at age 31.
	x.	**CORA ANNE KEARNEY** (Immigrant) b. 10 Sep 1880 in Four Corners, Parrsboro, Cumberland Co., Nova Scotia. Cora Anne married Joseph Harley Frazer of Prince Edward Island in Rhode Island in 1902. Cora and Joe had 4 children. Her daughter Anne and my father Albert were close cousins and enjoyed getting together in Cambridge, Massachusetts. Anne's daughter Dorothy and this author were also quite close. Cora Anne died on December 10, 1970, at the age of 90. She and her husband Joseph are buried in the Melrose Cemetery, Brockton, Massachusetts.
	xi.	**GORDON KEARNEY** b. circa 1884 in Four Corners, Parrsboro, Cumberland Co., Nova Scotia. Gordon died in 1901 at the age of approx. 17. He is buried in the Four Corners Cemetery in Parrsboro, Nova Scotia.

Cora Kearney Fraser was my paternal Great Aunt. She lived in Brockton, Massachusetts when I was growing up. She was a delightful woman. We never knew when she would visit—she just showed up and stayed about a week or two. She never announced when she would be leaving—she would just leave! She certainly had a mind of her own. She would take over the kitchen when she visited and always had a great sense of humor.

One day, I remember I came home from school and found her in the kitchen with her hair on fire! That was very scary! I was not aware that she was coming. She had arrived while I was at school. She was baking some cookies and bent her head down near the pilot light of the gas stove. Then her hair went up in flames! That was the moment I came home from school and witnessed the horrific event which she was going through! She immediately ran to the kitchen sink and put her head under the water faucet. Terrible experience!

A good memory of Aunt Cora, my never knowing my paternal grandfather, James Kearney, and Cora Anne Kearney Frazer was his sister, I of course always had a million questions for her every time she visited. She knew a lot about the family and was always willing to share and answer all my questions. She came to my grammar school graduation. I loved her very much.

She gave me this Land Grant (see above document) that her father George W. Kearney had given to her, which had been handed down to him by his father George Kearney of Donegal, Ireland. What a treasure it is, as it disclosed so much interesting information about our original Kearney ancestor George Kearney who was born circa 1800 in Donegal, Ireland. He was our Kearney Immigrant who had come to North America. My paternal cousin Libbie Merrow, on a trip to Europe with her husband George Merrow, visited Donegal, Ireland and found our Kearney cousins still living in that same area of Clondahorky. I would love to travel to Ireland someday and visit them as well. She said they didn't have much concrete information for us—just that one of their ancestors had gone to America years ago.

3. James Wintfield Kearney

JAMES WINTFIELD[3] KEARNEY (George W.[2], George[1])

- Born 26 November 1862 at Diligent River, Cumberland Co., Nova Scotia, Canada.
- Married 28 December 1898 Alberta Buchanan Atkinson, daughter of Rufus Atkinson and Margaret Buchanan in Southampton, Cumberland Co., Nova Scotia.
- Died 5 April 1905 in Parrsboro, Cumberland Co., Nova Scotia, at the age of 42.
- Buried. Four Corners Methodist Cemetery, Parrsboro, Cumberland Co., Nova Scotia.

James Wintfield Kearney
1862-1905

James Wintfield was an interior and exterior home painter. He was painting the outside of someone's home on a cold day in March and caught a bad cold which turned into pneumonia. This was in the days before antibiotics had been discovered and he died leaving 4 children under the age of 6.

The Kearney Home on Weston Avenue in Parrsboro, Nova Scotia, Canada

This information is from an interview (author's interview with Lena Yorke Erb on the cousins' trip to Parrsboro, July 1990). Lena is a cousin of Libbie, Joyce, Diane, and Mary-Louise. She is a third cousin once removed. Lena Yorke Erb was a young girl when she and her family moved into this home after Alberta Atkinson Kearney and her family had moved to the States in 1918. This interview contains Lena's memory of this home. There is no picture of the house, but these are Lena's special memories of personally living in that home when she was a young girl.

It was a wonderful home to grow up in. Lena's dad Edson DeMille Yorke bought the house from Alberta Atkinson Kearney in 1919 when she and her family moved away to Cambridge, Massachusetts to be near her siblings. The outside of this home was yellow with white trim. It had a shingled roof. It had a small gable on one side. Gorgeous purple lilacs were to the left of the house. There was a big porch and a veranda on both sides of the home. They stored the wood on the porch. The floors inside were all hardwood.

It had a circular stairway leading to the second floor where there were 5 bedrooms. Another winding stairway led up to the attic. Up in the attic, when they first moved in, they found some dolls so they could tell little girls had a wonderful time playing up there in the attic.

Downstairs was a large living room and a large dining room. There also was a hallway leading to a large kitchen. This memory led Lena to tell the author what happened on that horrible March day in 1935.

Lena said she had baked some bread in the morning and the chimney somehow overheated and caught on fire. The fire was out of control and ended up burning the entire house down. Everyone escaped unharmed but they lost everything inside.

Lena also added the house was on a large piece of land. When she was growing up, they had chickens and cows. They were selling 1500 eggs and 200 quarts of milk every day. After the fire they had to move and never rebuilt the house. At that point many of the kids were grown and had moved to their own homes. The land stood vacant and wild blueberries were grown on the land and still are growing there every summer.

Lena's memories of the author's paternal grandmother, Alberta Atkinson Kearney:

Alberta was a little woman with a sweet personality. Her hair was very long and quite fair, but she always wore it up with a little pug on the top of her head. When they first moved in, they found thread and homemade patterns of Alberta's which she had left behind in the house when she sold her home. Lena continued to say, "I could tell Alberta was a real genuine homemaker."

Alberta has also told her grandchildren of how when she was living in that home on Weston Avenue, her small children would make designs on the frosted windowpanes with her sewing thimbles.

The Kearney homestead on Weston Avenue in Parrsboro, Nova Scotia, this author believes was built by my great grandfather (James' Kearney's father, George W. Kearney) who was a professional carpenter. As a wedding gift to his son James and his new daughter in-law Alberta, he built this beautiful home known as the homestead. It was located across the street from the Field family who were cousins. (See Margery Kearney, daughter of George Carney & Catherine Cecelia Sherry who married Robert Dickey Field.) These Field descendants lived across the street from Alberta and James Kearney's homestead on Weston Avenue. Next door to the Kearney homestead was the home of Stanley McCurdy & Nora Leighton. Stanley's parents had also lived there before their deaths and were very good friends of Alberta as well. Stanley's father was Harry McCurdy who died 8 January 1936. Stanley's mother was Rebecca McCurdy who died 30 June 1955. They were not related to the Kearney family but were great friends. Stanley and Nora were cousins and they lived together for many years. Stanley and Nora both died within a day of each other. Stanley died 10 September 1964 and Nora died 11 September 1964. They were such great neighbors. They always told Alberta, "If you ever need help, just put a light in the window." At Christmas time, someone always left footprints leading to the Kearney's home and they always left a few Christmas packages at the Kearneys' door.

Children of JAMES WINTFIELD[3] KEARNEY and ALBERTA BUCHANAN ATKINSON were:

4.	i.	**ALBERT WINTFIELD KEARNEY** (IMMIGRANT) b. 6 November 1899 in Parrsboro, Cumberland Co., Nova Scotia. He married Sylvia Mary-Louise Grasser on 11 September 1938 in Portsmouth, Rockingham Co., New Hampshire. Sylvia (1903-1984) was the daughter of Michael Grasser II and Wilhelmina Rades. Albert attended Wentworth College in Boston which was a place to learn a trade. There he studied how to become a printer. After his schooling he became an apprentice for Louis Weston in Central Square in Cambridge. In Mr. Weston's later years, he sold the printing business to Albert and in 1936 he bought the Weston Printing Company, which he operated for the next 50 years. Albert and Sylvia had 2 children during their marriage (this author Mary-Louise and her sister Diane). Albert Wintfield died 29 December 1989 in Cambridge, Middlesex Co., Massachusetts, at age 90 years. He and his wife Sylvia are both buried in the Mount Hope Cemetery, Acton, Middlesex Co., Massachusetts.
	ii.	**ANNE ETTER KEARNEY** (IMMIGRANT) b. 18 May 1901 in Parrsboro, Cumberland Co., Nova Scotia. Anne married Dr. Sanford Hiram Moses Jr. 4 September 1926 in the home of the bride at 53 Oxford Street, Cambridge, Middlesex Co., Massachusetts. They met at the Harvard Epworth Church, known at that time as the Epworth Methodist Church located at 155 Massachusetts Avenue, Cambridge, Massachusetts. In 1941 this church became the Harvard Epworth Methodist Church which is still there today. This was the church that Anne, her mother, and her siblings attended every Sunday. Sanford also attended that church when he was a student at Harvard University Medical School. It was there, according to family knowledge, that they met, but they were married in the bride's home nearby on Oxford street. Dr. Moses later on became an OB/GYN physician at the Winchester Hospital in nearby Winchester, Massachusetts. Dr. Sandford Hiram Moses (1903-1985) was the son of Sanford Hiram Moses Sr. and Elizabeth Maria Kennedy of Troy, New York. Anne and Sanford had two children during their marriage. Anne had a respiratory illness which plagued her most of her

		adult life. They owned a beautiful summer home in Clifton Heights, Marblehead, Massachusetts, which is where the Kearney family reunions known as "K. Day" are held each year. After Anne Etter died, Sanford married again and married Anne's sister, Freda Kearney. Anne Etter died 26 October 1966 at the age of 65. She and her husband Dr. Sanford are both buried in the Wildwood Cemetery, Winchester, Middlesex Co. Massachusetts, as is Freda.
	iii.	**MARGARET SALINA KEARNEY** (IMMIGRANT) b. 26 August 1904 in Parrsboro, Cumberland Co., Nova Scotia, Canada. She married William McKinley Matheson (son of William Matheson and Mary A. Thompson) on 12 April 1932 in Los Angeles, Los Angeles Co., California. They had two children in their marriage. Margaret was of the Methodist Faith. Margaret Salina died 16 September 1987 at the age of 83 in Torrance, Los Angeles Co., California. She is buried in Inglewood, Los Angeles Co., California.
	iv.	**ALFREDA MAUD "FREDA" KEARNEY** (IMMIGRANT) b. 12 November 1905 in Parrsboro, Cumberland Co., Nova Scotia. Freda married Dr. Sanford Hiram Moses 23 December 1967 at 8 Prospect Street (at their home), Winchester, Middlesex Co., Massachusetts. This was a second marriage for Sanford Moses as he had been married to Freda's sister Anne. There were no children born to Freda and Sandford. Freda attended the Cambridge Latin High School and Miss Husted's School of Occupational Therapy in Cambridge and she interned at Massachusetts General Hospital and worked at Westboro Mental. Hospital. Following this she became a dentist's assistant and later became an assistant for her brother-in-law who had a GYN obstetrical practice in Winchester, Massachusetts. Freda died 24 June 1977 in Winchester, Middlesex Co., Massachusetts, at the age of age 71. She is buried in Wildwood Cemetery, Winchester, Middlesex Co., Massachusetts.

Children, Grandchildren & Great Grandchildren
of James Kearney and Alberta Atkinson

ALBERT WINTFIELD KEARNEY (IMMIGRANT) married SYLVIA MARY-LOUISE GRASSER

Their offspring were:

Mary-Louise Alberta Kearney

(13 September 1940-living) m. Charles Albert McComas (27 May 1938- Living) m. 4 August 1962.

Couple divorced.

Their 5 children:

- Adopted Anthony Joseph Bravo McComas (16 April 1961-living).
    Tony's 3 children are:

            Mitchell Anthony McComas (6 September 1982- living).
            LaRena Marie McComas (7 July 1987-living).
            Vanessa Louise McComas (19 January 1989-living).
    Tony's grandchildren:

            Mitchell's daughter is Caleigh McComas (18 Feb. 2009-living).

LaRena's daughter Rebecca Ann Milewski (14 Jan. 2008-living).
Vanessa (Nessy)'s 6 children:
>   Xavier Scott Gomes (3 April 2008-living).
>   Zacorra Helen Gomes (28 November 2010-living).
>   Analise Marie Hamilton (10 December 2013-living).
>   Jiralya Scott Gomes (16 November 2018-living).
>   Twin Legend Alexander Gomes (19 November 2021-living).
>   Twin Lennon Matthew Gomes (19 November 2021-living).

- Adopted David Michael Bravo McComas (21 September 1964-living).
  David's only child is James Michael Ross (20 May 1985) m. Barbie Dickson.
  David's grandchild is Alexis MacKinzie Ross (13 March 2007-living).

- Selena Elizabeth McComas (1 June 1966-living).
  m. John Paul Maciejewski (20 March 1958-living) m. 25 April 2005.
  No children in this marriage.
- Anne Mary-Louise McComas (16 May 1968-living).
  m. Jerome Jude Front (22 May 1958) m. 27 February 1999.
  Anne & Jerome's children are:
  >   Vincenty Jude Front (11 November 2000- living).
  >   Sophie Katherine Front (7 February 2002-living).
- Albert Charles McComas (10 September 1970-living).
  Remained single – No children.

Diane Wilhelmina Kearney

(8 November 1944- living) m. David Norman Gray (7 June 1939-living) m. 10 August 1968.

Their 2 children:

- Carolyn Elizabeth Gray (18 June 1975-living).
  Remained single – No children.
- David Sullivan Gray (6 September 1977l-living).
  m. Gayle Ann Hess (25 July 1977-living) m. 5 June 1999.
  David and Gayle's children are.
  >   Anna Elizabeth Gray (20 April 2004-living).
  >   Ethan David Gray (20 March 2006-living).
  >   Twin: Sullivan Dean Gray (14 November 2007-living).
  >   Twin: Sylvia Claire Gray (14 November 2007-living).

Anne Etter Kearney (Immigrant) m. Dr. Sanford Hiram Moses

Their offspring were:

Elizabeth Anne "Libbie" Moses

(2 December 1929-living) m. George Woodbridge Merrow (13 July 1928- 5 October 2018). m. 11 November 1950.

Their 3 children:
1) Eleanor Elizabeth "Lori" (5 October 1954-living).
   m. Thomas Eugene DuVal (4 May 1951-living) m. 12 June 1982.
   Lori & Tom's Children are
   - Rosalind Alberta DuVal (14 May 1985).
   m. Benjamin David Sloan (9 September 1998-living).
   m. 8 August 2010.
   - Samuel Henry Duval (4 March 1988-living).
   m. Heather Michelle Tillery (18 July 1988-living).
   m. 13 July 2013.

   Lori & Tom's grandchildren are
          Elizabeth Xochitl Sloan (9 March 2016- living).
          Mariellen Rose Sloan (26 August 2018- living).
          Ashur Landon DuVal (2 December 2015-living).
          Gabrielle Ayita DuVal (28 September 2017-living).

2) Martha Wolcott Merrow (9 July 1957-living).
   m. James Woodbridge Merrow (20 Aug. 1950-living) m. 2 January 1982.
   Couple divorced.
   Martha & Jim's children are
   - Elizabeth Howell "Lizzie" Merrow (3 March 1988-living).
   - Harriet Moses "Hattie" Merrow (20 March 1991-living).

3) George Sanford "Jed" Merrow (11 August 1959 -living).
   m. Katherine Tolman Buckland "Katie" (29 Deember1957-living).
   m. 24 August 1985.
   Jed and Katie's children are
   - William Buckland Merrow (27 December1988-living).
   - Joseph Lawrence Merrow (30 July 1991-living).
   - Henry Wolcott Merrow (28 June 1995-living).

Jed's nickname was given to him before he was born. His mom states that they knew a charismatic skier in the Northwest whose name was Jed. The beginning and ending of "Jed" sounds are the same as his first two names George and Sanford. The name Jed stuck!

Hiram Sanford Moses (two nicknames: early on he was called "Hi" and later on "Sandy").

b. 28 September 1934 – d. 2 January. 2008.

> m. 1st Barbara Ann Stumpf "Bobbi" m. 13 June 1959. Couple divorced.

> m. 2nd Susan Candice Wilhite (1949-living) No children.

> Hiram Sanford & Bobbie's two children are:

- Sanford Hiram Moses "Tripp" (25 December. 1960- living). Remained Single – No children.

- Allison Elizabeth Moses (8 January1965-14 March 2018).
  m. John J. Nistico (circa 1965-living).
  m. 2 October 1999. Couple divorced.
  Allison and John had one child:
  Austin Nistico (13 October 2000-living).

MARGARET SALINA KEARNEY (Immigrant) married William McKinley Matheson

Their offspring were:

Joyce Darlene Matheson
(21 May 1940-3 May 2019) m. Allen Frederick Greif (28 January 1931-17 August 2014).
    m. 28 April 1962.
    Their 2 children:

- Gregory Michael Greif (7 March 1964-living).
  m. Bernadette Michelle Boyer (3 September 19__-living)

    Greg & Bernadette's 2 children are:
        Paige Kelsey Greif (11 January 1996-living).
        Jake Allen Greif (14 April 1999-living).

- Stephanie Erika Greif (20 February 1967-living).
  Remains single with no children.

Jack William Matheson

(27 July 1944 -28 March 2017) married 1st Karen Freeman circa 1962.
                    married 2nd Joella Augusta Krol 19 Oct. 1971.
    Jack and Karen' 2 Children:

- Daughter Matheson _____ name unknown: (circa 1966-living).

- Kevin Matheson (circa 1968 -living).
  Married and has 2 daughters (names unknown)
  _____ and
  _____.

ALFREDA MAUDE "FREDA" KEARNEY (Immigrant) m. Dr. Sandford H. Moses
m. 23 December 1967.

> NOTE: Dr. Sanford Moses, a widower, married his first wife Anne Etter Kearney's sister who was Alfreda Maude "Freda" Kearney.

There were no offspring from this marriage.

4. Albert Wintfield Kearney

ALBERT WINTFIELD[4] KEARNEY (James[3], George W.[2], George[1])

- Born 6 Nov 1899 in Parrsboro, Cumberland Co., Nova Scotia, Canada.
- Married 11 September 1938 Sylvia Mary-Louise Grasser, daughter of Michael Grasser II and Wilhelmina Rades in Portsmouth, Rockingham Co., New Hampshire.
- Died 29 December 1989 in Cambridge, Middlesex Co., Massachusetts, at age 90 years.
- Buried Mount Hope Cemetery, Acton, Middlesex Co., Massachusetts.

Albert Wintfield Kearney and Sylvia Mary-Louise Grasser

Albert, having lost his father at the age of 6, struggled with this loss for years. However, he became a huge help to his mother amidst all the females in the home. His elderly paternal grandfather had moved in with them to help the family as well. Albert loved his grandfather very much and missed him greatly in 1913 when his grandfather died in their home. Albert stayed at the homestead for an additional year after his mother and sisters had left to go to the United States of America to seek a better education for the family. After a year of winding up things at the homestead in Parrsboro, Canada, Albert joined them in New England. He moved in with his mother who had rented a boarding house on Oxford Street in Cambridge, Massachusetts and was taking in boarders to support herself and her family. Albert was accepted at Wentworth College in Boston, Massachusetts. He had no idea of what he wanted to do for a living. The year was 1919. He ran his finger down the application page, staring at his options of what to study and suddenly decided on printing. "That sounds remarkably interesting," he exclaimed. He completed his education at Wentworth and upon graduation Mr. Weston of Cambridge offered Albert an apprenticeship at his printing company. Albert accepted this position and worked hard for Mr. Weston for years until Mr. Weston retired in 1936 and he sold the business to Albert. Albert kept the original name of the printing company, "The Weston Printing Company."

Albert was single for a long time and then one day his best friend Kenneth Bell, who was getting married to a young lady named Elsie, had an idea. Elsie's best friend was Sylvia Grasser, so Ken and Elsie decided to set up a blind date for their best friends! Well, it worked! Albert fell in love with Sylvia, and I (this writer) have some of their love correspondences. Albert signed his notes, "Oceans and oceans of love, dear Sylvia. Signed Al." They were both in Ken and Elsie's wedding. Albert was Ken's best man and Sylvia was Elsie's maid of honor. Before long, Albert and Sylvia also tied the knot of marriage.

Sylvia's brother (Rev. Raymond Grasser) married Albert and Sylvia in Portsmouth, New Hampshire where Raymond was minister of a church there. The date was 11 September 1938. Al and Sylvia went on their honeymoon to upstate New York in the Lake George region and visited Troy, New York while they were in that area. Shortly after they arrived home, a terrible hurricane hit (known later as the Hurricane of '38). Many trees came down, streets were closed off and homes were destroyed. They said it was like a war had hit but fortunately their apartment at 236 Lexington Avenue in Cambridge, Massachusetts was intact and not destroyed.

Albert was a "hand type" printer. He was now married in 1938. Albert and his wife, Sylvia operated and owned The Weston Printing Company for almost 50 years. Sylvia did all the bookkeeping and managed the front office. This printing shop was located in Central Square, on Massachusetts Avenue, Cambridge, Middlesex Co., Massachusetts. Albert's prize possession at their printing shop was the Heidelberg Printing Press, for which they had saved money for years and finally purchased the prized printing press in 1950! When his daughter Mary-Louise made a trip to Germany in 2013, she discovered the Heidelberg Press was very similar to the printing press machine that the Gutenberg Bible had been printed on in the 1500s. Printing technology had not advanced much from 1500-1950 but then with the advent of computers, printing technology had also advanced at a record-breaking speed. Albert was absolutely amazed in 1960 with the advancements. Albert continued to work at his printing shop. He died at the age of 90 years in 1989 with a sudden cardiac arrest while getting dressed for work. He had died instantly. Sylvia also had died of a major heart attack, five years earlier in 1984.

Children of ALBERT WINTFIELD[4] KEARNEY and SYLVIA MARY-LOUISE GRASSER were:

| 5. | i. | **MARY-LOUISE ALBERTA KEARNEY** b. 13 September 1940 in Cambridge, Middlesex Co., Massachusetts. She married Charles Albert McComas (1938-living) on 4 August 1962 at the Harvard-Epworth Methodist Church in Cambridge. Charles Albert McComas is a son of Charles McComas Jr. and Florence Hollomon. Mary-Louise and Charles Albert adopted two older boys and had 3 biological children as well. They are listed earlier in this chapter. Mary-Louise is a registered nurse and Charles Albert was a computer programmer. The couple divorced 25 March 2005. Both are now retired and living in Massachusetts and California. |
| | ii. | **DIANE WILHELMINA KEARNEY** b. 8 November 1944 in Winchester, Middlesex Co., Massachusetts. Diane married David Normas Gray (1939- living) on 10 August 1968 at the Harvard Epworth Methodist Church in Cambridge. David Norman Gray is the son of Norman Harry Gray and Carolyn Elizabeth Banks. Diane and David had two children in their marriage. They are listed earlier in this chapter. Diane was a special needs elementary school teacher and David was a banker in Boston. Both are now retired and are residing in Maine. |

5. Mary-Louise Alberta Kearney

MARY-LOUISE ALBERTA[5] KEARNEY (Albert[4], James[3], George W.[2], George[1])

- Born 13 September 1940 in Cambridge, Middlesex Co., and Massachusetts.
- Married 4 August 1962 Charles Albert McComas in the Harvard Epworth Methodist Church, Cambridge, Middlesex Co., Massachusetts. Charles Albert is the son of Charles McComas Jr. and Florence Hollomon McComas.
- Died (Living)

Mary-Louise and Charles Albert McComas were engaged 13 April 1959 in Brookline, Suffolk Co., Massachusetts while she was still in nursing school. They were married as soon as she had completed her nursing school education. The couple divorced 25 March 2005. She is a registered nurse and has worked in several medical and surgical nursing units for 4 years, an orthopaedic nursing unit for 8 years and a psychiatric nursing unit for 25 years. She also worked in a group home caring for chronically disabled clients for 4 years. Mary-Louise is currently now retired and is living in Massachusetts.

Children of MARY-LOUISE ALBERTA KEARNEY and CHARLES ALBERT MCCOMAS are documented in Volume II in the McComas chapter.

Source Citations for this Chapter

Paper Copy of Land Grant Document which is in the Author's Kearney file in her study.

Albert W. Kearney (1899-1989) Obituary found at the following ancestry site:

https://www.ancestry.com/mediaui-viewer/tree/7982833/person/170005246296/media/933bbea9--9318-4e69-ba67-7c91194662674?destTreeId=16080...

Letters from Gary Vickery in the Author's file.

Verbal information from Cora Kearney Fraser.

Genealogical Letters from Marion Kyle of Parrsboro, Cumberland Co., Nova Scotia (in Author's file).

Kearney Genealogical Records at PANS (Public Archives of Nova Scotia).

Ireland Records of Ulster, Donegal, Barony of Kilmacrenan, Diocese Rapho, Parish Clondahorky, Poor Law Union Dunfanaghy, Civil Parish Raymunterdoney (Catholic) Dunfanaghy.

Vital Records of Nova Scotia Federal Canadian Census of 1881, 1901 and 1911 Censuses.

Jenks Journal of Parrsboro, Nova Scotia, Canada.

Churches' Business Map of West Brook, Cumberland Co., Nova Scotia.

Diligent River, Advocate Harbor, and Apple River Nova Scotia Land Grants.

Correspondence with Cousin and fellow Genealogist Kenneth Jeffrey Kearney kjeffk@hotmail.com

Correspondence with Cousin and fellow Genealogist Peter Newton sirisaacnuclear@gmail.com

Chapter 18: The Lathams

The Latham Family Line

Lewis Latham 1584-1655		Elizabeth ____ Ca 1584-1619
Frances Latham 1609-1677		William Dungan Sr. 1611-1636

1. Lewis Latham (Royal Sergeant Falconer for King Charles I)

LEWIS[1] LATHAM

- Born 2 October 1584 in Elstow, Bedford Co., England.
- Married 1606 Wife #1 Ann ____ (circa 1584 - 1607).
- Married 1607 Wife #2: Elizabeth ____ (circa 1584 - 1619).
- Married 1619 Wife #3: Winifred Downes (1590-1620).
- Died 15 May 1655 in London, Middlesex Co., England at age 71.

"Master of the Hawks"
Lewis Latham
1584-1655

Lewis Latham was the son of John Latham Jr. (1554-1592) and his wife Mary____ Latham. Little is known of his early childhood. However, it is known that he had two brothers named William and Simon (Symon). Simon also was a falconer and published two books which have three editions (1615, 1633, and 1652.) They are all in the British Museum. In two books, the title page reads "Latham's Falconry – the Falconer's Lure and Cure." Lewis Latham was married three times. His first wife Ann ____ died shortly after the birth of their firstborn. They were married circa 1606. Lewis's second wife was Elizabeth ____. They were married in 1607 and Elizabeth died in 1619. Lewis' third wife was Winifred Downes. They married but shortly after their marriage, Winifred died giving birth to their only child. The child, Winifred, lived, but Winifred the mother died.

A Falcon in Flight

Lewis Latham was a Master in Falconry. He learned the art of falconry at an early age. In 1612 he was hired to be a falconer for Prince Henry. Lewis was a young man of 28 years at that time. It was not long, before he was promoted to be the Sergeant Falconer for King Charles I, a very prestigious position of work.

The Job of Falconry

Falconry is the hunting of wild animals in their natural state and habitant by means of a trained bird of prey. Small animals are hunted, including squirrels and rabbits, who often fall prey to the falcon. The practice of hunting with a conditioned falcon is called hawking or game hawking. They used this method of gaining food from animals in the dead of winter when food was scarce as well as a sport that the king of England and his royal subjects enjoyed watching.

Three Marriages of Lewis Latham and their children.

Married #1: Ann ____ (circa 1584 - 1607) m. 1606.

Child of LEWIS[1] LATHAM and ANN ____ was:

		ANN LEWIS circa b. 1607 in London, Middlesex Co., England. Ann died stillborn. Both the mother (Ann) and her daughter (also named Ann) died during the birth of this daughter in 1607.

Married #2: Elizabeth ____ (circa 1584 - 1619) m.1607.

Children of Lewis[1] Latham and Elizabeth ___ were:

	i.	**OLIVER Lewis** b. 1608 in London, Middlesex Co., England. He died stillborn at birth.
2.	ii.	**FRANCES LEWIS (Immigrant)** b. 15 February 1610 in Kempston, Bedfordshire, England. She married 4 times. Husband #1 Lord ____ Weston. They were married in 1625 in London, Middlesex Co., England. Husband #2 William Dungan Sr. They were married in 1627 in London, Middlesex Co., England and had 4 children during this marriage. Following William's death, Frances married yet again, this time Husband #3 Jeremiah Clarke. They were married in London, Middlesex Co., England circa 1635. They immigrated to America circa 1638. Following Jeremiah's death, Frances married a fourth time. Husband #4 Rev. William Vaughan married in Newport, Newport Co., Rhode Island. They were married circa 1654 in Newport, Rhode Island. Frances died 2 September 1677 in Newport, Newport Co., Rhode Island. She is buried in the Common Burying Ground Cemetery on Farewell Street in Newport, Rhode Island. Frances was known as "The Mother of the Governors."
	iii.	**JOHN Lewis** circa 1611 in London, Middlesex Co., England. He married Martha Fernand circa 1630. It is not known if they had any children. John's death date and location at death are also unknown.
	iv.	**HENRY Lewis** b. circa 1612 in London, Middlesex Co., England. Henry married twice. Wife #1 ____ ____ circa 1633. He also married Wife #2 Ann Goodwin in 1656. It is unknown if Henry had any children during either of these two marriages and his date of death and location at death are also unknown.
	v.	**MARIA Lewis** b. circa 1613 in London, Middlesex Co., England. She died at birth as stillborn.
	vi.	**KATHERINE LEWIS** b. 1615 in London, Middlesex Co; England. Katherine married William Garnett circa 1640. It is unknown if the couple had any children during their marriage and her death date and location at death are also unknown.
	vii.	**ELIZABETH Lewis** b. September 1617 in London, Middlesex Co., England. Elizabeth married ____ Bibbee circa 1637. It is unknown if the couple had any children during their marriage and Elizabeth's death date and her location at death are unknown.
	viii.	**ANN Lewis** b. circa 1618 in London, Middlesex Co; England. Ann married ____ Seager circa 1640. It is unknown if the couple had any children during their marriage. Also unknown are their death dates and their location at death.
	ix.	**SARAH Lewis** b. October 1618 in London, Middlesex Co., England. No further information known. Unknown if married, unknown if any children, unknown death date and unknown location.
	x.	**HELEN called "ELLEN" LEWIS (Immigrant)** b. 1619 in London, Middlesex Co., England. She married twice: Husband #1 ____ Sheringham circa 1640. Husband #2 Rev. William Wickenden 1663 in Providence, Providence Co., Rhode Island. It is unknown if she ever had any children during either marriage. She died in Providence, Rhode Island but date of death is unknown.

Married #3: Winifred Downes (1590-1620) m. 1619

There was one child of LEWIS[1] LATHAM and WINIFRED DOWNES.

		WINIFRED Downes Lewis b. 1620 in London, Middlesex Co., England. The child Winifred lived on until 1655 but her mother Winifred died giving birth to her in 1620. The child Winifred lived to be 35 years old.

Lewis Latham continued with his work as the Falconer for King Charles I until Lewis' death on 15 May 1655. He is buried at Elstow, the town where Lewis was born. Elstow is two miles from Bedford, in Bedfordshire, England. It is the same area where the famous preacher Reverend John Bunyan was born in 1628. It is most likely that they both knew each other during that same period.

2. Frances Latham (Immigrant) "Mother of the Governors"

FRANCES[2] LATHAM (*Lewis*[1])

- Born 15 February 1610 in Kempston, Bedfordshire, England.
- Married 1625 Husband #1 Lord ____ Weston. They married in London, Middlesex Co., England.
- Married 1627 Husband #2 William Dungan Sr. They married in London, Middlesex Co., England.
- Married circa 1635 Husband #3 Jeremiah Clarke in London, Middlesex Co., England.
- Arrived in America circa 1638.
- Married circa 1654 Husband #4 Rev. William Vaughan in Newport, Newport Co., Rhode Island.
- Died 2 September 1677 in Newport, Newport Co., Rhode Island at the age of 67.
- Buried in Common Burying Ground Cemetery located on Farewell Street, Newport, Newport Co., Rhode Island.

Since Frances Latham had 4 husbands, let me explain her life here. I normally add only an ancestor's children under the father's surname, but I am also adding them here as well for clarification.

Marriage #1 Frances Latham married **Lord Weston** (first name unknown) circa 1625. Frances was approx. 15 yrs. old. Shortly after they were married, Lord Weston died suddenly and left Francis a widow.

There were no children of Frances[2] Latham and Lord ____ Weston.

Marriage #2 Frances Latham Weston married **William Dungan Sr.** on 27 August 1629 in Westminster Cathedral in London, England. Frances was now approx. 19 years old. William Dungan Sr. was 18 years old. This marriage produced four children. William Dungan Sr. was a "Perfumer" and sold different perfumes which were a necessity at that period as people only bathed very infrequently. The months of May and June were popular months to be married as the brides would bathe in the rivers and lakes during the springtime when the weather was warmer. Ordinarily, people would use perfume to cover their body odor. William Dungan Sr. died in September 1636 at the age of 25, leaving Frances a widow yet again at age 26 but now with four children ages 8 yrs., 7 yrs., 6 yrs. and 4 yrs.

Children of William Dungan Sr. and Frances Latham Weston Dungan are documented in the Dungan chapter, but I have listed them here as well.

Children of WILLIAM DUNGAN SR. and FRANCES LATHAM WESTON DUNGAN were:

The Four Dungan Children

	i.	**BARBARA DUNGAN** (Immigrant) b. 1628 in London, Middlesex Co., England. Barbara married James Baker in Rhode Island in 1644. It is unknown if they had any children during their marriage. Barbara died in 1702 in America at age 74.
	ii.	**WILLIAM DUNGAN JR.** (Immigrant) b. 1629 in London, Middlesex Co., England. William Jr. died unknown date but died in America.
3.	iii.	**FRANCES DUNGAN** (Immigrant) b. circa 1630 in London, Middlesex Co., England. Frances married Captain Randall Holden Sr. in 1648 in Warwick, Rhode Island. They had 11 children during their marriage. Frances died in 1692 in Rhode Island at age 62.
	iv.	**REV. THOMAS DUNGAN** (Immigrant) b. 1632 in London, Middlesex Co., England. Rev. Thomas married Elizabeth Weaver in 1650 Newport, Rhode Island. Rev. Thomas and his wife moved to Pennsylvania. It is unknown if they had any children during their marriage. Rev. Thomas established the First Baptist Church there in Cold Spring, Pennsylvania and was their very first minister. Rev. Thomas died in 1688 in Old Cold Spring, Pennsylvania at the age of 56.

Marriage #3 Frances Latham Weston Dungan married **Jeremiah Clarke in** 1635. Frances married again at the age of 25 years. She affectionally referred to Jeremiah as "Jeremy." Jeremiah Clarke was the son of William Clarke and Mary Weston. Jeremy was born in central Kent in southeastern England. His maternal grandfather was Sir Jerome Weston, Baron of the Exchequer and his uncle was Richard Weston, 1st Earl of Portland, Lord High Treasurer of England. Jeremy was a simple merchant in London. He and Frances made the decision to sail to the colonies with Frances' four children.

They arrived and first settled in Aquidneck (later known as Rhode Island); He is listed as an inhabitant there in 1638. In April 1639 while living in Portsmouth, Rhode Island, Jeremy Clark was one of the nine men who signed the famous Portsmouth of Rhode Island Contract agreeing to establishing a government there. Shortly thereafter, Jeremy became one of the founders of Newport, Rhode Island and he held a variety of positions from 1639 to 1649, including Treasurer and Constable. In March 1640 Jeremy had 116 acres of land in Newport.

In 1642 he was chosen Lieutenant of the Military in Newport and in 1644 he became Captain. Jeremy Clark became the Governor of Rhode Island and during his administration they granted the charter to the town of Providence, Rhode Island on 14 March 1649. The new town of Providence, Rhode Island had been the Providence Plantation in the Narragansett Bay in New England. This new charter of civil incorporation gave the free inhabitants of the town the full power and authority to govern and rule themselves. Today the town of Providence is a huge city and is the capital of Rhode Island.

Jeremy Clark died of unspecific causes at the age of 47 leaving his wife again a widow. Jeremiah and Frances had an additional 7 children together. Later, at Frances' wife's grave site, there would be an inscription which reads as follows:

Here lyeth ye body of Mrs. Frances Vaughan, alias Clarke, ye mother of ye only children of Captain Jeremiah Clarke."

Frances Latham Weston Dungan Clarke is known as "The Mother of the Governors." The reason she had this title was because she became the ancestor of at least (10) Governors and (2) Deputy Governors and is related by marriage to an additional (6) Governors and (1) Deputy Governors. There are many Governors across America over the history of our country who were descended from her middle two marriages.

The Seven Clarke Children

Children of JEREMIAH CLARKE and FRANCES LATHAM WESTON DUNGAN CLARKE were:

	i.	**WALTER CLARKE** b. in Rhode Island in Newport, Rhode Island, became a future colonial Governor of Rhode Island.
	ii.	**MARY CLARKE** b. in Rhode Island married John Cranston who was another future Governor
	iii	**Jeremiah Clarke Jr.** b. in Rhode Island.
	iv.	**LATHAM CLARKE** b. in Rhode Island.
	v.	**WESTON CLARKE** b. in Rhode Island married Mary Easton who was the granddaughter of two other future Governors (John Coggeshall & Nicholas Easton).
	vii.	**JAMES CLARKE** b. Rhode Island.
	vii.	**SARAH CLARKE** b. 1632 in Rhode Island married future colonial Governor Caleb Carr as her second husband.

Marriage #4 Frances Latham Weston Dungan Clarke Vaughn married the **Reverend William Vaughan** in 1654 in Newport, Rhode Island. Frances was then 44 years old, and William was 47 years old. Rev. William was born in 1607 in England, and he too was an Immigrant. He had been ordained as a Baptist minister in 1648 in Newport, Rhode Island.

In 1656 he, along with others, formed the Second Baptist Church. He was a highly respected citizen of Newport, so much that in August 1676, during King Philip's War, he was one of 16 colonial leaders whose counsel was requested by the General Assembly during those troubled times.

It is thought by several writers of that early colonial time that Rev. William Vaugh was Frances' pastor and they had become good friends. Rev. William Vaughn died at the age of 70 years and Frances was again for the fourth time a widow. However, she died just several short weeks following her deceased husband, Rev. William Vaughan.

They had no children together in this marriage. Frances died on 2 September 1677 at the age of 67. She is buried in the Common Burying Ground, which is located on Farewell Street in Newport, Rhode Island. Her tombstone is pictured here.

**Gravestone of
Frances Latham Weston Dungan Clarke Vaughan
"Mother of the Governors"
1610-1677
Died at age 67**

Source Citations for this Chapter

The Last Will and Testametn of Lewis Latham:

https://www.ancestry.com/mediaui-viewer/tree/3588995/person/-1554705360/media/612fd75e-d37a-424e-a242-a7639e67c535?destTreeId=62293685..

Direct Ancestors and Direct Descendants of English Lathams:

https://www.ancestry.com/imageviewer/collections/12129/immages/dvm_GenMono001573-00080-0?treeid=62293685&personid=172225907054&hintid...

Lathan Genealogy and Lathan Family History Information:

https://www.geni.com/surnames/latham

Hybrid Falcons:

https://en.wikipedia.org/wiki/Falconry

Dungan Ancesry:

http://freepages.genealogy.rootsweb.com/-mylines/dungan074.htm

Lewis Latham Portrait (from the original by Sir Peter Lely).

Lewis Latham, Sergeant Falconer to Charels I of England.

Copy of the Orginal Portrait Paining is in the Newport Rhode Island Library.

Ancestry of Thirty Three Rhode Islanders born in the 18th Century by John O. Austin, 1889.

Genealogies of Rhode Island Families Volume I, Baltimore Genealogical Publishing Company Inc. 1983., Randall Holden and His Family, contributed by John O. Austin of Provicence , Rhode Island pgs 472-477.

Genealogies of Rhode Island Families Volume I, Baltimore Genealogical Publishing Company Inc. 1983., Latham Family Notes, contributed by John O. Austin of Provicence , Rhode Island pgs 591-594.

Chapter 19: The Laytons

The Layton Family Line

William Layton Sr. 1708-Aft 1730	Ann Sandrson Ca 1705-____
William Layton Jr. 1726-Aft 1745	____ Ca 1725-____
John Layton 1741-Aft 1774	Ann Boynton Ca 1740-____
Mary Layton 1755-1836	Thomas Bowser Jr. 1743-1816

Dread shame

layton

The name Layton is an old Anglo-Saxon name. It comes from where geographically the family lived in the place called Leighton. This habitation name was originally derived from the Old English word "Leac-tun," which referred to the homestead where leeks were grown in the Waltham Forest of Essex, England.

1. William "Will" Layton Sr.

WILLIAM[1] "Will" LAYTON SR.

- Born 1708 in All Saints, Wakefield, Yorkshire, England.
- Married 3 April 1722 Ann Sanderson, (circa 1705 -____) in Bishop Wilton, Yorkshire, England.
- Died after 1730 in Bishop Wilton, Yorkshire, England at the age of 22+.

Children of WILLIAM[1] "WILL" LAYTON and ANN SANDERSON were:

2.	i.	**WILLIAM LAYTON JR.** b. 17 May 1726 in All Saints, Wakefield, Yorkshire, England. William married ____ Surname unknown, date of marriage unknown in Yorkshire, England. William Jr. and ___ had 3 children during their marriage. Willian Jr. died after 1745 in Yorkshire, England at the age of approx. 19+.
	ii.	**THOMAS LAYTON** b. 1728 in Bishop Wilton, Yorkshire, England, married Mary ___Surname unknown. Thomas died date unknown.
	iii.	**ANN LAYTON** b. 1730 Bishop Wilton, Yorkshire, England. It is unknown if she ever married and had any children. Her death date and location at death are both unknown.

2. William Layton Jr.

WILLIAM[2] LAYTON JR. (William[1])

- Born 17 May 1726 in All Saints, Wakefield, and Yorkshire, England.
- Married circa 1740 ____Surname unknown and marriage date unknown in Yorkshire, England.
- Died after 1745 in Yorkshire, England at the age of 19+.

Children of WILLIAM[2] LAYTON JR. and _____ were:

3.	i.	**JOHN LAYTON (Immigrant)** b. 1741 Leavening, Yorkshire, England. John married Ann Boynton on 14 July 1742. Ann Boynton (1725-__). She was the daughter of James Boynton) of Yorkshire, England. John Layton and Ann Boynton were married in Leavening, Yorkshire, England. John and Ann had 1 child during their marriage. They Immigrated to Canada and arrived 9 May 1774 in Halifax, Nova Scotia on the ship *Two Friends*. John died after 1774 in Nova Scotia., Canada at the age of 43+.
	ii.	**THOMAS LAYTON** b. 1743 in Acklam, North Yorkshire, England. It is unknown if he ever married and had any children. His death date and his location at death are unknown.
	iii.	**LAYTON (FEMALE) LAYTON** b. 1745 in Bishop Wilton, Acklam, Yorkshire, England. It is unknown if she ever married and had any children. Her death date and her location at death are unknown.

Two Friends Sailing Ship
Departed Hull, England between
28 February 1774 - 7 March 1774
Arrived in Halifax, Nova Scotia, Canada
9 May 1774

Two Friends was a medium-sized wooden sailing ship that served the British government for transporting troops to garrisons across the British Empire during the Napoleonic Wars. On 22 October 1805 _Two Friends_ was wrecked on the coast of Cape Breton Island with the loss of three lives.

The ship was carrying around 80 passengers, 40 soldiers, 30 crew and all the baggage and heavy equipment of the 100th Regiment. Early in the morning of 22 October 1805, the ship was driven ashore by high winds and in dense fog on the south coast of Cape Breton Island close to Louisburg.

The ship lost her masts and frantic efforts were made to prevent it drifting off into deep water, where it would have sunk with all hands. Some hours after it was wrecked, local people spotted the disaster and made dozens of trips in small boats to the battered ship, managing to rescue all but three of those aboard, who had drowned trying to reach shore some hours before. Later that day, the remains of the ship drifted off the reef and sank in deep water, taking all the regiment's equipment with it.

3. John Layton (Immigrant)

JOHN[3] LAYTON (William[2], William[1])

- Born. 1741 in Leavening, Yorkshire; England.
- Married 14 July 1742 Ann Boynton (1725-__) Ann was the daughter of James Boynton of Yorkshire, England. John Layton and Ann Boynton were married in Leavening, Yorkshire, England.
- Arrived 9 May 1774 in Halifax, Nova Scotia on the ship _Two Friends_.
- Died after 1774 in Nova Scotia., Canada at the age of 43+.

Two Friends is the name of the ship John Layton and his wife sailed to Halifax on from February to May of 1774. It is interesting to note that the John Smith Family who also lived in Yorkshire,

158

England, sailed on that very ship, the same year and settled in Nova Scotia. Canada. They also intermarried into our family. (See the Smith chapter of Nova Scotia.) I wonder if they knew each other before both families sailed aboard the *Two Friends,* voyaging across the Atlantic to Canada.

The ship's passenger list states for both our families aboard the *Two Friends* the reasons they were leaving England, in their own words:

John Smith, Farmer: "Leaving on account of the rents being raised too high." (!)

John Layton, Farmer: "Leaving, going to seek a better livelihood."

The 1770s were years of turbulence for the tenant farmers of England's Yorkshire Country. The "Enclosure Movement" and the demands of the developing Industrial. Revolution were transforming a rural society which had changed little since the feudal era of the Middle Ages. After centuries of attachment to the land, the peasants were being forced off in the interests of the landlords who now had a large market in the new industrial towns for their produce. The peasants were no longer needed as new methods of large-scale farming demanded the end of scattered peasant plots and labor-intensive agriculture.

The peasants had a right to their tenancy but appeals to the English Parliament brought acts entitling the landlords to fence their large estates. The next step was to force the peasants off the land. Rents were raised to impossible levels and the peasants left the land, facing the prospect of low-paid labor in the factories and life in the industrial slums. Out of this prospect grew the great Yorkshire Migration to Nova Scotia during the years 1770-1775. Now years later, here in the 21st century, we as a modern society are leaving the Industrial Era and heading into a Technology Era with more changes and challenges ahead on the horizon. We, like our ancestors, will endure as we face more turbulent times once again!

Child of JOHN[3] LAYTON and ANN BOYNTON was:

4.	i.	**MARY LAYTON** (Immigrant) b. 28 December 1755 in Leavening, Yorkshire. She married "The Pioneer" Thomas Bowser Jr. in Acklam, Yorkshire, England in 1773. They had 12 children during their marriage. Mary died 26 May 1836 in Sackville, Westmoreland Co., New Brunswick, Canada at the age of 81.

4. Mary Layton (Immigrant)

MARY[4] LAYTON (John[3], William[2], William[1])

- Born 28 December 1755 in Leavening, Yorkshire, England.
- Married 13 January 1773 "The Pioneer" Thomas Bowser Jr., (1743-1816) , son of Thomas Bowser Sr. and Ann Wilkinson, Mary and Thomas Jr. were married in Acklam, Yorkshire, England.
- Arrived 9 May 1774 in Halifax, Nova Scotia.
- Died 26 May 1836 in Sackville, Westmorland Co., New Brunswick, Canada at age 81.

Children of MARY[4] LAYTON and "THE PIONEER" THOMAS BOWSER JR. are documented in the Bowser chapter.

Source Citations for this Chapter

The Heirs of Francis Layton, The Story of a Nova Scotia Family compiled by Jack F. Layton, 1986. NEHGS Library CS/90/L35/1986.

My Heritage: https://www.myheritage.com/research/record-1-198493471-7-3732/ann-layton-born-bointon-in-myheritage-family-trees

Ancestry:

https://www.ancestry.com/familytree/pt/PersonMatch.aspx?tid=62293685&pid=40085166199 &-phsrc=jJ07932&-phstart=default&usePUBJs=true&cu...

Chapter 20: The Lords

The Lord Family Line

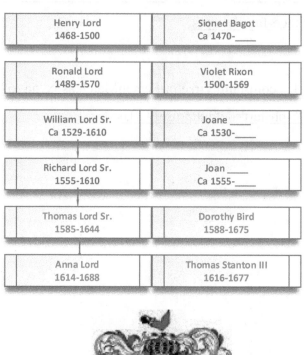

Henry Lord 1468-1500	Sioned Bagot Ca 1470-____
Ronald Lord 1489-1570	Violet Rixon 1500-1569
William Lord Sr. Ca 1529-1610	Joane ____ Ca 1530-____
Richard Lord Sr. 1555-1610	Joan ____ Ca 1555-____
Thomas Lord Sr. 1585-1644	Dorothy Bird 1588-1675
Anna Lord 1614-1688	Thomas Stanton III 1616-1677

The Surname Lord

The surname of Lord was derived from the Old English word "hlalord," a nickname which meant "loaf-keeper"—an occupational name for a servant in the household of the lord of the manor since the lord or chief of a clan was responsible for providing food for his dependants. It was also used as a status name for a "landlord" (property owner) or the lord of the manor himself. Occupational surnames originally denoted the actual occupation followed by the individual. At what period they became hereditary is a difficult problem. Many of the occupation names were descriptive and could be varied. In the Middle Ages, at least among the Christian population, people did not usually pursue specialized occupations exclusively to the extent that we do today, and they would, in fact, turn their hand to any form of work that needed to be done, particularly in a large house or mansion, or on farms and smallholdings. In early documents, surnames often refer to the actual holder of an office, whether the church or state. Early records of the name mention William le Lalord who was documented in the year 1198 in County Suffolk and John le Lord appears in 1252 in County Lancashire. Roger le Lord was recorded in County Cambridge, 1273. A later instance of the name mentions Judith Lord who was baptized at St. James's, Clerkenwell, London in 1642. In many parts of central and western Europe, hereditary surnames began to become fixed at around the 12th century and have developed and changed slowly over the years. As society became more complex, and such matters as the management of tenure, and in particular the collection of taxes, were delegated to special functionaries, it became imperative to distinguish a more complex system of nomenclature to differentiate one individual from another.

In the early part of the seventeenth century, there were four "Lord" families who settled in this country of America. They all came from England and are believed to be paternal cousins, **not** brothers.

Nathan Lord who landed in Kittery, Maine

> >> Thomas Lord who landed in Boston, Massachusetts >>>

Robert Lord who landed in Ipswich, Massachusetts

William Lord who landed in Salem, Massachusetts

>>> Thomas Lord >>>

Is this author's family line.

1. Henry Lord

HENRY[1] LORD

- Born 1468 in Stafford, Staffordshire, England.
- Married 1487 Sioned Bagot in Staffordshire, England.
- Died 1500 in Towcester, County of Northampton, England at the age of 32.
- Buried in Towcester, County of Northampton, England.

Children of HENRY[1] LORD and SIONED BAGOT were:

2.	i.	**Ronald Lord** b 1489 in Towcester, Northampton, England. He married Violet M. Rixon (1500-1569) daughter of William Henry and Theresa Sarah Meredith Rixon. They were married in 1528. Ronald and Violet had 1 child, a son, during their marriage. Ronald died 19 October 1570 in Towcester, Northampton, England at the age of 81.
	ii.	**Thomas Lord Sr.** b. 1490 in Towcester, Northampton, England. Thomas married Elspeth Ann Brereton (1486-1558). They were married in 1511. It is unknown how many children they had. Thomas Sr. died January 1560 in Staffordshire, England.

2. Ronald Lord

RONALD[2] LORD (Henry[1])

- Born 1489 in Towcester, Northampton, England.
- Married 1528 Violet M. Rixon (1500-1569), daughter of William Henry and Theresa Sarah Meredith Rixon in Towcester, Northampton, England.
- Died 19 October 1570 in Towcester, Northampton, England at the age of 81.
- Buried in Towcester, Northampton, England.

Child of RONALD[2] LORD and VIOLET M. RIXON was:

3	i.	**WILLIAM LORD** b. 1529 Towcester, Northampton, England. William married Joane __. They were married in 1554. They had 2 sons during their marriage. William Sr. died 30 May 1610 in Towcester, Northampton, England.

3. William Lord Sr.

WILLIAM[3] LORD SR. (Ronald[2], Henry[1])

- Born circa 1529 in Towcester, Northampton, England.
- Married 1554 Joane _____ in England.
- Died 30 May 1610 in Towcester, Northampton, England at the age of 81.
- Buried in Towcester, Northampton, England.

Children of WILLIAM[3] LORD SR. and JOANE _____ were:

4.	i.	Richard Thomas Lord b. 7 February 1555 in Towcester, Northampton, England. Richard married Joan ___ in 1582 in Towcester, Northampton, England. Richard and Joan had 4 children during their marriage. Richard died 14 October 1610 Towcester, Northampton, England at the age of 55.
	ii.	William Lord Jr. b. 1557 in Towcester, Northampton, England. William Jr. died young in 1560 at the age of 3 years old.

4. Richard Thomas Lord Sr.

RICHARD THOMAS[4] LORD (William[3], Ronald[2], Henry[1])

- Born 7 February 1555 in Towcester, Northampton, England.
- Married circa 1582 Joan _____ in Towcester, Northampton, England.
- Died 14 October 1610 in Towcester, Northampton, England at the age of 55 years.
- Buried in Towcester, County of Northampton, England.

Children of RICHARD THOMAS[4] LORD and JOAN _____ were:

	i.	**Elizabeth Lord** b. 1583 in Towcester, Northampton, England. Elizabeth married Robert Marriot. It is unknown if they had any children. Elizabeth died in 1667 at the age of 84. Her location at death is unknown.
5.	ii.	**THOMAS LORD SR.** (Immigrant) b. 1585 in Towcester, Northampton, England. Thomas Sr, married Dorothy Bird (1588-1675). They were married on 23 February 1610 near Towcester, Peterborough, Northampton, England. They had 8 children during their marriage. Dorothy was the daughter of Robert Bird and Amy ___. They

		immigrated to the Bay State in Cambridgeport, Massachusetts in 1635. From there, they walked to an area known today as Hartford, Connecticut. It took them two weeks of walking through the forests, carrying with them their entire earthly possessions which were essential items for living in their new wilderness surroundings. Thomas Sr. died on 17 May 1644 in Hartford, Hartford Co., Connecticut at the age of 59.
	iii.	**Ellen Lord** b.1589 in Towcester, Northampton, England. It is unknown if she married and had any children. Also unknown are her death date and location at death.
	iv.	**Alice Lord** b. 1591 in Towcester, Northampton, England. Alice married Richard Morris on 20 May 1611 in Towcester, Northampton, England. It is unknown if they had any children. Their death dates and location at death are unknown.

5. Thomas Lord Sr. (Immigrant)

THOMAS^5 LORD SR. (Richard^4, William^3, Ronald^2, Henry^1)

- Born 1585 in Towcester, Northampton, England.
- Married 23 February 1610 Dorothy Bird, daughter of Robert Bird and Amy ____(near Towcester), Peterborough, Northampton, England. Dorothy died in 1675 at the age of 86 years. Thomas Sr. and Dorothy are buried in the graveyard in the rear of the First Church of Hartford which is called the "Ancient Cemetery." There is a large tombstone there marking the site (see the tombstone picture in the Bird chapter.)
- Immigrated in 1635 to the Bay Colony and settled in New-town, later known as Cambridgeport. Still later, it is known today as Cambridge, Middlesex Co., Massachusetts.
- Died 17 May 1644 in Hartford, Hartford Co., and Connecticut at the age of 59.

The Ship
Elizabeth and Ann

From Hotten's "Original Lists" we learn that "on 29th of April 1635 there were registered for transportation from the port of London to New England in the ship 'Elizabeth and Ann' of which Capt. Robert Cooper was master, Thomas Lord, aged fifty; his wife Dorothy, aged forty-six; and their children Thomas, aged sixteen; Ann aged fourteen; William, aged twelve, John, aged ten; Robert, aged nine, Aymie aged six; and Dorothy aged four." They landed in Boston and joined Richard Lord at New-town (Cambridge, Massachusetts). The ages of the children as given on the ship's register are only approximate, as they vary from the actual baptismal records.

Early Settlers of Hartford, Connecticut

"In 1636, with his entire family, Thomas Lord joined the party of Rev. Mr. Hooker and Mr. Stone and one hundred men, women, and children, which took its departure from New Town to form a new settlement on the Connecticut River. They traveled more than a hundred miles, through a hideous and trackless wilderness to Hartford. They had no guide but their compass; and made their way over mountains, through swamps, thickets, and rivers, which were passable with great difficulty. They had no cover but the heavens and no lodging but such as nature afforded them. They drove with them one hundred and sixty head of cattle and subsisted on the milk of their cows. Mrs. Hooker was carried through the wilderness on a litter [later the "Litter" was known as a stretcher]. The people carried their packs, arms, and some utensils. They were a fortnight (2 weeks) on their journey. This adventure was the more remarkable as many of this company were persons of figure, who in England had lived in honor, affluence, and delicacy, and were strangers to fatigue and danger."

Thomas Lord thus became an original proprietor and one of the first settlers of Hartford. He lived on the north side of the highway on the bank of the Little River (now Wells Street), a near neighbor of Gov. Haynes, Rev. Mr. Hooker, Mr. Goodwin, Gov. Wyllys, and others of the prominent inhabitants. His sons Richard, and Thomas had lots next to his. Thomas Lord Sr. was a merchant and a mill owner. He lived in a part of Hartford, Connecticut that is still called to this day "Lord's Hill." This area was named after his family name. He owned 8 parcels of land and was a man of position and influence. The Hartford settlers were people of some culture propelled into raw conditions, and there was a mingling of high breeding and rough life.

Tombstone inscription: Founder's Monument found in the Ancient Cemetery in Hartford, Hartford Co., Connecticut where he is believed to be buried. The tombstone inscription reads:

"In Memory of Mr. Thomas Lord Born 1585. One of ye original proprietors of Hartford."

The Founders of Hartford, Connecticut Monument

Children of THOMAS² LORD SR. and DOROTHY BIRD were:

	i.	**CAPTAIN RICHARD LORD** (IMMIGRANT) b. January 1611 in Towcester, Northampton, England. He was baptized 5 January 1611. He married ___. The name of his wife is unknown as well as the names of his children. He came to America in 1632, four years earlier than his father. who came in 1636. Richard died 17 May 1662 in Hartford, Hartford Co., Connecticut at the age of 51.
6.	ii.	**ANNA LORD** (IMMIGRANT) b. 18 September 1614 in Towcester, Northampton, England. Anna married Thomas Stanton Jr. (1616-1677). Anna and Thomas Jr. were married in 1637 in Hartford, Hartford Co., Connecticut. They had 9 children during their marriage. Anna died on 4 September 1688 in Stonington, New London Co., Connecticut at the age of 74.
	iii.	**DR. THOMAS LORD JR.** (IMMIGRANT) b. November 1616 in Towcester, Northampton, England: baptized 15 November 1616. He married Hannah Thurston in Boston, Suffolk Co., Massachusetts. They were married on 28 September 1652. They settled five years later in Wethersfield, Connecticut on the Connecticut River, a few miles south of where Hartford, Connecticut is today. Dr. Thomas and Hannah had 3 daughters during their marriage. Dr. Thomas Jr. died in March 1662 in Wethersfield, Hartford Co., Connecticut at the age of 46. His Last Will &Testament was written 28 October 1661.
	iv.	**WILLIAM LORD** (IMMIGRANT) b. December 1618 in Towcester, Northampton, England: baptized 27 December 1618. William married Lydia Buckland (ca. 1637-ca 1699). William and Lydia were married on 3 January 1664 in Lyme, New London Co., Connecticut. (Note: See the Kearney Chapter Volume I: *Lydia Buckland is a direct ancestor of Jed Merrow's wife Katie Buckland Merrow; see Elizabeth "Libbie" Moses Merrow. Libbie's son is Jed Merrow).* William Lord died 17 May 1678 in Lyme, New London, Connecticut at the age of 60.
	v.	**ROBERT LORD** (IMMIGRANT) b. May 1620 in Towcester, Northampton, England: baptized 12 May 1620. Robert married Rebecca Stanley on 16 August 1648. It is unknown if they had any children during their marriage. Robert died 15 June 1676 at the age of 56. Location in America at his death is unknown.
	vi.	**JOHN LORD** (IMMIGRANT) b. January 1623 in Towcester, Northampton, England. He was baptized 21 January 1623. John married 3 times: Wife #1 Elizabeth Vincen; Wife #2 Adrian Busey; Wife #3 Rebecca Bushnell. It is unknown if he had any children during any of his 3 marriages. John died in 1692 at the age of 69 in the Colony of Virginia.
	vii.	**AYMIE LORD** (IMMIGRANT) b. November 1626 in Towcester, Northampton, England. She was baptized 30 November 1626. Aymie married John Gilbert on 6 May 1647. Aymie died 8 January 1691 in Hartford, Hartford Co., Connecticut at the age of 65.
	viii.	**DOROTHY LORD** (IMMIGRANT) b. June 1629 in Towcester, Northampton, England. She was baptized on 1 July 1629. Dorothy Lord married John Ingersoll in 1651. Dorothy died 3 January 1657 at the age of 28 in Northampton, Massachusetts Bay Colony.

6. Anna Lord

ANNA[6] LORD (Thomas[5], Richard[4], William[3], Ronald[2], Henry[1])

- Born September 1614 in Towcester, Northampton, England.
- Baptized 18 September 1614 in St. Laurence Church, Towcester, and Northampton, England.
- Married Thomas Stanton Jr., who was the son of Thomas Stanton Sr. and Katherine Washington. Thomas Jr. and Anna were married in 1637 in Hartford, Hartford Co., Connecticut.
- Died 1688 in Stonington, New London Co., and Connecticut at the age of 74.

Children of ANNA[6] LORD and THOMAS STANTON JR. are documented in the Stanton chapter.

Source Citations for this Chapter

Descendants of Thomas Lord – an original Proprietor and Founder of Hartford, Connecticut in 1636 by Kenneth Lord, Published in New York, 1946.

The Founding of New England by Ernest Flagg.

Lords of Towcester, England by Garvin L. Payne: Essex Institute Volume LIV.

https://www.wikitree.com/wiki/Lord-69

https//www.ancestry.com/family-tree/pt/PersonMatch.aspx?tid=62293685&pid=40085165835&-phsrc=jJ06526&-phstart=default&usePUBJs=true&cu...

https://ancestry.com/imageviewer/collections/21484/images/dvm_GenMono005167-00165-1?treeid=62293685&personnid=40085165859&hintid=...

https://ancestors.familysearch.org/en/G386-SCR/henry-lord-1468-1500

New England, The Great Migration and The Great Migration Begins (1620-1635) by Robert Charles Anderson, 2005 NEHGS, Boston, Massachusetts.

Hartford, Connecticut Probate Records, 1639-1700.

US New England Marriages Prior to 1700.

Northamptonshire, England, Church of England Baptisms, Marriages, and Burials 1532-1812.

Tombstone Inscription: Ancient Cemetery in Hartford, Hartford Co., Connecticut.

Founder's Monument: Hartford, Hartford Co., Connecticut.

Chapter 21: The Meads

The Mead Family Line

| William Mead | Rebecca ____ |
| Ca 1630-1683 | Ca 1630- ____ |

| Hannah Mead | Joseph Stanton Sr |
| 1655-1676 | 1646-1714) |

Mead Family's Shield

The Mead family extends back to England and goes back to Francois de la Mede born 1175. There are many Medes, Mead, Meade families scattered throughout England and many of them have not been proven yet to be connected to each other. Either they are connected, and the documentation has been lost over the years, or there are other reasons for the disconnect, unknown to this writer.

For this chapter I will concentrate only on the Mead family who arrived in the Massachusetts Bay Colony early on and their one descendant, a daughter, Hannah who did not live very long in her short marriage.

We do not know how William Mead's parents came to America if they ever did and do not know with whom William Mead arrived. He came as a young adult with his brother, Richard, and two cousins with the same last name. I will now concentrate on the facts I have and the new land where they arrived in the Bay State Colony.

There were four men who arrived in America in the same area of New England at the same time, all with the same last name of Mead. They were ***Gabriel Mead, Henry Mead, William Mead, and Richard Mead***. This author believes that two of them were paternal cousins and two of them were brothers. **William Mead**, our ancestor of study in this chapter, was in Gloucester and was one of their selectmen in 1647. Both William and his brother Richard Mead went on and settled in Roxbury, where one died in 1683 and the other in 1690. Gabriel Mead, son of Thomas Mead (b. 1550), had three brothers named John Mead, Andrew Mead, and Edward Mead, all of whom were not with him in his journey to America. Gabriel became a Freeman in 1638 in Dorchester, which is the community in

Boston that is right next door to Roxbury. Henry also became a Freeman in Massachusetts in 1665 but it is not known which town. This Gabriel Mead and Henry Mead, this writer believes, are both paternal cousins of our **two brothers William and Richard Mead.**

Our William Mead, who was in Gloucester, was also in Charlestown, Massachusetts with his wife Rebecca and later in New London, Connecticut.

1. William Mead (Immigrant)

WILLIAM[1] MEAD:

- Born circa 1630 in England.
- Married circa 1650 Rebecca _____ in Boston, Suffolk Co., Massachusetts.
  Rebecca died 6 November 1683 at the age of approx. 53.
- Died 29 October 1683 in Roxbury, Suffolk Co., Massachusetts at approx. 53.

William Mead emigrated from England and was in Roxbury along with his brother Richard Mead, who was a mariner. They were in Roxbury, circa 1650. William resided there with his wife Rebecca. Richard was a Freemason in 1665. Years later it was there in Roxbury that both William and his wife Rebecca died. William died 29 October 1683. His wife Rebecca died 8 days later on 6 November 1683. One wonders if they died of the same disease. William wrote his Last Will and Testament the very day that he died. In his will, he mentions his brother Richard and he mentions his own wife, Rebecca. He also mentions his son-in-law Joseph Stanton in this same Last Will & Testament.

Richard Mead (William's brother) died in Roxbury a few years later in 1690.

Where Is Roxbury? A Short History of the Town:

Roxbury was and still is a community of Boston in the Massachusetts Bay Colony. It is in a southern residential section of Boston, Massachusetts. Prior to becoming part of the city of Boston in 1868, it was a town (township) of Norfolk County, located between Boston and Dorchester. Early spellings include Rocksbury, Roxburie, and Rocsbury.

While the northeastern section was becoming one of America's first streetcar suburbs, the rural southwestern section became home to Brook Farm in 1841, a utopian commune based of the ideals of the Transcendentalist movement. English, Irish, and German immigrants were attracted to the industrial sections in the north and arrived by the mid-1800s. The town was split in 1851 and the rural western two-thirds was established as a new town of *West Roxbury*. The east become more integrated with the city until it was annexed to Boston in 1868, after which it was referred to as *Boston Highlands*. The Irish concentrated in the *Dudley Square* area and *Neponset*. After 1900, a large Jewish community settled along the *Blue Hill Avenue Corridor* (before annexation called *Grove Hall Avenue*). Twenty years prior to the Great Depression and after World War II through the 1950s, there was a massive migration of African Americans from the South to the northeast. In Boston, the community settled in **Roxbury**.

Village or section names include Dudley Square, Egleston Square, Grove Hall, Highland Park, Jamaica Plain (until 1851), Lower Roxbury, Mission Hill, Punch Bowl (now Brookline Village), Roslindale (until 1851), Roxbury Crossing, South End (partially in downtown Boston), Washington Park, and West Roxbury (until 1851).

Roxbury was one of several towns settled by the passengers from the Winthrop Fleet in 1630. The settlement grew when the famed Rev. John Eliot (called "the Apostle to the Indians") arrived in 1632 with a group of his followers called "Nazeing Christians." It is under Eliot that the church was established (with residents who attended Dorchester's church before his arrival). Some settlers moved away when the wealthiest resident, William Pynchon, moved in 1636 to establish Springfield. The leadership void was filled by Thomas Dudley moving to town. There were strong connections to East Anglia among the residents. The land was distributed quickly, unlike in other surrounding towns. It was not until the town was granted more land in 1660 by Massachusetts Bay Colony that this situation changed. The grant, called New Roxbury, was later renamed Woodstock and eventually became part of Connecticut.

In 1629 Thomas Dudley obtained from King Charles I a charter empowering the company to trade and colonize in New England between the Charles and Merrimack rivers. The grant was like that of the Virginia Company in 1609. This charter became the beginning of the Massachusetts Bay Colony, of which Boston was the central area of origin.

Thomas Dudley (born 1576, Northampton, England — died July 31, 1653, Roxbury, Mass.), British colonial governor of Massachusetts, for many years was the most influential man in the Massachusetts Bay Colony, save for John Winthrop.

Dudley was the son of a country gentleman in England. After being converted to Puritanism he joined with other Lincolnshire gentlemen in the Cambridge Agreement to settle in New England and take the charter of the Massachusetts Bay Company with them. In April 1630 Dudley sailed to America in the same ship with Winthrop. Dudley was elected deputy governor 13 times between 1629 and 1650 and served as governor 4 times.

Soon after his arrival in the colony, Dudley settled at New Towne (later Cambridge), which he helped found. He was also one of the promoters of the plan to establish Harvard College. Winthrop's decision to make Boston instead of New Towne the capital precipitated the first of many quarrels between the two and prompted Dudley to move his residence to Roxbury.

Men came exploring from Naumkeag (now Salem) and arrived at a place called Mishawum by the local Indians in 1628. A group of more than one hundred persons from Naumkeag moved to Mishawum to settle in 1629. It is now known as Charlestown, Massachusetts. This was another area of Boston where William Mead had been early on.

A mere decade later after the landing of the Pilgrims in Plymouth, another group of Puritan colonists, led by John Winthrop, arrived in North America. They first landed in Salem in June of 1630, but continued down the coast in search of clean, fresh water. The Shawmut Peninsula became their eventual home, as the town of Boston was officially founded in September of 1630. The Puritans came upon the lone resident of the Shawmut Peninsula, Reverend William Blackstone – an Anglican priest who had left England in 1623 on a quest to find peace and quiet. He welcomed the Puritans onto "his land," sharing the location of the freshwater spring. For his generosity, the Puritans granted him 50 acres of his own land, which he sold back to them 4 years later. Blackstone decided to leave Boston for present-day Cumberland, Rhode Island, saying, "I left England on account of the bishops, and I leave Boston on account of the brethren."

Significant Events

1630 The first church in Boston was established by John Winthrop's settlement.

1630 Boston's first cemetery, King's Chapel Burying Ground, was founded.

1634 The first tavern/inn was opened in Boston by Puritan settler Samuel Cole.

1635 Boston Latin School opened; it was the first American public school.

1636 "New College," or "the College at New Towne," was founded by vote of the Great and General Court of the Massachusetts Bay Colony. This school would be renamed Harvard College in 1639.

1689 Today's stone structure of King's Chapel was built.

1680 The building now known as the Paul Revere House was built. Paul owned this home from 1770-1800.

<u>**In Roxbury:**</u>

Eliot Burying Ground – Eustis Street:

This has been the oldest cemetery in Roxbury. It was established in 1630 and named after Reverend John Eliot. He is buried in the Parish Tomb, along with other early ministers of the First Parish of Roxbury.

First Church of Roxbury – John Eliot Square:

The oldest wood frame church in Boston, this 1804 building is the fifth meetinghouse on this site since the first church was built in 1632. The architect, William Blaney, was a church member. The land around it is a fragment of the original town commons. Its most famous pastor was Reverend John Eliot, the missionary to the Algonquin Native American tribe. Due to Eliot's work, First Church in Roxbury was one of only three churches in the Puritan Massachusetts era to admit Native Americans as full-fledged members.

Child of WILLIAM[1] MEAD and REBECCA ___ was:

2.	i.	**HANNAH MEAD** b. 1655 in Roxbury, Suffolk Co., Massachusetts. Hannah married Joseph Stanton Sr. (1646-1714). Joseph was the son of Thomas Stanton Jr. and Anna Lord. Hannah and Joseph married in 1673. They had 2 children. Hannah died in 1676 at the age of 21 years, giving birth to their second child in Stonington, New London Co., Connecticut.

Note:

Hannah Mead Stanton the Mother & Hannah Mead the Baby

Hannah Mead Stanton: The Mother

Hannah Mead Stanton was Joseph Stanton Sr.'s wife. She died giving birth to her second child, a daughter also named Hannah. Hannah Mead Stanton and Joseph Stanton Sr. had a 2-year-old son named Joseph Stanton Jr. The children of Hannah Mead Stanton, the mother, are listed in the Stanton chapter. Following the sad death of Joseph Stanton Sr.'s first wife Hannah Mead, Joseph married again, this time to his maternal cousin, Hannah Lord.

Hannah Stanton: The Baby

Baby Hannah Stanton lived on to the age of 39 years. She married James Yorke III. She gave birth to 9 children. She died in 1715. Her children are listed in the Yorke chapter.

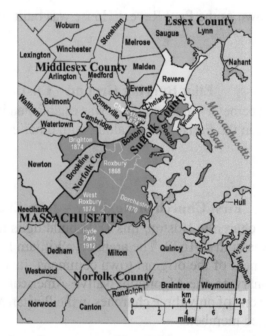

Metropolitan Boston showing the surrounding Townships in reference to Boston proper.

2. Hannah Mead

HANNAH[2] MEAD (*William*[1])

- Born 1652 in Roxbury, Suffolk Co., Massachusetts.
- Married 19 June 1673 Joseph Stanton Sr., son of Thomas Stanton Jr. and Anna Lord. Hannah and Joseph Sr. were married in Roxbury, Suffolk Co., Massachusetts.
- Died 1676 in Stonington, New London Co., Connecticut at the age of 24 years while giving birth to the couple's second child.

Children of HANNAH[2] MEAD and JOSEPH STANTON SR are documented in the Stanton chapter.

Source Citations for this Chapter

The First Settlers of New England, Surnames M-N-O Broderbund Software, Inc, Banner Blue Division, January 28, 2004.

New England Marriages Prior to 1700 page 501.

Genealogical Dictionary of the First Settlers of New England by James Savage Vol. III page 191.

Roxbury Deaths -- Massachusetts Vital Records up to 1850 Vol. II page 591.

https://www.ancestors.familysearch.org/en/LZN3-8Q4/hannah-mead-1655-1676

http://search.ancestry.com/cgi-bin/sse.dll?db=genepool&fsco=2%2cUnited+States&gspl=...

Chapter 22: The Nickersons

The Nickerson Family Line

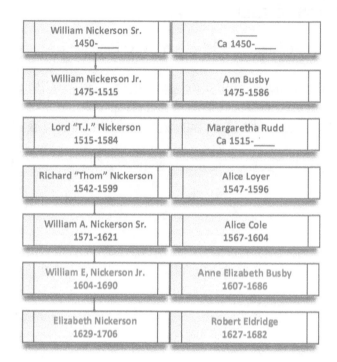

William Nickerson Sr. 1450-____	____ Ca 1450-____
William Nickerson Jr. 1475-1515	Ann Busby 1475-1586
Lord "T.J." Nickerson 1515-1584	Margaretha Rudd Ca 1515-____
Richard "Thom" Nickerson 1542-1599	Alice Loyer 1547-1596
William A. Nickerson Sr. 1571-1621	Alice Cole 1567-1604
William E, Nickerson Jr. 1604-1690	Anne Elizabeth Busby 1607-1686
Elizabeth Nickerson 1629-1706	Robert Eldridge 1627-1682

1. William Nickerson Sr.

WILLIAM [1] NICKERSON SR.

- Born 1450 in England.
- Married circa 1475. Her name is unknown (1450-___).
- Died _____ unknown date. William Sr. died in England at age approx. 25+.

Child of WILLIAM SR. and _____ was:

2.	i.	**WILLIAM NICKERSON JR.** b. 1475 in England. He married Ann Busby (1475-1586). William Jr. and Ann were married in 1515. They had 1 child during their marriage. William Jr. died in 1564 in England at the age of 40.

2. William Nickerson Jr.

WILLIAM [2] NICKERSON JR. (William Sr [1])

- Born 1475 England.
- Married 1515 Ann Busby (1475-1586) in England.
- Died 1515 England at the age of 40.

Child of WILLIAM NICKERSON JR. and ANNE BUSBY was:

| 3. | i. | **LORD THOMAS JEFFERSON. NICKERSON "TJ"** b. 1515 in England. He married Lady Margaretha Rudd (1520-1614). They had 5 children during their marriage. Lord TJ Nickerson died 25 February 1584 in St. John, Timberhill, Norwich, England at age 69. |

3. Lord Thomas Jefferson "TJ" Nickerson

LORD THOMAS JEFFERSON[3] "TJ" NICKERSON (William Jr.[2], William Sr.[1])

- Born 1515 in Norwich, Norfolk, England.
- Married 1536 Lady Margaretha Rudd.
- Died 25 February 1584 in St. John, Timberhill, Norwich, England age 69.

Children of LORD THOMAS JEFFERSON[3] NICKERSON and MARGARET RUDD WERE:

	i.	**Elizabeth Nickerson** b. 1537 in St. John, Timberhill. Norwich, England. It is unknown if she ever married and had any children. Her death date and location at death are both unknown. Age at death is unknown.
4.	ii.	**RICHARD THOMAS "THOM" NICKERSON** b. 15 December 1584 in St. John, Timberhill, Norwich, England married 1576 Alice Loyer (1547-1596). Richard and Alice were married in 1576. They had 7 children during their marriage. Richard Thomas died on 8 June 1599 St. Peter's Parish, Norwich, England at the age of 57.
	iii.	**John Nickerson** b. 1545 St. John, Timberhill, Norwich, England. It is unknown if he ever married and had any children. John died in 1596 at the age of 51. His location at death is unknown.
	iv.	**Richard Nickerson** b 1548 St. John, Timberhill, Norwich, England. It is unknown if he ever married and had any children. Richard died in 1599 at the age of 51. His location at death is unknown.
	v.	**William A. Nickerson.** B. 1571 St. John, Timberhill. Norwich, England. It is unknown if he ever married and had any children. William died in 1623 at the age of 52. His location at death is unknown.

4. Richard Thomas "Thom" Nickerson

RICHARD THOMAS [4] NICKERSON (Thomas Jefferson[3], William Jr.[2], William Sr.[1])

- Born 15 December 1542 in St. John, Timberhill, Norwich, Norfolk, England.
- Married 1576 Alice Loyer (1547-1596). They were married in Timberhill, Norwich, Norfolk, England.
- Died 8 June 1599 on St. Peter's Parish, Norwich, Norfolk, England age 57.

Children of RICHARD THOMAS[4] NICKERSON and ALICE LOYER were:

	i.	**TWIN: ALICE NICKERSON** b. 1567 St. Peter, Permontergate, England. It is unknown if she ever married and had any children. Alice died in 1604 at the age of 37.
	ii.	**TWIN: JOHN NICKERSON** b. 1567 St. Peter, Permontergate, England. John died as a stillborn in 1567.
	iii.	**JOHN NICKERSON** b.1568 St. Peter, Permontergate, England. A second son died, also named John. He died a year later in 1568 as a stillborn.
	iv	**TWIN: ROBERT NICKERSON I** b. 1570 St. Peter, Permontergate, England. Robert I died in 1570. Both twins died in 1570 stillborn.
	v.	**TWIN. ROBERT NICKERSON II** b. 1570 St. Peter, Permontergate, England. Robert II died 1570. Both twins died in 1570 stillborn.
5.	vi.	**WILLIAM A. NICKERSON SR.** b. 15 December 1571 in St. Peter, Permontergate, England. He married Twin Alice Cole (1567-1604). William A. Sr. and Alice married in 1593. They had 4 children during their marriage. William A. Sr. died after 28 April 1621 in Etheldred, Norwich, Norfolk, England at the age of 50.
	vii.	**RICHARD NICKERSON** b. 1573 in St. Peter, Permontergate, England. It is unknown if he ever married and had any children. Richard died in 1655 in England at the age of 82.

5. William A. Nickerson Sr.

WILLIAM A.[5] NICKERSON SR. (Richard Thomas [4], Thomas Jefferson[3], William Jr.[2], William Sr.[1])

- Born 15 December 1571 in St. Peter, Permontergate, England.
- Married 1593 Alice Cole (twin) (1567-1604) in Norwich, Norfolk, England.
- Died after 28 April 1621 in Etheldred, Norwich, Norfolk, England age 50.

Children of WILLIAM A. NICKERSON and ALICE COLE were:

	i.	**Twin: Margery Nickerson** b. 1602 the City of Norwich, Norfolk, England. It is unknown if she married and had any children. She died in 1634 in England at the age of 32.
	ii.	**Twin: Richard Nickerson** b. 1602 the City of Norwich, Norfolk, England. Richard died in 1606 at the age of 4 yrs. old.
6	iii.	**William Emory Nickerson** Jr. (Immigrant) b. 16 October 1604 in the City of Norwich, Norfolk, England. He married Anne Elizabeth Busby (1607-1686). They were married 24 June 1627 in Norfolk, England. They had 8 children prior to immigrating to America and then had an additional 6 more children after arriving in the new world of America. This totalled 14 children. William Emory was a weaver. He is known as "The Father of Chatham" as he was the first settler of Monomoit later known as Chatham, Massachusetts. He died on 8 August 1690 in Barnstable, Barnstable Co., Massachusetts at the age of 86.

	iv.	**Richard Nickerson** b. 1606 the City of Norwich, Norfolk, England. It is unknown if he married and had any children. It is also unknown if he ever immigrated to America and his death location in unknown. However, it is known that he died in 1699 at the age of 93.

6. William Emory Nickerson Jr. "The Weaver" (Immigrant)

WILLIAM EMORY [6] NICKERSON Jr. (William A.[5] Sr., Richard Thomas [4], Thomas Jefferson[3], William Jr.[2], William Sr.[1])

- Born 16 October 1604 in the City of Norwich, Norfolk, England.
- Married 24 June 1627 Anne Elizabeth Busby (1607-1686) in Norwich, Norfolk, England. Anne Elizabeth was daughter of Nicholas and Bridget (Cole) Busby.
- Arrived 1637 in the American Colonies.
- Died 8 August 1690 Monomoit (Chatham), Barnstable Co., Massachusetts at the age of 86.

William Emory Nickerson and his wife Anne Elizabeth Busby had a large family. They decided to make the trip across the water to the American colonies and brought their six children with them when they made the trip in 1637. Two of their eight children had died back in England before they made the voyage. The traveling party of about 100 people included William and Anne, their six children and Anne's parents Nicholas and Bridget Busby. They each carried with them all they could pack into a medium-size suitcase. Because of the persecutions of Bishop Wren of Norfolk, whose zealous efforts against Nonconformists drove over 3,000 small craftsmen out of the country, William Emory and his wife Anne Busby decided to go to America.

These hardy ancestors of ours left the English shoreline for various reasons. One was their hope for a better life free of oppression, and freedom to worship God as they chose to. They also had dreams of owning land in the New World which would make them landowners. William was a master of a needed trade, and I am sure he felt he would have a trade which would be an asset in the new community. He was a weaver and could take the raw product and turn it into clothing. William Jr. had been a tailor apprentice to his father William Sr. in 1621 and was admitted a worsted weaver and freeman in Norwich, England in 1632. He had learned this trade from his father and was now very skilled. His weaving loom accompanied him on their journey. Also, William's father-in-law Nicholas Busby (1590-1657) was a skilled weaver. I am sure both Nicolas and William Sr. were both skilled weavers back in Norwich, England and were very good friends.

Religious freedom was a primary motivating factor for William and Anne. They also were pushed to leave England for economic reasons as a major depression had covered the land where they all had been born. They knew the journey would be hard, but they were determined to leave. It would be a fresh start for them, which lured them forward. Aboard the ship called the *John & Dorothy* on 20 June 1637, they set sail for the American shore and said goodbye to the Yarmouth, England harbor shore and its English countryside!

The Ship John & Dorothy under Sail

They left with bright skies and high hopes, but out at sea after weeks on the long journey, they had become discouraged, and their moods were dimmed. They were cramped together in such a small space. One hundred people living in very close conditions in one ship made the trip frightful. I doubt that they had anticipated this stressful journey. Storms came up and rocked the ship to and fro, making matters even worse. It was a very trying and nerve-wracking experience. Days turned into nights and nights turned into more days. Food had spoiled. People had gotten extremely sick. Poor hygiene conditions were the way it was. Some passengers died along the way. It was an exceedingly difficult trip. There was no turning back. They also did not know the reality of what was ahead of them. What conditions they would face once they had arrived at their destination, they had no idea. They were headed into the complete unknown!

After weeks and weeks which turned into months, they finally arrived at their destination in the New World, but it was not where they had originally planned to land. A storm had arisen, throwing them off course. They had planned to land in the Salem and Marblehead Harbor area, but instead they faced an area that was a completely foreign sight to them all.

Getting off the ship, they now felt stranded. The ship had left and there they were, stranded and overwhelmed. I can imagine Anne saying to William, "Now what do we do"? What they faced was unlike anything they had ever seen or ever expected at the end of their treacherous journey. This is what they faced: TREES!

This was centuries before the invention of the "GPS." The Nickerson family had not prepared for this unexpected huge problem. England had very few trees and much of their land had been grazed over by all the sheep. They had never seen so many trees and it was a forest of confusion for them! A sidenote here: Once the colonists had settled, they cut down many trees and sold them to England which made income for the New World Colony. The wood was badly needed back in England for the country's lumber supply was extremely low. However, now back to the Nickerson party and their wandering in this huge forest, trying to find their way on foot. Nicholas Busby, Anne's father, who had been on a military trip to France years earlier, had learned some tricks of survival.

Nicholas Busby's Survival Skill:

He made a small hole in the ground and stuck his stick into it in a very vertical position. The stick's shadow became immediately apparent. He marked the tip with one rock. Then he said, "Let's all relax for about 15 minutes."

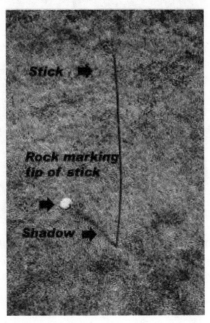

While this crowd of settlers stood around waiting, they saw the shadow move several feet.

Nicholas then marked the rock.

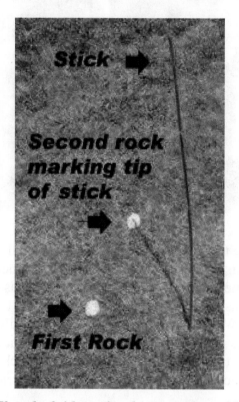

Then he laid a string between the pebbles.

"Now I will stand with the first rock on my left and that will be west and the rock on my right will be east," he said. "The direction I am facing is north, no matter where we are in the World. Now Will, pick up your loom and let's lead these people to the settlement in Salem!"

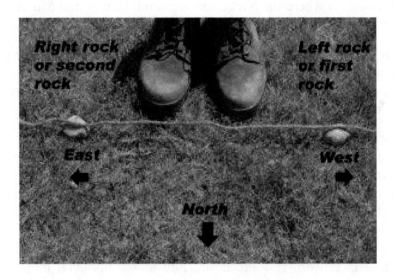

Nicholas and his military experience saved the day for our ancestors. How else could our intrepid ancestors navigate, especially as they traveled from Salem for Plymouth, Yarmouth and then finally to Chatham, all of which lacked roads and road signs? Just how many ways are there to navigate without our modern GPS or compasses? Here is another method they used to find their way. Looking to the heavens at night:

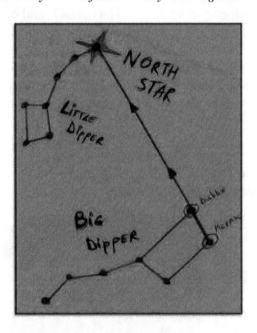

The above information is from the Nickerson Family Association Museum on Cape Cod, Massachusetts.

William and Anne finally made it to the Salem settlement but stayed only a few years there. They then travelled on to Plymouth and Yarmouth in 1641, and still later in the early 1640s, they settled in Monomoit which was what the Indians called this area. It was later known as Chatham. Both Yarmouth and Chatham are located on Cape Cod. The Nickerson family was one of the earliest English family settlers in that area. William tried to appeal to the Bay State court system to make the area a town, but this was rejected as they did not have a minister in that area. Until the time when there was an Association population sufficient to support a church, Monomoit would be known as a Constablewick. William gave each of his children land and built his home on Ryder's Cove in 1664 on the very spot that now is marked by the Nickerson's Family Research Center. This property on Orleans Road in

Chatham, Massachusetts is where the Nickerson Research Center and Museum now resides. There is much valuable history at that museum.

William's later life was full of conflict. Constantly he was in court, either suing someone or being sued himself. He caused a commotion in one of the Yarmouth Town Meetings and made fun of religion. On 3 June 1668 he and his three sons, Samuel, Joseph and William III, were forced to "Sit in the Stocks" for attacking the Constable of Yarmuth in the Constable's Court Office.

His Nonconformist religious views, partly responsible for his leaving England, also got him into trouble with the colonial authorities. In 1641, he was complained of as being "a scoffer and jeerer of religion." Records show that for the next few years he had several run-ins with the church authorities. His outspokenness and temper also caused problems with his fellow citizens. On 2 October 1650, several suits for defamation by and against William were brought before the court. In two of them, both parties were found at fault. In one by Edward Dillingham and sixteen others, "the court doe judge yet the said William Nickerson, in regard to his offensive speeches against sundry of the towne, to have carried himselfe therein unworthyly, and desire him to see his evell therein, and to been ready to acknowledge it; and yet those heed hath offended in that behalf should rest therein."

Despite these problems, he held a series of civil offices. In March of 1643/4, he was listed as able to bear arms in defense of the colony in Yarmouth, and he served on a committee chaired by Capt. Miles Standish to settle land boundary disputes. In 1641, 1647, and on 7 June 1651, he served on grand juries, and on 8 June 1655 he served as Deputy from Yarmouth to the General Court.

Around 1656, William purchased a sizable tract of land -- about 4,000 acres -- at a place called Monomoy (present-day Chatham). The sellers were a chief named Mattaquason and his son John Quason, and the deal was consummated without the permission of the colonial government, contrary to a law passed in 1643.

Years after William and his wife Anne had died, on the 11th day of June 1712, Chatham, Massachusetts was incorporated as a town and was no longer known as Monomoit, the Constablewick. Chatham was named after a seaport town in England.

**Plaque marking the site of William and Anne (Busby) Nickerson's home
in Monomoit (later known as Chatham), built in 1664.**

Children of WILLIAM EMORY [2] NICKERSON and ANNE ELIZABETH BUSBY were.

	i.	**Harriett "Hattie" Nickerson** (IMMIGRANT) b. 1621 Norwich, Norfolk, England. She married ___Lord. It is unknown if they had any children. Hattie died 1664 in New England at the age of 43.
	ii.	**"Nicho" Nickerson** I b. 1627 Norwich, Norfolk, England. Nicho was stillborn. He died in 1627 in Norwich, Norfolk, England.
	iii.	**Nicholas Nickerson** II (IMMIGRANT) b. 1628 Norwich, Norfolk, England. It is unknown if he married and had any children. He died in 1682 in Monomoit, Barnstable Co., Massachusetts at the age of 54.
7.	iv.	**HANNAH "ELIZABETH" NICKERSON** (IMMIGRANT) b. 1 January 1629 Norwich, Norfolk, England. Hannah "Elizabeth" married twice: Husband #1 Robert Eldridge (1627-1682). They were married in October 1649 and had 14 children. Husband #2 Samuel Russel November 1682. They had no children during their marriage. Hannah died on 3 May 1706 in Barnstable, Barnstable Co., Massachusetts at the age of 77.
	v.	**Anne Nickerson** (IMMIGRANT) b. 1635 Norwich, Norfolk, England. Anne married ___ Hedges. Their marriage date and place are unknown. It is also unknown if they had any children. Anne died 1681 in Monomoit, Barnstable Co., Massachusetts at the age of 46.
	vi.	**Twin: Joseph Nickerson** b. 1631 Norwich, Norfolk, England. It is unknown if he ever married and had any children. Joseph's death date and location at death are also unknown. It is also unknown if he ever immigrated or died young in England.
	vii.	**Twin: Robert Nickerson** (IMMIGRANT) b. 1631 Norwich, Norfolk, England It is unknown if he ever married and had any children. Robert died in 1710 in Monomoit, Barnstable Co., Massachusetts at the age of 79.
	viii.	**Thomas Nickerson** b. 1633 Norwich, Norfolk, England. He died as a stillborn in 1633 in Norwich, Norfolk, England.
	ix.	**Samuel Nickerson** b. 1638 Salem, Massachusetts It is unknown if he ever married and had any children. Samuel died in 1719 Chatham, Barnstable Co., Massachusetts at the age of 81.
	x.	**John Busby Nickerson** b. 1640 Salem, Suffolk Co., Massachusetts. It is unknown if he ever married and had any children. John Busby died in 1714 in Chatham, Barnstable Co., Massachusetts at the age of 74.
	xi.	**Sarah Nickerson** b. 1644 Yarmouth, Barnstable Co., Massachusetts It is unknown if she ever married and had any children. Sarah died in 1715 in Chatham, Barnstable Co., Massachusetts at the age of 71.
	xii.	**William Emery Nickerson** III b. 1646 Monomoit, Barnstable Co., Massachusetts. It is unknown if he ever married and had any children. William Emery III died in 1716 Chatham, Barnstable Co., Massachusetts at the age of 70.
	xiii.	**Joseph Nickerson** b. December 1647 Yarmouth, Barnstable Co., Massachusetts. It is unknown if he ever married and had any children. Joseph died 1729 in Chatham, Barnstable Co., Massachusetts at age 82.

	xiv.	**Esther Nickerson** b. 1656 Monomoit, Barnstable Co., Massachusetts. It is unknown if she ever married and had any children. Ester died in 1702 in Monomoit, Barnstable Co., Massachusetts at the age of 46.

7. Hannah "Elizabeth" Nickerson (Immigrant)

HANNAH ELIZABETH[7] NICKERSON (William Emory[6] Jr., William A.[5] Sr., Richard Thomas [4], Thomas Jefferson[3], William Jr.[2], William Sr.[1])

- Born 1 January 1629 in Norwich, Norfolk, England.
- Married October 1649 #1 Husband Robert Eldridge (1627-1682) in New England.
- Married November 1682 #2 Husband Samuel Russell in Marblehead, Massachusetts.
- Died 3 May 1706 in Barnstable, Barnstable Co., Massachusetts age 77.

Children of HANNAH ELIZABETH NICKERSON and ROBERT ELDRIDGE are documented in the Eldridge chapter.

There were no children born in the marriage of Hannah Elizabeth Nickerson and Samuel Russell.

Source Citations for this Chapter

Much of the information of this chapter was derived from:

The Museum of the Nickerson Family Association located at 1107 Orleans Road, Brewster, MA 02631 on Cape Cod. https://nickersonassoc.com/about/nickerson-history/

Cape Cod Museum of Natural History 869 Main Street (Route #6A) Brewster, MA 02631.

Nickerson State Park (Route #6A) Brewster, MA 02631

Brewster Historical Society 739 Lower Road Brewster, MA 02631

https://www.geni.com/people/William-Nickerson-II/6000000003490631675

From documents in the Bodleian Library, Oxford, and the Public Record Office, London. Passengers to New England on the John and Dorothy and the Rose, pp. 21-23.

Full Source Bibliography: JEWSON, CHARLES BOARDMAN. Transcript of Three Registers of Passengers from Great Yarmouth to Holland and New England, 1637-1639

(Norfolk Record Society Publications, 25.) Norwich: Norfolk Record Society, 1954. 98p. Reprinted by Genealogical Publishing Co., Baltimore, 1964. Page: 22

https://ancestors.familysearch.org/en/LB91-4HP/william-emory-nickerson-ii-1604-1690

Chapter 23: The Phippens

The Phippen Family Line

Henry Fitzpen Ca 1495-1562	Alice Pierce Ca 1495-___
John Fitz-Pen Sr. 1528-1583	Ann Holton Ca 1530-___
Robert Fitzpen Sr. 1555-1589	Cecily Jordan 1559-___
David Phippen Ca 1590-1650	Sarah Hull 1596-1659
Rebecca Phippen Ca 1615-1693	George Vickery Sr. 1620-1679

Mens cujusque is est quisque

Phippen

The Phippen Motto

The motto was originally a war cry or slogan. Mottoes first began to be shown with arms in the 14th and 15th centuries but were not in widespread use until the 17th century. Thus, the oldest coats of arms do not include a motto. Mottoes seldom form part of the grant of arms: Under most heraldic authorities, a motto is an optional component of the coat of arms and can be added later.

The Phippen Motto:
Mens cujusque is est quisque

Motto Translation:
As the mind of each, so is the man.

The Phippen Family Name was frequently called Fitzpen, and the early records referred to this family as Fitzpen or Fitz-Pen or later as Phippen. It is originally thought to have come from Philip or the family of the Phillips.

1. Henry Fitzpen

HENRY[1] FITZPEN

- Born circa 1495 in Ottery, East Devon District, Devon, England.
- Married 1527 Alice Pierce (circa 1495-____) of Ireland at Ottery, East Devon District, Devon, England.
- Died 1562 in England Ottery, East Devon District, Devon, England at age 67.
- Buried Ottery, St. Mary Church, East Devon District, Devon, England.

Henry Fittzpen married Alice Pierce of Ireland. Henry and Alice moved from Cornwallis, England to Scotland, then to Ireland, and then back to England again. Henry was a sailing merchant and owned the ship called *Seaweed*. Henry had lost property in Ireland. He had a huge thriving merchant business there in Ireland until the uprising. During the uprising, Henry lost a lot of money and property and he was forced to return to England. They settled in with his family in the East Devon District of Devon in England. He re-established his Merchant business there but died shortly thereafter.

Children of HENRY[1] FITSPEN and ALICE PIERCE were:

2.	i.	JOHN FITZ-PEN Sr. "Thickpenny" b. January 1528 at St. Mary, Overy, Devon, in Devonshire, England. John married Ann Holton (daughter of Robert and Constance Holton). John and Ann had 10 children. John was known as "John Thickpenny." John died in February 1583 in Weymouth, Dorset, England at the age of 55.
	ii.	JOSEPH FITZPEN b. 1530 at St. Mary, Overy, Devon, in Devonshire, England. Joseph married ____ in Devonshire, England. They married circa 1550. It is unknown if they had any children during their marriage. Joseph's death date and location at death are also unknown.

2. John Fitz-Pen Sr. "Thickpenny"

JOHN[2] FITZ-PEN SR. "THICKPENNY" (Henry[1])

- Born January 1528 in St. Mary, Overy, Devon, in Devonshire, England.
- Married circa 1554 Ann Holton (circa 1530-____). Ann was a daughter of Thomas and Constance Holton. John and Ann were married in Weymouth, Dorset, England.
- Died February 1583 Weymouth, Dorset, England at the age of 55.

188

Children of JOHN[1] FITZ-PEN "THICKPENNY" and ANN HOLTON were:

3.	i.	**ROBERT FITZ-PEN** circa 1555 in Weymouth, Dorsetshire, England. Robert married Cecily Jordan (1559-___). They had 5 children during their marriage. Robert and Cecily were married on 18 September 1580 in England. Robert died 12 October 1589 in Melcomb, Dorset, England at the age of 34.
	ii.	**JOHN FITZ-PEN Jr.** b. circa 1562 in Weymouth, Dorsetshire, England. It is unknown if he ever married and unknown if any children. His death date and location at death are unknown.
	iii.	**GEORGE FITZ-PEN** b. circa 1564 in Weymouth, Dorsetshire, England. It is unknown if he ever married and unknown if any children. His death date and location at death are unknown.
	iv.	**Unknown name FITZ-PEN** in England. Dates, marriage, children location all unknown.
	v.	**Unknown name FITZ-PEN** in England. Dates, marriage, children location all unknown.
	vi.	**Unknown name FITZ-PEN** in England. Dates, marriage, children location all unknown.
	vii.	**Unknown name FITZ-PEN** in England. Dates, marriage, children location all unknown.
	viii.	**Unknown name FITZ-PEN** in England. Dates, marriage, children location all unknown.
	ix.	**Unknown name FITZ-PEN** in England. Dates, marriage, children location all unknown.
	x.	**Unknown name FITZ-PEN** in England. Dates, marriage, children location all unknown.

John Fitz-Pen "Thickpenny"

John owned a small fleet of sailing vessels including the *Ventura*, *Roma*, *Anne*, and *Ascension*. In the early 1560s John received a few Fiaints (warrants) from Queen Elizabeth granting him commission to import wine into Ireland. The contract was to supply wine to the garrisons in Ireland. He was also given 21 land leases in Ireland and one of these leases covered the island and abbey of Molana. He also had an address at Glassmore, Co. Waterford. After John Thickpenny died, his business was taken over by his son Robert Fitzpen Thigpen. John and Ann had ten children but for many of them, their names, dates, and places of events are unknown at this time.

3. Robert Fitzpen "Thigpen" Phippen Sr.

ROBERT[3] FITZPEN PHIPPEN SR. "THIGPEN" (John[2], Henry[1])

- Born 1555 in Weymouth, Dorsetshire, England.
- Married on Sunday 18 September 1580 Cecily Jordan (1559-__).
- Died 12 October 1589 in Melcomb, Dorset, England at age 34. Robert died in the King's service.
- Buried St. Mary's Graveyard, Melcombe Regis, Weymouth & Portland Borough, Dorset, England.

"Thigpen" Shortened Version of "Thickpenny"

The meaning of the word Thigpen is from the German word which means "one who begs for coins." This family was quite poor. Robert died serving his country in the Anglo-Spanish War (1585-1602). He died in service to the King at the early age of 34 years, leaving a widow and five young children ages 2 years. 4 years, 6 years, 7 years, and 9 years.

Children of Robert[3] FITZPEN PHIPPEN and CECILY JORDAN were:

	i.	**Cecily Phippen** b. 1580 in Melcomb, Dorset, England. It is unknown if Cecily ever married and unknown if she had any children. Cicely died after 1604 in England at approx. age of 24+.
	ii.	**OWEN PHIPPEN ** b. 1582 in Melcomb, Dorset, England. He married Anne Coiners on 3 July 1605 in England. Anne (b. 1582 died date unknown). They had 3 children during their marriage. Owen died 17 March 1636 in the village of Lamorran near Cornwall in England at the age of 54.
	iii.	**Robert Phippen Jr**. b. 1583 in Melcomb, Dorset, England. It is unknown if he ever married and had any children. Robert Jr. died in 1610 in England age 27.
4.	iv.	**David Phippen** (Immigrant) b. 1585 in Melcomb, Dorset, England. He married Sarah ___. They were married circa 1610 in England. David and Sarah had 6 children during their marriage. They immigrated to America circa 1630. David died on 31 October 1650 in Boston, Suffolk Co., Massachusetts at the age of 60. After David's death Sarah remarried to a Mr. George Hull.
	v.	**REV. GEORGE PHIPPEN** b.1587 in Melcomb, Dorset, England. It is unknown if Rev. George ever married and had any children. George became the first Master of the Truro Grammar School (1621-1635) and then was a Rector at St. Mary's Church in Truro, England. He served in that church for the next 26 years. Rev. George died in 1650 in Truro, England at the age of 63.

** Owen Phippen was taken captive by Turkish Pirates on 24 March 1620 when he was 38 years old. He was on a trading voyage in the Mediterranean Sea. For seven years Owen and several other Christian captives served as slaves to the Turks near the present-day Algiers, Algeria. Their chance for freedom came when Owen and ten other Christian captives (Dutch and French) were herded aboard a corsair with 65 Turks to set sail for their next assignment. Owen and the ten other captives fought against the Turks for three hours. They suffered. Five of their number were slain before the surviving Turks surrendered; Owen and his crew sailed the ship to Cartagena, Spain, where news of the mutiny reached the King. Owen was summoned to Madrid where the King offered him a Captain's position and great favor if he would convert to Catholicism. Owen respectfully declined, sold the ship for 6,000 pounds sterling, and made his way back to England where he settled near his brother George in Cornwall. Owen died at the village of Lamorran on 17 March 1636 at the age of 54. George had the memorial put in St. Mary's Church shortly thereafter.

4. David Phippen (Immigrant)

DAVID[4] PHIPPEN (Robert[3], John[2], Henry[1])

- Born circa 1590 in Melcombe Regis, Dorset Co., England.
- Married circa 1615 Sarah ___ (1596 - 1659). They were married in England.
- Arrived in America 31 March 1634 aboard the *Recovery*.
- Died 31 October 1650 in Boston, Suffolk Co., Massachusetts at the age of 60.

David Phippen was an artisan from Weymouth, Dorset who came to Massachusetts Bay aboard the *Recovery* 31 March 1634. He is recorded to be on the passenger list for that date. He and his wife Sarah Hull arrived in Boston, Massachusetts and first settled in Hingham, Massachusetts. David died on 31 October 1650 in Boston, Massachusetts. Following David's death, his wife Sarah remarried to a man named George Hull. She died nine years later in 1659. Note in the Phippen records it states many times that the Phippens' signature was written first name & then "Fitzpen alias Phippen."

Children of DAVID[4] PHIPPEN and SARAH ___ were:

5.	i.	**REBECCA PHIPPEN** (IMMIGRANT) b. 1615 Weymouth, Dorset, England. Rebecca married George Vickery Sr. (1620-1679). Rebecca and George were married circa 1647 in Hull, Suffolk Co., Massachusetts. They had 12 children during their marriage. Rebecca died 1693 in Massachusetts at the age of 78.
	ii.	**JOSEPH PHIPPEN** b. 1620 Weymouth, Dorset, England. It is unknown if he ever married and had any children. Joseph died in 1687 at age 67. His location at death is unknown.
	iii.	**TWIN: GAMALIEL PHIPPEN** b. 1625 Weymouth, Dorset, England. It is unknown if he ever married and had any children. Gamaliel died in 1672 at the age of 47. His location at death is unknown.
	iv.	**TWIN: BENJAMIN PHIPPEN** b. 1625 Weymouth, Dorset, England. It is unknown if he ever married and had any children. Benjamin died in 1678 at the age of 53. His location at death is unknown.
	v.	**SARAH PHIPPEN** b. 1633 Weymouth, Dorset, England. Sarah married ___ Gold. It is unknown if they had any children during their marriage. Sarah died 1692 at the age of 59. Her location at death is unknown.

5. Rebecca Phippen (Immigrant)

REBECCA PHIPPEN (David[4], Robert[3], John[2], Henry[1])

- Born circa 1615 Weymouth, Dorset, England.
- Married circa 1647 George Vickery Sr. (1620-1679) in Hull, Suffolk Co., Massachusetts. George Sr. was the son of John "Short" Vickery and Jane Agnes Orchard.
- Died 1693 in Massachusetts at the age of 78.

Children of REBECCA[2] PHIPPEN and GEORGE VICKERY SR. are documented in the Vickery chapter.

Source Citations for this Chapter

https://www.geni.com/people/Henry-Phippen-Fitzpen/357875854260004933

https://irelandxo.com/ireland-xo/history-and-genealogy/ancestor-database/john-fitzpen-thickpenny

https://www.ancestry.com/family-tree/pt/PersonMatch.aspx?tid=62293685pif=172126072144&_phstart=default&usePUBJs=true&c...

https://ancestry.com/imageviewer/collections/12663/images/dvm_GenMono001877-00131?treeid=62293685&personid=172126072144&hintid...

http://www.findagrave.com/memorial/93830569/henry-fitzpen

https://ww.ancestry.com/mediaui-viewer/tree/23846215/person/26110317126/media/868beefc-2e57-45f3-baeb-b42c7fc1ae53

http://www.findagrave.com/memorial/157156384/john-'fitzpen'-phippen

https://www.ancestry.com/mediaui-viewer.tree/6379025/person/621984761/media/45266e77-e0ce-490c-ab1c-b611316b2a25

Chapter 24: The Reeves (Ryves) (Rives)

The Reeves Family Line

(The Cousins Connection Chapter)

(The Kearney – McComas Cousin Connection)

Lucy Ryves (b. 1535) and Sir Richard Ryves
(b. 1547) are sister & brother.

They are children of Sir John Ryves (1514-1549)

Lucy Ryves' Line

This line is the Author's Line of Ancestors

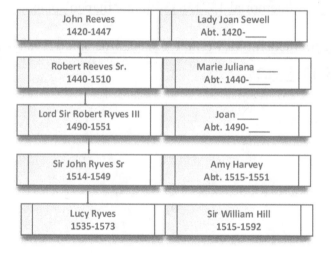

John Reeves 1420-1447	Lady Joan Sewell Abt. 1420-____
Robert Reeves Sr. 1440-1510	Marie Juliana ____ Abt. 1440-____
Lord Sir Robert Ryves III 1490-1551	Joan ____ Abt. 1490-____
Sir John Ryves Sr 1514-1549	Amy Harvey Abt. 1515-1551
Lucy Ryves 1535-1573	Sir William Hill 1515-1592

Sir Richard Ryves' Line

This line is the Author's Husband's Line of Ancestors

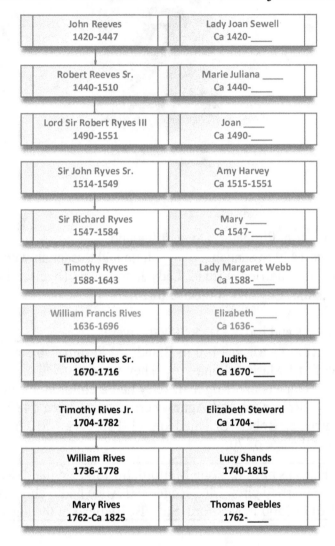

John Reeves 1420-1447	Lady Joan Sewell Ca 1420-____
Robert Reeves Sr. 1440-1510	Marie Juliana ____ Ca 1440-____
Lord Sir Robert Ryves III 1490-1551	Joan ____ Ca 1490-____
Sir John Ryves Sr. 1514-1549	Amy Harvey Ca 1515-1551
Sir Richard Ryves 1547-1584	Mary ____ Ca 1547-____
Timothy Ryves 1588-1643	Lady Margaret Webb Ca 1588-____
William Francis Rives 1636-1696	Elizabeth ____ Ca 1636-____
Timothy Rives Sr. 1670-1716	Judith ____ Ca 1670-____
Timothy Rives Jr. 1704-1782	Elizabeth Steward Ca 1704-____
William Rives 1736-1778	Lucy Shands 1740-1815
Mary Rives 1762-Ca 1825	Thomas Peebles 1762-____

The Reeves Family

The Reeves family name is the Anglicization of the old word "Rives" pronounced the same way it is today. Older English documents spell the family name as "Ryves." Many descendants took their surname from their profession of Reeve or Shire Reeve (the origin of the word "sheriff," which was a law enforcing judiciary in pre-Elizabethan times). Many have asserted that such is the case with the Reeves family of Dorset, England. However, evidence strongly suggests that the Rives of Dorset were of Norman descent. The name is of French derivation which is the family's point of origin. Given the derivation of Shire Reeve, it seems that our Reeves line of Dorset is the oldest one that survives today.

1. John (Reeves)

JOHN[1] RYVES (Reeves)

- Born 1420 in France Farm, Pimpemr, Dorset. England.
- Married Wife #1 circa 1439 Susannah _____. John and Susannah were married in Blandford Forum, Dorset, England. Married Wife #2 Lady Joan Sewell (b. circa 1420).
- Died 1447 in Dorsetshire, England at the age of 27.

Children of ROBERT[1] RYVES and LADY LOAN SEWELL were:

2	i.	ROBERT REEVES SR. b 1440 in Blandford Forum, Dorset, England. Robert married twice. Wife #1 Marie Juliana____. They were married circa 1459 at Damory Castle, Blandford, Dorsetshire, England. They had 2 children during their marriage. Wife #2 Agnes ___. Robert Sr. and Agnes were married circa 1489 They had 1 child during their marriage, Robert Sr. died on 11 February 1510 in Blandford, Dorsetshire, England at the age of 70.
	ii.	ROGER REEVES b. 1442 Long Melford, Suffolk, England. Roger married Alice ___. They were married circa 1462 Roger and Alice had 6 children during their marriage. Roger died in 1500 in Medford, Suffolk, England at the age of 58.

2. Robert (Reeves) Sr.

ROBERT[2] REEVES SR. (John[1])

- Born 1440 in Blandford Forum, Dorset, England., England.
- Married circa 1459 Wife #1 Marie Juliana _____. Robert Sr. and Marie Juliana ___ were married at Damory Castle, Blandford, Dorsetshire, England.
- Married circa 1489 Wife #2 Agnes _____. Robert Sr. and Agnes were married at Damory Castle, Blandford, Dorsetshire, England.
- Died 11 February 1510 in Blandford, Dorsetshire, England at the age of 70.

Children of ROBERT[2] REEVES SR. and MARIE JULIANA ___ were:

	i.	ROBERT REEVES JR. b. 1460 in Blandford Forum, Dorset, England. Robert Jr. died in 1465 at the age of 5 years old.
3.	ii.	LORD SIR ROBERT RYVES III b. 4 August 1490 in Blandford Forum, Dorset, England. Sir Robert III married Joan ___ circa 1510. Sir Robert III and Joan had 3 children during their marriage. Sir Robert III died on 11 February 1551 at Damory

		Castle, Blandford, Dorsetshire, England at the age of 61. He is buried in the church cemetery at the Old St. Peter and St. Paul Church in Blandford Forum, Dorset, England.

Children of ROBERT[2] REEVES SR. and AGNES ___ were:

	iii.	JOHN REEVES SR. b. 1495 in Blandford Forum, Dorset, England. John Sr. married ____. They were married circa 1515. They had 1 son named John Jr. Ryves. John Sr. death date is unknown, but he died at Blanford Forum, Dorset, England at age unknown.

3. Lord Sir Robert Ryves III (Note name changes to Ryves)

LORD SIR ROBERT[3] RYVES III (Robert[2] John[1])

- Born 4 August 1490 in, Dorset, England.
- Married circa 1510 Joan ____.
- Died 11 February 1551 Dorset, England at age 61.
- Buried in the church cemetery at the Old St. Peter and St. Paul Church, Blandford Forum, Dorset, England.

Lord Sir Robert Ryves III was a very wealthy man. He and his only son Sir John Ryves, Knight of Damory Court, both purchased large areas of land. Both became extremely wealthy!

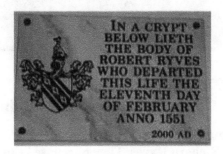

Children of Lord Sir ROBERT[3] RYVES III and JOAN ____ were:

	i.	AGNES RYVES b. 1511 in Blandford Forum, Dorset, England. Agnes married twice: Husband #1 Thomas Swayne and Husband #2 John Swayne. Agnes had a total of 8 children during the two marriages. Agnes died in February 1591 at the age of 80 in England.
4.	ii.	SIR JOHN RYVES (KNIGHT OF THE DAMORY COURT) b. 1514 in Blandford Forum, Dorset, England. Sir John married Amy Harvey of Tarrant, Lancaster, England. They built the Damory Court home and raised 8 children there (children listed) including two children who are our cousin connection! Sir John died on 20 October 1549 at age 35 at Damory Court in Blandford, Dorsetshire, England.
	iii.	N.H. (DAUGHTER) RYNES b. circa 1516 in Blandford Forum, Dorset, England. N.H. married William Hunton. It is unknown if the couple ever had any children. N.H.'s death date and death place are both unknown.

Damory Castle – Note from a current Ryves family member:

"It is not a castle, but a street name and it exists in Blandford with the Damory name. It was originally d'Amorie, and it was Damory Court. It was later owned by the Ryves family. This court later became a farm, but today it is known as the Damory Hotel."

Note was written by a current Ryves family member named "Peter."

Damory Court, Blandford, Dorsetshire, England

It is here that Sir John Ryves and his wife Amy Harvey raised their 8 children, including our cousins, Lucy Ryves and her brother Sir Richard Ryves. They purchased this property and built this home shortly after their first child, Lucy, was born. They raised all their children here. Sir John and his father (Sir Robert Ryves Jr.) had purchased a considerable number of lands in Dorsetshire including the property here at Damory Court. Sir John Ryves was a nobleman and a knight. They were a very wealthy family.

4. Sir John Ryves Sr. Knight, of Damory Court

ROBERT,[4] RYVES SR. (Robert[3], Robert[2], John[1])
- Born 1514 in Blandford Forum, Dorset, England.
- Married 1533 Amy Harvey (1515-1551) of Tarrant, Lancaster England.
- Died 20 October 1549 at Damory Court, Blandford, Dorsetshire, England at age 35.

Our Cousin Connection:

The Author is designated as (ml). She descends from Lucy Ryves.

Author's husband is designated as (cam). He descends from Sir Richard Ryves, who is Lucy's brother.

The siblings listed below are where the cousin connection is.

Children of Sir JOHN[4] RYVES SR. KNIGHT OF DAMORY COURT and AMY HARVEY were:

5. ml	i.	**LUCY RYVES** b. April 1535 Poundsford, Somerset, England. Lucy married Sir William Hill (1515-1592) of Poundsford. They had 7 children. One of their children was Dr. John Allyxander Hall (1575-1635). He married in his 2nd marriage Susannah Shakespeare (who was the daughter of William Shakespeare of Stratford-upon-Avon, England). Lucy died 1573 at the age of 38. She is buried in the Saint Andrew & Saint Mary Church Graveyard in Pitminster, Taunton Deane Borough, Somerset, England.
	ii.	**JOHN RYVES** b. 24 June 1536 Damory Court, Blandford, Dorsetshire, England. Being first son, after his father's death, he inherited his paternal grandparents' fortune. He attended Oxford University and became a reputable lawyer. John married Elizabeth ___. John and Elizabeth had 10 children. John died 15 May 1587 at the age of 51 at Dorsetshire, England.
	iii.	**MARY RYVES** b. 1538 Damory Court, Blandford, Dorsetshire, England. She married William Adeyn. It is unknown if they had any children. Mary's death date and location at her death are both unknown. Her age at death is unknown.
	iv.	**MARGARET RYVES** b. 1540 Damory Court, Blandford, Dorsetshire, England. She married Richard Lawrence. They had 1 son named, Richard Jr. Margaret died 31 December 1618 in Winterbourne, Dorset, England at the age of 78.
	v.	**JANE RYVES** b. 1542 Damory Court, Blandford, Dorsetshire, England. She married Thomas Sydenham. They had two sons George and Charles. Jane died 31 December 1618 at the age of 76. Her death location is unknown.
	vi.	**ROBERT RYVES** b. 1544 Damory Court, Blandford, Dorsetshire, England. He married Margaret ___. They had 7 children including twins (John & James). Robert died on 27 July 1576 at the age of 32. His death location is unknown.
5. cam	vii.	**SIR RICHARD RYES** b. 24 June 1547 Damory Court, Blandford, Dorsetshire, England. he married Mary ___. They had one son Timothy. Sir Richard died 20 October 1588 at the age of 41. He died at Damory Court, Blandford, Dorsetshire, England in the very home where he had been born.
	viii.	**THOMAS RYVES** b. 1549 Damory Court, Blandford, Dorsetshire, England. He married Jane ___. They had 5 children. Thomas died in 1597 at Shaftsbury, Dorset, England at the age of 48.

Following the death of Amy's husband, Sir John Ryves, Amy Harvey remarried, to John Thomas Mann. They had 1 son (Edward Mann) who was a half-brother to the children listed above.

Child of JOHN THOMAS MANN and AMY HARVEY RIVES was:

	ix.	**EDWARD MANN** b. 11 May 1551 in Dorset, England. Edward married Eleanor ____. Edward and Eleanor had 2 children. Edward died 22 December 1622 in Dorset, England at the age of 71.

<u>Lucy Reeves & William Hill's son</u> was:

<u>Dr. John Alexander Hall (medical physician)</u>

Born 1575 in Carlton, Bedfordshire, England.

Married 1602 Wife #1 Jane Gaud (1575-1682). They had 6 children.

Married 1607 Wife #2 Susanna Shakespeare (1583-1649).

They had 1 child, a daughter Elizabeth Hall (1608-1670).

Wife #2 **Susanna was the daughter of William Shakespeare (1564-1616).**

Dr. John A. Hall died 25 November 1635 Stratford-upon-Avon, Warwickshire, England.

The black and gold plaque above reads:

The Grave of
John Hall
Physician
Son in law of
William Shakespeare
1575-1635
https://youtu.be/VmrEHyfgskk

5. (ml) Lucy Ryves Hill and her husband William Hill's line continues in the Hill ancestry.

———

(Following below is the Author's Husband's Line (cam) which can also be found in Volume II)

5. (cam) Sir Richard Ryves

SIR RICHARD[5] RYVES (John[4], Robert[3], Robert[2], John[1])

- Born 24 June 1547 at Damory Court, Dorsetshire, England.
- Married circa 1587 Mary Elizabeth Bagshaw at Damory Court, Dorsetshire, England.
- Died 20 October 1588 at Damory Court, Dorsetshire, England at the age of 41.

Child of SIR RICHARD[5] RYVES JR. and MARY ELIZABETH BAGSHAW was:

6.	i.	**TIMOTHY RYVES** b. 1588 in Oxford, Oxfordshire, England. Timothy married three times: Wife #1 Mary Elizabeth ____. Timothy and Mary Elizabeth had 2 sons during their marriage. Wife #2 Lady Margaret Webb. Wife Timothy and Lady Margaret had 2 sons also during their marriage. #3 Mary ___. They had 3 children during their marriage. Timothy had a total of 7 children in his three marriages. Timothy was a very distinguished and prominent man of his community. He attended Oxford University. Timothy died 30 September 1643 in Oxford, Oxfordshire, England at the age of 55. He is buried in the St. Mary Magdalene Church Cemetery in Oxford, England.

6. Timothy Ryves (Immigrant)

TIMOTHY[6] RYVES (Richard[5], John[4], Robert[3], Robert[2], John[1])

- Born 1588 Oxford, Oxfordshire, England.
- Married circa 1622 Wife #1 Mary Elizabeth ___. Timothy and Mary Elizabeth were married in Oxford, Oxfordshire, England. (They had 2 children).
- Married circa 1631 Wife #2 Lady Margaret Webb. Timothy and Lady Margaret were married in Oxford, Oxfordshire, England. (They had 2 children).
- Married circa 1637 Wife #3 Mary ____. Timothy and Mary were married in Oxford, Oxfordshire, England. (They had 3 children).
- Arrived circa 1638 in America (Virginia Colony). He returned to England and died there the same year his youngest son was born in Virginia (1643).
- Died 30 September 1643 at Oxford, Oxfordshire, England at the age of 55.
- Buried St. Mary Magdalene Church, Oxford, Oxfordshire, England.

Timothy Ryves of Oxfordshire, England -- This is a Timothy from a later era, but perhaps he bears a resemblance to his Elizabethan ancestors.

Children of TIMOTHY[6] RYVES and MARY ELIZABETH _____ were:

	i.	**Timothy Ryves Jr.** b. 1623 at Oxford, Oxfordshire, England. Timothy Jr. died in 1643 at the young age of 20 in England.
	ii.	**Timothy Ryves III** b. 1625 at Oxford, Oxfordshire, England. He died in 1643 at the young age of 18 in England.

Both boys died the same year. They may have been in a tragic accident together.

Children of TIMOTHY[6] RYVES and LADY MARGARET WEBB were:

	i.	**GEORGE RYVES** b. 1632 in Woodstock, Oxfordshire, England. George married Joan ___ circa 1642. George and Joan had 8 children. George died in 1677 in Woodstock, Oxfordshire, England at the age of 45.
7.	ii.	**WILLIAM FRANCIS RIVES (Immigrant)** b.1636 in Woodstock, Oxfordshire, England. He immigrated to America, settling in Virginia with his family in 1638 at the young age of 2 years. William Francis married Elizabeth ___. They had 4 children. William Francis died in 1696 in Surry, Surry Co., Virginia at the age of 60.

Children of TIMOTHY[6] RIVES SR. and MARY ___ were:

	i.	**WILLIAM RIVES** b. 1640 in Virginia. William married ____. They had 1 child; a son named Timothy. William died in Virginia; death date is unknown.
	ii.	**ELIZABETH RIVES** b. 1641 in Virginia. She married Michael McKinney. It is unknown if Elizabeth and Michael had any children during their marriage. Elizabeth died in 1701 in Virginia at the age of 60

	iii.	**TIMOTHY RIVES JR.** b. 1643 in Virginia. Timothy Jr. married Judith ___. It is unknown if Timothy Jr. and Judith had any children during their marriage. Timothy Jr. died in Charles City, Virginia but his death date is unknown.

Timothy Rives Sr and his wife Mary ___ Rives immigrated to America circa 1638. When they made the crossing to the new colony of Virginia their **name was changed from RYVES to RIVES**.

7. William Francis Rives – note name changes to Rives (Immigrant)

WILLIAM FRANCIS[7] RIVES (Timothy[6], Richard[5], John[4], Robert[3], Robert[2], John[1])

- Born 1636 Woodstock, Oxfordshire, England.
- Arrived circa 1638 in America (Virginia Colony) age 2 years old.
- Married circa 1659 Elizabeth ____.
- Died 1695 in Surry Co., Virginia at age 59.

Children of WILLIAM FRANCIS[7] RIVES and ELIZABETH ____ were:

	i.	**GEORGE RIVES** b. 1660 in Albemarle Parish, Sussex Co., Virginia. George married twice: Wife #1 Frances ___. Wife #2 Grace ___. George had 10 children altogether with both wives. George died 8 September 1719 in Bristol Parish, Prince George Co., Virginia at the age of 59.
	ii.	**ROBERT RIVES.** b. 1662 in Surry, Surry Co., Virginia. Robert married Sarah Culpepper. They had 1 child a daughter who married a Mr. ___ Jones. Robert died 1735 in Surry, Surry Co., Virginia at the age of 73.
8.	iii.	**TIMOTHY RIVES SR.** b. 1670 in Virginia. He married Judith___ circa 1689, They had 5 children. Timothy died in 1716 in Surry, Surry Co., Virginia at the age of 46.
	iv.	**WILLIAM RIVES** b. 1680 in Surry, Surry Co., Virginia. He married twice. Wife #1 Margaret Frances, Wife #2 Marta ____. He had twelve children altogether between both wives. William died November 1761 in Granville, Granville Co., North Carolina.

8. Timothy Rives Sr.

TIMOTHY[8] RIVES SR. (William Francis[7], Timothy[6], Richard[5], John[4], Robert[3], Robert[2], John[1])

- Born 1670 in Virginia.
- Married circa 1689 Judith ____.
- Died 1716 in Surry, Surry Co., Virginia at age 46.

Children of Timothy[8] Rives and JUDITH ___ were:

	i.	**URSULA RIVES** b. 1690 Surry, Surry Co., Virginia. Ursula never married and there is no death date for her. She died in Surry, Surry Co., Virginia at age unknown.

	ii.	**REBECCA RIVES** b. 1692 Surry Co., Virginia. Rebecca married John Hicks. They had 2 children Abigail Rose and Robert. Rebecca died 1729 in Surry, Surry Co., Virginia at the age of 37.
	iii.	**GEORGE RIVES** b. 1698 in Surry, Surry Co., Virginia. GEORGE married Frances ____. They had 1 child a son named Timothy. George died 1 June 1746 in Surry, Surry Co., Virginia at the age of 48.
9.	iv.	**TIMOTHY RIVES JR.** b. 1704 in Surry Co., Virginia. Timothy married Mary Elizabeth Steward in 1735. They had 2 sons during their marriage. Their sons were William and **Colonel Timothy III who fought in the Revolutionary War**. Timothy Jr. died 1782 in Virginia at the age of 78.
.	v.	**WILLIAM RIVES** b. 1706 in Surry, Surry Co., Virginia. William married Priscilla ___. They had 1 child during their marriage, a daughter named Elizabeth. William died in 1777 in Surry, Surry Co., Virginia at the age of 71.

9. Timothy Rives Jr.

TIMOTHY[9] RIVES JR. (Timothy[8], William Francis[7], Timothy[6], Richard[5], John[4], Robert[3], and Robert[2], John[1])

- Born 1704 in Surry, Surry Co., Virginia.
- Married 1735 Mary Elizabeth Steward in Surry, Surrey Co., Virginia.
- Died 1782 in Virginia at the age of 78.

Children of TIMOTHY[9] RIVES and MARY ELIZABETH STEWARD were:

10.	i.	**WILLIAM RIVES** b. 1736 in Prince George Co., Virginia. William married Lucy Shands (1740-1815). William and Lucy were married in 1760. Lucy was the daughter of William Shands and Priscilla Moss. William and Lucy had 8 children during their marriage. William died 21 May 1778 in Albemarle Parish Sussex Co. Virginia at age 42.
	ii.	**COLONEL TIMOTHY RIVES** III **(Revolutionary War)** b. 1740 in Sussex, Sussex Co., Virginia. It is not known if he ever married and had any children. Colonel Timothy III died in 1782 in Sussex, Sussex Co, Virginia at the age of 42.
	iii.	**URSILLA RIVES** B. 6 July 1743 in Bristol Parish Virginia. Ursilla's death date and location at death are both unknown. Her age at death is unknown.

10. William Rives

WILLIAM[10] RIVES (Timothy [9], Timothy [8], William Francis [7], Timothy [6], Richard [5], John[4], Robert[3], Robert[2], John[1])

- Born 1736 in Prince George Co., Virginia.
- Married 1760 Lucy Shands (1740-1815) Virginia (daughter of William Shands & Priscilla Moss).
- Died 21 May 1778 in Albemarle Parish, Sussex Co., Virginia at the age of 42.

Children of WILLIAM[10] RIVES and LUCY SHANDS were:

	i.	**JOEL RIVES** b. 6 April 1761in Prince George Co., Virginia. Joel married Jemima ___. They had 1 son, Henry during their marriage. Joel died in 1829 in Virginia at age 68.
11.	ii.	**MARY RIVES** b. 18 November 1762 in Surry, Surry Co., Virginia. Mary married Thomas Peebles on 28 March 1785 in Sussex Co., Virginia. They had 1 son named William Rives Peebles. Mary died 1825 at an unknown location at the age of 73.
	iii.	**ROBERT RIVES SR.** b. 11 March 1764 in Albemarle Parish, Surry Co., Virginia. Robert married Margaret Jordan. Robert and Margaret had 11 children. Robert Sr. died on 9 March 1845 in Oak Ridge, Nelson, Virginia at the age of 81.
	iv.	**CHARLES RIVES** b. 25 August 1766 in Surry, Surry Co., Virginia. It is unknown if he married and had any children. His death date and location at death are unknown.
	v.	**HENRY RIVES** b. 12 May 1768 in Surry, Surry Co., Virginia. Henry married Anne Anderson. They had 7 children during their marriage. Henry died 19 October 1824 at the age of 56. His location at death is unknown.
	vi..	**LAVINA RIVES** b. 21 February 1779 in Surrey, Surrey Co., Virginia. It is unknown if she ever married and had any children. Her death date and location at death are both unknown.
.	vii..	**HARTWELL RIVES** b. 29 October 1772 in Surrey, Surrey Co., Virginia. It is unknown if he ever married and had any children. His death date and location at death are both unknown.
	viii.	**PHOEBE RIVES** b. 22 December 1774 in Surrey, Surrey Co., Virginia. It is unknown if she ever married and had any children. Her death date and location at death are both unknown.

11. Mary Rives

MARY[11] RIVES (William[10], Timothy[9], Timothy[8], William Francis[7], Timothy[6], Richard[5], John[4], Robert[3], Robert[2], John[1])

- Born 18 November 1762 in Surrey, Surrey Co., Virginia.
- Married 25 March 1785 Thomas Peebles.in Sussex Co., Virginia.
- Died circa 1825 at age approx. 63. Location of death is unknown.

Children of MARY[11] RIVES and THOMAS PEEBLES are documented in the Peebles chapter in Volume II.

Paths to find the Ancestral Rives Cousins

Volume I:

mi (Author) –> Albert Kearney (Immigrant)-> James Kearney -> George Kearney/Salina Smith➔William Smith/Amelia Yorke-> Fones Yorke-> Capt. Edward Yorke/Mary Fones->

Capt. Daniel Fones Sr./Mary Remington->Thomas W. Remington Jr. ->

Thomas Remington Sr/Mary Allen->William J. Allen V/Elizabeth Hill->Lt. John E. Hill->

John Ellis Hill->Dr. John A. Hill->Sir William Hill/Lucy Ryves->Lucy's parents are:

Lord Sir John Ryves Jr./Amy Harvey.

Cousins

Lucy Ryves sister of Sir Richard Ryves

ML side   CAM side

Volume II:

cam (Author's husband) – Charles McComas/Florence Hollomon-> Albert E. Hollomon->

Albert Sidney Hollomon/Ada Florence Alston ->Joseph John Alston->

John Solomon Alston/Mary Peebles->Thomas Peebles/Mary Rives->William Rives->

Timothy Rives Jr.->Timothy Rives Sr.->William Francis Rives Immigrant)->

Timothy Ryves->Sir Richard Ryves' parents -> Lord Sir John Ryves Jr./Amy Harvey

Cousins

Sir Richard Ryves brother of Lucy Ryves

CAM side   ML side

Author's Note:

I have included the spouse's' name *only* when the ancestral search switched over to the maternal path.

Source Citations for this Chapter

The Reeves Review edited by Jonathan Floyd Reeves & Emma Barrett Reeves, 1976 privately published, Pineywood Printing, Lufkin Texas.

Triune Methodist Church Cemetery Records, 18th District, Williamson Co., Tennessee.

https://www.ancestry.com/familytree/62293685/person/172237765588/familyview/print?_phsrc=WLs9&usePUBJs=true

https://youtu.be/VmrEHyfgskk

https://www.wikitree.com/wiki/Hall-10505

Chapter 25: The Sands

The Sands Family Line

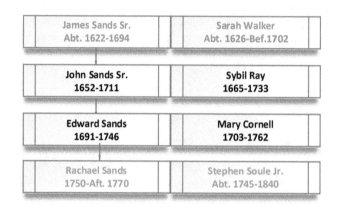

1. Captain James Sands Sr. (Immigrant)

CAPTAIN JAMES[1] SANDS SR.

- Born 1622 in Reading, Berkshire, England.
- Arrival circa 1638 with the Hutchinson Family landed in Plymouth, Plymouth Co., Massachusetts.
- Married 1645 Dr. Sarah Walker (circa 1622-1709). Dr. Sarah Walker was known as the first female doctor in New England. They were married in Portsmouth, Newport, Rhode Island. Doctor Sarah was the daughter of John Walker and Katherine Hutchinson.
- Founder of Block Island, Rhode Island in 1648.
- Died 13 March 1694 in New Shoreham, Block Island, Newport Co., Rhode Island age 73.

Captain James Sands Senior was a sea captain. He made the journey across the Atlantic Ocean and landed in Plymouth, Plymouth Co., Massachusetts circa 1638. He came with the Hutchinson family, but Captain James was single and not married yet at the time of the trip. Sarah Walker, along with her parents, also made the trip with him. Sarah's mother was Katherine Hutchinson. Doctor Sarah Walker married our Captain James Sands Sr. in 1645. Captain James was one of the first 16 settlers who founded Block Island in 1645 and he himself is noted as the founder of Block Island.

Three years after arriving from England, landing in Plymouth, Plymouth Co., Massachusetts, Captain James built a home for Ann Hutchinson, who was one of his future wife's cousins. Ann Hutchinson was the woman who caused a lot of disturbance in Massachusetts, and they banished her from the Bay Colony for antinomian preaching. She fled to East Chester, New York and it was there she employed Captain James to build her a house, which he did. Soon after the house was completed, she and sixteen members of her family moved in. Ann Hutchinson was murdered by the Indians.

Soon after that James Sands Sr. moved to what is now Block Island; he was one of the first European people there. Being also a carpenter, he built his own home for his new wife Dr. Sarah Walker Sands, and he settled there becoming the founder of Block Island. His wife Dr. Sarah Walker Sands was the first female doctor in New England.

His garrisoned stone home was close to the mill and close to a bridge on the road from the harbor to the center of town where a Baptist church was later constructed. According to his grandson, the Rev. Samuel Niles, Captain James Sands Sr. was a brave, humane, and devoted Christian as well as an enterprising citizen. He was the first representative to sit in the General Court of Commissioner of Rhode Island. He was foremost in presenting the petition to have the Island incorporated under the name New Shoreham. The General Assembly granted the request but in doing so, the old name of Block Island stayed, and the chartered name became "New Shoreham, otherwise "Block Island." He was of the Baptist faith and before the Baptist church's building was completed, Captain James turned his house into a house of worship every Sunday to which the citizens of Block Island came. It was noted in the history of Block Island that Captain James Sands was referred to as "Mr. Sands was an enterprising citizen, had a plentiful estate, and gave free entertainment to all gentlemen that came to the Island." When his house became garrisoned, it also became "a hospital for several poor people resorted thither." Mr. Sands was the first Freeman on the Island, and he was also a close intimae friend of the now-famous Roger Williams. James Sands had a large farm on Block Island and raised sheep. He died in his 72nd year and above his grave is erected a monument which reads:

Hre Lyes Intvrred the

Body of Mr James Sands Seniovr

Aged 73 Years Who Departed This

Life March 13 A.D. 1695

Children of Captain JAMES[1] SANDS SR. and DR. SARAH WALKER were:

	i.	SARAH SANDS b. 15 August 1645 in Portsmouth, Newport Co., Rhode Island. Sarah married Nathaniel Niles on 14 February 1671 in New Shoreham (Block Island), Newport Co., Rhode Island. Sarah and Nathaniel had 7 children during their marriage. Sarah died on 15 May 1726 in Cow Neck Peninsula, Port Washington, Nassau Co., New York at the age of 81.
	ii.	MARGARET SANDS b. 1647 in Portsmouth, Newport Co., Rhode Island. It is not known if she ever married and had any children. Margaret died on 6 April 1758 at the age of 81 on Block Island, Newport Co., Rhode Island.
2.	iii.	CAPTAIN JOHN SANDS SR. b. 1652 in Portsmouth, Newport Co., Rhode Island. Captain John Sr. married Sybil Ray on 19 March 1665 in New Shoreham (Block Island) Newport, Rhode Island. Sybil Ray (circa 1650-23 December 1733). She was the daughter of Simon Ray III and Mary Thomas. Captain John and Sybil were married on 19 March 1665 in New Shoreham (Block Island), Rhode Island. They had 8 children during their marriage. Captain John Sr. died on 15 March 1711 at the age of 59 in Cow Neck Peninsula, Port Washington, Nassau Co., New York.
	iv.	SAMUEL SANDS b. 1656 in Portsmouth, Newport Co., Rhode Island. Samuel married twice: Wife #1 Mary Ray Kenyon in Block Island, Washington Co., Rhode Island (marriage date unknown). Wife #2 Dorothy Ray (who was a sister of his brother Captain John's wife Sybil Ray). Samuel had 6 children between both his wives. Samuel died in 1739 at the age of 83 in Cow Neck Peninsula, Port Washington, Nassau Co., New York.

	v.	**JAMES SANDS** Jr. b. 1662 in Block Island, Newport Co., Rhode Island. James married Mary Cornell in 1697 in Block Island Newport Co., Rhode Island. James and Mary had 10 children during their marriage. James died on 21 September 1732 in Cow Neck Peninsula, Port Washington, Nassau Co., New York, at the age of 70.
	vi.	**MERCY SANDS** b. 1665 in Block Island, Newport Co., Rhode Island. Mercy married Joshua Raymond Jr. on 29 April 1683 in New London, New London Co., Connecticut. They had 4 children during their marriage. Mercy died on 3 May 1741 in Lyme, New London, Connecticut at the age of 76.
	vii.	**JOB SANDS** b. 1667 in Block Island, Newport Co., Rhode Island. It is unknown if he ever married and had any children. His death date and location at death are both unknown.
	viii.	**EDWARD SANDS** b. 1672 in Block Island, Newport Co., Rhode Island. Edward married Mary Williams (circa 1675-1708). They were married circa 1693 and had 1 daughter. Edward died on 14 June 1708 in New Shoreham, Newport, Rhode Island.

2. John Sands Sr.

JOHN^2 SANDS SR. (James^{1}Sr.)

- Born 1652 in Portsmouth, Newport, Rhode Island.
- Married circa 1690 Sybil Ray (1665-23 December 1733). Sybil was the daughter of Simon Ray III and Mary Thomas.
- Died 15 March 1711 in Cow Neck, Long Island at the age of 59.

Children of JOHN^2 SANDS SR. and SYBIL RAY were:

	i.	John Sands Jr. b. 22 January 1684 in Cow Neck, Long Island, Sands Point, Queens Co., New York. John married Catherine Guthrie. John Jr. and Catherine were married on 9 September 1706 in Newport, Newport Co., Rhode Island. They had 4 children during their marriage. John Jr. died 30 August 1763 Cow Neck, Lewis, New York at the age of 22.
	ii.	Nathaniel Sands b. 1687 in Cow Neck, Long Island, Sands Point, Queens Co. New York. It is unknown if he ever married and had any children. His death date is unknown. However, he died in Block Island, Newport, Rhode Island.
3.	iii.	Edward Sands b. 1691 in Block Island, Washington Co., Rhode Island. Edward married Mary Cornell. Edward and Mary were married in 1725. They had 5 children during their marriage who were all born at Sands Point, New York. Edward died on 9 March 1746 in Sands Point, Queens Co., New York at the age of 55.
	iv.	George Sands b. 1694 in Block Island, Washington Co., Rhode Island. George died in 1704 in Long Island City, Queens, New York at the age of 10 years.
	v.	Mary Sands b. 1697 in Long Island City, Queens Co., New York. Mary married Nathan Selleck on 2 December 1710. It is unknown if they had any children during their marriage. Mary died on 15 July 1712 in Stamford, Fairfield Co., Connecticut at age 15.

	vi.	Catherine Sands b. 1700 in Long Island City, Queens Co., New York. Catherine married Edmund Mott on 2 April 1726 in Cow Neck, Hempstead, Queens, New York. They had 4 children during their marriage. Catherine died in 1758 at the age of 58. Her death location is unknown.
	vii.	Dorothy Sands b. 1703 in Long Island City, Queens Co., New York. It is unknown if she ever married and had any children. Dorothy died on 15 June 1765 at the age of 62. Her death location is unknown.
	viii.	Abigail Sands b. 1708 in Long Island City, Queens Co., New York. Abigail married John Thomas (1707-1777). Abigail and Thomas were married in 1733 and moved to Rye, Westchester Co., New York. They had 4 children during their marriage. Abigail died on 4 August 1782 at the age of 74. She is buried in the Trinity Churchyard in Manhattan, New York City, New York.

3. Edward Sands

EDWARD[3] SANDS (John[2] Sr., James[1] Sr.)

- Born 1691 Block Island, Washington Co., Rhode Island.
- Married 1725 Mary Cornell (10 July 1703-15 September 1762). Mary was the daughter of Richard Cornell and Harriet Thorne.
- Died 9 March 1746 in Cow Neck, Long Island, Sands Point, Queens Co., New York at age 55.

Children of EDWARD[3] SANDS SR. and MARY CORNELL were:

	i.	**SYBIL SANDS** b. 13 September 1727 in Sands Point, North Hampstead, New York. Sybil married Captain Stephen Thorn on 27 July 1746 at the St. George's Church in Hempstead, Long Island, New York. Sybil and Stephen had 6 children during their marriage. **Captain Stephen was a Loyalist and served in the British militia during the Revolutionary War. Following the war, after Sybil had died, he moved to Canada. He died in Granville, Nova Scotia on 11 December 1800.** Sybil died on 1 March 1759 in Port Washington, North Hempstead, Nassau, New York at age 32
	ii.	**RICHARD SANDS** b. 3 February 1729 in Sands Point, North Hampstead, New York. Richard married Deborah Griffin. Richard and Deborah had 6 children during their marriage. Richard died on 26 October 1798 at Sands Point, Long Island, New York at the age of 69.
	iii.	**GEORGE H. SANDS** b. 17 April 1733 in Cow Neck, Long Island, Sands Point, Queens Co., New York. George married Jemima Smith in April 1757 in Poughkeepsie, New York Jemima was the daughter of Abel Smith Jr, and Ruth Jackson. George and Jemima had 12 children during their marriage. George died on 8 October 1816 at the age of 83 in Cow Neck Peninsula, Port Washington, Nassau Co., New York,
	iv.	**RAY SANDS** b. 1738 in Cow Neck, Long Island, Sands Point, Queens Co., New York. It is unknown if Ray ever married and had any children. Also unknown is Ray's death date and location at death. His age at death is also unknown.
4.	v.	**RACHAEL SANDS** b. 1740 in Cow Neck, Long Island, Sands Point, Queens Co., New York. **Rachael arrived circa 1765 in New Brunswick, Canada.** Rachael married Stephen Soules Jr. in 1767 in St. John, St. John Co., New Brunswick, Canada. Rachael

		and Stephen Jr. had 2 children during their marriage. Rachael died after 1770 at the age of approx. 30 in St. John, St. John Co., New Brunswick, Canada.

4. Rachael Sands

RACHAEL[4] SANDS (Edward[3], John[2] Sr., James[1] Sr.)

- Born 1740 in Cow Neck, Long Island, Sands Point, and Queens New York.
- Circa 1730 moved to Dutchess Co., New York where other family members had moved to.
- Arrived circa 1765 in New Brunswick, Canada.
- Married in 1767 Stephen Soule Jr. Rachel and Stephen Jr. were married in St. John, St. John Co., New Brunswick, Canada. (They had 2 daughters during their marriage.)
- Died after 1770 in St. John, St. John Co., New Brunswick, Canada at the age of approx. 30.

Both Rachael and her husband, Stephen, left their country of origin (America), Rachael from New York state and Stephen from the Commonwealth of Massachusetts. See the Soules of Canada chapter for the possible reason of their abandoning their country of origin.

The children of Rachael[4] Sands and Stephen Soule Jr. are documented in the Soules of N.B. & N.S. Canada chapter.

Source Citations for this Chapter

https://en.wikipedia.org/wiki/Block_Island

https://www.blockislandtimes.com/article/week-block-islands-history-november-8-1660-goat-tale/29291

The New England Historical and Genealogical Register. Boston, MA: New England Historic Genealogical Society, 1847-. (Online database: AmericanAncestors.org, New England Historic Genealogical Society, 2001-2013.), Vol. 13, page 37-38.

Early Settlers of Block Island, R. I., J.D. Champlin, Jr., of Stonington, Conn.

Wilson, Malcolm, Sands, Descendants of James Sands of Block Island with notes on Hutchinson, Cornell, Walker, and related Families. 1749, New York.

Find A Grave: Memorial #24866274

Niles, Samuel. *Indian and French Wars*, Collections of the Massachusetts Historical Society (Massachusetts Historical Society, 1837) Third Series, Vol. 6, Page 221.

Harris, Edward Doubleday. *A Copy of The Old Epitaphs in The Burying Ground of Block-Island, R.I.* (John Wilson & Son, Cambridge, Mass., 1883) Page 5. Also see footnote.

Colonial Families of the United States of America, Volume I. Page 461.

Seventeenth Century Colonial Ancestors, Vol. I, Page 220.

Filby, P. William. *Passenger and Immigration Lists Index, 1500s-1900s* (Gale Research, Farmington Hills, MI, USA, 2012).

Letters and a Sands Pedigree Chart of Mrs. Barbara Haskell of Gansevoort, New York.

Chapter 26: The Smiths of Nova Scotia

The Smith Family Line

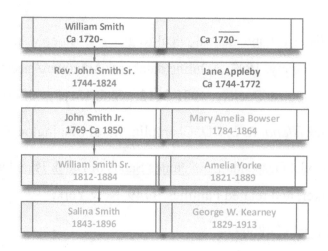

1. William Smith

WILLIAM[1] SMITH

- Born circa 1720 in Yorkshire, England.
- Married circa 1740 Unknown full name ____. William and ____ were married in Yorkshire, England.
- Died _____ unknown date and place.

Child of WILLIAM[1] SMITH and ____ was:

2.		i.	**REV. JOHN SMITH SR.** (Immigrant) b. 20 March 1744 in a village 10 miles north of York, Sheriff Hutton, Yorkshire. Rev. John married twice. Wife #1 Jane Appleby. Rev. John and Jane had 2 children during their marriage. Wife #2 Mary Bowser. Rev. John and Mary had 7 children during their marriage. Rev. John Sr. died 30 January 1824 in Parrsboro, Cumberland Co., Nova Scotia, Canada at the age of 79.

NOTE

Before entering the history of Rev. John Sr. and John Smith Jr., it may be best to note the remarkable fact:

John Smith Jr. married his stepmother's (Mary Bowser's) niece, Mary Amelia Bowser!

Rev. John Smith Sr.'s second wife (whom he married after his first wife, Jane Appleby, died) was Mary Bowser, which made her John Smith Jr.'s stepmother. She was the sister of Captain Thomas Bowser. Captain Thomas Bowser's daughter was Mary Amelia Smith, who was Mary Bowser's niece. John Smith Jr. married Mary Amelia Bowser, who was his stepmother's paternal niece.

2. Rev. John Smith Sr. (Immigrant)

REV. JOHN^2 SMITH SR. (*William^1*)

- Born 20 March 1744 in a village 10 miles north of York, Sheriff Hutton, Yorkshire, England.
- Married 24 September 1768 Wife #1 Jane Appleby in Hutton's Ambo, Yorkshire. Jane Appleby was born circa 1744 in Hutton's Ambo, Yorkshire, England. She died 16 Apr 1772 in Yorkshire in childbirth with her second son, George Smith. Jane Appleby is buried in Yorkshire, England. She bore Rev. John Smith two children, John Smith Jr., and George Smith.
- Married 29 September 1772 Wife #2 Mary Bowser. Mary was the daughter of Thomas Bowser Sr. and Ann Wilkinson, in Yorkshire. Mary Bowser b. July 1750 in England – d. after 1783 in Nova Scotia
- Immigrated 1774 from the Port of Hull. Yorkshire, England on the vessel *Two Friends*, arrival at the Fort of Cumberland, Nova Scotia, Canada.
- Died 30 January 1824 in Parrsboro, Cumberland Co., Nova Scotia, at the age of 79.
- Buried in an unmarked grave in Methodist Cemetery in Parrsboro, Nova Scotia.

Note:

John Smith Jr.'s Stepmother was Mary Bowser.
Mary Bowser was the sister of Thomas Bowser Jr. "The Pioneer"
Thomas Bowser "The Pioneer" was the father of John Smith Jr.'s wife Mary Amelia Bowser.
John Smith Jr. married his stepmother's paternal niece Mary Amelia Bowser.

Rev. John Sr. at the age of 22 years was a farmer and a Methodist preacher in Yorkshire. He married Jane Appleby 24 September 1768 and she bore him two sons, but she died a few weeks after giving birth to their second son, George Smith. Six months later, Rev. John remarried, to Mary Bowser. He needed a wife to help raise his two sons. In the coming year, Mary Bowser, now Smith, bore Rev. John Sr.'s third son, William.

Rev. John was a preacher and a farmer. His preaching ministry in the Methodist faith, plus being a farmer and raising his sons, was quite stressful. He followed the teachings of John Wesley (1703-1791) and his brother, Charles Wesley, who were the famous evangelists who started the Methodist movement in England at about that same time. There was an evangelical spiritual awakening spreading all over England. Times were hard for Rev. John and when he married Mary Bowser, his new brother-in-law Thomas Bowser Jr. was very influential in convincing Rev. John and wife Mary to join him in leaving England and planting new roots in the new land across the water.

Two years later they sailed with their 3 sons: John Jr. age 4, George age 2, and William now 1 year old. According to the Port of Hull Emigration Paperwork, John and Mary with their three sons had left the Port of Hull, England and made the trip across the ocean aboard the ship *Two Friends*. Rev. John Sr. was now 29 years old, and he states according to this paperwork the reason he was leaving England was due to "rents raised too high to live." Also, on this journey was Mary Bowser Smith's sister, Ann Bowser (who was single on the journey but later married a John Hutchinson in Halifax, Nova Scotia), and a brother Richard Bowser. Mary Bowser's brother Captain Thomas Bowser had sailed with his family on the ship called the *Duke of Yorke*. Both arrived the same year of 1774. For further details see the Bowser chapter. The Smith family arrived in Halifax, Nova Scotia but moved on and settled first in Windsor Township, now Hants County, Nova Scotia.

Rev. John Smith Sr.'s family increased, and they eventually settled on Lot #76 in Parrsborough Township, Nova Scotia. It is interesting to note that Rev. John Smith Sr.'s sons were continually active in preparing the land in the next lot over, Lot #77, for the site of a Methodist chapel. The name of the town Parrsborough was later shortened to read Parrsboro. A new and promising life was now before them all. This area where they settled is close to Wharton, Cumberland County, Nova Scotia, which is where Rev. John Smith Sr and his wife Mary (Bowser) Smith years later are believed to have been buried, in the Wharton Cemetery in unmarked graves.

Note: To clarify the above see the Bowser Family chapter for further details.

John Smith Jr.'s stepmother was Mary Bowser.

Mary Bowser was the sister of Thomas Bowser Jr. "The Pioneer."

Captain Thomas Bowser, Jr. "The Pioneer" was the father of John Smith Jr.'s wife Mary Amelia Bowser. Therefore John Smith Jr.'s wife's paternal aunt was his stepmother.

Children of Rev. John[2] Smith Sr. and Jane Appleby were:

1st Marriage

3.	i.	JOHN SMITH JR. (IMMIGRANT) b. 20 Aug 1769 in Yorkshire Co., England. John Jr. married Mary Amelia Bowser. John Jr. and Mary Amelia Bowser were married March 1806 in Sackville, New Brunswick, Canada. They had 9 children during their marriage. John Jr. died circa 1850 at the age of 91 at Diligent River, Cumberland Co., Nova Scotia.
	ii.	GEORGE SMITH (IMMIGRANT) b. 28 Mar 1772 in Yorkshire Co., England. He immigrated with his parents to Canada at the age of 2 years. It is unknown if George ever married and unknown if he had any children. George died before 1812 in Cumberland Co., Nova Scotia at age approx. 40.

Children of Rev. John[2] Smith Sr. and Mary Bowser were:

2nd Marriage

	i.	WILLIAM SMITH (IMMIGRANT) b. 1773 in Acklam, Yorkshire Co., England. William died circa 1778 in Falmouth, Hants Co., Nova Scotia at age approx. 5 years.
	ii.	DAVID SMITH b. 26 May 1776 in Windsor, Hants Co., Nova Scotia. David married Esther Pugsley circa 1805 in Cumberland Co., Nova Scotia; Marriage Bond dated 26 December 1804 in Halifax, Nova Scotia. Marriage was in Cumberland Co.; David died circa 1844 in Kirk's Hill, Cumberland Co., Nova Scotia at the age of 68. He and his wife are buried in Methodist Crossroads Cemetery, Parrsboro. Cumberland Co., Nova Scotia.
	iii.	ELIZABETH SMITH b. 12 June 1777 in Windsor, Hants Co., Nova Scotia. Elizabeth married Richard Black on 19 February 1821 in Parrsboro, Cumberland Co., Nova Scotia. This was Richard's 2nd marriage. His first wife, Sally Chapman bore him 11 children. There were no children from the marriage with Elizabeth Smith. Richard died in 1834 and in his Will, he left his "dear and beloved" 2nd wife (Elizabeth Smith) the following: 20 pounds a year, a bay horse, and a cow. Also "the use and benefit of the best room in the dwelling house," several other rooms and furnishings therein and "the bed belonging to the best bedroom" was to be for "her own proper and absolute

		use, benefit and disposal." Elizabeth died in 1861 in Amherst, Cumberland Co., Nova Scotia at the age of 84.
	iv.	**SARAH SMITH** b. 22 October 1778 in Windsor, Hants Co., Nova Scotia. Sarah married John Craig (a soldier) married circa 1800. It is unknown if they had any children. Also unknown is her death date and location at death. Age at death is unknown.
	v.	**MARY SMITH** b. 1780 in Windsor, Hants Co., Nova Scotia. Mary married Edward Dixon in 1802 in Windsor, Hants Co., Nova Scotia. It is unknown if Mary and Edward had any children during their marriage. Mary died in 1854 in Sackville, Westmorland Co., New Brunswick at the age of 74.
	vi.	**MATTHEW SMITH** b. 1781 in Windsor, Hants Co., Nova Scotia. Matthew married Mary Elizabeth Holstead on 21 Sep 1821 in Amherst, Cumberland Co., Nova Scotia. Matthew and Mary Elizabeth had 5 children during their marriage. Matthew died on 18 February 1870 at the age of 89 at Fox River, Cumberland Co., Nova Scotia. He and his wife are buried in Port Greville, Cumberland Co., Nova Scotia.
	vii.	**HANNAH SMITH** b. circa 1783 in Windsor, Hants Co., Nova Scotia. Hannah married Duncan McArthur November 1813 in Parrsboro, Cumberland Co., Nova Scotia. It is unknown if Hannah and Duncan had any children during their marriage. Hannah died after 1824 at the age of approx. 41 in Eastport, Washington Co., Maine.

3. John Smith Jr. (Immigrant)

JOHN[3] SMITH JR. (*John Sr.*[2], *William*[1])

- Born 20 August 1769 in Yorkshire Co., England.
- Married 14 March 1806 Mary Amelia Bowser. Mary Amelia was the daughter of "The Pioneer" Thomas Bowser Jr. and Mary Layton, in Sackville, New Brunswick, Canada.
- Died circa 1850 in Diligent River, Cumberland Co., Nova Scotia at the age of approx. 91.
- Buried in an unmarked grave at Diligent River, Nova Scotia.

Children of JOHN[3] SMITH JR. and MARY AMELIA BOWSER were:

	i.	**GEORGE SMITH** b. 1805 at Diligent River, Cumberland Co., Nova Scotia. George married twice: Wife #1 Mary Hatfield. They were married circa 1830 at Diligent River, Cumberland Co., Nova Scotia. Wife #2 Caroline McKin 2 December 1872 in Five Islands, Colchester Co., Nova Scotia. It is unknown if George had any children between the two marriages. George died 15 April 1880 in Diligent River, Cumberland Co., Nova Scotia at the age of 75.
	ii.	**JOHN T. SMITH** b. 17 April 1807 at Diligent River, Cumberland Co., Nova Scotia. John T. married Phoebe Williams 31 January 1843 in Diligent River, Cumberland Co., Nova Scotia. John T. died 17 January 1875 at Diligent River, Cumberland Co., Nova Scotia, at age 67. He and his wife are buried in the Wharton Cemetery, Wharton, Cumberland Co., Nova Scotia.
4.	iii.	**WILLIAM SMITH SR.** b. 1812 at Diligent River, Cumberland Co., Nova Scotia. William Sr. married Amelia Yorke (1821-1889). They were married circa 1837 at Diligent River, Cumberland Co., Nova Scotia. Amelia York was the daughter of Fones York and Susannah Vickery. Amelia York was born 26 November 1821. She

		died 29 October 1889. William Smith Sr. died 22 December 1884 at the age of 72. Both William Sr. and his wife are buried in the Wesleyan Methodist Cemetery at Diligent River, in Cumberland Co., Nova Scotia.
	iv.	**SYDNEY SMITH** b. 1812 in Diligent River, Cumberland Co., Nova Scotia. Sydney (female) never married. She died 3 April 1868 at Diligent River, Cumberland Co., Nova Scotia at the age of 56.
	v.	**TWIN BOY SMITH** b. September 1819 at Diligent River, Cumberland Co., Nova Scotia. Died September 1819. Died stillborn.
	vi.	**TWIN GIRL SMITH** b. September 1819 at Diligent River, Cumberland Co., Nova Scotia. Died September 1819 at Diligent River, Cumberland Co., Nova Scotia. A letter dated 15 October 1819 from Reverend John Smith to his daughter Mary Dixon refers to other children born to John Jr. and his wife "bout 4 weeks ago John's wife was brought to bed with twins a boy and a girl. The girl is dead, and the boy is not very rugged. Their other girl cannot walk yet so her hand is full." She died at a very young age.
	vii.	**CHARLES APPLEBY SMITH** b. 1821 at Diligent River, Cumberland Co., Nova Scotia. Charles Appleby married Elizabeth Yorke on 2 September 1841 in Cumberland Co. Nova Scotia. Charles Appleby Hannah Hatfield married 29 August 1871. Charles Appleby died 5 July 1882 at the age of 47.
	viii.	**MATILDA SMITH** b. 1825 at Diligent River, Cumberland Co., Nova Scotia. Matilda married John Yorke 4 November 1847 at Diligent River, Cumberland Co., Nova Scotia. It is unknown if the couple had any children during their marriage. Matilda died after 1872 age approx. 47 at Diligent River, Cumberland Co., Nova Scotia.
	ix.	**CHARLES EDWARD SMITH** b. 1838 at Diligent River, Cumberland Co., Nova Scotia. Charles Edward married Elizabeth Annie Spicer on 1 February 1859 in Parrsboro, Cumberland Co., Nova Scotia. It is unknown if they had any children. Charles Edward died on 8 May 1889 the age of 53.

4. William Smith Sr.

WILLIAM[4] SMITH (*John[3], John[2], William[1]*)

- Born 1812 at Diligent River, Cumberland Co., Nova Scotia.
- Married circa 1837 Amelia Yorke (1816-1883). Amelia was the daughter of Fones Yorke and Susannah Vickery. William Sr. and Amelia were married at Diligent River, Cumberland Co., Nova Scotia. William Sr. and Amelia had 6 children during their marriage.
- Died 22 December 1889 at Diligent River, Cumberland Co., Nova Scotia at the age of 77.
- Buried Wharton Cemetery, Wharton, Cumberland Co., Nova Scotia.

William Smith Sr. was a farmer in the town of Diligent River. He had a large farm and financially he and his family were doing very well. Suddenly in their midst, a huge tragedy! The year 1873.

Incredibly early in the morning on April 1, 1873, the villagers of the Lower Prospect and Terrace Bay, Nova Scotia, near where William Smith Sr. (63 years old and his wife Amelia (Yorke) Smith 56 years old) were living nearby when this tragic event happened. They suddenly awoke to a gunshot. The men of the area leaped out of bed, understanding the signal immediately – a shipwreck on their coast! When they reached the shore, they saw the wreckage of the RMS *Atlantic*.

The RMS *Atlantic* Ocean Liner on its way from Liverpool to New York City.

April 1st, 1873, Tragic Disaster

The passengers were struggling in the water as the crew attempted to help them reach the shore. The villagers, including William Smith Sr. and his wife Amelia, launched their rowboats. Of the 952 crew and passengers on board, only 371 survived, making it the worst civilian loss of life in the Northern Atlantic to that date. Now today it is regarded as the second-worst such disaster, with the first being the sinking of the *Titanic* in 1912. The RMS *Atlantic* disaster could have been avoided as the vessel was 13 miles off course when she wrecked. The officers did not spot the Sambro Island Lighthouse, which was warning the ships of the rocky shoals along the coast. The RMS *Atlantic* struck an underwater rock and quickly capsized. In the weeks following the disaster the villagers recovered the many bodies of the dead. It had been the 19th voyage of this transatlantic ocean liner of the White Star Company, which operated between Liverpool in the United Kingdom of Britain and New York City in the United States.

Children of WILLIAM[4] SMITH SR. and AMELIA YORKE were:

	i.	**JAMES GEORGE SMITH** b. 1838 at Diligent River, Cumberland Co., Nova Scotia. He married Mary Elizabeth Dean on 5 January 1859. Mary Elizabeth was the daughter of John Edward Dean. James George and Mary Elizabeth had 3 children during their

		marriage. James George died in 1870 at the age of 32 (the same year that his youngest son was born).
	ii.	**WILLIAM SMITH JR.** b. 1839 at Diligent River, Cumberland Co., Nova Scotia. William Jr. married Sarah Ann ____ (1843-4 March 1893). They were married circa 1859 at Diligent River, Cumberland Co., Nova Scotia. They had 3 children (all daughters) during their marriage. Two daughters died early, one at age 7 years and the other was 10 years old. Both died tragically of measles. A year after losing their two daughters they were blessed with a third daughter (Annie Laurie). Annie Laurie lived to maturity, and she married William A. Yorke, who was the son of James F. Yorke. Sarah Ann died on 4 March 1893at the age of 50. William Smith Jr. died 29 December 1909 at the age of 70.
5.	iii.	**SALINA SMITH** b. 17 August 1843 at Diligent River, Cumberland Co., Nova Scotia. Salina married George W. Kearney on 12 January 1858 in Westbrook Methodist Church, Westbrook, Cumberland Co., Nova Scotia. George W. was the son of George Kearney and Catherine Cecelia Sherry. George W. was born January 1829 – died 25 August 1917 at the age of 88. Salina and George W. had 11 children during their marriage. Salina Smith died on 29 March 1896 at the age of 56 at Diligent River, Cumberland Co., Nova Scotia. Salina preceded her husband in death and is not buried with him. Instead, she is buried in the same cemetery as her parents, the Wharton Cemetery in Wharton Cumberland Co., Nova Scotia.
	iv.	**SARAH A. SMITH** b. 1851 at Diligent River, Cumberland Co., Nova Scotia. She died of scarlet fever on 12 February 1872 at Diligent River, Cumberland Co., Nova Scotia at the age of. 22. She was buried the next day on 13 February. Her grave was dug and was only 2 feet deep because the ground was frozen. Sarah was a seamstress. She never married nor had had any children.
	v.	**ALLISON E. SMITH** b. 1853 at Diligent River, Cumberland Co., Nova Scotia. Allison E. married Charlotte Sanford on 16 June 1875 in Windsor, Hants Co., Nova Scotia. Allison E. and Charlotte had 4 children during their marriage. One of his children was Lee Stanley Freeman Smith (1876-1946) who married Blanche Vickery Smith (1885-1960). They had two daughters Alice Josephine Smith (1906-1966) and Gertrude Bessie Smith (1908-1985). Blanche and her daughter Alice lived together in Parrsboro for many years and stayed connected with author's parents over many years after Albert Kearney had moved to Boston, Massachusetts. When this author and her husband went to Nova Scotia on our honeymoon, we visited the last remaining branch of this family in Parrsboro which was Alice. It was a delightful visit with Alice at her home. Alice died four years later in 1966 at the age of 60. Alice's grandfather Allison E. Smith died on 23 May 1885 of influenza at the age of 33.
	vi.	**ALMINA E. SMITH** b. 6 October 1855 at Diligent River, Cumberland Co., Nova Scotia. Almina married Captain George Newcombe on 26 December 1875 in Cumberland Co., Nova Scotia. It is unknown if Almina and Captain George had any children during their marriage. Almina E. died circa 1918 at the age of approx. 63. Her location at her death is unknown.

In the Nova Scotia 1871 Census it states that William Smith Jr. age 31 (son of William Smith Sr.) was a farmer and owned 800 acres of land, of which 200 acres were cultivated. On this land was one house, one barn and two carriages, two wagons and 40 pastures.

William Smith Sr. and his wife Amelia had a very distinguished gravestone which showed their wealth; the Census reports also confirmed that they were very well-to-do.

Tombstone of
William Smith Sr. & Amelia (Yorke) Smith
(1812-1884)   (1821-1889)

5. Salina Smith

SALINA[5] SMITH (*William⁴, John Jr³, John Sr², William¹*)
- Born 17 August 1843 at Diligent River, Cumberland Co., Nova Scotia.
- Married 12 January 1858 George W. Kearney, son of George Kearney and Catherine Cecelia Sherry. Salina and George W. were married in the Westbrook Methodist Church, Westbrook, Cumberland Co., Nova Scotia. George W. Kearney b. January 1829 - d. 25 August 1913.
- Died 29 March 1896 in Diligent River, Cumberland Co., Nova Scotia, at the age of 52.
- Buried Wharton Cemetery, Wharton, Cumberland Co., Nova Scotia.

Children of SALINA⁵ SMITH and GEORGE W. KEARNEY are documented in the Kearney chapter.

Note: The author and her husband named our firstborn daughter after Salina Smith. However, we changed our daughter's spelling of her name to Selena.

Source of Citations for this Chapter

Personal verbal recollections of Author's Paternal Grandmother (Alberta Atkinson Kearney) of Parrsboro, Nova Scotia and Cambridge, Massachusetts.

Personal verbal and written letters of Author's Paternal Cousin Alice Smith of Parrsboro, Nova Scotia.

Personal verbal and written letters of Author's Paternal Cousin Elizabeth Moses Merrow of Bloomfield, Connecticut.

Written research of Retired Lt. Col R. F. Kirkpatrick of Orange City, Florida.

Written letters from Odilite Juvelis of Swampscott, Massachusetts.

Oral Smith History and written letters from Heather Smith Robinson, Ottawa Historical Research House of Parrsboro, Nova Scotia.

The Descendants of Rev. John Smith, Yorkshire Settler of Diligent River, Nova Scotia by

Heather Smith Robinson, 1991, Ottawa House, Parrsboro, Nova Scotia.

Written research Letters from Marion Kyle (Genealogist of Parrsboro, Nova Scotia Canada).

Written Smith Research from Heather Wardlow of Grande Prairie, Alberta, Canada.

Written Smith Research from Mrs. George Manzer of Paarrsboro, Nova Scotia.

Written Smith Research from Kathy Norton of Enfield, Nova Scotia.

Emigrants from England to the American Colonies (1773-1776) Port of Hull, England Records

https://www.ancestry.com/imageviewer/collections/49141/images/FLHG_EmigrantsEnglandtoAmericaColonies-0023?ssrc=pt&treeid=62293685&perso...

Catalogue of Some of the Smiths at Parrsboro, Cumberland County, Nova Scotia, Canada

Supplements A & B.

Jenks Journal of Nova Scotia.

The Chignecto Isthmus by Howard Trueman book found at P.A.N.S. (Public Archives of Nova Scotia).

Registry of deeds: Amherst, Nova Scotia.

Land Registry Information Service, Property Mapping & Record Division, New Glasgow, Nova Scotia,

Census of 1861 Cumberland Co., Nova Scotia, Canada. Microfilm Reel #5, Polling District #10.

Census of 1871 Mill Village (now Parrsboro, Nova Scotia, Canada). Microfilm Reel #1 and #2.

Census of 1881 Parrsboro, Nova Scotia, Canada). Census book found at P.A.N.S. (Public Archives of Nova Scotia).

Sinking of the R.M.S. Atlantic Ship – Nova Scotia, Canada of April 1, 1873. Loose Papers found at P.A.N.S. (Public Archives of Nova Scotia).

Chapter 27: The Smiths of Rhode Island

The Smith Family Line of Rhode Island

John Smith Sr.	Margaret ____
Ca 1625-1677	Ca 1625-____

Hannah Smith	Joseph Case Sr.
Ca 1655-1712	Ca 1654-1741

Except for Hannah Smith, at this point there does not appear to be a direction connection with the Smiths of Rhode Island and the Smiths of Canada. If there is a further direct connection, it is in England but unknown to this author currently.

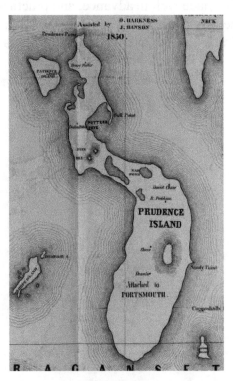

The Smith Family lived here on Prudence Island

Circa 1647-1720

Where is Prudence Island?

Prudence Island is in the Narragansett Bay and is northeast of Newport, Rhode Island. In colonial times, the island was used for farming. During the American Revolution, the British forces were there under Captain James Wallace. Today, 385 years after Roger Williams, the founder of Rhode Island, bought the land from the Narragansett Indians in 1637, Prudence Island remains one of the best-kept secrets in southern New England.

Prudence is smack in the middle of Narragansett Bay, between Bristol to the north and Newport to the south. Six and a half miles long and a mile and a half wide, the island is about as big as its better-known ocean relative, Block Island, but it gets nowhere near the attention. In part that is because it has no nightlife and because most of its beaches have rocky bottoms. But there are other reasons why it has not fallen to the ravages of boutiques, gift shops, bars, and fancy restaurants. The most obvious is the fierce protectiveness with which its residents guard the island. Nobody among the 60 to 70 year-round dwellers thinks Prudence needs more than the 1,500 people it now counts in its summer population.

On that score residents have advantages working in their favor. The principal transportation to the island, the ferry run by Prudence Island Navigation Company from Bristol, has room for only one vehicle. Car reservations must be made well in advance, and practically speaking a customer cannot be sure that he can get a car off the island when he wants to. Most vacationers bring a bicycle or rely on their own two feet. You can bring a Sailfish or similar small sailboat, or a motor scooter or motorbike.

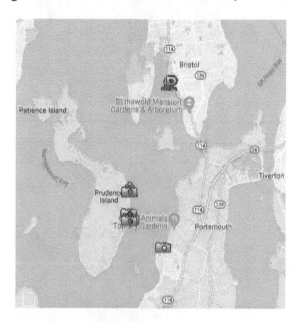

**This Prudence Island is where our John Smith Sr. circa 1645 settled and lived. John married Margaret ____. They had five children in their marriage.
They were all raised on Prudence Island.**

Interesting documentation of Prudence Island

5 May 1664

John Smith Sr.'s wife Margaret, having been fined L5 = 5 Pounds by the Last Court of Trials, and presented a petition to the Assembly for the Court's favor and mercy in remitting fine and said fine was there upon remitted.

19 August 1673

John Smith Sr., Willian Allen and John Snook all witnessed a deed from John Paine of Boston of certain land on Prudence Island bounded partly by lands of John Smith.

Note

John Smith Sr. died in 1677.

Following John Smith Sr's death, his widow married John Snook of Prudence Island.

24 October 1677

John Smith Sr.'s widow, Margaret executrix, Margaret Smith recovered L25, in money and L37, 10s in country pay in a suit against John Paine.

12 June 1678

Margaret Smith's former sentence of being incapable of giving evidence in any case and thereby stands as a perjured person is remitted, null and void.

XXXXXXXXXXX

More Interesting Early Notes about Prudence Island

1637

Governor John Winthrop, on his visit to Prudence Island, noticed that many large trees had been cut down by the Indians to make canoes. He wrote a letter to Roger Williams asking him to notify Miantonomi to order his tribe to cease cutting down the trees on this island.

1642

Prudence (Island) was heavily forested when the first white settlers arrived there.

1659

Roger Williams to John Winthrop Jr.

"Good Mr. Parker, of Boston. Passing from Prudence Island, at his coming on shore, on Seekink land, trod awry, upon a stone or stick, and fell, and broke the small bone of his leg. He hath lain by of it all this winter, and the last week was carried to Boston in a horse litter."

1661

As early as 1661 there were records of drownings off the Prudence shore.

1. John Smith Sr. (Immigrant)

JOHN[1] SMITH SR

Born circa 1625 in England.

- Married circa 1645 Margaret ____. They married in Prudence Island, Newport Co., Rhode Island.
- Died 1677 in Prudence Island, Newport Co., Rhode Island at age 52.

Children of John[1] Smith Sr. and Margaret ____ were:

	i.	**JOHN Smith JR**. b. circa 1646 in Prudence Island, Newport Co., Rhode Island. John Jr. married Phyllis Gereardy. They were married on Prudence Island circa 1666. It is unknown if John Jr. and Phyllis had any children. John Jr. died in 1730 at the age of approx. 84. Location at death is unknown.
	ii.	**JEREMIAH SMITH** b. circa 1649 in Prudence Island, Newport Co., Rhode Island. Jeremiah married Mary Gereardy on 2 January 1672 in Prudence Island, Newport Co., Rhode Island. It is unknown if Jeremiah and Mary had any children during their marriage. It is believed that Mary and Phyllis were sisters who married the Smith brothers. Jeremiah died in 1720 at the age of approx.71 in Prudence Island, Newport Co., Rhode Island.
	iii.	**MERCY SMITH**; b. circa 1652 in Prudence Island, Newport Co., Rhode Island. Mercy married Benjamin Clarke. They were married circa 1672 in Prudence Island, Newport Co., Rhode Island. It is unknown if they had any children during their marriage. Mercy's death date and location at death are also unknown.
2.	iv.	**HANNAH SMITH**, b. circa 1655 in Prudence Island, Newport Co., Rhode Island. Hannah married Joseph Case Sr. (1654-1741). Hannah and Joseph Sr. were married circa 1677 in Kings Town, Rhode Island. Hannah's husband **Joseph Case Sr. fought in King Philip's War in the Rhode Island area in 1675 shortly before they were married.** They had 7 children during their marriage. Hannah died in 1712 at the age of approx. 57 in South Kingstown, Washington Co., Rhode Island.
	v.	**DANIEL SMITH** b. circa 1660 in Prudence Island, Newport Co., Rhode Island. It is unknown if Daniel ever married and had any children. Daniel died in 1707 at the age of approx. 47 in Kingstown, Washington Co., Rhode Island.

2. Hannah Smith

HANNAH[2] SMITH (*John[1]*)

- Born circa 1655 in Prudence Island, Newport Co., Rhode Island.
- Married circa 1677 Joseph Case Sr. (circa 1654-1741). Joseph Sr. was the son of William Case Sr. and Mary ____. Hannah and Joseph Sr. were married in Kings Town, Washington Co., Rhode Island.
- Died 1712 in South Kings Town, Washington Co., Rhode Island at the age of 57.

Hannah's husband **Joseph Case Sr. fought in King Philip's War in the Rhode Island area in 1675, shortly before they were married.**

Children of Hannah[2] Smith and Joseph Case Sr. are documented in the Case chapter.

Source Citations for this Chapter

The Genealogical Dictionary of Rhode Island by John Osborne Austin. Book was found in
The New England Historical Genealogical Society Library REF F A935 – 1969.

Rhode Island Vital Records (1636-1850) Volume 4, Newport Co., Rhode Island.
The New England Historical Genealogical Society Book Loan F, 78, A75, Volume 4.

Ancestry of Thirty-Three Rhode Islanders Born in the 18th Century by J. O. Austin, 1889.
The New England Historical Genealogical Society Book Loan F, 78, A93. Prudence Island

Prudence Island   https://en.wikipedia.org/wiki/Main_Page

Chapter 28: The Soules of Massachusetts

The Soule Family Line

This gentleman serves as a representative of what George Soule looked like. He plays the role of George Soule in the live daily recreations of 17th-century life at the Plimouth Plantation in Plymouth, Massachusetts.

1. George Soule Sr. "THE PILGRIM" (Immigrant)

GEORGE[1] SOULE SR. "THE PILGRIM"

- Born circa 1600 in Elkington, Worcestershire, England.
- Married circa 1626 Mary Becket in Plymouth, Plymouth Co., Massachusetts. Mary Becket Soule died in December 1676 at the age of approx. 51 in Duxbury, Plymouth Co., Massachusetts.
- Died 22 January 1679 in Duxbury, Plymouth Co., Massachusetts at the age of 79.

George Soule lived in Plymouth, Massachusetts from 1620 to circa 1640 as Plymouth is where four of his nine children were born. The other five children were born in Duxbury, Massachusetts (about 19 miles north of Plymouth) and this is where the family moved to. It is in Duxbury that both George and his wife Mary Becket Soule died. The George Soule family lived in Duxbury from circa 1640 to circa 1679, a period of approx. 39 years.

11 November 1620
The Signing of the Mayflower Compact
George Soule was one of the signers.

It is known that George came on the *Mayflower* and was credited to the household of Edward Winslow as a manservant or apprentice, along with Elias Story and a little girl Ellen More, who both died in the first winter. George Soule was mentioned in Bradford's recollections of the Winslow group: "Mr. Edward Winslow; Elizabeth, his wife; and 2 men servants, called Georg Sowle and Elias Story; also a little girl was put to him, called Ellen, sister of Richard More." He continues: "Mr. Ed. Winslow his wife dyed the first winter; and he is married with the widow of Mr. White, and hath 2 children living by her marriageable besides sundry that are dead. One of his servants dyed, as also the little girl, soon after the ships arrival. But this man Georg Sowle, is still living and hath 9 children."

Earlier researchers into Soule's origin believed in the London association of Winslow and Soule. Thus, based on this belief, and for five years ending in 2009, *Mayflower* researcher and biographer Caleb Johnson, managed an intensive search for Soule's English origins; he examined several likely "George Soules" in various parts of England and subsequently concluded that the most promising candidate of all the "George Soules" he reviewed was that of Tingrith, Bedfordshire, baptized in February 1594/5.

More recent work in 2017 has identified the parents of George Soule through a high-quality YDNA match of Soule with families in Scotland and Australia. Following up on research published by Louise Walsh Throop in 2009, the DNA study pointed to Soule's parents as Jan Sol and his wife Mayken Labis, who are identified by their marriage as Protestant refugees in London, England, in 1586 and by the baptisms of their children before 1600 in Haarlem, Holland. Their eldest known son Johannes Sol is identified by his baptism in 1591, as well as by his permissions in both Haarlem and Leyden to marry in Leyden. Johannes Sol, a printer in Leyden with one known publication, died suddenly, probably while helping William Brewster in the presswork for the Perth Assembly. His apprentice, Edward Raban, fled to Scotland in 1619 to avoid being apprehended by agents of the King of England. He was accompanied by the pregnant widow of his master and took with him the missing press of Brewster, as well as the tell-tales type and initials from Brewster; Raban also apparently took with him the Sol press and type. Edward Raban in 1622 published a very veiled version of his master's shocking death, well hidden in a discussion of drunkenness and resultant chaos. It would appear all helpers in the press work and distribution of "Perth Assembly" took an oath of silence that was never breached, even after King James I died in 1625.

It is likely that George's presumed father Jan Sol, who married as a refugee in 1586 in London, was the grandson of Jan van Sol. This Jan van Sol was a zealous opponent of Anabaptism, which he saw in

1550 as divided into three movements: the Melchiorites (the peaceful Mennonite group), the Davidites, and the Batenburgers. Jan van Sol was born at Dordrecht, in South Holland, but left the Netherlands in 1530 because of debts (he kept an inn there) and went east to Danzig. There he was known as Johann/Jan Solius (the Latin version of his name). In 1536 he bought the "Robitten" estate near Bardeyn in East Prussia. He returned in 1550 to Brussels but may have spent his last years, until about 1556, in the territory of Preussisch-Holland. A presumed son born about 1525, and by naming patterns was named Georg, would have married about 1555 in Brussels, and thus would have been the father of Jan Sol of the 1586 marriage record in London. This Jan Sol and wife Maecken had seven children baptized in the Dutch Reformed Church of Haarlem in 1590–99.

The *Mayflower* departed Plymouth, England on 16 September 1620. The small, 100-foot ship had 102 passengers and a crew of about 30–40 in extremely cramped conditions. By the second month out, the ship was being buffeted by strong westerly gales, causing the ship's timbers to be badly shaken with the caulking failing to keep out sea water, and with passengers, even in their berths, lying wet and ill. These conditions, combined with a lack of proper rations and unsanitary conditions for several months, contributed to the high number of fatalities in the first winter, especially for the women and children. On the voyage, there were two deaths, being just a crew member and a passenger. The worst was yet to come after arriving at their destination when, in the space of several months, almost half the passengers perished in the cold, harsh, unfamiliar New England winter.

On 9 November 1620, after about 2 months at sea, preceded by a month of delays in and around England, they spotted land, which was the Cape Cod Hook, now called Provincetown Harbor. After several days of trying to get south to their planned destination of the Colony of Virginia, strong winter seas forced them to return to the harbour at Cape Cod, where they anchored on 11 November 1620.

On 11 November 1620, George Soule and others signed the Mayflower Compact. Soule and three others were under 21 years of age, and one of the three had a baptismal record showing he was just 20 years old at the time of signing. The signers were members of a church group, where the age of membership was 18. The original compact was lost. It was published, without any signers' names appended, several times after 1620. It was not until almost 50 years after the signing that the Compact was published with the names of the signers. Thus, the print work crew of Brewster, Winslow, Soule, and others was sheltered from exposure to the agents of King James I of England. When finally published with all names of signers, only Soule was still alive from the print work crew. From George Soule's signature on the Mayflower Compact and the inventory of his home after he died, both proved that he was literate and could read and write.

I must add a note here about my husband's ancestor John Edward Clark. If it were not for him and his skilled navigational expertise, the *Mayflower* would have never had a successful landing in Plymouth. There will be more about his ancestry in Volume II but here is a brief sketch of his life. He never signed the Mayflower Compact because he was of the Quaker faith and he did not agree with the Separatists movement; thus, he refused to sign it. However, he did his job as a skilled pilot, and he brought the *Mayflower* to a safe landing. We have much to be grateful for and our deep gratitude to John Edward Clark, the pilot of "The 1620 *Mayflower* Ship."

Master Mate: John Edward Clark, Pilot of the *Mayflower* (1620)

John Edward Clark (Immigrant) was the pilot of the *Mayflower*. He was born in 1575 in Surrey England. John Edward married 4 times and had four children within these four marriages. He first went to Jamestown, Virginia in March 1610 as a ship's pilot. There, at Point Comfort, Virginia he was captured by the unfriendly Spanish in June 1611. He was taken captive to Havana, Cuba, where he was interrogated, for several years and then sent to Seville, Spain. He was then sent on to Madrid in 1613. There he was held as a prisoner until he was exchanged for a Spanish prisoner held by the English in 1616. He immediately went back to his occupation as a ship's pilot, and took a shipment of cattle to Jamestown, Virginia in 1619 under the pirate Thomas Jones. In 1620, he was hired to be the master's mate and pilot of the *Mayflower*, on its intended voyage to Northern Virginia. However, the storms sorely tested the crew. The storms with their violent winds forced the ship in a more northern route up the coast toward to what is now known as New England. The ship could not use any of its sails at times with the severity of the wind and the waves.

The ship arrived in December 1620 at what is now known as "First Encounter Beach" in Eastham, Cape Cod, Massachusetts. However, the Indians there were very hostile to the colonists, and they were forced to leave, After leaving, the Pilgrims were again exploring Cape Cod and the Plymouth Harbour, shuttling in and around the shoreland, when their shallop (a small boat they were exploring in) once again was caught in a terrible storm and Clark brought them safely ashore on an island, which is known to this day as Clark's Island which is in Duxbury Bay in Massachusetts. However, it was only an island and not the mainland, so they rowed back to the *Mayflower* leaving the small Clark Island, and finally, they landed at Plymouth, in the Bay State of Massachusetts and set foot on dry solid land. The Indians there were much more favorable to them and helped them settle in.

John Edward Clark was given 2 shares in the Virginia Company for his service. He never signed the Mayflower Compact and he did not stay with the Puritans exceptionally long. He was a Quaker and because of his Quaker faith he did not really settle in comfortably with the Puritans of Plymouth. John Edward left the Bay Colony with the plan of returning to England but changed his mind and decided to settle in Jamestown, Virginia himself, where there was a strong Quaker settlement. Three years later he set sail for Jamestown, Virginia on 10 April 1623 on Daniel Gookin's ship *Providence*, with the intention of settling there in Jamestown. However, he was caught up in a massacre organized and conducted by the Powhatan Indians in Virginia. John Smith wrote that the Powhatan Indians "came unarmed into our houses with deer, turkeys, fish, fruits, and other provisions to sell us." It was absolutely ruthless; all men, women, and children were killed, and their crops burned to the ground. The Powhattan Indians approached the colonists pretending to trade with them, but when they got within striking distance, they fought the colonists at the Jamestown settlement and massacred ¼ of the settlement there, including our John Edward Clark. He was murdered in this massacre not too long after his arrival in April of 1623 in Jamestown, Virginia. Word reached the Pilgrims of Plymouth that the pilot of their *Mayflower*, John Edward Clark, had been killed on that fateful day in April 1623 in Jamestown, Virginia.

Plymouth Colony

George Soule first lived with his employer, Edward Winslow, whose first-house in Plymouth was located on the site of what is now the 1749 Count House Museum in the Town Square in downtown Plymouth. As a servant of Edward Winslow, George had been given the responsibility of taking care of an 8-year-old orphan named Ellen More during the journey across the ocean. He also travelled and lived with Elias Story who was also a servant of Edward Winslow. Elias was much younger than 21 years of age, so he was not allowed to sign the Mayflower Compact.

The first winter the Pilgrims had in America was brutal! There were 102 passengers on the *Mayflower* and by springtime about half the Pilgrim group had perished! In the household of Edward Winslow, only Edward Winslow himself and George Soule had survived. Edward's wife was the last person to die that first terrible winter. Both Elias Story and the little girl Ellen More also had died.

In 1623, the Division of Land at Plymouth provided one acre for George Soule to live on. It was between the property of Frances Cooke and Mr. Isaak Allerton. George was not married at this time; married men were given 2 acres of land and single men were only given one acre of land.

About 1626, George Soule married a woman by the name of Mary. It is known that the only Mary in Plymouth who was then unmarried was Mary Bucket (Buckett). In 1623, "Marie" Buckett, as a single woman, had received one acre of land.

In 1626 George Soule was one of twenty-seven Purchasers involved with the colony joint-stock company which afterwards was turned over to the control of senior colony members. That group was called Undertakers and was made up of such Pilgrim leaders as Bradford, Standish, and Allerton initially, who were later joined by other leaders Winslow, Brewster, Howland, Alden, Prence and others from London who were former merchant adventurers. On the agreement, dated 26 October 1626, his name appears as "Georg Soule."

In the 1627 Division of Cattle, George and Mary Soule and their first son Zachariah (all with the recorded surname of "Sowle") were listed with the Richard Warren family. They were allotted several animals that arrived on the ship *Jacob* in 1625.

Historical records indicate Soule became a freeman prior to 1632/33 and was on the 1633 list of freemen.

In 1633/34 Soule (as "Sowle") was taxed at the lowest rate which indicates that his estate was without much significance.

Per Plymouth records, Soule's life with his family appears to have been lived quietly in a Puritan home. He obtained some land holdings throughout the years which he would later provide for his large family. He was never involved in any criminal or civil court dispute and did participate in several public service situations, one being his volunteering to fight in the Pequot War in 1637, which was over before the Plymouth Company could get organized.

Land records note that in 1637 he was assigned "a garden place…on Duxbury side, by Samuel Nash's, to lie to his ground at Powder Point."

The 1638 land records note that "one acre of land is granted to George Soule at the watering place…and also a parcel of Stony Marsh at Powder Point, containing two acres." The land at the "watering place" in south Plymouth was sold the next year, possibly as he was living in Duxbury at that time and did not need his property in south Plymouth. In 1640 he was granted a meadow at Green's Harbour – now Marshfield. His land holdings included property in several towns, those being Nantasket, Middleboro and Dartmouth.

First in 1642 and last in 1662, he was assigned to at least five grand and petty juries. He was deputy for Duxbury for several years.

In the 1643 "Able to Bear Arms" (ATBA) List, George, and his son Zachariah (listed as "Georg" and "Zachary") appear with those bearing arms from Duxbury (written as "Duxbarrow").

In October 1645 the General Court granted to Duxbury inhabitants lands "about Saughtuckquett" and nominated "Captain, Mr John Alden, George Soul..." and others for "equal dividing and laying forth of the said lands to their inhabitants." The purpose of this committee was to divide property in the Duxbury area for its inhabitants. Soule was also on a similar committee in 1640.

On 20 October 1646 Soule, with Anthony Thatcher, was chosen to be on a "committee to draw up an order concerning disorderly drinking (smoking) of tobacco." The law, as drawn up, provided strict limitations on where tobacco could be smoked and what fines could be levied against lawbreakers.

George Soule's Wife Mary Beckett

Marie/Mary Beckett was the wife of George Soule. The young woman known to Plymouth Colony history as "Marie Beckett" arrived in Plymouth in July 1623 as a single woman passenger on the ship named *Anne*. She may have been about age 18 (born c. 1604) and appears to have travelled with some Alden relatives of her mother, or with members of the possible Warren family with whom she may have lived after the death of her father. Earlier researchers have been stymied in their efforts to prove her ancestry, or from where she came, whether Holland or England.

She first appears in Plymouth Colony records in the 1627 Division of Cattle with passengers of the *Anne* as "Marie Beckett" where she received one lot of her own "adjoining to Joseph Rogers" ..."on the other side of town towards the eele-riuer."

Author Caleb Johnson estimates she married George Soule about 1625 or 1626 as George Soule was born in 1601, and he would have had to wait to marry until released as Winslow's servant at age 25. The marriage of George and Mary was in 1626.

In the 1627 Division of Cattle, she is listed with her husband George and young son "Zakariah" as "Mary Sowle."

Noted *Mayflower* researcher and author Caleb H. Johnson writes in *The Mayflower Quarterly* of December 2013 that the origin of Mary Beckett, wife of *Mayflower* passenger George Soule, has not been conclusively proven by his, or any previous research. What Johnson did find in England, through extensive research and a lengthy process of elimination, was a Mary Beckett in the parish of Watford, Hertfordshire. This Mary was born about 1605 and fits the right age to have been on the *Anne* in 1623. Also, she was in a family using the name Nathaniel, which is found in her later naming one of her own children. Her mother had a *Mayflower*-sounding name – Alden. She and her husband George were grouped with the Warrens in the 1627 Division of Cattle, with Mrs. Warren coming from Hertfordshire, as did Mary Beckett. Mary's home parish register of St. Mary's Church, Watford, has several sixteenth-century Warren family entries of names which all appear in the *Mayflower* Warren family. Johnson considers the following to be among the most important information in considering Marie Beckett's ancestry.

Mary Beckett Soule's Ancestry

Mary Beckett's father died in 1619 when she was only about 14 years old. As a custom of the time, she and her siblings were apprenticed out to relatives, neighbors, acquaintances, etc. Her mother remained a widow until at least 1622 (listed in that year as "Widow Buckett") – further increasing the chance that her children would be sent to other families. Johnson concludes by stating that the following could have put Mary Beckett on the ship *Anne* sailing to America in 1623: the right age, associated with families of *Mayflower* surnames, within a family using the name Nathaniel, and could have had the opportunity to be transferred to another family that would eventually sail to America on the ship *Anne*. Johnson notes after this time, Mary Beckett is not found again in Watford records, based on recent research.

**George Soule's gravestone in
Duxbury within the Myles Standish Burial Ground**

George Soule's Last Will & Testament

"George Soule made his will on 11 August 1677 and mentions his eldest son John: "my eldest son John Soule and his family hath in my extreme old age and weakness been tender and careful of me and very helpful to me." John was his executor and the person to whom was given nearly all of Soule's estate. But after he wrote his will, on 12 September 1677, George seemed to have second thoughts and made a codicil to the will to the effect that if John or any family member were to trouble his daughter Patience or her heirs, the will would be void. And if such happened, Patience would then become the executor of his last will and testament with virtually all that he owned becoming hers. To put his youngest daughter to inherit his estate ahead of his eldest son would have been a major humiliation for John Soule. But John must have done well in his father's eyes since after his father's death, he did inherit the Duxbury estate. Twenty years later, Patience and her husband sold the Middleboro estate they had received from her father." From *The Mayflower and Her Passengers*, Caleb H. Johnson (Xlibris Corp: 2006), p. 208, https://en.wikipedia.org/wiki/George_Soule_(Mayflower_passenger).

George Soule's will was dated 11 August 1677, with a codicil dated 20 September 1677 and with the will proved in 1679. His will named his sons Nathaniel, George and John, and daughters Elizabeth, Patience, Susannah, and Mary. His sons Zachariah and Benjamin had predeceased him. George Soule died shortly before 22 January 1679, when inventory was taken of his estate. He was buried at Myles Standish Burial Ground in Duxbury, Massachusetts, as his wife Mary Becket Soule had predeceased him in 1676.

Caleb H. Johnson notes: "The codicil is quite interesting as it gives a little insight into a family squabble between son John and daughter Patience: If my son John Soule above-named or his heirs or assigns or any of them shall at any time disturb my daughter Patience or her heirs or assigns or any of them in peaceable possession or enjoyment of the lands I have given her at 'Nemasket' alias Middleboro and recover the same from her or her heirs or assigns or any of them; that then my gift to my son John Soule shall be void; and that then my will is my daughter Patience shall have all my lands at Duxbury and she shall be my sole executrix of this my last will and testament and enter into my housing lands and meadows at Duxbury".

The Mayflower History Documentary by Caleb H. Johnson does state that history reveals that John did not violate his father George Soule's wishes and indeed was the recipient of his father's estate. See and listen to this fascinating documentary by Caleb H. Johnson at www.mayflowerhistory.com.

There are two Soule connections to our family. One is in this chapter marked 2B. and the other is in the Soules of Canada chapter which is marked 2A. They are both children of George Soule "The Pilgrim," resulting in my paternal grandparents, James Kearney and Alberta Atkinson being cousins!

Children of George Soule, Sr. "The Pilgrim" and Mary Beckett were:

	i.	ZACHARIAH SOULE b. 22 May 1627 in Plymouth, Plymouth Co., Massachusetts. Zachariah married Margaret Ford. They were married circa 1650 in Plymouth Co., Massachusetts. There are no recorded children from this marriage. Zachariah's death date and location at death are also unknown.
	ii.	JOHN SOULE b. circa 1632 in Plymouth, Plymouth Co., Massachusetts. John married twice. Wife #1 Rebecca Simonson. They were married circa 1656 in Duxbury, Plymouth Co., Massachusetts. John and Rebecca had 9 children during their marriage. Wife #2 Esther Nash Sampson. They were married in 1678 in Duxbury, Plymouth Co., Massachusetts. Esther had been a widow of Samuel Sampson who was killed in King Philip's War.
2A.	iii.	NATHANIEL SOULE SR. b. circa 1637 in Plymouth, Plymouth Co., Massachusetts. *Nathaniel may have caused the most colony trouble of any of his siblings. See below. Nathaniel married Rose Thorn. They were married circa 1681 in Plymouth Co., Massachusetts. Nathaniel fathered a child by an Indian woman prior to this marriage. Nathaniel and Rose had 5 children during their marriage. Nathaniel died circa 1699 at the age of approx. 62 in Dartmouth, Plymouth Co., Massachusetts.
	iv.	GEORGE SOULE JR. b. circa 1639 in Plymouth, Plymouth Co., Massachusetts. George Jr. married Deborah Thomas. They were married circa 1665 in Dartmouth, Plymouth Co., and Massachusetts. They had 8 children in this marriage. George died circa 1704 at the age of approx. 65 in Dartmouth, Plymouth Co., and Massachusetts.
2B.	v.	SUSANNA SOULE b. circa 1642 in Duxbury, Plymouth Co., Massachusetts. Susanna married Francis West Sr. They had 9 children during this marriage. Susanna died on 2 January 1707 in Kings Towne, Washington Co., Rhode Island at the age of 65.
	vi.	MARY SOULE b. circa 1644 in Duxbury, Plymouth Co., Massachusetts. Mary married John Peterson circa 1666 in Duxbury, Plymouth Co., Massachusetts. Mary died after 1720 at the age of approx. 76 in Plymouth, Plymouth., Massachusetts.
	vii.	ELIZABETH SOULE b. circa 1645 in Duxbury, Plymouth Co., Massachusetts. **Elizabeth, like her brother Nathaniel, also got into some mischief. See below.

		Elizabeth had been charged and whipped for fornication twice prior to marriage. Following this incident, a year later, she married Francis Walker circa 1668 in Duxbury, Plymouth Co., Massachusetts. It is unknown if Elizabeth and Francis had any children. Elizabeth died circa 1700 at approx. age 55 in Middleboro "Namassakett," Plymouth Co., Massachusetts.
	viii.	**PATIENCE SOULE** b. circa 1648 in Duxbury, Plymouth Co., Massachusetts. Patience married John Haskell in January 1666 in Middleboro "Namassakett," Plymouth Co., Massachusetts. Patience and John had 8 children in their marriage. Patience died on 11 March 1705 at the age of approx. 57 in Middleboro "Namassakett," Plymouth Co., Massachusetts.
	ix.	**BENJAMIN SOULE** b. circa 1652 in Duxbury, Plymouth Co., Massachusetts. Benjamin died on 26 March 1676 at the age of approx. 24 in Kings Philip's War in Pawtucket, Providence Co., Rhode Island. Benjamin died unmarried and had no children.

*Nathaniel may have caused the most colony trouble of any of his siblings. On 5 March 1667/8, he made an appearance in Plymouth Court to "answer for his abusing of Mr. John Holmes, teacher of the church of Christ at Duxbury, by many false, scandalous and opprobrious speeches." He was sentenced to make a public apology for his actions, find sureties for future good behaviour and to sit in the stocks, with the stock sentence remitted. His father George and brother John had to pay surety for Nathaniel's behaviour with his being bound for monies and to pay a fine. Three years later, on 5 June 1671, he was fined for "telling several lies which tended greatly to the hurt of the Colony in reference to some particulars about the Indians." And then on 1 March 1674/5 he was sentenced to be whipped for "lying with an Indian woman," and had to pay a fine in the form of bushels of corn to the Indian woman towards the keeping of her child.

**Elizabeth, like her brother Nathaniel, also had her share of problems with the Plymouth Court. On 3 March 1662/3, the Court fined Elizabeth and Nathaniel Church for committing fornication. Elizabeth then in turn sued Nathaniel Church "for committing an act of fornication with her ... and then denying marrying her." The jury awarded her damages plus court costs.

On 2 July 1667 Elizabeth was sentenced to be whipped at the post "for committing fornication the second time." And although the man with whom she committed the act was not named, Elizabeth did marry Francis Walker within the following year.

2B. Susannah Soule

SUSANNAH[2] SOULE (George[1])

- Born circa 1642 in Duxbury, Plymouth Co., Massachusetts.
- Married circa 1660 Francis West Sr. in Plymouth Co., Massachusetts.
- Died 2 January 1707 in Kings Towne, Washington Co., Rhodes Island at the age of approx. 65.

Susanna Soule was mentioned in her father's will. She and her sister received 12 pence and then Susanna disappeared from the Duxbury records. This was due to the fact she married Francis West Sr. and moved with him to Kings Towne in Washington Co., Rhode Island, where they raised their 9 children. Susanna and Francis had their first 6 children in Duxbury, Plymouth Co., Massachusetts.

Susanna's father George Soule died in 1679. Susanna and Francis' 7th child, William West, was born 31 May 1681 in Kings Town, Washington Co., Rhode Island. Their 8th and 9th children were also born in Kings Town which is also where Susanna later died in 1707 at the age of approx. 65.

In 1924 an old diary was found in a home near Boston. In the diary it mentions Susannah and her husband Francis West. For more information about this diary writing, see the West chapter.

Children of Susanna[2] Soule and Francis West Sr. are documented in the West chapter.

Source Citations for this Chapter

Genealogies of Mayflower Families by Gary Boyd Roberts, New England Historical& Genealogical Register, Volume II Reprinted for the Clearfield Company Inc. by the Genealogical Publishing Co., Baltimore, Maryland, 2000.

Mayflower Marriages by Susan E. Roser, Mayflower Marriages form the files of George Earnest Bowman at the Massachusetts Society of Mayflower Descendants, Genealogical Publishing Company, Baltimore, Maryland, 1990.

Of Plymouth Plantation 1620-1647 by William Bradford, edited with an Introduction & Notes by Samuel Eliot Morison. Alfred A. Knopf, New York, 1993.

Mayflower, Voyage, Community, War by Nathaniel Philbrick, Penguin Books, 2020.

The Pilgrims A Documentary Film by Ric Burns, PBS edition, "The American Experience." (DVD)

The Mayflower History Documentary by Caleb. H. Johnson www.mayflowerhistory.com

The Mayflower and Her Passengers by Caleb H. Johnson, 2005.

The Signers of the Mayflower Compact by Annie Arnoux Haxton Part II, New York, 1897.

The History of the Town of Plymouth published by the Plymouth Historical Society, 1885.

The "Silver Books" Mayflower Families Through Five Generations Volume III, George Soule, Published by the General Society of Mayflower Descendants, 1980.

Saga of the Pilgrims: From Europe to the New World. by John Harris, The Globe Pequot Press, Chester, Connecticut, 1990.

The Plymouth Collection Genealogy at the Plymouth Public Library 132 South Street, Plymouth, Massachusetts 02360 Phone (508) 830-4250.

Plimouth Plantation www.plimoth.org

Author is a Life Member of the General Society of Mayflower Descendants, the Massachusetts chapter as well as The Soule Kindred in America, Duxbury, Massachusetts.

Chapter 29: The Soules of N.B. & N.S., Canada

The Soule Family Line of Canada

George Soule "Pilgrim" Abt. 1600-1679	Mary Becket Abt. 1600-1676
Nathaniel Soule Abt. 1637-1699	Rose Thorne Abt. 1635-1705
Jacob Soule 1687-1748	Rebecca Gifford 1689-1747
Stephen Soule Sr. 1726-Abt. 1789	Sarah Potter 1724-1789
Stephen Soule Jr. Abt. 1745-1840	Rachael Sands Abt. 1740-Aft. 1770
Amy Frances Soule 1770-Aft. 1821	Michael Atkinson Sr. 1771-Aft. 1840

1. George Soule Sr. "THE PILGRIM" (Immigrant)

GEORGE[1] SOULE SR. "THE PILGRIM"

- Born circa 1600 in Elkington, Worcestershire, England.
- Married circa 1626 Mary Becket in Plymouth, Plymouth Co., Massachusetts. Mary Becket Soule died in December 1676 at the age of approx. 51 in Duxbury, Plymouth Co., Massachusetts.
- Died 22 January 1679 in Duxbury, Plymouth Co., Massachusetts at the age of 79.

George Soule lived in Plymouth, Massachusetts from 1620 to circa 1640 as Plymouth is where four of his nine children were born. The other five children were born in Duxbury, Massachusetts (about 19 miles north of Plymouth) and this is where the family moved to. It is in Duxbury that both George and his wife Mary Becket Soule died. The George Soule family lived in Duxbury from circa 1640 to circa 1679, a period of approx. 39 years.

For much more information on George Soule "THE PILGRIM" and his wife Mary Becket, see the Soule of Massachusetts Chapter in this Volume.

Children of GEORGE[1] SOULE SR. "THE PILGRIM" and MARY BECKET were:

	i.	**ZACHARIAH** Soule b. 22 May 1627 in Plymouth, Plymouth Co., Massachusetts. Zachariah married Margaret Ford. They were married circa 1650 in Plymouth Co., Massachusetts. There are no recorded children from this marriage. Zachariah's death date and location at death are also unknown.
	ii.	**JOHN** Soule b. circa 1632 in Plymouth, Plymouth Co., Massachusetts. John married twice. Wife #1 Rebecca Simonson. They were married circa 1656 in Duxbury,

		Plymouth Co., Massachusetts. John and Rebecca had 9 children during their marriage. Wife #2 Esther Nash Sampson. They were married in 1678 in Duxbury, Plymouth Co. Massachusetts. Esther had been a widow of **Samuel Sampson who was killed in King Philip's War.**
2A	iii.	**NATHANIEL SOULE** b. circa 1637 in Plymouth, Plymouth Co., Massachusetts. Nathaniel may have caused the most colony trouble of any of his siblings. See 2A. Nathaniel married Rose Thorn. They were married circa 1681 in Plymouth Co., Massachusetts. Nathaniel fathered a child by an Indian woman prior to this marriage. Nathaniel and Rose had 5 children during their marriage. Nathaniel died circa 1699 at the age of approx. 62 in Dartmouth, Plymouth Co., Massachusetts.
	iv.	**GEORGE Soule JR.** b. circa 1639 in Plymouth, Plymouth Co., Massachusetts. George Jr. married Deborah Thomas. They were married circa 1665 in Dartmouth, Plymouth Co., Massachusetts. They had 8 children in this marriage. George died circa 1704 at the age of approx. 65 in Dartmouth, Plymouth Co., Massachusetts.
2B.	v.	**SUSANNA Soule** b. circa 1642 in Duxbury, Plymouth Co., Massachusetts. Susanna married Francis West Sr. They had 9 children during this marriage. Susanna died on 2 January 1707 in Kings Towne, Washington Co., Rhode Island at the age of 65.
	vi.	**MARY SOULE** b. circa 1644 in Duxbury, Plymouth Co., Massachusetts. Mary married John Peterson circa 1666 in Duxbury, Plymouth Co., Massachusetts. Mary died after 1720 at the age of approx. 76 in Plymouth, Plymouth., Massachusetts.
	vii.	**ELIZABETH SOULE** b. circa 1645 in Duxbury, Plymouth Co., Massachusetts. **Elizabeth, like her brother Nathaniel, also got into some mischief. See below. Elizabeth had been charged and whipped for fornication twice prior to marriage. Following this incident, a year later, she married Francis Walker circa 1668 in Duxbury, Plymouth Co., Massachusetts. It is unknown if Elizabeth and Francis had any children. Elizabeth died circa 1700 at approx. age 55 in Middleboro "Namassakett," Plymouth Co., Massachusetts.
	viii.	**PATIENCE SOULE** b. circa 1648 in Duxbury, Plymouth Co., Massachusetts. Patience married John Haskell in January 1666 in Middleboro "Namassakett," Plymouth Co., Massachusetts. Patience and John had 8 children in their marriage. Patience died on 11 March 1705 at the age of approx. 57 in Middleboro "Namassakett," Plymouth Co., Massachusetts.
	ix.	**BENJAMIN SOULE** b. circa 1652 in Duxbury, Plymouth Co., Massachusetts. **Benjamin died on 26 March 1676 at the age of approx. 24 in King Philip's War in Pawtucket, Providence Co., Rhode Island.** Benjamin died unmarried and had no children.

2A. Nathaniel Soule

NATHANIEL[2A] SOULE (George[1])

- Born circa 1637 in Plymouth, Plymouth Co., Massachusetts.
- Married circa 1681 Rose Thorne (circa 1635-December 1705). Nathaniel and Rose were married in Plymouth, Plymouth Co., Massachusetts.
- Died 12 October 1699 Dartmouth, Plymouth Co., Massachusetts at the age of approx. 62.

Nathaniel may have caused the newest colony more trouble than any of his siblings. On 5 March 1667/8, he made an appearance in Plymouth court to "answer for his abusing of Mr. John Holmes, teacher of the church of Christ at Duxbury, by many false, scandalous and opprobrious speeches." He was sentenced to make a public apology for his actions, find sureties for future good behavior and to sit in the stocks, with the stock sentence remitted. His father George and brother John had to pay surety for Nathaniel's good behavior with he is being bound for monies and to pay a fine. Three years later, on 5 June 1671, he was fined for "telling several lies which tended greatly to the hurt of the Colony in reference to some particulars about the Indians."

Nathaniel fathered a child by an Indian woman prior his marriage with Rose Thorne. For this, he was punished. On 1 March 1674/5 he was sentenced to be whipped for "lying with an Indian woman," and had to pay a fine in the form of bushels of corn to the Indian woman towards the keeping of her child.

Child of NATHANEIL[2A] SOULE SR. and a NATIVE INDIAN WOMAN ____ was:

	i.	**INDIAN CHILD ___** b. 1673 in Plymouth, Plymouth Co., Massachusetts. This child was born out of wedlock. Nathaniel (his/her father) was 36 years old when this child was born. The Indian woman kept her child and Nathaniel was punished with a whipping and he had to pay a fine in the form of bushels of corn to the Indian woman for child support. No further information is known about this child.

Children of NATHANEIL[2A] SOULE SR. and ROSE THORNE were:

	i.	**NATHANIEL SOULE JR.** b. 12 January 1681 in Dartmouth, Bristol Co., Massachusetts Nathaniel Jr. married Meribah Gifford (1687-ca.1732). Meribah had been born on 31 October 1687 in Sandwich, Barnstable Co., Massachusetts. They were married 20 July 1708 in Dartmouth, Bristol Co., Massachusetts. Meribah was the daughter of Christopher Gifford and Deborah Perry. Nathaniel Jr. was 27 at the time of his marriage and Meribah was 21. They had 4 children during their marriage, all born in Dartmouth, Massachusetts. Nathaniel Jr. died 2 June 1766 at the age of 85 in Dartmouth, Bristol Co., Massachusetts.
	ii.	**SYLVANUS SOULE** b. 1683 in Dartmouth, Bristol Co., Massachusetts. It is not known if he ever married and had any children. His death date and location at death are also both unknown. Age at death is unknown.
	iii.	**MARY SOULE** b. 1684 in Dartmouth, Bristol Co., Massachusetts. It is not known if she ever married and had any children. Her death date and location at death are also both unknown. Age at death is unknown.
	iv.	**SUSANNAH SOULE** b. 1685 in Dartmouth, Bristol Co., Massachusetts. It is not known if she ever married and had any children. Her death date and location at death are also both unknown. Age at death is unknown.
	v.	**SARAH SOULE** b. 1686 in Dartmouth, Bristol Co., Massachusetts. It is not known if she ever married and had any children. Her death date and location at death are also both unknown. Age at death is unknown.

3A.	vi.	**JACOB SOULE** b. 1687 in Dartmouth, Bristol Co., Massachusetts. Jacob married Rebecca Gifford (1689-1747). They were married 22 January 1709 in Dartmouth, Bristol Co., Massachusetts. Jacob and Rebecca had 8 children during their marriage. Jacob died 3 May 1748 at the age of 61 in Dartmouth, Bristol Co., Massachusetts.
	vi.	**MYLES SOULE** b. 1690 in Dartmouth, Bristol Co., Massachusetts. It is not known if he ever married and had any children. His death date and location at death are also both unknown. Age at his death is unknown.

3A. Jacob Soule

JACOB[3A] SOULE (Nathanuel[2A], George[1])

- Born 1687 in Dartmouth, Bristol Co., Massachusetts.
- Married 22 January 1709 Rebecca Gifford (1689-12 August 1747). Rebecca died at the age of 38. She was the daughter of Robert Gifford and Sarah Wing.
- Died 3 May 1748 in Dartmouth, Bristol Co., Massachusetts at the age of 61.

Children of JACOB[3A] SOULE and REBECCA GIFFORD were:

	i.	**JOSEPH SOULE** b. 16 February 1710 in Dartmouth, Bristol Co., Massachusetts. Joseph married Mary Davis (1710-1749). Joseph and Mary were married 8 April 1736 in Dartmouth, Bristol Co., Massachusetts. They had 4 children during their marriage. Joseph died before 7 May 1793 at the age of 83 in Westport, Bristol Co., Massachusetts.
	ii.	**ELIZABETH SOULE** b. 14 November 1712 in Dartmouth, Bristol Co., Massachusetts. Elizabeth married Caleb Tripp (1714-1780). Elizabeth and Caleb were married in 1735. They had 3 children during their marriage. Elizabeth died after her last child Rebecca was born on 9 June 11, 1744, in Dartmouth, Bristol Co., Massachusetts. Elizabeth was 32 at the time of her death.
	iii.	**OLIVER SOULE** b. 7 September 714 in Dartmouth, Bristol Co., Massachusetts. Oliver died on 4 January 1715 at the age of 3 days short of being 4 months old. He died in Dartmouth, Bristol Co., Massachusetts.
	iv.	**REBECCA SOULE** b. 18 December 1715 in Dartmouth, Bristol Co., Massachusetts. Rebecca married Reuben Waite (circa 1715-1757). Rebecca and Reuben were married circa 1735 in Dartmouth, Bristol Co., Massachusetts. They had 2 children during their marriage. Rebecca died before March of 1745 at the age of approx. 30 in Dartmouth, Bristol Co., Massachusetts.
	v.	**NATHANIEL SOULE** b. 23 January 1717 in Dartmouth, Bristol Co., Massachusetts. Nathaniel married Jane Potter (1717-1807). Nathaniel and Jane were married in 1741 in Dartmouth, Bristol Co., Massachusetts. They had 3 children during their marriage. Nathaniel died 20 November 1769 at the age of 52 in Dartmouth, Bristol Co., Massachusetts.
	vi.	**BENJAMIN SOULE** b. 18 November 1719 in Dartmouth, Bristol Co., Massachusetts. Benjamin married Meribah Waite in 1742 They had 2 children during this marriage. Benjamin died 31 January 1803 at the age of 83 in Westport, Bristol Co., Massachusetts.
	vii.	**ROSEMOND SOULE** b. 28 July 1723 in Dartmouth, Bristol Co., Massachusetts.

		Rosemond married Nathaniel Potter (1719-1801). Rosemond and Nathaniel married in 1743. They had 6 children during their marriage. Rosemond died circa 1801 at the age of 77. Her location at death is unknown.
4A.	viii	**STEPHEN SOULE SR.** b. 1 January 1726 in Dartmouth, Bristol Co., Massachusetts. Stephen Sr. married Sarah Potter (1724-1789). Sarah was the daughter of William Potter and Mary Fish. Stephen and Sarah were married in 1744 and had 6 children during their marriage. Stephen Sr. died circa April 1789 at the age of approx. 63 in Westport, Bristol Co., Massachusetts.

Several of the Soule children and the Potter children intermarried. Also, several Soule children and the Waite children also intermarried. They all lived in Dartmouth, Bristol Co., Massachusetts.

Soule siblings married Potter siblings

Nathaniel Soule married Jane Potter in 1741.

Rosemond Soule married Nathaniel Potter in 1743.

Stephen Soule Sr. married Sarah Potter in 1744.

Soule siblings married Waite siblings

Rebecca Soule married Reuben Waite in 1735.

Benjamin Soule married Meribah Waite in 1742.

4A. Stephen Soule Sr.

STEPHEN^{4A} SOULE SR. (Jacob^{3A}, Nathanuel^{2A}, George^{1})

- Born 1 January 1726 in Dartmouth, Bristol Co., Massachusetts.
- Married Sarah Potter (1724-1789). Stephen Sr. and Sarah were married in 1744. Sarah was the daughter of William Potter and Mary Fish. They were married in Dartmouth, Bristol Co., Massachusetts.
- Died circa April 1789 in Westport, Bristol Co., Massachusetts at the age of 63.

Children of STEPHEN^{4A} SOULE SR. and SARAH POTTER were:

5A.	i.	**STEPHEN SOULE JR.** b. circa 1745 in Dartmouth, Bristol Co., Massachusetts. Stephen Jr. married Rachael Sands (1750-after 1770). They were married in 1767 and had 2 children during their marriage. Stephen Sr. died circa April 1789 at the age of approx. 63 in Westport, Bristol Co., Massachusetts.
	ii.	**Phebe Soule** b. circa 1750 in Dartmouth, Bristol Co., Massachusetts. Phebe married Gideon Church. They were married 29 March 1772 and moved to Sydney, Maine and later moved to Gardiner, Maine. They had 1 child named Eliza during their marriage. Phebe died after 12 June 1819 in Gardiner, Maine at age approx. 69.
	ii.	**OLIVER SOULE** b. circa 1755 in Dartmouth, Bristol Co., Massachusetts. Oliver married twice. Wife #1 Eleanor Potter on 5 September 1776 in Dartmouth, Bristol Co., Massachusetts. Oliver and Eleanor had 6 children during their marriage. Wife #2 Susannah Trafford. They were married on 12 November 1815 in Westport, Bristol Co.,

		Massachusetts. There were no children born during their marriage. Oliver died in Westport, Massachusetts circa 1830 at the age of approx. 75.
	iv.	**JACOB SOULE** (Revolutionary War) b. circa 1760 in Dartmouth, Bristol Co., Massachusetts. Jacob married Abigail Tripp on 28 August 1783 in Dartmouth, Bristol Co., Massachusetts. Jacob and Abigail had 3 children during their marriage. Jacob died 15 April 1825 in Westport, Bristol Co., Massachusetts at the age of 75.
	v.	**SARAH SOULE** b. circa 1765 in Dartmouth, Bristol Co., Massachusetts. It is not known whom Sarah married or if she had any children. She is mentioned in her father's will so she lived following her father's death in 1726. Her actual death date and her location at death are both unknown.
	vi.	**BENJAMIN SOULE** b. December 1767 in Dartmouth, Bristol Co., Massachusetts. Benjamin married Sarah Potter on 24 July 1793 in Westport, Bristol Co., Massachusetts. They had 3 children during their marriage. Their son Israel and daughters Ruby and Miriam are all mentioned in Benjamin's will. Benjamin Soule died 26 January 1838 at the age of 63 in Westport, Bristol Co., Massachusetts.

5A. Stephen Soule Jr. (Emigrated)

STEPHEN^{5A} SOULE (Stephen Jr.^{4A}, Jacob^{3A}, Nathanuel^{2A}, George^1)

- Born circa 1745 in Duxbury, Plymouth Co., Massachusetts.
- Emigrated circa 1765 to St. John, St. John Co, New Brunswick, Canada from Massachusetts, United States.
- Married 1767 Rachael Sands (1750–after 1770). They were married at River St. John, New Brunswick, Canada.
- Died 16 January 1840 St. John, St. John Co., New Brunswick, Canada at age approx. 95.

Two Possible Reasons Why He Left His Country of Origin

As did many colonists of the 1760-1770 era in the New England area, land grants were offered to them in New Brunswick and Nova Scotia. It may have been this call that Stephen responded to. He met his bride (Rachael Sands) in New Brunswick and his two daughters met their husbands in Nova Scotia.

However, Stephen Jr. could have been a Loyalist and left New England because of a Loyalist viewpoint regarding the Crown of England. His oldest daughter (Mary Soule Clark) was buried years later in the Loyalist Cemetery in New Brunswick. She died in Nova Scotia, but she made plans for her body to be returned to St. John, New Brunswick. She could have been buried there next to her husband or near her parents. The true reason for her being buried in a Loyalist Cemetery is still very much unknown.

Stephen Soule Jr. is <u>not</u> mentioned in his father Stephen Sr.'s will, so there may have been some difficulties in family relationships at this time, resulting also in Stephen Jr.'s leaving his country of origin.

Children of STEPHEN^{5A} SOULE JR. and RACHAEL SANDS were:

	i.	**Mary Soule** b. 1768 in River St. John. Mary married William S. Clark (1764-___). Mary and William married 8 June 1793 in Maccan, Cumberland Co., Nova Scotia. Mary and William S. had 2 children (Sally and James) during their marriage. Mary died 6 October 1856 at the age of 88 as a widow. William had preceded her in death.

		She died in Southampton, Cumberland Co., Nova Scotia. She is buried in the United Empire Loyalist Cemetery in St. John, St. John Co., New Brunswick. See Cemetery Sign below. She and her husband were of the Church of England (high Episcopal faith).
6A.	ii.	**Amy Frances Soule** b. 1770 in River St. John, St. John Co., New Brunswick. Amy Frances married Michael Atkinson Sr. (Immigrant) (1771-1849). They were married 3 January 1797 in Southampton, Cumberland Co., Nova Scotia, Canada. Amy Frances and Michael Sr. had 13 children. Amy Frances died after 1821 at the age of approx. 51 in Southampton, Cumberland Co., Nova Scotia. Amy and her husband were of the United Baptist faith.

Mary Soule Clark (1768-1856) is buried here:

Church of England Cemetery
St. John, St. John Co., New Brunswick
Plot # SW120

6A. Amy Frances Soule

AMY[6A] FRANCES SOULE (Stephen Jr.[5A], Stephen Jr.[4A], Jacob[3A], Nathanuel[2A], George[1])

- Born 1770 in River St. John, St. John Co., New Brunswick, Canada.
- Married 3 January 1797 Michael Atkinson Sr. (Immigrant) in Southampton, Cumberland Co., Nova Scotia. Michael Sr. was the son of John Atkinson Sr. and his wife Frances ___. Michael Sr. and Amy Frances had 13 children.
- Died after 1821 in Southampton, Cumberland Co., Nova Scotia at the age of approx. 51.

Children of AMY[6A] FRANCES SOULE and MICHAEL ATKINSON SR. documented in the Atkinson chapter.

Amy's father, Stephen Soule, was a direct ancestor of George Soule, the Pilgrim Father who settled in Duxbury, Plymouth Co., Massachusetts in the 1620 era.

The George Soule "The Pilgrim" Genealogy is that of the Author's Paternal **Grandfather James Wintfield Kearney** through George Soule the Pilgrim's daughter **Susanna Soule**.

The George Soule "The Pilgrim" Genealogy is that of Authors' Paternal **Grandmother Alberta Atkinson (who was James W. Kearney's wife)** through George Soule (The Pilgrim)'s son **Nathaniel Soule**.

244

The connection is with George Soule, The Pilgrim's two children Nathaniel and Susanna:

Nathaniel Soule -> Alberta Atkinson (Author's paternal grandmother).

Susanna Soule -> James Wintfield Kearney (Author's paternal grandfather).

*Nathaniel Soule and **Susanna Soule were brother and sister.

*Nathaniel Soule->Jacob Soule->Stephen Soule Sr.->Stephen Soule Jr.->Amy Frances Soule married Michael Atkinson Sr.->John William Atkinson->Rufus Atkinson->Alberta Atkinson who married James W. Kearney.

**Susanna Soule married Francis West->Martha West married Jeremiah Fones->Captain Daniel Fones->Mary Fones married Johnathan Vickery IV->Susannah Vickery married

Fones Yorke->Amelia Yorke married William Smith->Salina Smith married George W. Kearney-> James W. Kearney married Alberta Atkinson.

So, there is a double Soule connection here. James and Alberta never realized that they were cousins. This was discovered by this author just recently, which is many years after both James and Alberta (author's paternal grandparents) had died.

Source Citations for this Chapter

Genealogies of Mayflower Families by Gary Boyd Roberts, New England Historical& Genealogical Register, Volume II Reprinted for the Clearfield Company Inc. by the Genealogical Publishing Co., Baltimore, Maryland, 2000.

Mayflower Marriages by Susan E. Roser, Mayflower Marriages form the files of George Earnest Bowman at the Massachusetts Society of Mayflower Descendants, Genealogical Publishing Company, Baltimore, Maryland, 1990.

Of Plymouth Plantation 1620-1647 by William Bradford, edited with an Introduction & Notes by Samuel Eliot Morison. Alfred A. Knopf, New York, 1993.

Mayflower, Voyage, Community, War by Nathaniel Philbrick, Penguin Books, 2020.

The Pilgrims A Documentary Film by Ric Burns, PBS edition, "The American Experience." (DVD)

The Mayflower History Documentary by Caleb. H. Johnson www.mayflowerhistory.com

The Mayflower and Her Passengers by Caleb H. Johnson, 2005.

The Signers of the Mayflower Compact by Annie Arnoux Haxton Part II, New York, 1897.

The History of the Town of Plymouth published by the Plymouth Historical Society, 1885.

The "Silver Books" Mayflower Families Through Five Generations Volume III, George Soule, Published by the General Society of Mayflower Descendants, 1980.

Saga of the Pilgrims: From Europe to the New World. by John Harris, The Globe Pequot Press, Chester, Connecticut, 1990.

The Plymouth Collection Genealogy at the Plymouth Public Library 132 South Street, Plymouth, Massachusetts 02360 Phone (508) 830-4250.

Plimouth Plantation www.plimoth.org

Author is a Life Member of the General Society of Mayflower Descendants, the Massachusetts chapter as well as The Soule Kindred in America, Duxbury, Massachusetts.

Chapter 30: The Staffords

The Stafford Family Line

Lord Henry Stafford 1501-1563	Lady Ursula Pole 1504-1570
Richard Stafford Sr. 1539-1632	Maria Corbet 1550-1634
Baron Roger Stafford 1572-1640	Baroness Ellen Earle 1583-1625
Thomas Stafford Sr. 1605-1677	Elizabeth Isabelle Leigh Ca 1605-1677
Joseph Stafford Sr. 1648-1697	Sarah Holden 1658-1731
Elizabeth Stafford 1682-1756	William Case Sr. 1681-1739

1. Lord Henry Stafford – 1st Baron of Stafford

LORD HENRY[1] STAFFORD SR.

- Born 18 September 1501 in Abergraveary, Monmouthshire, Wales.
- Married 16 February 1519 Lady Ursula Pole. Lord Henry and Lady Ursula were married in London, Middlesex, England. Lady Ursula Pole was born 1504 in Congletom, Asbury, Chestershire, England. She died on 12 August 1570 Warwickshire, England at age 66.
- Died 30 April 1563 Cases Castle, Salop, England age of 62.

What is a Baron and a Baroness?

An English Baron is a rank of nobility, often hereditary. Typically, the title denotes an aristocrat who ranks higher that a Lord or Knight but lower than a Viscount or Count. Ranking from highest to lowest is Duke, Marquess, Earl, Viscount and Baron, Lord, Knight. Many times, their title regardless of ranking status, is referred to as Lord. Baroness is a wife or a widow of a Baron.

Lord Henry De Stafford 1st Baron of Stafford
2nd Duke of Buckingham

Parents of Lord Henry Stafford 1st Baron of Stafford:
<u>Lord Henry's Father Edward Stafford 3rd Duke of Buckingham</u>
Born: 3 February 1477 Breaknock Castle in Breconshire, Wales
Married: 14 December 1490 Leconfield, Yorkshire, England
Died: 15 May 1521 in London, Greater City of London, England age 44

<u>Lord Henry's Mother was Lady Eleanor Percy, Duchess of Buckingham</u>
Born: 1474 in Leconfield, East Riding, Yorkshire, England
Died: 13 February 1530 in Grey Friars, London, Middlesex. England age 56

Lady Ursula Pole -- 1st Baroness of Stafford
Wife of Lord Henry De Stafford 1st Baron of Stafford

Born 16 February 1504 Isleworth, Middlesex, England
Married 16 February 1524 age 20
Died 12 Aug 1570 age 66

Parents of Ursula Pole:

Ursula's Father was Sir Richard Pole "Knight of the Garter."

He was a valiant and expert commander in the wars of Scotland. He was the Constable of Harlech and Montgomery Castles. He was also the High Sheriff of Merinethshire and Chief Gentleman of the Privy Chamber of Arthur. He was also Prince of Wales.

Born: 1462 Mendlesham, Buckingham, England.
Married: 22 September 1494 Isleworth, Middlesex, England.
Died: 18 December 1505 beheaded the Tower of London, Middlesex, England age 43.

Ursula's Mother was Lady Margaret Plantagenet, 3rd Countess of Salisbury.
She was called "Blessed Margaret." She was the daughter of the Duke of Clarence who was a brother of King Edward IV. Lady Margaret was among the few surviving members of the Plantagenet Dynasty.
Born: 14 August 1473 Farley Castle, Bath, Avon, England.
Died: 28 May 1541 beheaded the Tower of London, Middlesex, England age 68.

House of Plantagenet
Royal House

Armorial of Plantagenet

The House of Plantagenet
1154-1485

The House of Plantagenet was a royal house which originated from the lands of Anjou in France. They held the English throne from 1154 with the accession of Henry II at the end of the Anarchy crisis until 1485 when Richard III died in battle. Under the reign of the Plantagenet House, England was transformed. They were in power when the Magna Carta was signed. There was rivalry between the House of Plantagenet's two cadet branches of York and Lancaster which brought, about the famous **War of Roses**, a decade-long fight for English succession, culminating in the Battle of Bosworth Field in 1485, when the reign of the Plantagenets and the English Middle Ages both met their end with the death of King Richard III. Henry VII, of Lancastrian descent, became king of England. Five months later he married Elizabeth of York, thus ending the War of the Roses, and giving rise to the Tudor Dynasty. The Tudors worked to centralize English royal power, which allowed them to avoid some of the problems that had plagued the last Plantagenet rulers. The resulting stability allowed for the English Renaissance, and the advent of the early modern Britain which is in power today.

Children of LORD HENRY[1] STAFFORD and LADY URSULA POLE were:

	i.	**DOROTHY STAFFORD** b. 1 October 1526. Dorothy married Sir William Stafford of Grafton, Baron of Chelsey. It is not known if they had any children. Dorothy died on 22 September 1604 at St Margaret Church Westminster, London, England at age 78.
	ii.	**THOMAS STAFFORD "THE REBEL"** b. 1531 at Caus Castle, Shropshire, England. Thomas was never married and had no children. Thomas died 28 May 1557 at the Tower of London, London, Middlesex, England at the age of 26. *
	iii.	**SIR HENRY STAFFORD 2ND BARON** b. 1534 at Shropshire, England. Sir Henry married Elizabeth ____. It is unknown if they had any children. Henry died 7 January 1565 in Staffordshire, England at the age of 31.
	iv.	**EDWARD STAFFORD 4TH BARON** 7 January 1535 at Stafford Castle in Staffordshire, England. Edward married Mary Stanley at the Stafford castle. The couple married on 23 November 1558. It is not known if they had any children. Edward died 18 October 1603 at the Stafford Castle, in Staffordshire, England at the age of 68.
.	v..	**MARGARET STAFFORD** b. 1536 Isleworth, London, England. It is unknown if she ever married and had any children. Her death date and location at death are also unknown.
	vi.	**TWIN: WALTER STAFFORD 3RD BARON** b. 1539. Walter never married. He died in 1571 at the Stafford Castle, in Staffordshire, England at age 32.
2.	vii.	**TWIN: HONORABLE RICHARD STAFFORD SR. 5TH BARON** b. 1539 in Staffordshire, England. Richard Sr. married twice: Wife #1 Maria Corbet. Richard and Maria were married in 1559 in Warwickshire, England. They had 4 children during their marriage. Wife #2 Ann Jeffrey. Richard and Ann were married on 29 October 1580. They had 1 child during their marriage, Richard died on 1 October 1632 Congleton, Asbury, Chestershire, England at the age of 93.
	viii.	**JANE STAFFORD** b. 1547 Jane never married and had no children. Her death date and place of death are both unknown.

- **Thomas "The Rebel" Stafford (1531-1557)**

Thomas was known as "The Rebel." He travelled to both Italy and Poland and made it well known that he opposed Queen Mary's Spanish marriage. He claimed he was from royal descent on both sides of his family (which was true). He had two ships and sailed from his travels into Scarborough, England. There he was captured in April 1557 and was taken to the Tower of London where he was hanged for treason on 28 May 1557. He was 26 years old.

2. Honorable Richard Stafford Sr. 5th Baron

HONORABLE RICHARD[2] STAFFORD SR. (Lord Henry[1])

- Born 1539 Congleton, Asbury, Chestershire, England.
- Married 1559 Wife #1 Baroness Maria Corbet (b. 1550 -18 June 1634). Richard and Maria were married in Congleton, Asbury, Chestershire, England. Maria died at the age of 84. (There were 4 children during this marriage.)
- Married 29 October 1580 Wife #2 Ann Jeffrey. Richard and Ann were married in Exhall near Coventry, Warwickshire, England. (There was 1 child during this marriage.)
- Died 1 October 1632 Congleton, Asbury, Chestershire, England at the age of 93.

Remnant of the 1400 Corbet Castle, still standing in Salop, England

Children of HONORABLE RICHARD[2] STAFFORD and MARIA CORBET were:

	i.	**RICHARD STAFFORD JR.** b. 1568 in Avon, Warwickshire, England. It is unknown if he ever married or had any children. Richard died 15 October 1737 in Bakewell, Derbyshire, England at the age of 69.
	ii.	**ROBERT STAFFORD** b. 1571 in Avon, Warwickshire, England. It is unknown if he ever married and had any children. Robert died in 1640 England at the age of 69.
	iii.	**TWIN: JOHN STAFFORD** b. 2 February 1572 in Warwick, Warwickshire, England. It is unknown if he ever married and had any children. John died in 1620 in Avon, Warwickshire, England at the age of 48.
3.	iv.	**TWIN: ROGER STAFFORD** b. 2 February 1572 Warwick, Warwickshire, England. Roger was married twice: Wife #1 Ellen Earle (1583-1625). They were married on 27 November 1595 in Warwickshire, England. Roger and Ellen had 3 sons during their marriage. Wife #2 Margaret Woodward were married on 1 May 1615 in Derbyshire, England. Roger and Margaret had no children during their marriage. Roger died in 1640 Warwickshire, England at the age of 68.

Child of HONORABLE RICHARD STAFFORD and AN JEFFREY was:

	i.	**LADY JANE STAFFORD** b. 1581 Malpas, Chestershire, England. Lady Jane married. Thomas Beaumont circa 1600 Malpas, Chestershire, England. It is unknown if Jane and Thomas had any children. Jane died 1637 in Malpas, Chestershire. England at age 56.

3. Baron Roger Stafford 6th Baron

ROGER[3] STAFFORD SR: 6TH BARON (Richard[2] Sr., Lord Henry[1])

- Born 2 February 1572 in Warwick, Warwickshire, England. Roger was a twin of John Stafford.
- Married 1600 Wife #1 Baroness Ellen Earle (1583-1625). Roger and Ellen were married on 27 November 1595 in Warwickshire, England. They had 3 children during this marriage.
- Married Wife #2 Margaret Woodward (1586-1626). Roger and Margaret were married in 1625. There were no children by this 2nd marriage.
- Died 1640 in Warwickshire, England age of 68.

Children of BARON ROGER[3] STAFFORD SR. and BARONESS ELLEN EARLE were:

	i.	**JOHN STAFFORD JR.** b. 1602 in Avon, Warwickshire, England. It is unknown if he ever married and had any children. John Jr. died in 1674 at St. Laurence Heavor, Derbyshire, England at the age of 72.
4.	ii.	**THOMAS STAFFORD SR.** (IMMIGRANT) b. 1605 in Warwickshire, England. Thomas Sr. married Elizabeth Isabelle Leigh (1614-1677). Thomas and Elizabeth Isabelle were married in 1631 in England. They immigrated to the new colony in America and arrived in Rhode Island circa 1632. They had 6 children during their marriage. Thomas died 4 November 1677 in Warwick, Kent Co., Rhode Island at the age of 72.
	iii..	**WILLIAM STAFFORD** (IMMIGRANT) b. 1606 in Avon, Warwickshire, England. It is unknown if he ever married and had any children. William died in 1655 in Elizabethtown, Bladen Co., North Carolina at the age of 49.

The Medieval Castle of our Stafford Family
The Stafford Castle in Staffordshire, England
Circa 1400

4. Thomas Stafford Sr. (Immigrant)

THOMAS[4] STAFFORD SR (Baron Roger[3], Richard[2] Sr., Lord Henry[1])

- Born 1605 in Warwickshire, England.
- Married circa 1631 Elizabeth Isabelle Leigh (1614-1677). Thomas and Elizabeth married in Warwickshire, England.
- Arrived circa 1632 in Rhode Island.
- Died 1677 in Warwick, Kent Co., Rhode Island at the age of 72 years.

The year was about 1626 when Thomas Stafford, a young man, came from Warwickshire, England to the new colony and became an inhabitant of Plymouth. From there he moved to Providence, Rhode Island, where he erected the first grist mill in Rhode Island. The mill was situated at the north end of town near the mill bridge. It is not known how long he lived there, but from there he moved to Old Warwick, in Rhode Island. There he obtained a considerable tract of land at the head of Mill Cove, including the present mill site, where he erected another grist mill. It was there in Old Warwick where he spent the remainder of his days and died there in 1677 at the age of 72 years.

Children of THOMAS[4] STAFFORD SR. and ELIZABETH ISABELLE LEIGH were:

	i.	**THOMAS STAFFORD JR.** b. circa 1632 in Newport, Newport Co., Rhode Island. Thomas Jr. married twice: Wife #1 Jane Dodge. Thomas and Jane were married on 21 December 1671 in Warwick, Kent Co., Rhode Island. Wife #2 Sarah _____ married circa 1700 in Warwick, Kent Co., Rhode Island. It is unknown how many children Thomas Jr. had in either marriage. Thomas died. 20 January 1723 in Warwick, Kent Co., Rhode Island at the age of approx. 91.
	ii.	**SAMUEL STAFFORD** b. 1636 in Warwick, Kent Co., Rhode Island, married Mercy Westcott circa 1656 in Warwick, Kent Co., Rhode Island. It is unknown if they had any children during their marriage. Samuel died on 20 March 1718 in Warwick, Kent Co., Rhode Island at the age of 82.
	iii.	**HANNAH STAFFORD** b. circa 1640 in Warwick, Kent Co., Rhode Island. Hannah married Luke Bromley circa 1660 in Warwick, Kent Co., Rhode Island. It is unknown if they had any children during their marriage. Hannah died circa 1692 in Warwick, Kent Co., Rhode Island at the age of approx. 52.
	iv.	**SARAH STAFFORD** b. circa 1645 in Warwick, Kent Co., Rhode Island. Sarah married Amos Westcott 13 July 1667 in Warwick, Kent Co., Rhode Island. It is unknown if they had any children during their short marriage. They were only married for 2 years when Sarah died in 1669 in Warwick, Kent Co. Rhode Island at the age of 24.
5	v.	**JOSEPH STAFFORD SR.** b. 21 March 1648 in Warwick, Kent Co., Rhode Island. Joseph Sr. married Sarah Holden 21 March 1678 in Warwick, Kent Co., Rhode Island. Sarah was the daughter of Captain Randall Holden Jr. and Frances Dungan. They had 9 children during their marriage. Joseph died 1697 in Warwick, Kent Co., Rhode Island at age 49.
	vi.	**DEBORAH STAFFORD** b. 1651 in Warwick, Kent Co., Rhode Island. Deborah married Amos Westcott on 9 June 1670 in Warwick, Kent Co., Rhode Island. It is unknown if they had any children during their marriage. Deborah died in 1706 in Warwick, Kent Co., Rhode Island at the age of 55.

5. Joseph Stafford Sr.

JOSEPH[5] STAFFORD SR. (Thomas[4] Sr., Baron Roger[3], Richard[2] Sr., Lord Henry[1])

- Born 21 March 1648 in Warwick, Kent Co., Rhode Island.
- Married 21 March 1678 Sarah Holden in Warwick, Kent Co., Rhode Island. Sarah was the daughter of Captain Randall Holden Jr. and Frances Dungan.
- Died 1697 in Warwick, Kent Co, Rhode Island at age of 49.

Children of JOSEPH[5] STAFFORD SR and SARAH HOLDEN were:

	i.	**Joseph Stafford Jr.** b. 1676 in Warwick, Kent Co., Rhode Island. Joseph Jr. married twice: Wife #1 Susanna Gorton circ1715. Joseph Jr. married Wife #2 Margaret Havens circa 1736. It is unknown how many children he had during either marriage. Joseph Jr. died in 1773 at the age of 97. Location at death is unknown.
	ii.	**Frances Stafford** b. 1679 in Warwick, Kent Co., Rhode Island. Frances married Benjamin Congdon on 1 December 1701 in Warwick, Kent Co., Rhode Island. It is unknown if they had any children during their marriage. Frances died in 1774 at the age of 95. Location at death is unknown.
	iii.	**Thomas Stafford** b. 1680 in Warwick, Kent Co., Rhode Island. It is unknown if he ever married and had any children. Thomas died in 1740 at the age of 60. Location at death is unknown.
	iv.	**Twin: Captain John Stafford** b. 1682 in Warwick, Kent Co., Rhode Island. Captain married Elizabeth _____ circa 1705 in Warwick, Kent Co., Rhode Island. It is unknown if they had any children during their marriage, Captain John died in 1753 in Warwick, Kent Co., Rhode Island at the age of 71.
6.	v.	**Twin: Elizabeth Stafford** b. 1682 in Warwick, Kent Co., Rhode Island. Elizabeth married twice: Husband #1 William Case (son of Joseph Case Sr. and Hannah Smith). Elizabeth and William Sr. were married circa 1704 in South Kingston, Rhode Island. They had had 7 children during their marriage. Married Husband #2 Israel Arnold. They were married on 27 June 1730 in Rhode Island. They had 1 child during their marriage. Elizabeth died on 21 August 1756 in Rhode Island at the age of 74.
	vi.	**Mary Stafford** b. 1684 in Warwick, Kent Co., Rhode Island. Mary married Pasco Whiteford circa 1700. It is unknown if they had any children during their marriage. Mary died in 1741 at the age of 57. Location at death is unknown.
	vii.	**Stukeley Stafford** b. 1685 in Warwick, Kent Co., Rhode Island. Stukeley married Elizabeth Waterman circa 1712. It is unknown if they had any children during their marriage. Stukeley died 4 June 1790 in Warwick, Kent Co., Rhode Island at age 115!
	viii.	**Sarah Stafford** b. 1686 in Warwick, Kent Co., Rhode Island. Sarah married Joseph Smith circa 1705. It is unknown if they had any children during their marriage. Sarah died in 1727 at the age of 39.

		ix.	**MARGARET STAFFORD** b. 1688 in Warwick, Kent Co., Rhode Island. Margaret married circa 1710 but her spouse's name is unknown. It is unknown if they had any children during their marriage. Her age at death is 39.

6. Elizabeth Stafford

ELIZABETH^6 STAFFORD (Joseph^5 Sr., Thomas^4 Sr., Baron Roger^3, Richard^2 Sr., Lord Henry^1)

- Born 1682 in Warwick, Kent Co., Rhode Island.
- Married circa 1704 Husband #1 William Case Sr. Elizabeth and William Sr. were married in South Kingston, Rhode Island. William Case Sr. (1681-1739) was the son of Joseph Case Sr. and Hannah Smith. Elizabeth and William Sr. had 7 children during their marriage.
- Married 27 June 1730 Husband #2 Israel Arnold. Elizabeth and Israel were married in Rhode Island. They had 1 child during their marriage.
- Died 21 August 1756 in Rhode Island at the age of 74.

Children of Elizabeth^6 Stafford and William Case are documented in the Case Family chapter.

Child of Elizabeth^6 Stafford and Israel Arnold was:

		i.	**BATHSHEBA ARNOLD.** b. October 1732. No further information is known about her.

Source Citations for this Chapter

https://en.wikipedia.or/wiki/House_of_Plantagener#

The Genealogical Dictionary of Rhode Island by John Osborne Austin 1969 NEHGS Library Ref.
F.78/A935.

History of Warwick, Rhode Island (Settlement in 1642 to Present Time) by Oliver Payson Fuller B.A,
Providence, Rhode Island, Angell, Burlingence & Co. Printers 1875.

http://www.gbnf.com/genealog4/hansen/html/d0018/12650.HTM

Vital Records of Rhode Island: Newport Marriages. NEHGS Library, Boston, Massachusetts.

http://www.geocities.com/Heartland/Garden/7021/millardmiller/dat146.html

https://www.ancestry.com/family-tree/person/tree/173084079/person/172259902734/facts

Chapter 31: The Stantons

The Stanton Family Line

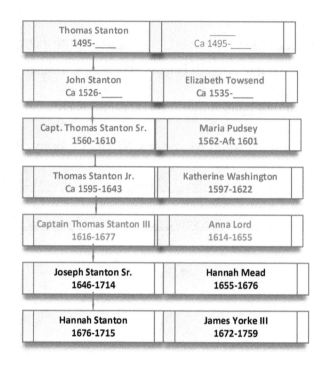

Thomas Stanton
1495-____ | Ca 1495-____

John Stanton
Ca 1526-____ | Elizabeth Towsend
Ca 1535-____

Capt. Thomas Stanton Sr.
1560-1610 | Maria Pudsey
1562-Aft 1601

Thomas Stanton Jr.
Ca 1595-1643 | Katherine Washington
1597-1622

Captain Thomas Stanton III
1616-1677 | Anna Lord
1614-1655

Joseph Stanton Sr.
1646-1714 | Hannah Mead
1655-1676

Hannah Stanton
1676-1715 | James Yorke III
1672-1759

1. Thomas Stanton

THOMAS[1] STANTON

- Born circa 1495 in Longbridge, Warwickshire, England.
- Married circa 1525 _____ Unknown.
- Died _____ date and place unknown most likely England. Age at death is unknown.

Child of THOMAS[1] STANTON and _____ was:

2.		i.	JOHN STANTON b. circa 1526-1530 in Longbridge, Warwickshire, England. John married Elizabeth Townsend in 1559. John and Elizabeth had 5 children during their marriage. John died _____ unknown date in England. Age at death is unknown.

2. John Stanton

JOHN[2] STANTON SR. (Thomas[1])

- Born circa 1526-1530 in Longbridge, Warwickshire, England.
- Married 1559 Elizabeth Townsend (born circa 1635 in Wallisdown, Dorsetshire, England. Elizabeth died at date unknown).
- Died _____ date and place unknown most likely England. Age at death unknown.

Children of JOHN[2] STANTON and ELIZABETH TOWNSEND were:

3.	i.	**CAPTAIN THOMAS STANTON SR.** b. 1560 Longbridge, Warwickshire, England. Captain Thomas Sr. married Wife #1 Susanna Fisher. Thomas Sr. and Susanna married in 1580. Susanna died in 1582. They had no children during their marriage. Wife #2 Maria Pudsey. Thomas and Maria were married in 1592. They had 4 children during their marriage. Captain Thomas died in 1610 Wolverton, Warwickshire, England at the age of 50.
	ii.	**Robert Stanton** b. 1563. Longbridge, Warwickshire, England. It is unknown if he ever married and had any children. Also, unknown is death date and location at his death.
	iii.	**RICHARD STANTON** b. 1567 Longbridge, Warwickshire, England. It is unknown if he ever married and had any children. Also, unknown is death date and location at his death.
	iv.	**ELIZABETH STANTON** b. 1567 Longbridge, Warwickshire, England. It is unknown if she ever married and had any children. Also, unknown is death date and location at death.
	v.	**MARGARETA STANTON** b. 1573 Longbridge, Warwickshire, England. It is unknown if she ever married and had any children. Also, unknown is her death date and location at her death.

3. Captain Thomas Stanton Sr.

CAPTAIN THOMAS[3] STANTON SR. (John[2], Thomas[1])

- Born circa 1560 Longbridge, Warwickshire, England.
- Married 1580 Wife #1 Susanna Fisher in Wolverton, Warwickshire, England. Susanna died in 1582.
- Married 1591 Wife #2 Maria Pudsey in Langley, Warwickshire, England. (b. 1562-__).
- Died 1610 Wolverton, Warwickshire, England at the age of 50.

No children born in the marriage of Captain Thomas Stanton Sr. and Susanna Fisher.

Children of CAPTAIN THOMAS[3] STANTON and MARIA PUDSEY were:

	i.	**DOROTHEA STANTON** b. 1591 Wolverton, Warwickshire, England. Dorothea married Walter Peyton. It is unknown if they ever had any children. Also, unknown is her death date and location at death.
	ii.	**MARIA STANTON** b. 1593 Wolverton, Warwickshire, England. It is unknown if Maria ever married and had any children. Also, unknown is her death date and location at her death.
4.	iii.	**THOMAS STANTON JR.** b. 1595 Wolverton, Warwickshire, England. Thomas Jr. married Katherine Washington in Stratford-on-Avon, Warwickshire, England in 1610. Thomas Jr. and Katherine had 3 children during their marriage. Thomas died in 1643 Wolverton, Warwickshire, England at the age of 48.
	iv.	**William Stanton** b. 1599 Wolverton, Warwickshire, England. It is unknown if William ever married and had any children. Also, unknown is his death date and location at death.

4. Thomas Stanton Jr.

THOMAS⁴ STANTON JR. (Captain Thomas³ Sr., John², Thomas¹)

- Born circa 1595 in Wolverton, Warwickshire, England.
- Married 30 July 1616 Katherine Washington (1597-1622). They were married in the Holy Trinity Church, Stratford on-Avon, Warwickshire, England. Katherine was the daughter of Walter Washington and Alice Murden. (Walter's brother was Lawrence Washington, which is President George Washington's ancestral line.) See the Washington chapter.
- Died 1643 Wolverton, Warwickshire, England at age 48.

Children of THOMAS⁴ STANTON and KATHERINE WASHINGTON were:

5.	i.	**CAPTAIN THOMAS STANTON III** (IMMIGRANT) b. 1616 Longbridge, Warwickshire, England. Captain Thomas III married Anna Lord (1614-1688) in 1637 in Hartford, Hartford Co., Connecticut. They had 10 children during their marriage. Captain Thomas III died 2 December 1677 in Stonington, New London Co., Connecticut at the age of 59.
	ii.	**Alicia Stanton** b. 1618 Longbridge, Warwickshire, England. Alicia married John Wagstaff. It is unknown how many children they had during their marriage. Alicia's death date and her location at death are also unknown.
	iii.	**THOMAS STANTON IV** b. 1621 Longbridge, Warwickshire, England. Thomas IV married Elizabeth Cooke on 28 May 1645 in Claverdon, Warwickshire, England. It is unknown if they had any children. Also, unknown is his death date and location at death.

5. Captain Thomas Stanton III (Immigrant)

(Famous Indian Interpreter)

CAPTAIN THOMAS⁵ STANTON III (Thomas⁴ Jr., Captain Thomas³ Sr., John², Thomas¹)

- Born 30 July 1616 in Wolverton, Stratford-on-Avon District, Warwickshire, England.
- Arrival 1635 in Virginia. He crossed the ocean aboard the ship *Bonaventura*.
- Arrival 1636, came to Boston in the Bay Colony per request of Gov. Winthrop.
- Married 1637 Anna Lord, (1614-1655) daughter of Thomas Lord Sr. and Dorothy Bird, in Hartford, Hartford Co., Connecticut. Anna died 4 September 1655 in Stonington, New London Co., Connecticut.
- Died 2 December 1677 in Stonington, New London Co., Connecticut at the age of 62.
- Buried Wequetequock Burial Ground, Stonington Cemetery, Stonington, New London Co., Connecticut.

Thomas Stanton III was born on 30 July 1616 in Wolverton, Stratford-on-Avon District of Warwickshire, England. He was educated for a military cadet and became a captain. However, he did not like the profession of arms and took a deep interest in the religious principles of the migrating Puritans.

In 1635 Captain Thomas Stanton III sailed from London, England aboard the ship *Bonaventura* to the colonies of America and landed in Virginia. From there he intermingled with the Indians in such a positive manner that word spread up to New England that he was a great communicator with the Indian tribes. His communication skills with the Indian tribes were outstanding. He was a young man who understood the Indians and their customs and language very well. Within two years, word spread of his amazing skill all the way up to Boston, Massachusetts and to the ears of Gov. John Winthrop. The Massachusetts Bay colony was struggling with the Indian tribes of the northeast. He was sent for by Gov. Winthrop and the young colonies of the north to help them out. Thomas accepted their offer and moved north to Boston in 1636, and onto Hartford, Connecticut in 1637 and later into the new area of Stonington, Connecticut in 1650.

It was there in Hartford, Connecticut he met Anna Lord. They fell in love and the next year they married. They had 10 children during their marriage. They set up their home in Stonington, Connecticut, which was at that time called Pawcatuck. In 1650 Thomas established a trading post in Pawcatuck. It was during this time that he became Interpreter General for the Colonies. He was also Marshall of the Colony, County Commissioner, Member of the General Court and one of the first founders of the First Church of Stonington, Connecticut. Thomas Stanton was a man of widespread and lasting importance to the colonies, and he has been identified with every major transaction between the natives and the colonists up to the year of his death in 1677.

Indian Interpreter General for the New England Colonies

"The Wequetequock Burial Ground Association on August 31, 1899, dedicated a monument which had been elected as a memorial to the first four settlers of Wequetequock – William Chesebrough, Thomas Minor, Walter Palmer, and Thomas Stanton. Each side of the monument carries an epitaph, above which has been carved a coat of arms. The Stanton epitaph reads as follows:

"THOMAS STANTON

Interpreter General for the
New England Colonies,
Died December 2, 1677, aged 62 Years.
He came from England in 1635,
Was of Boston in 1636, Hartford 1637,
and Stonington in 1650.
Was Marshall of the Colony,
County Commissioner,
Member of the General Court
and one of the Founders of the First Church in Stonington.
A Man of Widespread and Lasting Importance to the Colonies
And Identified with every transaction between
The natives and Colonists up to the Year of His Death."

"When their early market or fair was established, there were in Hartford several merchants, who had in their homes or outbuildings such articles as were used in trade or were sold to the settlers. Their early traffic was with the Indians for corn or beaver skins. The General Court sent out its agents to obtain corn, in 1638, the exclusive right to trade for beaver on the river was given to certain individuals. William Whiting and Thomas Stanton secured it for Hartford. Governor Hopkins obtained a special privilege of trade at Warranoke in 1640. Traffic with the Indians on Long Island was restrained in 1642, though Thomas Stanton and Richard Lord [this may have been, Thomas' brother-in-law – his wife Anne's brother, Richard, or it may have been his father-in-law, Anne's dad, as both were named Richard Lord – *author's note*] could have make one voyage. The settlers were then in need of articles and goods, which they hoped to secure in the older colonies. Protests were made, however, by Massachusetts and Plymouth, that their markets were being overfilled. Hence, Connecticut traders sought a foreign market."

Dr. George D. Stanton [a descendant of Thomas Stanton] writes about Thomas Stanton his ancestor: "Thomas Stanton, the Indian Interpreter-General for the New England Colonies. His record is fully set forth on the pages of the history of his time. Nothing that we can say will add to the character and the honor of those brave pioneer settlers, William Cheesebrough, Thomas Minor, Walter Palmer, and Thomas Stanton (named in the order of their settlement here), who left comfortable homes in the mother country to seek and establish civil and religious liberty in a new country inhabited by savage barbarians. We may well reflect and admire the moral courage and heroism of those pioneers, the result of whose labors, dangers, and self-denial contributed to formulate and perfect one of the most liberal, successful, and powerful systems of self-government ever established by man...."

Here was full liberty under reasonable restrictions. Thomas Stanton's whole life – from the time of his arrival in this country in 1635 to the time of his death, December 2, 1677 – was continuously devoted to public service. If there was a disagreement between the natives and the colonists, a treaty was made, and 99% of the time, it was Captain Thomas Stanton III who was behind each treaty.

**One of the original buildings
in the Stonington Community.
It is now a fascinating museum.**

**Tombstone of
Thomas Stanton (1616-December 2, 1677)
and his wife
Anna Lord (1614-September 4, 1655)**

Children of Captain Thomas[5] Stanton III and Anna Lord were:

	i.	**Thomas Stanton IV**; b. 1638 in Hartford, Hartford Co., Connecticut. Thomas IV married Sarah Denison in 1659 in Connecticut. It is unknown if they ever had any children during their marriage. Thomas IV died on 11 April 1718 in Connecticut at age 80.
	ii.	**Captain John Stanton** b. 1641 in Hartford, Hartford Co., Connecticut. It is unknown if he ever married and had any children. Captain John died on 3 October 1713 in Stonington, New London Co., Connecticut at the age of 72.
	iii.	**Mary Stanton**; b. 1643 in Hartford, Hartford Co., Connecticut. Mary married Samuel Rogers on 17 November 1662 in New London, New London Co., Connecticut. It is unknown how many children they had during their marriage. Mary died in 1713 in Connecticut at the age of 70.
	iv.	**Hannah Stanton** b. 1644 in Hartford, Hartford Co., Connecticut. Hannah married Nehemiah Palmer on 19 November 1662 in Connecticut. It is unknown how many children they had during their marriage. Hannah died on 17 October 1727 in Stonington, New London Co., Connecticut at the age of 83.
3.	v.	**Joseph Stanton Sr.**, b. 1646 in Hartford, Hartford Co., Connecticut. Joseph Sr. married four times: Wife #1 Hannah Mead. Joseph Sr. and Hannah Mead had 2 children during their marriage. Wife #2. Hannah Lord. Joseph Sr. and Hannah Lord had 2 children during their marriage. Wife #3_____. Joseph Sr. and ___ had 0 children during their marriage. Wife #4 ___ Prentice. Joseph Sr. and ___ Prentice had 3 children during their marriage. Joseph Sr. died in 1714 in Stonington, New London, Connecticut at the age of 68.
	vi.	**Daniel Stanton** b. 1648 in Hartford, Hartford Co., Connecticut. Daniel married Sarah Wheeler on 1 June 1671 in Stonington, New London Co., Connecticut. It is unknown how many children they had during their marriage. Daniel died in 1681 in Barbados, West Indies at the age of 43.
	vii.	**Dorothy Stanton** b. 1651 in Hartford, Hartford Co., Connecticut. Dorothy married Rev. James Noyes Jr. on 11 September 1674 in Stonington, New London Co., Connecticut. It is unknown how many children they had during their marriage. Dorothy died on 19 January 1743 in Stonington, New London Co., Connecticut at the age of 92.
	viii.	**Robert Stanton**; b. 1653 in Pequot, New London Co., Connecticut. Robert married Joanna Gardiner on 12 September 1677 in Stonington, New London Co., Connecticut. It is unknown how many children they had during their marriage. Robert died on 25 October 1724 in Connecticut at the age of 71.
	ix.	**Sarah Stanton** b. 1655 in Pequot, New London Co., Connecticut. Sarah married twice. Husband #1 Thomas Prentice Jr. Sarah and Thomas were married on 20 March 1675. Husband #2 Lieut. William Denison. Sarah and Lieut. William were married in May 1686. It is unknown how many children Sarah had in either one of her marriages. Sarah died on 7 August 1713 in Connecticut at the age of 58.

	x.	**SAMUEL STANTON** b. 1658 in Pequot, New London Co., Connecticut. It is unknown if he ever married and had any children. Samuel died in 1732 at the age of 74. Location at his death is unknown.

6. Joseph Stanton Sr.

JOSEPH[6] STANTON SR. (Captain Thomas[5] III Thomas[4] Jr., Captain Thomas[3] Sr., John[2], Thomas[1])

- Born 1646 in Hartford, Hartford Co., Connecticut.
- Married 19 June 1673 Wife #1 Hannah Mead, daughter of William Mead and Rebecca ____, Joseph Sr. and Hannah were married in Roxbury, Suffolk Co., Massachusetts. Hannah Mead Stanton died in 1676 giving birth to their second child, a daughter named Hannah Stanton.
- Married 13 August 1677 Wife #2 Hannah Lord. Joseph Sr. and Hannah were married in Hartford, Hartford Co., Connecticut. They had 2 children during their marriage.
- Married circa 1682 Wife #3 Joseph Sr. and were married in Stonington, New London Co., Connecticut. They had no children during their marriage.
- Married circa 1690 Wife #4 Prentice. Joseph Sr. and were married in Westerly, Washington Co., Rhode Island. They had 3 children during their marriage.
- Died 1714 in Stonington, New London Co., Connecticut at the age of 68.

Joseph Stanton's first wife:

Children of Joseph[6] Stanton Sr. and Hannah Mead were:

	i.	**JOSEPH STANTON JR.** b. 1674 Stonington, New London Co., Connecticut. Joseph Jr. married Hester Gallup on 3 January 1705 in Stonington, New London Co., Connecticut. It is unknown how many children they had during their marriage. It is also unknown when and where Joseph Jr. died. Age at death is unknown.
7.	ii.	**HANNAH STANTON** b. 1676 Stonington, New London Co., Connecticut. Hannah married James Yorke III. They had children 3 during their marriage. Hannah died in 1715 at the age of 39.

Joseph Stanton's second wife:
Children of Joseph[6] Stanton Sr. and Hannah Lord were:

	i.	**THOMAS STANTON I** b. 16 December 1677 Stonington, New London Co., Connecticut. Thomas I died circa 1685 in Stonington, New London Co., Connecticut at the age of approx. 8 years old.
	ii.	**REBECCA STANTON** b. April 1678 Stonington, New London Co., Connecticut. Rebecca married Joseph Babcock circa 1698. It is unknown how many children they had during their marriage. It is also unknown as to when and where Rebecca died. Her age at death is unknown.

Joseph[6] Stanton's third wife ____.
There were no children of Joseph[6] Stanton Sr. and _____.

Joseph[6] Stanton's fourth wife ____Prentice.

Children of Joseph[6] Stanton Sr. and _____ Prentice were:

	i.	**THOMAS Stanton II** baptized on 5 April 1691 in Stonington, New London Co., Connecticut. Thomas II married Esther Babcock circa 1710 in Westerly, Washington Co., Rhode Island. It is unknown as to how many children they had during their marriage. It is also unknown as to when and where Thomas II died. His age at death is unknown.
	ii.	**DANIEL STANTON** b. 1694 in Stonington, New London Co., Connecticut. Daniel was baptized on 1 April 1694. He married twice: Daniel married Wife #1 Mercy Babcock circa 1714 in Westerly, Washington Co., Rhode Island. Daniel married Wife #2 Elizabeth Brown circa 1722 in Westerly, Washington Co., Rhode Island. It is unknown how many children Daniel had in either one of his marriages. When and where he died is unknown as is his age at death.
	iii.	**SAMUEL STANTON** b. 1698 and was baptized on 17 July 1698 in Stonington, New London Co, Connecticut. Samuel died circa 1710 in Stonington, New London, Connecticut. He died at age approx. 12 years old.

7. Hannah Stanton

HANNAH[7] STANTON (Joseph[6], Captain Thomas[5], III Thomas[4] Jr., Captain Thomas[3] Sr., John[2], Thomas[1])

- Born 1676 in Stonington, New London Co., Connecticut.
- Married 13 November 1695 James Yorke III. James III was the son of James Yorke II and Deborah Bell. Hannah and James Yorke III were married in Stonington, New London Co., Connecticut. They had 9 children during their marriage.
- Died circa 1715 Stonington, Connecticut at approx. 39.

Note: Hannah's mother Hannah Mead Stanton (1655-1676) died giving birth to her second child, a daughter also named Hannah, who is this Hannah Stanton Yorke.

Children of Hannah[7] Stanton and James Yorke III are documented in the Yorke chapter.

Source Citations for this Chapter

Genealogies of Connecticut Families, From the New England Historical and Genealogical Register, Volume III, Baltimore Genealogical Publishing Co., Inc. 1983.

Stonington Graveyards Map Stonington Historical Society, Stonington, Connecticut.

Representative Men and Old Families of Rhode Island Volume II, J.H. Beers & Co., Chicago, 1908.

https://www.ancestry.com-family Stanton Family Tree.

Gravestone Photos and Epitaphs with Genealogical Data, 1650 Wequetequock Burial Ground, Stonington Founders Cemetery by Frederick E. Burdick, 2002. CD – WBGA, c/o Fred Burdick,

595 Augmon Road, Stonington, Connecticut 06378.

www.stantondavishomestead.org Thomas Stanton Book.

https://www.findagrave.com/memorial/7930907/thomas-stanton

https://stantonsociety.org/tsgenealogy.html

Vital Records of Rhode Island – Newport Marriages – NEHSG Library, Boston, Massachusetts.

A Record, Genealogical, Biographical, Statistical of Thomas Stanton of Connecticut and His Descendants (1635-1891) by William A. Stanton, PH. D., D. D., Albany, New York, Joel Munsell's Sons, Publishers, 1891.

The Genealogical Dictionary of Rhode Island by John Osborne Austin, 1969, NEHGS Ref. F, 78, A935.

The History of the Wequetequock Burial Ground and Stonington's First Families by Mary Thacher & Jody Wren, 2001.

Descendants of Thomas Lord by Kenneth Lord, 1946, NEHGS, CS, 71, L873, c.2.

The History of Stonington, Connecticut, County of New London, Connecticut. First Settlement in 1649 with a Genealogical Register, Genealogical Publishing Co., Baltimore, Maryland, 1977.

New England Marriages Prior to 1700 by Clarence Almon Torrey, NEHGS Library, Boston, Massachusetts.

Chapter 32: The Vickerys

The Vickery Family Line

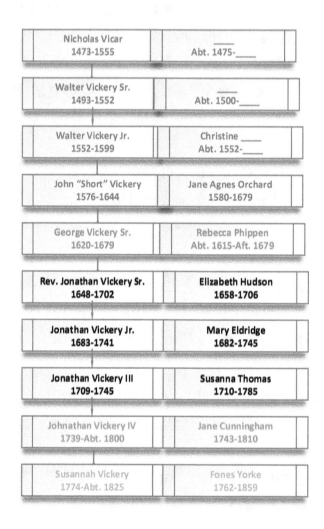

Nicholas Vicar
1473-1555

_____
Abt. 1475-_____

Walter Vickery Sr.
1493-1552

_____
Abt. 1500-_____

Walter Vickery Jr.
1552-1599

Christine _____
Abt. 1552-_____

John "Short" Vickery
1576-1644

Jane Agnes Orchard
1580-1679

George Vickery Sr.
1620-1679

Rebecca Phippen
Abt. 1615-Aft. 1679

Rev. Jonathan Vickery Sr.
1648-1702

Elizabeth Hudson
1658-1706

Jonathan Vickery Jr.
1683-1741

Mary Eldridge
1682-1745

Jonathan Vickery III
1709-1745

Susanna Thomas
1710-1785

Johnathan Vickery IV
1739-Abt. 1800

Jane Cunningham
1743-1810

Susannah Vickery
1774-Abt. 1825

Fones Yorke
1762-1859

1. Nicholas Vicar

NICHOLAS[1] VICAR

- Born 1473 London, Middlesex, England.
- Married circa 1492. They were married in Devonshire, England.
- Died 1555 in Devonshire, England at the age of 82.

Child of NICHOLAS[1] VICAR and _____ was:

2.	i.	**WALTER VICKERY SR.** b. 1493 in Devonshire, England. Walter married _____. Walter Sr. and his wife ___ had 1 son named Walter Jr. during their marriage. Walter Sr. died in 1552 in Kirton, Devonshire, England at the age of 59.

Note: Name changes from Vicar to Vickery

2. Walter Vickery Sr.

WALTER[2] VICKERY SR. (Nicholas[1])

- Born 1493 in Devonshire, England.
- Married circa 1550. Walter Sr. and his wife were married in Halberton, Devonshire, England.
- Died 1552 in Kirton, Devonshire, England at age 59.

Child of WALTER[2] VICKERY SR. and _____ was:

3.	i.	Walter Vickery Jr., b. 1552 in Halberton, Devonshire, England. Walter Jr. married Christine _____ circa 1575. They had 1 child during their marriage. Walter Jr. died in 1599 in Halberton, Devonshire, England at the age of 47.

3. Walter Vickery Jr.

WALTER[3] VICKERY JR. (Walter [2]Sr., Nicholas[1])

- Born 1552 Halberton, Devonshire, England.
- Married circa 1575 Christine. Walter Jr. and Christine were married in Halberton, Devonshire, England.
- Died 1599 in Halberton, Devonshire, England at the age of 47.

Child of WALTER[3] VICKERY SR. and CHRISTINE _____ was:

4.	i.	**JOHN "SHORT" VICKERY** b. 1576 in Halberton, Devonshire, England. John "Short" married twice. He married Wife #1 Joan Dayve (1586-1612) in 1605 in Halberton, Devonshire, England. John "Short" and Joan had 1 child during this marriage. Following Joan's death, he married again, this time to Wife #2 Agnes Orchard (1580-1679). They were married in Halberton, Devonshire, England. They had 4 children during this marriage. John "Short" died in 1644 in Halberton, Devonshire, England at the age of 68.

4. John "Short" Vickery

JOHN "SHORT"[4] VICKERY (Walter[3] Jr., Walter[2] Sr., Nicholas[1])

- Born 1576 in Halberton, Devonshire, England.
- Married 1605 Wife #1: Joane Davye (1586-1612). They were married in Halberton, Devonshire, England. ("Short" and Joane had 1 child during this marriage.)
- Married 23 September 1612 Wife #2: Jane Agnes Orchard (1580-1679). They were married in Halberton, Devonshire, England. Jane Agnes Orchard was the daughter of Johannas Orchard Jr. and Agnes Mary Crouche Orchard. ("Short" and Jane Agnes had 4 children during this marriage.)
- Died 1644 in Halberton, Devonshire, England at age 68.

John "Short's first wife was Joane Dayve. She and John had one child together, a daughter named Elizabeth Vickery who was born in 1605 and died in 1606. They had no other children. Joane died in 1612. After Joane's death that very year, John Short again married, this time to Jane Agnes Orchard. However, they did not start having a family for eight more years until 1620 when George Vickery was born. When George became a young man, he was the first Vickery to cross the "great water" to America at about 16 years of age. It is unclear still with whom 16-year-old George made the journey, but it is clear from the records that he was in Salem, Massachusetts in 1636.

Child of JOHN "SHORT"[4] VICKERY and JOANE DAYVE was:

	i.	**ELIZABETH VICKERY** b. 1605 in in Halberton, Devonshire, England. Elizabeth died in 1606 in Halberton, Devonshire, England at the age of 1 year old.

Children of JOHN "SHORT"[4] VICKERY and JANE AGNES ORCHARD were:

5.	i.	**GEORGE VICKERY SR. (Immigrant)** b. August 1620 in Dunkerswell, Devonshire, England. George married Rebecca Phippen circa 1647 in America. Rebecca was the daughter of David Pippen and Sarah ____. George and Rebecca were married in Hull, Plymouth Co., Massachusetts. They had 12 children during their marriage. George died on 12 July 1679 in Hull, Plymouth Co., Massachusetts at the age of 59.
	ii.	**Elizabeth Vickery** b. circa 1622 in England. It is unknown if she ever married and had any children. Her death date and location at death are both unknown. Her age at death is also unknown.
	iii.	**John Vickery** b. circa 1624 in England. It is unknown if he ever married and had any children. His death date and location at death are both unknown. His age at death is also unknown.
	iv.	**Amos Vickery** b. circa 1626 in England. It is unknown if he ever married and had any children. His death date and location at death are both unknown. His age at death is also unknown.

5. George Vickery Sr. (Immigrant)

GEORGE⁵ VICKERY SR. (John⁴, Walter³ Jr, Walter² Sr, Nicholas¹)

- Born August 1620 in Dunkerswell, Devonshire, England.
- Arrival circa 1636 in Salem, Essex Co., Massachusetts.
- Married circa 1647 Rebecca Phippen (circa 1615-1693). Rebecca was the daughter of David Phippen and Sarah ____. George Sr. and Rebecca were married in Nantasket (Hull), Plymouth Co., Massachusetts.
- Died 12 July 1679 in Hull, Plymouth Co., Massachusetts at age 59.

George Vickery came over to the American colonies at a young age. He was first seen in Salem, Massachusetts in 1636 and then in neighboring Marblehead in 1637 as one of their first settlers. He owned several parcels of land there in Marblehead and then moved on to Nantasket (later known as Hull) in 1650. He was a fisherman and sailed up and down the coast of New England (from Cape Ann to the shores of Rhode Island) quite frequently. He and his wife Rebecca finally settled in Hull, Massachusetts and raised their family there. Rebecca Phippen was the daughter of David and Sarah ____ Phippen. George and Rebecca raised twelve children during their marriage.

In the *New England Historical Genealogical Register* of October 1989, pages 338-339, it states:

> "Shortly before the King Philip War had erupted, the town of Nantasket (Hull) prepared a beacon light and watch house, the account of which has been preserved in the Massachusetts Archives. It notes the cost of the buildings. Among the sixteen men of Hull who awarded the beacon light were George and Isaac Vickery. On 3 March 1675, a petition by two men of Hull, including George, Isaac, Israel, and Johnathan Vickery, asked that they be provided for, since they were cut off from their trade of fishing by military order, due to the country's exposure to the wasting fury of the most barbarous heathen."

George Vickey died very suddenly in June of 1679 at the age 59 years. His inventory as of 31 July 1679 included 220 pounds, household furnishings, the livestock, one third of a shallop, the house, and the farm home lot, several house lots at Nantasket (Hull), and nearby islands, and a single horse.

Children of GEORGE[5] VICKERY and REBECCA PHIPPEN are:

6.	i.	**REV. JONATHAN VICKERY SR.** b. 1648 in Hull, Plymouth Co., Massachusetts. Rev. Jonathan married Elizabeth Hudson in 1678 in Hull, Suffolk Co., Massachusetts. They had 7 children during their marriage. Rev. Johnathan died 1702 in Chatham, Massachusetts in a drowning (boating) accident at the age of 54.
	ii.	**HANNAH VICKERY** b. 1648 in Hull, Plymouth Co., Massachusetts. It is unknown if she ever married and had any children. Her death date and location at death are both unknown. Her age at death is also unknown.
	iii.	**REBECCA VICKERY** b. 1650 in Hull, Plymouth Co., Massachusetts. Rebecca married ____ Prince. The date of their marriage is unknown. It is also unknown if they had any children during their marriage. Also unknown is Rebecca's death date and location at death. Her age at death also unknown.
	iv.	**GEORGE VICKERY JR.**; b 1651 in, Hull, Plymouth Co., Massachusetts. George Jr. married Lucy Hudson circa 1671. It is unknown if they had any children during their marriage. George's death date and location at death are both unknown. His age at death is also unknown.
	v.	**ISAAC VICKERY** b. circa 1654 in Hull, Plymouth Co., Massachusetts. He married twice: Wife #1 Elizabeth Cromwell Price. They were married circa 1674. Wife #2 Lydia Jones circa 1685. It is unknown if Isaac ever had any children with either of his two wives. His death date and location at death are unknown, as is his age at death.
	vi.	**SETH VICKERY** b. 1655 in Hull, Plymouth Co., Massachusetts. It is unknown if he ever married and had any children. His death date and location at death are both unknown. His age at death is also unknown.
	vii.	**JOHN VICKERY** b. 1657 in Hull, Plymouth Co., Massachusetts. John married Sarah Croakum circa 1682. It is unknown if they ever had any children during their marriage. John's death date and location at death are both unknown. His age at death also is unknown.
	viii.	**ISRAEL VICKERY** b. circa 1660 in Hull, Plymouth Co., Massachusetts. Israel married Judith Hersey in 1680. It is unknown if they ever had any children during their marriage. Israel's death date and location at death are both unknown. His age at death is also unknown.
	ix.	**BENJAMIN VICKERY SR.** b. 1664 in Hull, Plymouth Co., Massachusetts. Benjamin married twice: Wife #1 Dorcas Paine. Benjamin and Dorcus were married circa 1684. Wife #2 Mary Coom. Benjamin and Mary were married circa 1710. It is unknown if Benjamin ever had any children with either wife. Benjamin's death date and location at death are both unknown. His age at death is also unknown.
	x.	**JOSEPH VICKERY** b. 1666 in Hull, Plymouth Co., Massachusetts. Joseph married Abigail ____ circa 1686. It is unknown if they ever had any children during their marriage. His death date and location at death are both unknown. His age at death is also unknown.
	xi.	**MARY VICKERY** b. date unknown in Hull, Plymouth Co., Massachusetts. It is unknown if she ever married and had any children. Her death date and location at death are both unknown. Her age at death is also unknown.
	xii.	**ROGER VICKERY** b. date unknown in Hull, Plymouth Co., Massachusetts. It is unknown if he ever married and had any children. His death date and location at death are unknown,

6. Rev. Jonathan Vickery Sr.

REV. JONATHAN[6] VICKERY SR. (George [5,] John [4], Walter[3] Jr, Walter [2] Sr., Nicholas [1])

- Born 1648 in Hull, Plymouth Co., Massachusetts.
- Married 1678 Elizabeth Hudson (1658-1706). Elizabeth was the daughter of John Hudson and Ann Rogers. Rev. Jonathan Sr. were married in Hull, Plymouth Co., Massachusetts.
- Died 30 Apr 1702 in Chatham, Barnstable Co., Massachusetts at the age of 52. (Drowning due to a boating accident.)

Reverend Jonathan Sr. was born in Hull and was a fisherman by trade. He was made a freeman there in Hull in 1678. It was about that time when he and Elizabeth Hudson were married in Hull. They had seven children during their marriage. On 19 June 1693 Jonathan Sr. and his wife Elizabeth were in Boston. While Elizabeth was visiting her husband's maternal aunt (Elizabeth Phippen), a man named Samuel White grabbed Elizabeth by the throat and robbed her. It was a horrifying and traumatic experience!

A few years later in 1697, Jonathan and his family moved from Hull to Chatham and Johnathan Sr. became the first minister of the settlement there in Monomoit, now known as Chatham. They sold their house lot in Hull to a man named John Steel for the sum of 25 pounds. Reverend Jonathan Sr. was not an educated man at all, nor was he an ordained clergyman. He was a simple fisherman. However, he was a Christian believer and a particularly good speaker. He was asked in 1699 and accepted the position to be the minister of the very first church in Monomoit. He was paid a supply of hay and wood for his family's use plus 20 pounds per year. He continued the ministry there in Monomoit for two years.

One sunny day in April (it was 30 April 1701), he and three other men went out on Pleasant Bay fishing. It was a large body of water leading into the ocean on the Bay side in Chatham. However, a storm came up suddenly and their open boat capsized. All four men drowned. These men were Lieutenant Nicholas Eldridge (who was Rev. Jonathan Sr.'s daughter in-law's father), William Cahoon, Edward Small and Rev. Jonathan Vickery Sr.! Such a tragic accident. Rev. Jonathan Sr. 's estate took about a year to be settled but before that was finalized, his widow Elizabeth, who was not well and had a lingering disease, died. They had seven children ranging from 22 years to 8 years old when both parents died.

**Pleasant Bay on the Bay side of Cape Cod,
where the tragic Sunday afternoon
fishing boat accident occurred.**

Children of Rev. JONATHAN[6] VICKERY SR. and ELIZABETH HUDSON were:

	i.	**ELIZABETH VICKERY** b. 1679 Hull, Plymouth Co., Massachusetts. Elizabeth married Jonathan Collins on 27 January 1705 in Eastham, Barnstable Co., Massachusetts. It is unknown if they had any children during their marriage. Elizabeth's death date and location and age at death are unknown.
7.	ii.	**DEACON JOHNATHAN VICKERY JR.** b. 1683 Hull, Plymouth Co., Massachusetts. Deacon Jonathan Jr. married Mary Eldridge (1683-1745). They were married in 1706. Mary was the daughter of Lieutenant Nicholas Eldridge and Elizabeth Hawes. Deacon Jonathan Jr. and Mary had 6 children during their marriage. Deacon Jonathan Jr. died in 1741 at the age of 58.
	iii.	**DAVID VICKERY** b. 1685 Hull, Plymouth Co., Massachusetts. He was missing at sea, off the coast of Massachusetts. This happened circa 1714. He was 29. It was presumed he had died at sea.
	iv.	**JOANNA VICKERY** b. 1687 Hull, Plymouth Co., Massachusetts. Joanna married Samuel Treat Jr.. The couple married on 27 October 1708 in Eastham, Barnstable Co., Massachusetts. It is unknown how many children the couple had during their marriage. Joanna died on 26 August 1720 in Truro, Barnstable Co., Massachusetts at the age of 33.
	v.	**MARY VICKERY** b. 1672 Hull, Plymouth Co., Massachusetts. It is unknown if Mary ever married and had any children. Mary died circa 1708 in Hull, Suffolk Co., Massachusetts at the age of 36.
	vi.	**REBECCA VICKERY** b. 1691 Hull, Plymouth Co., Massachusetts. Rebecca married Samuel Bonney. Marriage date is unknown, and it is also unknown how many children Rebecca and Samuel had during their marriage. Rebecca's death date and location at death both unknown. Her age at death is unknown.
	vii.	**SARAH VICKERY** b. 1693 Hull, Plymouth Co., Massachusetts. Sarah married twice: Husband #1 _____ Nickerson circa 1725. She married Husband #2 Thomas Higgins (marriage date unknown). It is unknown how many children Sarah had within either marriage. Sarah's death date and location and age at death all unknown.

7. Deacon Johnathan Vickery Jr.

JOHNATHAN[7] VICKERY JR. (Rev. Johnathan [6] George [5,] John [4], Walter[3] Jr, Walter [2] Sr., Nicholas [1])

- Born circa 1683 in Hull, Plymouth Co., Massachusetts.
- Married 1703 Mary Eldridge (1683-1745) in Barnstable Co., Massachusetts. Mary was the daughter of Lieutenant Nicholas Eldridge and Elizabeth Hawes.
- Died 19 November 1741 in Truro, Barnstable Co., Massachusetts.
- Buried in the Old North Cemetery, Truro, Barnstable Co., Massachusetts.

Deacon Johnathan Vickery was born in Hull, Massachusetts and he moved to Cape Cod where he met Mary Eldridge who was born and raised in Truro, Massachusetts. For her family history please see the Eldridge chapter of this book. They fell in love and were married in 1703 in Truro. They had six children in this marriage. Jonathan and Mary were admitted to the church in Truro on 26 April 1713. Jonathan was chosen to be a Deacon in the church on 13 November 1713. This was during the time when the first meeting house was still standing. Jonathan and Mary were residents of Truro when it was incorporated in 1709. The first meeting house was constructed there between 1709 and 1710 in the Pond Village area. Johnathan was ordained on 22 December 1728. He died 19 November 1741 and Mary died four years later 13 November 1745. Their joint gravestone is still standing in Truro in the Old North Cemetery.

Tombstone of Deacon Jonathan Vickery II (d. 1741) and his wife Mary (Eldridge) Vickery (d.1745) Old North Cemetery, Truro, Barnstable Co., Massachusetts.

Children of DEACON JOHNATHAN[7] VICKERY JR. and MARY ELDRIDGE were:

	i.	**DAVID VICKERY** 4 March 1707 in Truro, Barnstable Co., Massachusetts. It is unknown if David ever married and had any children. His date of death and his location at death are unknown. Age at death is unknown.
8.	ii.	**JONATHAN VICKERY III** b. 27 May 1709 in Truro, Barnstable Co., Massachusetts. Johnathan III married Susanna Thomas (1710-1785). Jonathan III and Susanna were married on 6 February 1734. Susanna was the daughter of William Thomas & Susanna Bates of Marblehead, Essex Co., Massachusetts. Jonathan III and Susanna were married in Boston, Suffolk Co., Massachusetts, and they had 4 children during their marriage. Jonathan III was a fisherman and he died at sea when his boat was shipwrecked off the coast of Antigua in October of 1745. Jonathan III was 36 when he died at sea.
	iii.	**MATTHIAS VICKERY** b. 12 September 1711 in Truro, Barnstable Co., Massachusetts. It is unknown if Mathias ever married and had any children. His date of death and his location at death are unknown. Age at death is unknown.
	iv.	**MARY VICKERY** b. 12 November 1713 in Truro, Barnstable Co., Massachusetts. It is unknown if Mary ever married and had any children. Her date of death and her location at death are unknown. Age at death is unknown.

	v.	**ISAAC VICKERY** b. 10 February 1716 in Truro, Barnstable Co., Massachusetts. It is unknown if Isaac ever married and had any children. His date of death and his location at death are unknown. Age at death is unknown.
	vi.	**NATHANIEL VICKERY** b. 1 April 1718 in Truro, Barnstable Co., Massachusetts. It is unknown if Nathaniel ever married and had any children. His date of death and his location at death are unknown. Age at death is unknown.

8. Jonathan Vickery III

JONATHAN[8] VICKERY III (Deacon Johnathan[7], Rev. Johnathan [6], George [5,] John [4], Walter[3] Jr, Walter [2] Sr., Nicholas [1])

- Born 27 May 1709 in Truro, Barnstable Co., Massachusetts.
- Married 6 February 1734 Susanna Thomas (1710-1785) in Boston, Suffolk Co., Massachusetts.
- Died October 1745 Died at sea – shipwrecked at sea en route from Boston to the islands of Antigua and Barbados.

Jonathan Vickery III was born in Truro on Cape Cod, Massachusetts. As a young man he moved to Boston, the capital city of Massachusetts. There he met a young lady Susanna Thomas who was the daughter of William Thomas and Susannah (Bates) Thomas of Marblehead, Massachusetts. Susanna and Johnathan III fell in love and were married in Boston, Suffolk Co., Massachusetts on 6 February 1734. They settled in Hyde Park, an area of Boston, and raised 4 children during their short marriage. Johnathan was a fisherman and during the month of October 1745, he left Boston in his ship en route to the islands of Antigua and Barbados. Unfortunately, an unexpected storm arose. His ship was wrecked off the coast of Antigua. He and his fishing crew all died and were all lost at sea. Johnathan III was only 36 years old. His heartbroken widow moved from Hyde Park, Boston to Plymouth and lived another 40 years there. She died in Plymouth at age 75 on 15 May 1785.

Children of Jonathan[8] Vickery III and Susanna Thomas were:

	ii.	**Susannah Vickery** b. 1737 in Hyde Park, Suffolk Co., Massachusetts. It is unknown if Susannah ever married and had any children. Her date of death and her location at death are unknown. Age at death is unknown.
9.	ii.	**Jonathan Vickery IV** (Emigrated) b. 15 August 1739 in Hyde Park, Suffolk Co., Massachusetts. Jonathan IV married in 1764 to Jane Cunningham (1743-1810). Jane was the daughter of John Cunningham Sr. and Eleanor Helen Aird of Scotland & Ireland. Jonathan IV and Jane had 8 children during their marriage. Johnathan died in 1800 in Parrsboro, Cumberland Co., Nova Scotia, Canada.
	iii.	**Abigail Vickery** b. 16 May 1743 in Hyde Park, Suffolk Co., Massachusetts. It is unknown if Abigail ever married and had any children. Her date of death and her location at death are unknown. Age at death is unknown.
	iv.	**John Guttridge Vickery** b. 1744 in Hyde Park, Suffolk Co., Massachusetts. It is unknown if John Guttridge ever married and had any children. His date of death and his location at death are unknown. Age at death is unknown.

9. Jonathan Vickery IV (Emigrated)

Jonathan[9] Vickery IV (Jonathan III[8], Deacon Johnathan[7], Rev. Johnathan[6], George[5,] John[4], Walter[3] Jr, Walter[2] Sr., Nicholas[1])

- Born 15 August 1739 Hyde Park, Boston, Suffolk Co., Massachusetts.
- Married 17 April 1764 Jane Cunningham (1743-1810) in Falmouth, Nova Scotia., Canada.
- Died circa 1800 in Parrsboro, Cumberland Co., Nova Scotia.

Jonathan Vickery IV (Emigrated) was born in Hyde Park, an area of Boston, Massachusetts in 1739 and he grew up there. About the time (in the early 1760s) of the beginning of the huge movement of the Planters' settlement in Nova Scotia with more land being available to the north, a young woman named Jane Cunningham arrived in Boston from Ireland. She along with her family had been shipwrecked in a storm and the rescue vessel had brought her and her two sisters to the Boston Harbor. (You can read more about Jane in the Cunningham chapter of this book.) Well, Johnathan and Jane fell in love, and they traveled up to the new colony in Falmouth, Hants Co., Nova Scotia. There they were married in the spring of 1764 (17 April 1764) and were given a plot of land. Jonathan was a young, hard-working carpenter and was extremely helpful to their new community at Falmouth. They had eight children, all born in Falmouth, Nova Scotia between the years of 1764-1780. Shortly thereafter they are found to have moved to Parrsboro which is in Cumberland Co., Nova Scotia. There are records (their footprints) of several land plots which they bought in Parrsboro. There were many Vickery families who had moved onto Parrsboro, and Jonathan and Jane's names are among the original Vickery families. Jonathan died there in Parrsboro circa 1800. Jane survived him by ten years. She died in 1810. Both are buried in unmarked graves in a Parrsboro cemetery (exact location in Parrsboro of the cemetery where they are buried is unknown).

Map of Nova Scotia Canada
Note: The locations of where Jonathan and Jane moved from and where they moved to.

Children of JONATHAN[9] VICKERY IV and JANE CUNNINGHAM were:

	i.	**WILLIAM VICKERY** b.10 November 1764 in Falmouth, Hants Co., Nova Scotia. It is unknown if William ever married and had any children. William died in 1862 at the age of 98.
	ii.	**JOHN VICKERY** b. 6 February 1767 in Falmouth, Hants Co., Nova Scotia. It is unknown if John ever married and had any children. John died in 1804 at the age of 37.
	iii.	**JONATHAN VICKERY V** b. 21 August 1769 in Falmouth, Hants Co., Nova Scotia. It is unknown if Jonathan V ever married and had any children. Jonathan V died in 1870 at the age of 101.
	iv.	**MARY VICKERY** b. 24 January 1772 in Falmouth, Hants Co., Nova Scotia. It is unknown if Mary ever married and had any children. Her date of death and her location at death are unknown. Age at death is unknown.
10.	v.	**SUSANNAH VICKERY** b. 18 June 1774 in Falmouth, Hants Co., Nova Scotia. Susannah married circa 1795 Fones Yorke in Falmouth, Hants Co., Nova Scotia. Fones Yorke (31 August 1762-1859) was the son of Captain Edward Yorke and Mary Fones. Susannah and Fones had 11 children during their marriage. Susannah died circa 1865 in Parrsboro, Cumberland Co., Nova Scotia age approx. 51.
	vi.	**CHRISTOPHER VICKERY** b. 1776 in Falmouth, Hants Co., Nova Scotia. It is unknown if Christopher ever married and had any children. Christopher died in 1837 at the age of 61. His location at death is unknown.
	vii.	**JAMES VICKERY** b. circa 1778 in Falmouth, Hants Co., Nova Scotia. It is unknown if James ever married and had any children. His date of death and his location at death are unknown. Age at death is unknown.

	viii.	**FONES VICKERY** b. circa 1780 in Falmouth, Hants Co., Nova Scotia. Fones married ____ Holmes circa 1800 in Nova Scotia. His date of death and his location at death are unknown. His age at death is unknown.

10. Susannah Vickery

SUSANNAH[10] VICKERY (Jonathan IV[9], Jonathan III [8], Deacon Johnathan[7], Rev. Johnathan [6], George[5], John [4], Walter[3] Jr., Walter[2] Sr., Nicholas[1])

- Born 18 June 1774 in Falmouth, Hants Co., Nova Scotia.
- Married circa 1795 Fones Yorke (31 August 1762-1859). Fones was the son of Captain Edward Yorke and Mary Fones. Susannah and Fones were married in Falmouth, Hants Co., Nova Scotia.
- Died circa 1825 in Parrsboro, Cumberland Co., Nova Scotia at the age of approx. 51.

Children of SUSANNAH[10] VICKERY and FONES YORKE are documented in the Yorke chapter.

Source Citations for this Chapter

https://www.geni.com/people/Nicholas-Vicar/6000000040214092235

https://www.ancestry.com/family-tree/person/tree/24847082/person/280135125525/facts

https://www.familysearch.org/tree/person/details/MK4W-QPT

https://www.findagrave.com/memorial/162239176/jonathan-vickery

https://ripleyresearch.weebly.com/the-vickery-family-in-falmouth.html

https://ripleyresearch.weebly.com/the-vickery-family-in-parrsboro-and-diligent-river.html

Vickery Land Grants at Yorke Settlement near Diligent River are visible on the Nova Scotia Land Map Number 51 at the public Archives of Nova Scotia, Canada in Halifax, Nova Scotia.

PANS Research (Public Archives of Nova Scotia) Vickery Family of Cumberland Co. Nova Scotia

MG #1 Volume 2596 Number 253/254

PANS The Vickery Family Papers

Verbal Information from Cousin Gary Vickery of Springhill, Cumberland Co., Nova Scotia.

1796-1800 A Number Came from Falmouth, Hants Co., to Parrsboro, Nova Scotia

by D. J. Taylor – "The Halifax Harold News," Halifax, Nova Scotia.

Verbal information from Marion Kyle, Genealogist from Parrsboro, Cumberland Co., Nova Scotia.

Vital Records of Wellfleet & Truro (Cape Cod), Massachusetts by John Harvey Trout.

The Founding of Marblehead, Massachusetts by Thomas E. Gray, 1984, George Vickery page 126.

Records of the Latter-Day Saints - Vital Records, Boston, Suffolk Co., Massachusetts.

New England Historical Genealogical Society the Register VI #338 and the Register #34 (1880) 101 Newberry Street, Boston, Massachusetts.

The Early History of Chatham, Massachusetts (Under the Bay Colony), Formerly the Constablewick of Village of Monomoit by William C. Smith, Hyannis, Massachusetts, F.B.& F.P. Goss, Publishers 1909.

Suffolk Probate Records (The Estate of George Vickery). Court House, Boston, Massachusetts.

A Genealogical Dictionary of the First Settlers of New England based on the Farmers Register by James Savage's Vol III K-R and Vol. IV S-Z published in 1862, Book is in the NEHGS Library Reference Room. 101 Newbury Street, Boston, Massachusetts.

Pioneers of Massachusetts The Vickery Family, Lynnfield, Library, Genealogical Room Gen/F/63/P87, Lynnfield, Essex Co., Massachusetts.

Planters and Pioneers of Nova Scotia (1749-1775) Revised Edition by Ester Clark Wright, Hantsport, Nova Scotia, Lancelot Press Limited, 1982.

Township of Falmouth Nova Scotia by John V. Duncanson, Mika Publishing Co., Belleville, Ontario, 1990.

Chapter 33: The Waltons

The Walton Family Line

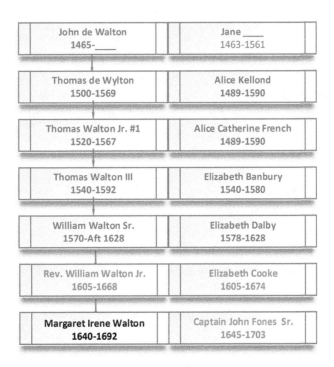

John de Walton 1465-____	Jane ____ 1463-1561
Thomas de Wylton 1500-1569	Alice Kellond 1489-1590
Thomas Walton Jr. #1 1520-1567	Alice Catherine French 1489-1590
Thomas Walton III 1540-1592	Elizabeth Banbury 1540-1580
William Walton Sr. 1570-Aft 1628	Elizabeth Dalby 1578-1628
Rev. William Walton Jr. 1605-1668	Elizabeth Cooke 1605-1674
Margaret Irene Walton 1640-1692	Captain John Fones Sr. 1645-1703

1. John de Walton

JOHN[1] DE WALTON

- Born 1465 in Southam, Warwickshire, England.
- Married circa 1499 Jane _____ (1463-1561).
- Died _date unknown, died in England. Age at death is unknown.

Child of John[1] de Walton and JANE ____ was:

2.	i.	Thomas Wylton Sr. b. March 1500 Southam, Warwickshire, England. Thomas married Alice Kellond (1489-1590). Thomas and Alice were married in 1545 in Southam, Warwickshire, England. Thomas died 2 September 1567 in Southam, Warwickshire, England at the age of 67.

2. Thomas de Wylton Sr.

THOMAS[2] DE WYLTON SR. (John[1])

- Born March 1500 in Southern Warwickshire, England.
- Married 1545 Alice Kellond (1489-1590) in Southam, Warwickshire, England.
- Died 2 September 1567 Southam, Warwickshire, England at the age of 67.

Thomas[2] de Wylton Sr. and his wife Alice had three sons, all born different years and died at different times, but they named them all Thomas after their father! This must have been very confusing in their home, but maybe they gave them all nicknames!

280

Children of Thomas[2] de Wylton Sr. and ALICE KELLOND were:

3.	i.	**THOMAS DE WYLTON JR. #1** b. 1520 Southam, Warwickshire, England. Thomas married Lady Alice Catherine French (1489-1590). They were married in 1539. They had 1 child in this marriage. Thomas #1 died in 1567 in Southam, Warwickshire, England at the age of 47.
	ii.	**THOMAS DE WYLTON JR. #2** b. 1523 Southam, Warwickshire, England. It is unknown if Thomas #2 ever married and had any children. Thomas #2 died in 1592 at the age of 69. His location at death is unknown.
	iii.	**THOMAS DE WYLTON JR. #3**. b. 1524 Southam, Warwickshire, England. It is unknown if Thomas #3 ever married and had any children, Thomas #3 died in 1571 at the age of 47. His location at death is unknown.

3. Thomas Walton Jr. #1

THOMAS[3] WALTON JR. #1 (Thomas[2], John [1])
- Born 1520 in Southam, Warwickshire, England.
- Married 1539 Lady Alice Catherine French (1489-1590).
- Died 1567 in Southam, Warwickshire, England at the age of 47.

Child of Thomas[3] Walton Jr. #1 and LADY ALICE CATHERINE FRENCH was:

4.	i.	Thomas Walton III. b. 1540 at Oxhill, Warwickshire, England. Thomas III married Elizabeth Banbury (1540-1580). Thomas III and Elizabeth were married 25 June 1565 at Oxhill, Warwickshire, England. They had 6 children during their marriage. Thomas III died in 1592 Oxhill, Warwickshire, England at the age of 52.

4. Thomas Walton III of Oxhill, England

THOMAS [4] WALTON III (Thomas[3] Jr. Thomas[2] Sr., John[1])
- Born 1540 in Oxhill, Warwickshire, England.
- Married 25 June 1565 Elizabeth Banbury (1540-1580) at Oxhill, Warwickshire, England.
- Died 1592 Oxhill, Warwickshire, England at the age of 52.

Children of THOMAS[4] WALTON III and ELIZABETH BANBURY were:

	i.	**EMMA WALTON** b. 1568 in Oxhill, Warwickshire, England. It is unknown if she ever married and had any children. Emma died in 1616 at age 48, location at death is unknown.
5.	ii.	**WILLIAM WALTON SR.** b. 1570 in Oxhill, Warwickshire, England. William Sr. married Elizabeth Dalby (1578-1628). William Sr. and Elizabeth were married in 1590 in Warwickshire, England. They had 8 children during their marriage. William Sr. died in 1628 at the age of 58. His location at death is unknown.
	iii.	**MARIA WALTON** b. 1574 in Oxhill, Warwickshire, England. Maria married _____ Savage. It is unknown if they had any children during their marriage. Maria died in 1616 at the age of 42. Her location at her death is unknown.

	iv.	**THOMAS WALTON JR.** b. 1574 in Oxhill, Warwickshire, England. It is unknown if he ever married and had any children. Thomas died in 1592 at the age of 18. His location at death is unknown.
	v.	**JOANNE WALTON** b. 1579 in Oxhill, Warwickshire, England. It is unknown if she ever married and had any children. Joanne died in 1632 at the age of 53. Her location at death is unknown.
	vi.	**ANNE WALTON** b. 1580 in Oxhill, Warwickshire, England. It is unknown if she ever married and had any children. Anne died in 1616 at the age of 36. Her location at death is unknown.

5. William Walton Sr. of Oxhill, England

WILLIAM [5] WALTON SR. (Thomas III[4], Thomas[3] Jr., Thomas[2] Sr., John[1])

- Born 21 May 1570 in Oxhill, Warwickshire, England.
- Married 1590 Elizabeth Dalby (1578-1628) in Kineton by Oxhill, Warwick, England.
- Died after 1628 in Oxhill Parish, Warwickshire, England. approx. 58.

Children of William[5] Walton SR. and ELIZABETH DALBY were:

	i.	**TWIN: DANIEL WALTON** b. 1600 in Oxhill, Warwickshire, England. It is unknown if he ever married and had any children. His death date and his location at death are unknown. Age at death is unknown.
	ii.	**TWIN: NATHANIEL WALTON** b. 1600 in Oxhill, Warwickshire, England. It is unknown if he ever married and had any children. His death date and his location at death are unknown. Age at death is unknown.
	iii.	**THOMAS WALTON** b. 1602 in Oxhill, Warwickshire, England. It is unknown if he ever married and had any children. His death date and his location at death are unknown. Age at death is unknown.
6.	iv.	**REV. WILLIAM WALTON JR.** (Immigrant) b. 1605 in Devonshire, England. Rev. William Jr. married Elizabeth Cooke (1603-1674). Rev. William Jr. and Elizabeth were married 10 April 1627. They immigrated to America and arrived in the Bay State Colony, New England in 1636. They had 9 children during their marriage. Rev. William Jr. died in 1668 Marblehead, Essex Co., Massachusetts at the age of 53.
	v.	**ELIZABETH WALTON** b. 1606 in Devonshire, England. It is unknown if she ever married and had any children. Her death date and location at death are unknown. Age at death is unknown.
	vi.	**GEORGE WALTON** b. 1615 in Devonshire, England. It is unknown if he ever married and had any children. George died in 1686 at the age of 71. His location at death is unknown.
	vii.	**RICHARD WALTON** b. 1615 in Devonshire, England. It is unknown if he ever married and had any children. His death date and his location at death are unknown. Age at his death is unknown.

	viii.	**JOHN WALTON** b. 1617 in Devonshire, England. It is unknown if he ever married and had any children. John died in 1669 at the age of 52. Location at death unknown. Age at his death is unknown.

6. Rev. William Walton Jr. (Immigrant)

REV. WILLIAM [6] WALTON JR. (William[5]Sr. Thomas III[4], Thomas[3] Jr., Thomas[2] Sr., John[1])

- Born 13 September 1605 in Devonshire, England.
- Married 10 April 1627 Elizabeth Cooke in Matravers, Dorset, England.
- 1636 Arrived in Bay State Colony, New England.
- Died 6 November 1658 Marblehead, Essex Co., Massachusetts at the age of 53.

The Great Migration

1620 - 1640

Reverend William Walton was born in Devonshire, England. He attended the Emmanuel College in Cambridge, England. He received degrees in 1621 and again in 1625. He became a "Separatist Minister" after he completed the University studies. He was ordained and served as clergy in a church in Seaton, Devon England.

In 1636 he and his wife and their small family sailed to Massachusetts with other Puritans during the "Great Migration" – the year of 1636. This movement of several thousand families brought some of the earliest New England settlers. He went to Hingham, Massachusetts after landing in Boston. He later moved to Salem, then an area later called Manchester by-the-Sea and still later in his life moved to nearby Marblehead where he died in 1668. In records it was noted that Rev. William founded an establishment called "Jeffery's Cove" in Manchester. Records also indicate that he and his wife had no great wealth. He was a teacher there during the winter months.

Manchester by-the Sea in early colonial days (1626) was known as the town of Jeffrey's Creek. It changed its name to Manchester in 1645. It was settled by Pioneers from Salem. In 1640 the entire town consisted of 63 people. In modern days it changed its name yet again to distinguish this small town from the larger city of Manchester in New Hampshire. The small town in Massachusetts is known today as Manchester-by-the Sea. Rev. William Walton Jr. moved to Marblehead, and he died on 6 November 1668 in Marblehead, Essex Co., Massachusetts at the age of 63. He had apoplexy, which in modern-day terms is called a cerebral vascular accident (CVA), also known as a stroke. He is buried in the old section of Marblehead.

There is a memorial sign at Old Burial Hill which marks the area where he is most likely buried. It is in downtown Marblehead on Orne Street.

Children of Rev. William Walton JR and ELIZABETH COOKE were:

	i.	**JOHN WALTON** (Immigrant) b. 6 February 1627 in Seaton, Devon, England. It is unknown if he ever married and had any children. His death date is unknown. He died in America. His age at death is unknown.
	ii.	**ELIZABETH WALTON** (Immigrant) b. 27 August 1629 in Seaton, Devon, England. Elizabeth married twice: Husband #1 ____ Conant and later Elizabeth married Husband #2 ____ Mamsfield. Both marriage dates are unknown. Also, unknown is whether Elizabeth had any children during either of her marriages. Her death date is unknown. She died in America. Age at death is unknown.
	iii.	**MARTHA WALTON** (Immigrant) b. 26 February 1632 in Seaton, Devon, England. Martha married ____ Munjoy. Marriage date and place both unknown. Also, unknown is whether Martha had any children during her marriage. Her death date is unknown. She died in America. Age at death is unknown.
	iv.	**JANE WALTON** (Immigrant) b. 1634 in Seaton, Devon, England. It is unknown if she ever married and had any children. Her death date is unknown. She died in America. Her age at death is unknown.
	v.	**NATHANIEL WALTON** b. 3 January 1636 in Hingham, Massachusetts. It is unknown if he ever married and had any children. His death date is unknown. His age at death is unknown as well as his location at death.
	vi.	**SAMUEL WALTON** b. 5 April 1639 in Marblehead, Essex Co., Massachusetts. It is unknown if he ever married and had any children. Samuel died in 1717 at the age of 78. His location at death is unknown.

7.	vii.	**MARGARET IRENE WALTON** b. 2 October 1640 Kingston, Washington Co., Rhode Island. Margaret Irene married 1663 Captain Honorable John Fones (1645-1703), They were married in 1663 in Warwick, Kent, Rhode Island. They had 6 children during their marriage. Margaret Irene died 20 April 1692 in Kingston, Washington Co., Rhode Island at the age of 52.
	vii.	**JOSIAH WALTON** b.20 October 1641 in Marblehead, Massachusetts. Josiah married ___. Date and place of their wedding is unknown. It is also unknown if they ever had any children. Josiah died in 1673 at the age of 32. His location at death is unknown.
	ix.	**MARIE WALTON** b. 14 May 1644 in Marblehead, Essex Co., Massachusetts. Marie married Robert Bartlett. It is unknown if they ever had any children. Her death date and her location at death are unknown. Age at death is unknown.

7. Margaret Irene Walton

MARGARET IRENE WALTON. (Rev. William Jr. [6], William[5], Thomas[4], Thomas[3], Thomas[2], John[1])

- Born 1640 in Kingston, Washington Co., Rhode Island.
- Married 1663 Captain Honorable John Fones Sr. **(Immigrant)** in Warwick, Kent, Rhode Island. Captain John Fones Sr (1645-1703) was the son of Richard Fones and Joanne Twidall.
- Died 20 April 1692 Kingston, Washington Co., Rhode Island at the age of 52.

Children of MARGARET IRENE[7] WALTON and Captain HONORABLE JOHN[8] FONES SR. are in the Fones chapter.

Source Citations for this Chapter

www.thehennesseefamily.com/getperson.php?personID=137130&tree=hennessee Rev. Wm Walton the Immigrant

https://www.findagrave.com/memorial.29952166/william-walton Find a Grave William Walton

https://www.ancestry.com/family-tree/pt/PersonMatch.aspx?tid=62293685&pid=40085166259&_phsrc=jJ05793&_phstart=degault&usePUBJs=true&cu Walton Ancestry Page

https://magenweb.org/Essex/Manchester/history.html

Manchester, Essex Co., MA History.

https://www.ancestry.com/imageviewer/collections/48213/images/PioneersMA-000734-477

Pioneers of Massachusetts, 1620-1650.

https://www.familysearch.org/ark:/61903/2:2:3PPN-BDB

Pedigree of Walton Family.

https://www.geni.people/John-Fones

Public Sign at the Old Burial Hill in downtown Marblehead, Massachusetts on Orne Street.

Chapter 34: The Washingtons

The Washington Family Line

Acquiring the Washington Name

Year 1183

The Washington family name was acquired in 1183 when William fitz Patrick de Hertburn assumed tenancy of the Washington lands from the Bishop of Durham at a cost of four pounds over a year. It was to his advantage to accept Washington in exchange for the Stockton lands since he was already heir to the lands at Offerton, which lie just across the River Wear from Washington. It was upon the acquisition of the Washington lands in 1183 that Sir William fitz Patrick de Hertburn became William Wessynton. It is highly probable according to genealogists, that the Washingtons, known in earlier lines, as de Wessington, descended in direct male line from Crinan Hereditary Lay Abbot of Dunkeld and hs wife Bethoc, daughter of Malcolm II, King of Scots through Gospatrick, 1st Earl of Dunbar, son of Maldred, Lord of Allerdale, son of Crinan Gospatrick (alias, Sir Patric of the Hirsel and Patric de Offerton, a year son os Gospatirc, 3rd Earl of Dunbar, was probably the father of Sir William de Hertburn (Hartburn) alias Wessington, from whom the Washington line undoubetdly stems.

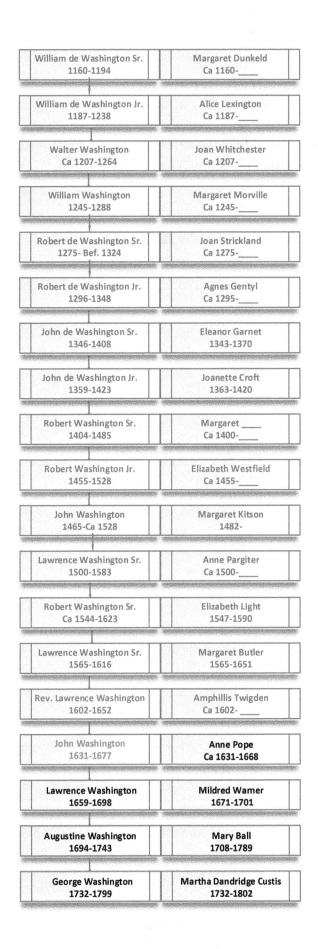

William de Washington Sr. 1160-1194	Margaret Dunkeld Ca 1160-____
William de Washington Jr. 1187-1238	Alice Lexington Ca 1187-____
Walter Washington Ca 1207-1264	Joan Whitchester Ca 1207-____
William Washington 1245-1288	Margaret Morville Ca 1245-____
Robert de Washington Sr. 1275- Bef. 1324	Joan Strickland Ca 1275-____
Robert de Washington Jr. 1296-1348	Agnes Gentyl Ca 1295-____
John de Washington Sr. 1346-1408	Eleanor Garnet 1343-1370
John de Washington Jr. 1359-1423	Joanette Croft 1363-1420
Robert Washington Sr. 1404-1485	Margaret ____ Ca 1400-____
Robert Washington Jr. 1455-1528	Elizabeth Westfield Ca 1455-____
John Washington 1465-Ca 1528	Margaret Kitson 1482-
Lawrence Washington Sr. 1500-1583	Anne Pargiter Ca 1500-____
Robert Washington Sr. Ca 1544-1623	Elizabeth Light 1547-1590
Lawrence Washington Sr. 1565-1616	Margaret Butler 1565-1651
Rev. Lawrence Washington 1602-1652	Amphillis Twigden Ca 1602-____
John Washington 1631-1677	**Anne Pope Ca 1631-1668**
Lawrence Washington 1659-1698	**Mildred Warner 1671-1701**
Augustine Washington 1694-1743	**Mary Ball 1708-1789**
George Washington 1732-1799	**Martha Dandridge Custis 1732-1802**

1. Sir William de Washington Sr.
AKA --- William Fitzpatrick Hertburn
WILLIAM[1] DE WASHINGTON SR.

- Born 1160 in England.
- Married circa 1186 Margaret Dunkeld of Huntington.
- Died 1194 in Washington Manor, Sutherland Co., Durham, England at the age of 34.

Child of WILLIAM[1] DE WASHINGTON and Margaret Dunkeld of Huntington was:

2.	I.	**WILLIAM DE WASHINGTON JR.** b. 1187 in Washington, England. William married Alice Lexington. William Jr. died 1238 in England at the age of 51.

2. William de Washington Jr.
WILLIAM[2] DE WASHINGTON JR. (William[1])

- Born 1187 in Durham, England.
- Married Alice Lexington.
- Died 1238 in England at the age of 51.

Child of WILLIAM[2] DE WASHINGTON and ALICE LEXINGTON was:

3.	i.	**WALTER DE WASHINGTON** b. 1207 in Washington, England. Walter married twice. Wife #1 _____. Walter and ___ had 4 children. Wife #2 Joan Whitchester. They were married circa 1244. The had I child during their marriage. **Walter died 14 May 1264 in the Battle of Lewes, Lewes, Sussex, England at the age of 57.**

There were also (four) half-siblings (mother unknown). Half-siblings' names are also unknown.

3. Walter de Washington The Battle of Lewes
WALTER[3] DE WASHINGTON (William[2], William[1]) **Fought in The Battle of Lewes**

- Born 1207 in Washington, England.
- Married circa 1227 Wife #1 ____. They had 4 children.
- Married circa 1244 Wife #2 Joan Whitchester. They were married in England. They had 1 child.
- **Died 14 May 1264 in The Battle of Lewes, Lewes, Sussex, England at age 57.**

The Battle of Lewes was one of two main battles of the conflict known as the Second Barons' War. It took place at Lewes in Sussex, on 14 May 1264. It marked the high point of the career of Simon de Montfort, 6th Earl of Leicester, and made him the "uncrowned King of England." Henry III left the safety of Lewes Castle and St. Pancras Priory to engage the barons in battle and was initially successful, with his son Prince Edward routing part of the baronial army with a cavalry charge. However, Edward pursued his quarry off the battlefield and left Henry's men exposed. Henry was forced to launch an infantry attack up Offham Hill where he was defeated by the barons' men defending the hilltop. The royalists fled back to the castle and priory and the King was forced to sign the Mise of Lewes, ceding many of his powers to Montfort.

There were 4 children born during the marriage of Walter Washington and ___. Their names are unknown.

Child of WALTER³ WASHINGTON and JOAN WHITCHESTER was:

4.	i.	SIR WILLIAM DE WASHINGTON b. 1245 in England. Sir William married Margaret Morville. Sir William and Margaret had 1 child during their marriage. Sir William died in 1288 in Washington, England at the age of 43.

4. Sir William De Washington

SIR WILLIAM⁴ DE WASHINGTON (Walter³, William², William¹)

- Born 1245 in England.
- Married 1274 Margaret Morville in England.
- Died 1288 in Washington, England at age 43.

Child of WILLIAM⁴ DE WASHINGTON and MARGARET MORVILLE was:

5.	i.	ROBERT DE WASHINGTON SR. b. 1275 in England. Robert married Joan Strickland in 1292. They had 2 children during their marriage. Robert died 18 August 1324 in England at the age of 49.

5. Robert De Washington Sr.

ROBERT⁵ DE WASHINGTON SR. (William⁴, Walter³, William², William¹)

- Born 1275 in England.
- Married 1292 Joan Strickland. They had 2 children.
- Died 18 August 1324 England at age 49.

Children of ROBERT⁵ DE WASHINGTON and JOAN STRICKLAND were:

6.	i.	ROBERT DE WASHINGTON JR. b. 1296 in Warner, Lancaster, England. Robert married Agnes Gentyl in 1341. They had 4 children during their marriage. Robert Jr. died in 1348 in England at the age of 52.
	ii.	John de Washington b. circa 1298 in Warner, Lancaster, England. It is unknown if John ever married and had any children. His death date and location at death are unknown. His age at death is unknown.

6. Robert de Washington Jr.

ROBERT⁶ DE WASHINGTON JR. (Robert⁵, William⁴, Walter³, William², William¹)

- Born1296 in Warner, Lancaster, England.
- Married 1341 Agnes Gentyl. They had 3 children.
- Died 1348 in England at the age of 52.

Children of ROBERT[6] DE WASHINGTON, and AGNES GENTYL were:

	i.	**AGNES DE WASHINGTON** b. circa 1342 in Warton, Lancaster, England. It is unknown if Agnes ever married and had any children. Her death date and location at death are unknown. Her age at death is unknown.
	ii.	**Robert De Washington** b. circa 1344 in Warton, Lancaster, England. It is unknown if Robert ever married and had any children. His death date and location at death are unknown. His age at death is unknown.
7.	iii.	**JOHN DE WASHINGTON SR.** b. circa 1346 in Warton, Lancaster, England. John Sr. married Eleanor Garnet. John Sr. and Eleanor had 3 children during their marriage. John Sr. died circa 1408 in Tewitfield, Warton, Lancaster, England at the age of 62.

7. John De Washington Sr.

JOHN[7] DE WASHINGTON SR. (Robert[6], Robert[5], William[4], Walter[3], William[2], William[1])
- Born circa 1348 in Warton, Lancaster, England.
- Married 1368 Eleanor Garnet. They had 3 children.
- Died circa 1408 in Tewitfield, Warton, Lancaster, England at age 62.

Children of JOHN[7] DE WASHINGTON and ELIZABETH WESTFIELD were:

8.	i.	**JOHN DE WASHINGTON JR.** b. 1369 Tewitfield, Warton, Lancaster, England. John Jr. married Joanette Croft (1363-1420). John Jr. and Joanette married circa 1400. They had 1 child during their marriage. John Jr. died 1423 Tewitfield, Warton, Lancaster, England at the age of 64.
	ii..	**Agnes De Washington** b. 1371 Tewitfield, Warton, Lancaster, England. It is unknown if Agnes ever married and had any children. Also, unknown is her death date and location at death. Her age at death is unknown.
	ii..	**LAWRENCE DE WASHINGTON** b.1373 Tewitfield, Warton, Lancaster, England. It is unknown if Lawrence ever married and had any children. Also, unknown is his death date and location at death. His age at death is unknown.

8. John De Washington Jr.
(Note – Last name with John Jr.'s son, Robert Sr., the "De" in the name Washington was dropped)

JOHN[8] DE WASHINGTON JR. (John[7], Robert[6], Robert[5], William[4], Walter[3], William[2], William[1])
- Born 1369 in Tewitfield, Warton, Lancaster, England.
- Married circa 1400 Joanette Croft (1363-1420). They had 1 child.
- Died 1423 in Tewitfield, Warton, Lancaster, England at age 64.

Child of ROBERT[8] WASHINGTON and ELIZABETH WESTFIELD was:

| 9 | I. | **ROBERT WASHINGTON SR.** b. 1401 in Warton, Lancaster, England. John Jr. married Margaret ___ circa 1434. They had 1 child during their marriage. Robert Sr. died on 7 December 1483 in Warton, Lancaster, England at the age of 79. |

9. Robert Washington Sr.

ROBEERT[9] WASHINGTON SR. (John[8], John[7], Robert[6], Robert[5], William[4], Walter[3], William[2], William[1])
- Born 1404 in Warton, Lancaster, England.
- Married circa 1434 Margaret _____. They had 1 child.
- Died 7 December 1483 in Warton, Lancaster, England at age 79.

Child of ROBERT[9] WASHINGTON Sr. and MARGARET ____ was:

| 10. | i. | **Robert Washington Jr.** b. 1435 in Warton, Lancaster, England. Robert Jr. married Elizabeth Westfield. Robert Jr. and Elizabeth were married circa 1464. They had 1 child during their marriage. Robert died 7 December 1483 in Warton, Lancaster, England at the age of 93. |

10. Robert Washington Jr.

ROBERT[10] LAWRENCE WASHINGTON JR. (Robert[9], John[8], John[7], Robert[6], Robert[5], William[4], Walter[3], William[2], William[1])
- Born circa 1435 in Warton, Lancaster, England.
- Married circa 1464 Elizabeth Westfield. They had 1 child.
- Died 1528 in Warton, Lancaster, England at age 93.

Child of ROBERT[10] WASHINGTON and ELIZABETH WESTFIELD was:

| 11. | I. | **John Washington** b. 1465 in Warton, Lancaster, England. John married Margaret Kitson. They were married circa 1500. They had 6 children during their marriage. John died before 1528 in Warton, Lancaster, England at the age of circa 63. |

11. John Washington

JOHN[11] WASHINGTON (Robert[10], Robert[9], John[8], John[7], Robert[6], Robert[5], William[4], Walter[3], William[2], William[1])
- Born 1465 in Warton, Lancaster, England.
- Married circa 1500 Margaret Kitson (b. 1482). They were married in Warton, Lancaster, England. They had 6 children.
- Died before 1528 in Warton, Lancaster, England at the age of circa 63.

Children of JOHN[11] WASHINGTON and MARGARET KITSON were:

	i.	**JANE WASHINGTON** b. 1502 in Lancaster, England. Jane married Humphrey Gardiner of Cockerham, Lancaster, England. It is unknown if they had any children during their marriage. They were married circa 1522, It is unknown when and where Jane died. Her age at death is unknown.
	ii.	**NICHOLAS WASHINGTON** b. 1504 in Tewitfield, Warton, Lancaster, England. It is unknown if he ever married and had any children. His death date and location at death are both unknown. His age at death is unknown.
	iii.	**LEONARD WASHINGTON** b. 1506 in Lancaster, England. Leonard married Elizabeth Croft. It is unknown if they had any children during their marriage. His death date and location at death are both unknown. His age at death is unknown.
	iv.	**PETER WASHINGTON** b. 1508 in Tewitfield, Warton, Lancaster, England. It is unknown if he ever married and had any children. His death date and location at death are both unknown. His age at death is unknown.
12	v.	**Lawrence WASHINGTON SR.** b. 1510 in Tewitfield, Warton, Lancaster, England. Lawrence married twice: Wife #1 Elizabeth ____ (Elizabeth was a widower of William Gough). Lawrence and Elizabeth had no children during their marriage. Wife #2 Anne Amy Pargiter. Lawrence and Anne Amy had 11 children during their marriage. Lawrence Sr. became the Mayor of Northampton in 1532. They were quite wealthy. Lawrence had the Tudor home, Sulgrave Manor, built. Lawrence died on 19 February 1583 at Sulgrave Manor, Northampton, England at the age of 73.
	vi.	Thomas Washington b. 1512 in Tewitfield, Warton, Lancaster, England. It is unknown if he ever married and had any children. His death date and location at death are both unknown. His age at death is unknown.

12. Lawrence Washington Sr.

LAWRENCE[12] WASHINGTON SR. (John[11], Robert[10], Robert[9], John[8], John[7], Robert[6], Robert[5], William[4], Walter[3], William[2], William[1])

- Born 1510 in Tewitfield, Warton, Lancaster, England.
- Married circa 1530 Wife #1 Elizabeth ____ (she was a widow of William Gough). Lawrence and Elizabeth had no children.
- Sulgrave Manor built circa 1530.
- Married circa 1531 Wife #2 Anne Pargiter, daughter of Robert Pargiter and Anne Knight. Lawrence and Anne had 11 children.
- Mayor in 1532 of Northampton, England.
- Died 19 February 1583 at Sulgrave Manor, in Northampton, England at the age of 73.

Lawrence Washington Sr. was a wool merchant. He was also the Mayor of Northampton in 1532. He took advantage of the dissolution of the monasteries and purchased three manors from the Crown including Sulgrave, which was held by his descendants until late 1659.

Sulgrave Manor was built by Lawrence Washington in the 1500s and he raised his 11 children there. It was a Tudor architecture home and is still standing today. One can visit it if one is in Northampton, England.

Sulgrave Manor
Northampton, England

There were no children of the marriage of LAWRENCE[12] WASHINGTON SR. and ELIZABETH ___ GOUGH.

Children of LAWRENCE[12] WASHINGTON Sr. and ANNE PARGITER were:

	i.	**Lawrence Washington Jr. Esquire** b. circa 1531 in Northampton, England. It is unknown if he ever married and had any children. His death date and location at death are both unknown. His age at death is unknown.
	ii.	**Christopher Washington** b. circa 1533 in Northampton, England. It is unknown if he ever married and had any children. His death date and location at death are both unknown. His age at death is unknown.
	iii	**George Washington** b. circa 1535 in Northampton, England. It is unknown if he ever married and had any children. George died April 1625 at the age of approx. 99.
	iv.	**Amy Washington** b. circa 1537 in Northampton, England. It is unknown if she ever married and had any children. Her death date and location at death are both unknown. Her age at death is unknown.
	v.	**Frances Washington** b. circa 1539 in Northampton, England. It is unknown if she ever married and had any children. Her death date and location at death are both unknown. Her age at death is unknown.
	vi	**Twin: Elizabeth Washington** b. circa 1540 in Northampton, England. It is unknown if she ever married and had any children. Her death date and location at death are both unknown. Her age at death is unknown.

	vii.	**Twin: Barbara Washington** b. circa 1540 in Northampton, England. It is unknown if she ever married and had any children. Her death date and location at death are both unknown. Her age at death is unknown.
	viii.	**Magdalen Washington** b. circa 1542 in Northampton, England. It is unknown if she ever married and had any children. Her death date and location at death are both unknown. Her age at death is unknown.
	ix.	**Twin: Margaret Washington** b. circa 1544 in Northampton, England. It is unknown if she ever married and had any children. Her death date and location at death are both unknown. Her age at death is unknown.
	x.	**Twin: Mary Washington** b. circa 1544 in Northampton, England. It is unknown if she ever married and had any children. Mary died 1622 at the age of 80. Her location at death is unknown.
13.	xi.	**Robert Washington Esquire Sr.** b. circa 1546 in Northampton, England. Robert married twice: Wife #1 Elizabeth Light (1547-1590) daughter of Walter Light and Ursula Woodford. Robert and Elizabeth were married in 1564. They had 9 children during their marriage. Wife #2 Anne Fisher. Robert and Anne were married in 1599. They had 6 children during their marriage. Robert died 10 March 1623 at Sulgrave Manor, Northampton, Virginia at the age of approx. 79. (Note this is both US President George Washington's line and the author's line).

13. Robert Washington Sr. Esquire of Silgrave Manor ***> *Connection Point*

ROBERT[13] WASHINGTON ESQUIRE SR. (Lawrence[12], John[11], Robert[10], Robert[9], John[8], John[7], Robert[6], Robert[5], William[4], Walter[3], William[2], William[1])

- Born circa 1546 in Northampton, England.
- Married 1564 Wife #1 Elizabeth Light (1547-1590) daughter of Walter Light and Ursula Woodford. They had 9 children.
- Married 1599 Wife #2 Anne Fisher. They had 6 children.
- Died 10 March 1623 Sulgrave Manor, Northampton, England at the age of approx. 79.

Children of ROBERT[13] WASHINGTON SR., Esquire and ELIZABETH LIGHT were:

Geo14A	i.	**Lawrence Washington Sr.** b. 1565 at Sulgrave Manor, Northampton, England. Lawrence Sr. married twice: Wife #1 Elizabeth Lyte who was the daughter & heiress of Walter Lyte of Radway, Warwickshire, England. Lawrence Sr. and Elizabeth were married circa 1585. They had 9 children during their marriage. Wife #2 Margaret Butler who was the daughter of William Butler and Margaret Greeke. Margaret b. circa 1565 – died 16 March 1651. They were married circa 1599 and had 17 children during their marriage. Lawrence died 1616 at Sulgrave Manor, Northampton, England at age 51.

	ii.	**ROBERT WASHINGTON JR.** b. 1568 at Sulgrave Manor, Northampton, England. It is unknown if he ever married and had any children. Also unknown are death date and location at death. Age at death is unknown.
Aut 14B	iii.	**WALTER WASHINGTON** b. 1570 at Sulgrave Manor, Northampton, England. Walter married Alice Murden in 1593. Walter and Alice had only 1 child. Walter died in 1597 at age 27, the year that his only child Katherine was born.
	iv.	**CHRISTOPHER WASHINGTON** b. 1572 at Sulgrave Manor, Northampton, England. It is unknown if he ever married and had any children. Also, unknown is death date and location at death. Age at death is unknown.
	v.	**WILLIAM WASHINGTON** b. 1574 at Sulgrave Manor, Northampton, England. It is unknown if he ever married and had any children. Also unknown are death date and location at death. Age at death is unknown.
	vi.	**THOMAS WASHINGTON** b. 1576 at Sulgrave Manor, Northampton, England. It is unknown if he ever married and had any children. Also unknown are death date and location at death. Age at death is unknown.
	vii.	**ANNE AMY WASHINGTON** b. 1578 at Sulgrave Manor, Northampton, England. It is unknown if she ever married and had any children. Also unknown are death date and location at death. Age at death is unknown.
	viii.	**URSULA WASHINGTON** b. 1580 at Sulgrave Manor, Northampton, England. It is unknown if she ever married and had any children. Also unknown is death date and location at death. Age at death is unknown.
	ix.	**ELIZABETH WASHINGTON** b. 1582 at Sulgrave Manor, Northampton, England. It is unknown if she ever married and had any children. Also unknown are death date and location at death. Age at death is unknown.

Children of ROBERT[13] WASHINGTON and ANNE FISHER were:

	i.	**ALBANE WASHINGTON** b.1584 at Sulgrave Manor, Northampton, England. It is unknown if she ever married and had any children. Also unknown are death date and location at death. Age at death is unknown.
	ii.	**GUY WASHINGTON** b. 1586 at Sulgrave Manor, Northampton, England. It is unknown if he ever married and had any children. Also unknown are death date and location at death. Age at death is unknown.
	iii.	**ROBERT WASHINGTON** b. 1588 at Sulgrave Manor, Northampton, England. It is unknown if he ever married and had any children. Also unknown are death date and location at death. Age at death is unknown.
	iv.	**MARY WASHINGTON** b. 1590 at Sulgrave Manor, Northampton, England. Mary married Martin Eden of Banbury, England. It is unknown if they ever had any children in their marriage. Mary's death date and location at death are unknown. Age at death unknown.

	v.	**MARGARET WASHINGTON** b. 1592 at Sulgrave Manor, Northampton, England. Margaret married John Gardiner of London, England. It is unknown if they ever had any children. Also unknown are death date and location at death. Age at death is unknown.
	vi.	**CATHERINE WASHINGTON** b. 1594 at Sulgrave Manor, Northampton, England. It is unknown if she ever married and had any children. Also unknown are death date and location at death. Age at death is unknown.

14A. Lawrence Washington Sr. of Sulgrave Manor

(Note this is President George Washington's Line)
Lawrence is Brother of Walter Washington (1570-1597)

LAWRENCE[14A] WASHINGTON SR (Robert[13], Lawrence[12], John[11], Robert[10], Robert[9], John[8], John[7], Robert[6], Robert[5], William[4], Walter[3], William[2], William[1])

- Born 1565 at Sulgrave Manor, Northampton, England.
- Married circa 1585 Wife #1 Elizabeth Lyte (1565-1592) Elizabeth was the daughter and heiress of Walter Lyte of Radway, Warwickshire, England. (There were no children born to Lawrence and Elizabeth.)
- Married circa 1593 Wife #2 Margaret Butler, who was the daughter of William Butler and Margaret Greeke. Margaret b. circa 1565 – died 16 March 1651. (Lawrence Sr. and Margaret had 17 children.)
- Died 1616 at Sulgrave Manor, Northampton, England at age 51.

Note: There were no children born during the marriage of Lawrence Washington Sr. and Elizabeth Lyte.

Children of LAWRENCE[14A] WASHINGTON SR. and MARGARET BUTLER were:

	i.	**ROBERT WASHINGTON** b. 1594 at Sulgrave Manor, Northampton, England. It is unknown if he ever married and had any children. Also unknown are death date and location at death. Age at death is unknown.
	ii.	**SIR JOHN WASHINGTON** b. 1596 at Sulgrave Manor, Northampton, England. It is unknown if he ever married and had any children. Also unknown are death date and location at death. Age at death is unknown.
	iii.	**SIR WILLIAM WASHINGTON** b. 1598 at Sulgrave Manor, Northampton, England. Sir William married Anne Villiers. It is unknown how many children they had during their marriage. Also unknown are Sir William's death date and location at death. His age at death is unknown.
	iv.	**RICHARD WASHINGTON** b. 1600 at Sulgrave Manor, Northampton, England. It is unknown if he ever married and had any children. Also unknown are death date and location at death. Age at death is unknown.
15.	v.	**REV. LAWRENCE WASHINGTON JR.** b 1602 in Hertfordshire, England. Lawrence Jr. studied at Oxford University. He married Amphillis Twigden in December 1633. Amphillis was the daughter of John Twigden and Anne Dicken. Lawrence

		and Amphillis had 6 children during their marriage. Rev. Lawrence died 21 January 1652 in Malden, Essex, England at the age of 50. He is buried the in All Saints Church Cemetery in Malden, Essex, England.
	vi.	**THOMAS WASHINGTON** b. 1604 at Sulgrave Manor, Northampton, England. It is unknown if he ever married and had any children. Also unknown are death date and location at death. Age at death is unknown.
	vii.	**TWIN: GREGORY WASHINGTON** b. 1606 at Sulgrave Manor, Northampton, England. It is unknown if he ever married and had any children. Also unknown are death date and location at death. Age at death is unknown.
	viii.	**TWIN: GEORGE WASHINGTON** b. 1606 at Sulgrave Manor, Northampton, England. It is unknown if he ever married and had any children. Also unknown are death date and location at death. Age at death is unknown.
	ix.	**TWIN: ELIZABETH WASHINGTON** b. 1608 at Sulgrave Manor, Northampton, England. It is unknown if she ever married and had any children. Also unknown are death date and location at death. Age at death is unknown.
	x.	**TWIN: JOAN WASHINGTON** b. 1608 at Sulgrave Manor, Northampton, England. It is unknown if she ever married and had any children. Also unknown are death date and location at death. Age at death is unknown.
	xi.	**MARGARET WASHINGTON** b. 1609 at Sulgrave Manor, Northampton, England. It is unknown if she ever married and had any children. Also unknown are death date and location at death. Age at death is unknown.
	xii.	**TWIN: ALICE WASHINGTON** b. 1610 at Sulgrave Manor, Northampton, England. It is unknown if she ever married and had any children. Also unknown are death date and location at death. Age at death is unknown.
	xiii.	**TWIN: FRANCES WASHINGTON** b. 1610 at Sulgrave Manor, Northampton, England. It is unknown if she ever married and had any children. Also unknown are death date and location at death. Age at death is unknown.
	xiv.	**AMY WASHINGTON** b. 1611 at Sulgrave Manor, Northampton, England. It is unknown if she ever married and had any children. Also unknown are death date and location at death. Age at death is unknown.
	xv.	**LUCY WASHINGTON** b. 1612 at Sulgrave Manor, Northampton, England. It is unknown if she ever married and had any children. Also unknown are death date and location at death. Age at death is unknown.
	xvi.	**BARBARA WASHINGTON** b. 1614 at Sulgrave Manor, Northampton, England. It is unknown if she ever married and had any children. Also unknown are death date and location at death. Age at death is unknown.
	xvii.	**JANE WASHINGTON** b. 1616 at Sulgrave Manor, Northampton, England. It is unknown if she ever married and had any children. Also unknown are death date and location at death. Age at death is unknown.

14B. Walter Washington of Sulgrave Manor
(Note: This is Author's Line)
Walter is Brother of Lawrence Washington Sr. (1565-1616)

WALTER[14B] WASHINGTON (Lawrence[14A] Robert[13], Lawrence[12], John[11], Robert[10], Robert[9], John[8], John[7], Robert[6], Robert[5], William[4], Walter[3], William[2], William[1]) Born 1570 in Sulgrave Manor, Northampton, England.

- Born 1570 at Sulgrave Manor, Northampton, England.
- Married 1593 Alice Murden. They had 1 child.
- Died 1597 in Radway, Warwickshire, England at age 27.

Child of WALTER[14B] WASHINGTON and ALICE MURDEN was:

**	i.	**Katherine Washington** b. 1597 in Radway, Warwickshire, England. Katherine married Thomas Stanton Jr. 30 July 1616 in Stratford-on-Avon, Warwickshire, England. Katherine and Thomas Jr. had 4 children during their marriage. Katherine died in 1622 in England at the age of 25 after giving birth to their fourth child. Both the baby and Katherine died during childbirth.

** Katherine Washington was born the year that her father Walter Washington died. Katherine later married Thomas Stanton Jr. b. 1595. They were married 30 July 1616 in Holy Trinity Church, Stratford-on-Avon, Warwickshire, England. Their son, Thomas Stanton III, became the famous Indian interpreter for the New England Colonies in America. Katherine never reached America. She died in England at the age of 25 years giving birth to their fourth child. Having both the mother and the baby die was a tragic time for this young family.

For further information on this family, please see the Stanton chapter.

15. Rev. Lawrence Washington Jr.
REV. LAWRENCE[15] WASHINGTON JR. (Walter[14B], Lawrence[14A] Robert[13], Lawrence[12], John[11], Robert[10], Robert[9], John[8], John[7], Robert[6], Robert[5], William[4], Walter[3], William[2], William[1])
- Born 1602 in Hertfordshire, England.
- Married December 1633 Amphillis Twigden who was the daughter of John Twigden and Anne Dicken. Rev. Lawrence Jr. and Amphillis had 6 children.
- Died 21 January 1652 in Malden, Essex, England at age 50.
- Buried in All Saints Church, Malden, Essex, England.

Rev. Lawrence Washington Jr. studied at Oxford University. At the time of his marriage to Amphillis Twigden, he had completed his studies there and was called to be a Rector of Purleigh, in Essex, England in 1633. During the English Civil War in 1643, the royalist Washington was stripped of his clerical position by the Parliamentary Puritans. Rev. Lawrence was reduced to serving as a Vicar of an impoverished parish in Little Braxted, Essex. His wife Amphillis returned to her parents' home in Tring, Hertfordshire, England. Little John (later known as Lieutenant Colonial John Washington) was eight years old and was unable to attend the Charterhouse School in London that his father had signed him up for. He then became apprenticed with a London merchant through the help of his relatives. His father Rev. Lawrence Washington Jr. died in poverty and is buried in the All Saints Church graveyard in Malden, Essex, England.

Children of Rev. LAWRENCE[15] WASHINGTON JR. and AMPHILLIS TWIGDEN were:

16.	I.	**LIEUTENANT COLONEL JOHN WASHINGTON** (Immigrant) b. January 1634 in Tring, Hertfordshire, England. **Immigrated in 1656 to the Colony of Virginia.** He married three times. Wife #1 Anne Pope (circa 1633-1668). She was the daughter of Nathaniel Pope and Lucy Fox. John and Anne #1 were married in 1658. They had 5 children during their marriage. Wife #2 Anne _____. John and Anne were married after 1668 after his first wife died that year. John and Anne #2 had 2 children during their marriage. Wife #3 Frances Gerard. John and Frances had no children during their marriage. **Lieut. Col. John fought in the Native Indian War.** He died in 1677 in Virginia at the age of 43.
	ii.	**LAWRENCE WASHINGTON III** b. 1636 in Tring, Hertfordshire, England. It is unknown if he ever married and had any children. Also unknown are death date and location at death. Age at death is unknown.
	iii.	**WILLIAM WASHINGTON** b. 1638 in Tring, Hertfordshire, England. It is unknown if he ever married and had any children. Also unknown are death date and location at death. Age at death is unknown.
	iv.	**ELIZABETH WASHINGTON** b. 1640 in Tring, Hertfordshire, England. It is unknown if she ever married and had any children. Also unknown are death date and location at death. Age at death is unknown.
	v.	**MARGARET WASHINGTON** b. 1642 in Tring, Hertfordshire, England. It is unknown if she ever married and had any children. Also unknown are death date and location at death. Age at death is unknown.
	vi.	**MARTHA WASHINGTON** b. 1644 in Tring, Hertfordshire, England. It is unknown if she ever married and had any children. Also unknown are death date and location at death. Age at death is unknown.

16. Lieutenant Colonel John Washington (Immigrant) Local Virginia Militia

LIEUTENANT COLONEL JOHN[16] WASHINGTON (Rev. Lawrence[15], Walter[14B], Lawrence[14A] Robert[13], Lawrence[12], John[11], Robert[10], Robert[9], John[8], John[7], Robert[6], Robert[5], William[4], Walter[3], William[2], William[1])

- Born January 1631 in Tring, Hertfordshire, England.
- Immigrated 1656 to the Colony of Virginia.
- Lieutenant Colonel in the Local Colonist Militia of Virginia.
- Married 1658 Wife #1 Anne Pope (circa 1633-1668). She was the daughter of Nathaniel Pope and Lucy Fox. Lieut. Col. John and Anne Pope had 5 children.
- Married Wife #2 aft 1668 Anne ___. Lieut. Col. John and Anne __ had 2 children.
- Married Wife #3 Frances Gerard. Lieut. Col. John and Frances had no children.
- Died in 1677 (1 September 1675 date of his will), Westmoreland Co., Virginia at age 46.

In 1656 The Washington family immigrated to America from England. They arrived in the Colony of Virginia after being shipwrecked. The ship was called the *Seahorse*. John Washington was a planter and soldier as well as a politician in colonial Virginia. He was also a Lieutenant Colonel in the local militia. He and the Washington family settled in Westmoreland Co., Virginia.

Children of LIEUTENANT COLONEL JOHN[16] WASHINGTON (IMMIGRANT) and ANNE POPE were:

Wife #1

17.	i.	**LAWRENCE WASHINGTON** b. 1659 in Westmoreland Co., Virginia. He married Mildred Warner. Lawrence and Mildred had 3 children during their marriage. Lawrence died February 1698 at Warner Hall, Gloucester Co., Colony of Virginia at the age of 39. Lawrence and his wife Mildred were the grandparents of our 1st President of the United Staes, George Washington.
	ii.	**John Washington Jr.** b. 1661 in Westmoreland Co., Virginia. It is unknown if he ever married and had any children. Death date and location and age at death are all unknown.
See Vol.2.	iii.	**Anne Washington** b. 1662 in Westmoreland Co., Virginia. It is unknown if she ever married and had any children. Death date and location and age at death are all unknown. Anne married Major Francis Wright (1658-1713). They were married in 1682 in Westmoreland Co., Virginia. They had 1 child, a son named John Wright Sr. He was about 12 years old when his mother Anne Washington Wright died. She died before 1697 and was about 35 years old when she died. She is buried in the Washington Family Burying Ground on the original Washington Estate in Westmoreland Co., Virginia. There is a large granite marker which was erected years later by an Act of Congress which denotes where on the estate the cemetery is located.
	iv.	**Unknown Name** b. 1665 in Westmoreland Co., Virginia. Possible stillborn.
	v.	**Unknown Name** b. 1667 in Westmoreland Co., Virginia. Possible stillborn.

Children of LIEUTENANT COLONEL JOHN[16] WASHINGTON (IMMIGRANT) and ANNE _____ were:

Wife #2

| | vi. | **Unknown Name** b. 1670 in Westmoreland Co., Virginia. Possible stillborn. |
| | vii. | **Unknown Name** b. 1672 in Westmoreland Co., Virginia. Possible stillborn. |

These four children above "Unknown Name" all died at birth. There is no name listed for them.

There were no Children of LIEUTENANT COLONEL JOHN[16] WASHINGTON (IMMIGRANT) and FRANCES GERARD.

17. Captain Lawrence Washington Militia Captain

CAPTAIN LAWRENCE[17] WASHINGTON (John[16], Rev. Lawrence[15], Walter[14B], Lawrence[14A] Robert[13], Lawrence[12], John[11], Robert[10], Robert[9], John[8], John[7], Robert[6], Robert[5], William[4], Walter[3], William[2], William[1])

- Born 1659 in Westmoreland Co., Virginia.
- **Captain Lawrence was a Militia Captain in the Army of Virginia.**
- Married 1686 Mildred Warner (1671-1701) daughter of Augustine Warner Jr. and Mildred Reade. Captain Lawrence and Mildred had 3 children.
- Died February 1698 at Warner Hall, Gloucester Co., Colony of Virginia at the age of 39.

Captain Lawrence was a Militia Captain and a Member of the Virginia House of Burgesses. He was very wealthy and owned about 1,000 acres on Bridge Creek in Westmoreland County, Virginia, as well as the Little Creek Plantation in that same county. The Washington family rose to great economic prominence, especially regarding real estate. Lawrence owned several plantations, mostly for tobacco cultivation.

Note: The same year that Captain Lawrence and Mildred's third child was born, Captain Lawrence died. Following Captain Lawrence's death, his wife Mildred Warner Washington remarried to married George Gale who moved the family to Whitehaven, England, where Mildred died in 1701 at the age of 30 following a difficult childbirth.

Children of CAPTAIN LAWRENCE[17] WASHINGTON and MILDRED WARNER were:

	i.	John Washington III b. 1692 at Bridges Creek Plantation in Westmoreland Co., Virginia. It is unknown if John ever married and had any children. John died in 1746 at the age of 54. His location at death is unknown.
18.	ii.	Augustine Washington b. 12 November 1694 at Bridges Creek Plantation in Westmoreland Co., Virginia. He married twice: Wife #1 Jane Butler (1699-1726). They were married in 1715. Lawrence and Jane had 4 children during their marriage. Jane died in 1726 and four years later Lawrence married again. Wife #2 Mary Ball (1708-1789). They were married in 1730 in Virginia. Lawrence and Mary had 6 children during their marriage. Augustine died in 1743 in Virginia at the age of 43.
	iii.	Mildred Washington b. 1698 at Bridges Creek Plantation in Westmoreland Co., Virginia. It is unknown if she ever married and had any children. Mildred died in 1747 at the age of 59. Her location at death is unknown.

18. Augustine "Gus" Washington

AUGUSTINE[18] "GUS" WASHINGTON (Lawrence[17], John[16], Rev. Lawrence[15], Walter[14B], Lawrence[14A] Robert[13], Lawrence[12], John[11], Robert[10], Robert[9], John[8], John[7], Robert[6], Robert[5], William[4], Walter[3], William[2], William[1])

- Born 12 November 1694 at Bridges Creek Plantation in Westmoreland Co., Virginia.
- Married 1715 Wife #1 Jane Butler (1699-1726). They had 4 children.
- Married 1730 Wife #2 Mary Ball (1708-1789), daughter of Joseph Ball and Mary Johnson. They had 6 children.
- Died 1743 Westmoreland Co., Virginia at the age of 43.

Augustine Washington, known as "Gus," was only four years old when his father died. His mother remarried and went off to England and died there in childbirth. Gus inherited a large sum of land in Virginia from his deceased father and when he grew older, he belonged to the Colony of Virginia's landed gentry. Gus was a planter and a slaveholder. He was President George Washington's father.

Children AUGUSTINE[18] WASHINGTON and JANE BUTLER were:

Wife #1

	I.	**BUTLER WASHINGTON** b. 1716 at Bridges Creek Plantation in Westmoreland Co., Virginia. Butler died in 1716. He was stillborn; died at birth).

	ii.	**LAWRENCE WASHINGTON** b. 1718 at Bridges Creek Plantation in Westmoreland Co., Virginia. It is unknown if Lawrence ever married and had any children. Lawrence died in 1752 at the age of 34. Location at death is unknown.
	iii.	**AUGUSTINE WASHINGTON JR.** b. 1720 at Bridges Creek Plantation in Westmoreland Co., Virginia. It is unknown if Augustine ever married and had any children. Augustine died in 1762 at the age of 42. Location at death is unknown.
	iv.	**JANE WASHINGTON** b. 1722 at Bridges Creek Plantation in Westmoreland Co., Virginia. Jane died in 1735 at the age of 13 in Westmoreland Co., Virginia.

Children of AUGUSTINE[18] WASHINGTON and MARY BALL were:

Wife #2

19.	i.	**PRESIDENT GEORGE WASHINGTON** b. 22 February 1732 at Popes Creek, Westmoreland Co., Virginia. President George married Martha Dandridge Custis on 6 January 1759 at Mount Vernon, Virginia. Martha had been previously married to Colonel Daniel Parke Custis and was a widow. Martha and Daniel had 4 children during their marriage but two of the four died very early in life. The two who survived were known as Nellie and "Wash." George and Martha had no children during their marriage. **George fought as a General in the Revolutionary War of 1776.** He became the first President of the United States of America. George died 14 December 1799 at Mount Vernon, Virginia at the age of 67.
	ii.	**ELIZABETH "BETTY" WASHINGTON** b. 1733 at Popes Creek, Westmoreland Co., Virginia. Elizabeth married Fielding Lewis and had children, but their names and number of them are unknown. Betty died in 1797, location unknown, at the age of 64.
	iii.	**COLONIAL SAMUEL WASHINGTON** b. 1734 at Popes Creek, Westmoreland Co., Virginia. Colonel Samuel was married and had children, but his wife and his children's names are unknown. It has been noted that Samuel's finances were unstable, and George often helped Samuel and his family financially. Colonel Samuel died in Virginia in 1781 at age 47.
	iv.	**JOHN AUGUSTINE WASHINGTON.** b. 1736 at Popes Creek, Westmoreland Co., Virginia. He married Hannah Bushrod in 1756. They had 6 children during their marriage. John died in 1787 at the age of 51 in Virginia.
	v.	**CHARLES WASHINGTON** b. 1738 at Popes Creek, Westmoreland Co., Virginia. It is unknown if he ever married and had any children. Charles died in 1799, location unknown, at the age of 61.
	vi.	**MILDRED WASHINGTON** b. 1739 at Popes Creek, Westmoreland Co., Virginia. She died the very next year at home at age 1 year old.

George was the oldest of Mary Ball's children. His closest sibling in age, Samuel, was two years younger, but it does not appear that they were particularly close. Samuel's finances were unstable, and George often helped Samuel's family, including paying for the education of the children.

John Augustine, four years younger than George, was a particular favorite. George described him in a letter as "the intimate companion of my youth and the friend of my ripened age." John often handled George's business affairs when he was away serving in the military.

George's only sister, Betty, married Fielding Lewis; the families visited each other often and corresponded when apart. Lewis also had monetary problems, and once again, George helped them out financially.

19. President George Washington

GEORGE[19] WASHINGTON (Augustine[18], Lawrence[17], John[16], Rev. Lawrence[15], Walter[14B], Lawrence[14A] Robert[13], Lawrence[12], John[11], Robert[10], Robert[9], John[8], John[7], Robert[6], Robert[5], William[4], Walter[3], William[2], William[1])

- Born 22 December 1732 at Popes Creek, Virginia.
- Married 6 January 1759 Martha Dandridge Custis (1732-1802) daughter of John Dandridge and Frances Jones. Martha was the widow of Daniel Parke Custis who died 1757.
- Died 14 December 1799 at Mount Vernon, Virginia at the age of 67.
- Buried at Mount Vernon, Virginia.

Note:

George Washington and this author are cousins. George's ancestry and the author's connection to the Washington family are both listed below. You will see how George's family merges with the author's Washington family. There were four sons born to Robert Washington (born 1544) and his wife Elizabeth Light, two of which are where our connection is. Robert's son **Lawrence Washington (born 1565) is George's family line.**

This author's line is with Lawrence's brother **Walter Washington (born 1570)**. From this connection, the family tree merges into one line, straight back to the first known Washington family of **William de Washington (1160-1194).**

President George Washington

Born: February 22, 1732
Died: December 14, 1799

President George Washington had no direct **descendants**, and his wife Martha Custis was a widow when they married. However, George adopted Martha's children and grandchildren, "Washy" and his sister "Nellie." George and Martha raised them on their Mount Vernon estate.

Martha Dandridge Custis and George Washington

Married: 6 January 1759

On May 15, 1750, at age 18, Martha married Daniel Parke Custis, a rich planter two decades her senior, and moved to his residence, White House Plantation, located on the south shore of the Pamunkey River, a few miles upriver from Chestnut Grove. They had four children together: Daniel, Frances, John, and Martha. Daniel (November 19, 1751–February 19, 1754) and Frances (April 12, 1753–April 1, 1757) died in childhood. The other two children, John "Jacky" Parke Custis (November 27, 1754–November 5, 1781) and Martha "Patsy" Parke Custis (1756–June 19, 1773), survived to young adulthood. Her husband's death in 1757 left Martha, the mother, a rich young widow at age 26, with independent control over a dower inheritance for her lifetime, and trustee control over the inheritance of her minor children. In all, she was left in custody of some 17,500 acres of land and 300 slaves, apart from other investments and cash. According to her biographer, "she capably ran the five plantations left to her when her first husband died, bargaining with London merchants for the best tobacco prices."

Martha Dandridge Custis in 1757

Mezzotint by John Folwell (1863) after a portrait by John Wollaston

Martha Custis, age 27, and George Washington, age 26, married on January 6, 1759, at the White House Plantation. As a man who lived and owned property in the area, Washington had known both Martha and Daniel Parke Custis for some time before Daniel's death. During March 1758, he visited her twice at the White House Plantation; the second time, he came away with either an engagement of marriage or at least her promise to think about his proposal. At the time, she was also being courted by planter Charles Carter, who was even wealthier than Washington.

The wedding was grand. Washington's suit was of blue and silver cloth with red trimming and gold knee buckles. The bride wore purple silk shoes with spangled buckles, which are displayed at Mount Vernon. The couple honeymooned at the Custis family's White House Plantation for several weeks before setting up house at Washington's Mount Vernon estate. They appeared to have had a solid marriage. Martha and George Washington had no children together, but they raised Martha's two surviving children. In 1773, her daughter Patsy died when she was 16 during an epileptic seizure. John Parke "Jacky" Custis left King's College that fall and married Eleanor Calvert in February 1774.

John Parke Custis was serving as a civilian aide to George Washington during the siege of Yorktown in 1781 during the American Revolutionary War when he died of "camp fever" (epidemic typhus). After his death, the Washingtons raised the youngest two of John's four children, Eleanor "Nelly" Parke Custis (March 31, 1779 – July 15, 1852), and George Washington Parke "Washy" Custis (April 30, 1781 – October 10, 1857). The two older girls remained with their mother. The Washingtons also provided personal and financial support to nieces, nephews, and other family members in both the Dandridge and Washington families. Because Martha was not content to live a private life at Mount Vernon and her homes from the Custis estate, she followed Washington to his winter encampments for each of the eight years of the war. She helped keep up morale among the officers. Martha became an early celebrity with press reports about her travels and towns greeting her arrival by ringing bells.

President George Washington (February 22, 1732– December 14**, 1799)** was an American political leader, military general, statesman, and Founding Father of the United States, who served as the First President of the United States from 1789 to 1797. He led the Patriot forces to victory in the American Revolutionary War, and presided at the Constitutional Convention of 1787, which established the US Constitution and a federal government for the United States. Washington has been called the "Father of the Nation" for his leadership in the formative days of our country.

Washington's first public office was serving as official Surveyor of Culpeper County, Virginia from 1749 to 1750. Subsequently, he received his initial military training (as well as a command with the Virginia Regiment) during the French and Indian War. He was later elected to the Virginia House of Burgesses and was named a delegate to the Continental Congress, where he was appointed Commanding General of the Continental Army. He commanded American forces, allied with France, in the defeat and surrender of the British during the Siege of Yorktown. He resigned his commission after the Treaty of Paris was signed in 1783.

Washington played an indispensable role in adopting and ratifying the Constitution and was then twice elected president by the Electoral College. He implemented a strong, well-financed national government while remaining impartial in a fierce rivalry between cabinet members Thomas Jefferson and Alexander Hamilton. During the French Revolution, he proclaimed a policy of neutrality while sanctioning the Jay Treaty. He set enduring precedents for the office of president, including the title "Mr. President," and his Farewell Address is widely regarded as a preeminent statement on republicanism.

Washington owned slaves, and, to preserve national unity, he supported measures passed by Congress to protect slavery. He later became troubled with the institution of slavery and freed his slaves in a 1799 will. He endeavored to assimilate Native Americans into the Anglo-American culture but combated indigenous resistance during instances of violent conflict. He was a member of the Anglican Church and the Freemasons, and he urged broad religious freedom in his roles as general and president. Upon his death, he was eulogized as "first in war, first in peace, and first in the hearts of his countrymen". He has been memorialized by monuments, art, geographical locations, including the national capital, stamps, and currency, and many scholars and polls rank him among the greatest of all the United States presidents. On March 13, 1978, Washington was posthumously promoted to the military rank of General of the Armies. George Washington died at his home at Mount Vernon, Virginia on December 14, 1799. Martha died at Mount Vernon on May 22, 1802. They are both buried at Mount Vernon, Virginia.

There were no children of GEORGE[19] WASHINGTON and MARTHA DANDRIDGE CUSTIS.

However, George Washington adopted Martha Dandridge Custis' children following Daniel Parke Custis' death and the marriage of George and Martha.

Children of DANIEL PARKE CUSTIS and MARTHA DANDRIDGE were:

	I.	**Daniel Custis Jr.** b. 1751 at the White House Plantation, located on the south shore of the Pamunkey River, a few miles upriver from Chestnut Grove. White House Plantation, located on the south shore of the Pamunkey River, a few miles upriver from Chestnut Grove. Daniel died in 1754 at the age of 3 years.
	ii.	Francis Custis b. 1753 White House Plantation, located on the south shore of the Pamunkey River, a few miles upriver from Chestnut Grove. Francis died in 1757 at the age of 4 years in Virginia.
	iii.	**John "Jacky" Parker Custis** b. 1754. White House Plantation, located on the south shore of the Pamunkey River, a few miles upriver from Chestnut Grove. John "Jacky" married Eleanor Calvert. They had 4 children (2 girls who went to live with their mother after their father Daniel Custis' death) and two younger children named Eleanor "Nellie" (1779-1852) & George Washington Parke "Washy" Custis (1781-1857). Nellie and her

		brother "Washy" lived with their grandmother Martha and her new husband George Washington following the death of their father John "Jacky" Parke Custis, who died in 1781 at the age of 21 in Virginia. He died the very same year his youngest child, "Washy" was born.
	iv.	**MARTHA "PATSY" PARKE CUSTIS** b. 1756. White House Plantation, located on the south shore of the Pamunkey River, a few miles upriver from Chestnut Grove in Virginia. She died in 1773 at the age of 17 years in Virginia.

Interesting Notes

George Washington Parke Custis "Washy" (April 30, 1781 – October 10, 1857) was the son of John Parker Custis. John Parker Custis was the stepson of President George Washington and Martha Dandridge Custis Washington was his mother. G.W. Parke Custis was an American plantation owner, antiquarian, author, and playwright. As a small child after his father died, little "Washy" and his sister Eleanor "Nellie" grew up at Mount Vernon and they were part of the Washington presidential household.

Upon reaching age 21, Custis (known as "Washy") inherited a large fortune from his late father, John Parke Custis, including a plantation in what became Arlington, Virginia. High atop a hill overlooking the Potomac River and Washington, DC, Custis built the Greek Revival mansion Arlington House (1803–1860), as a shrine to George Washington. There he preserved and displayed many of Washington's belongings. Custis also wrote historical plays about Virginia, delivered a number of patriotic addresses, and was the author of the posthumously published *Recollections and Private Memoirs of George Washington* (1860).

"Washy's" daughter, Mary Anna Randolph Custis (1807-1873), married General Robert E. Lee in 1831 and they had 7 children during their marriage. They inherited Arlington House and the plantation surrounding it, but the property was soon confiscated by the federal government during the Civil War. After the war, the US Supreme Court determined the property to have been illegally confiscated and ordered it returned to Lee's heirs, after regaining Arlington.

Custis Lee immediately sold it back to the federal government for its market value. Arlington House is now a museum, interpreted by the National Park Service as the Robert E. Lee Memorial. Fort Myer and Arlington National Cemetery are also located on what had been Custis' plantation.

Mary Anna Randolph Custis Lee
b. 1 October 1807 – d. 5 November 1873
Married in 1831. Had 7 children.
(She was the wife of General Robert E. Lee)
She was the daughter of "Washy" Custis

Her dad, Washy, grew up in the home of President George & Martha Washington

Her paternal grandfather & guardian was President George Washington

Her paternal grandmother was Martha Dandridge Custis Washington

Source Citations for this Chapter

https://www.archives.com/genealogy/president-washington.html President George Washington's Family Genealogical Records

https://en.wikipedia.otg/wiki/John_Washington Lieutenant Jon Washington's Records.

https://www.geni.com/people/Lawrence-Washington-1st-of-Sulgrave/6000000007 Lawrence Washington Esquire.

https://history.wika.org/wiki/Augustine_Washington Augustine Washington's family life.

https://en.wikipedia.org/wiki/Washington_family Washington Family - Roots in England.

Westmoreland Co., Virginia Deed. Patents & Wills 1665-1677 Will of John Washington.

The History of Our Country: From its Discovery by Columbus to the Celebration of the Centennial Anniversary of The Declaration of Independence by Abby Sage Richardson, published in 1875. H.O. Houghton and Company.

Washington of Adwick: Origin of the Washington Family, Rotherhamweb.co.uk

https://web.arcive.org/web/20090105215727

https://www.rotherhamweb.co.uk//genealogy/washington.htm

https://en.wikipedia.org/wiki/George_Washington_Parke_Custis "Interesting Notes"

Chapter 35: The Wests

The West Family Line

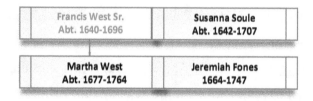

Francis West Sr. Abt. 1640-1696	Susanna Soule Abt. 1642-1707
Martha West Abt. 1677-1764	Jeremiah Fones 1664-1747

1. Francis West Sr. (Immigrant)

FRANCIS[1] WEST SR.

- Born circa 1640 in Hawes, Yorkshire, England.
- Arrival circa 1660 in Plymouth, Plymouth Co., Massachusetts.
- Married circa 1660 Susanna Soule in Plymouth, Plymouth Co., Massachusetts. Susanna was the daughter of George Soule "The Pilgrim" and Mary Beckett.
- Susanna was born circa 1642 and she died in January 1707 in Kings Towne, Washington Co., Rhode Island at the age of approx. 65.
- Died 2 January 1696 in North Kings Town, Washington Co., Rhode Island at age approx. 56.

West Family Name

The family name West has a special meaning both in middle Europe and in Germany. In both areas of the world, it refers to a topographical meaning as to where a family came from (a family who lived west of a settlement) or for a family who had migrated from an area further west in location.

Francis West's parents are unknown as of this writing despite much genealogical research. How Francis West came to America is also unknown and some believe he never immigrated but was born in Plymouth, Massachusetts with his parents unknown. However, the discovery of a family diary provides proof to this author that Francis West Sr. was born in Europe. (See the diary writing in following pages.)

The following is known:

- The year of the marriage of Francis West Sr. and George Soule's daughter Susanna Soule has been estimated by the birth of their children in the Plymouth Colony. (Estimated at 1661.)
- The West family back in the 1600s was called the "Wast" family, probably as that was how the West name was pronounced.

From the Kingston, Rhode Island courthouse records of the 1600s:
- "29 October 1668 Phillip, Sachem of Pocanokett, petitioned the court for justice against Francis Wast. Phillip complained that Wast had taken a gun and a hog from some of his men. The matter was referred to the selectmen at Taunton, and a report was made in court on 1 June 1669. Francis was to pay 30 shillings for the hog and to return the gun."

- "6 September 1687 Francis Sr. was on a list of inhabitants to be taxed in Kingstown, Rhode Island, then called Rochester. Francis Sr. was taxed 2 shillings 1 pence." His sons, Francis Wast Junior, and Richard Wast were also on the list, but not taxed. Note: It was written in the tax records Wast not West (written as it sounded).
- The *George Soule: Mayflower Families in Progress* book neglects to mention that a Francis West was made a freeman of Duxbarrow 29 May 1670. The elder Francis had long since been made freeman. This date is too early for the sons of Francis. Conclusion: this date belongs to Susanna's husband, Francis West Sr.
- From here we can speculate. His birth was not in America or Rhode Island, but in Europe, sometime between say 1630 and 1640. The Mayflower Society uses England about 1634. His marriage was around 1661, based on the estimated births of children about 1662, in Plymouth or Duxbury, both in Plymouth Colony. Francis West Sr.'s death was after the 1687 tax list. It may be 2 January 1696 in Kingstown or North Kingstown, Rhode Island, but the Mayflower Society failed to mention the significance of this date.
- Francis Sr. and Susannah and family may have left Plymouth Colony about the time of King Philip's War or after the death of Susannah's father George Soule about January 1678/9. The births of Francis' last three children were recorded in North Kingstown, Rhode Island, one in 1681 and twins in 1684. It is believed that they went to Kings Town, Rhode Island and settled there.

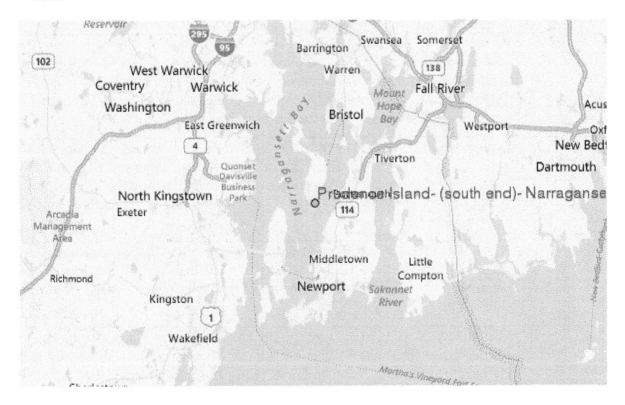

In 1924 an old diary was found in a home near Boston which mentions Francis West and his wife Susanna Soule (daughter of the Pilgrim Father George Soule). A facsimile of a page from the diary was published in the *Boston Evening Transcript*. It was found through the courtesy of Mrs. Elvira Jerusha (West) Coney of Ware, Massachusetts. It was written by her paternal grandfather Elder Samuel West.

"Samuel West's Memorandum Book"
1802 August 23rd

"My great grandfather Francis West Came from Europe to America Soon after the first Settlement at Plymouth and Soon after his arrival he married A young Lady By the name of Sole daughter of Mr George Sole (he came with his family to Plymouth in the first Vessel that Came there from Europe) by whom he had Seven Sons & 2 daughter "his Sons names ware Francis Thomas Peter William Richard Clemment & John his daughters names ware Martha & Susanna Martha married a Fones by whom she had Children Susann Married a Barber By Whom She had a number of Sons & daughters."

Children of FRANCIS[1] WEST SR. and SUSANNA SOULE are:

	i.	**FRANCIS WEST JR.** b. 1660 in Duxbury, Plymouth Co., Massachusetts. Francis Jr. married Mary ____. Francis Jr. and Mary were married circa 1682 in Kings Town, Washington Co., Rhode Island. It is unknown how many children they had during their marriage. Francis Jr. died before 13 October 1724 which is the date his will was proven in Westerly, Washington Co., Rhode Island. His age at death was 64.
	ii.	**RICHARD WEST** b. circa 1663 in Duxbury, Plymouth Co., Massachusetts. Richard married Mary Samson on 26 October 1693. It is unknown how many children they had during their marriage. Richard died 17 November 1727. His location at death is unknown. His age at death is approx. 63.
	iii.	**PETER WEST** b. circa 1665 in Duxbury, Plymouth Co., Massachusetts. Peter married Patience ____. They were married circa 1674. Peter and Patience had 9 children during their marriage. Patience died on 20 February 1721 in Plymouth, Massachusetts. Peter inherited his father's estate. Peter died on 29 February 1720 in Duxbury, Massachusetts at the age of approx. 55.
	iv.	**SUSANNAH ELIZABETH WEST** b. 23 October 1666 in Duxbury, Plymouth Co., Massachusetts. Susannah Elizabeth married Moses Barber on 24 March 1692. She and her husband did have children during their marriage, but their names are unknown. Susanna died on 4 April 1758. Her location at her death is unknown. Her age was 92.
	v.	**JOHN WEST** b. circa 1668 in Duxbury, Plymouth Co., Massachusetts. John married Deborah ____. It is unknown if they had any children during their marriage. It is also unknown when and where he died. His age at death is unknown.
2.	vi.	**MARTHA WEST** b. 1676 in Duxbury, Plymouth Co., Massachusetts. Martha married twice: Husband #1 James Card Sr. There were no children from this marriage. Husband #2 Jeremiah Fones (1664-1747). Martha and Jeremiah had 7 children during their marriage. Martha died 2 December 1764 in North Kings Towne, Rhode Island at the age of 88.
	vii.	**WILLIAM WEST** b. 31 May 1681 in Kings Town, Washington Co., Rhode Island. William married Jane Tanner. They were married circa 1700. Jane was the daughter of Francis Tanner and his wife ____ Babcock. William and Jane had 11 children during their marriage. William died after July 1742 in Charlestown, Washington Co., Rhode Island at the age of approx. 61.
	viii.	**TWIN: THOMAS WEST** b. 18 September 1684 in Kings Town, Washington Co.,

		Rhode Island. Thomas married Dorcas Rathbone. They were married on 20 September 1716. It is unknown how many children they had during their marriage. Thomas died in July 1744 at the age of 60. His location at death is unknown.
	ix.	**TWIN: CLEMENT WEST** b. 18 September 1684 in Kings Town, Washington Co., Rhode Island. Clement married Sarah ___. It is unknown if they had any children during their marriage. Clement died in 1749 at the age of 65. His location at death is unknown.

2. Martha West

MARTHA[2] WEST (*Francis*[1])

- Born circa 1677 in Duxbury, Plymouth Co., Massachusetts.
- Married Husband #1 James Card Sr. Martha and James were married on 4 March 1703.
- Married Husband #2 Jeremiah Fones (1664-1774). Martha and Jeremiah were married in November 1710 in Jamestown, Rhode Island.
- Died 2 December 1764 in North Kings Towne, Rhode Island at the age of approx. 87.

There were no children born during the marriage of Martha West and James Card Sr.

Children of MARTHA[2] WEST and JEREMIAH FONES are documented in the Fones chapter.

Source Citations for this Chapter

https://www.findagrave.com/memorial/62782199/francis-john-west

https://www.findagrave.com/memorial/627821621/susannah-west

https://www.ancestry.com/mediaui-viewer/tree/40149383/person/28650362444/media/3743e3c0-ff42-4921-b6f9-39d849ebabbd?destTreeId=6229368... Samuel West's Memorandum Book.

https://www.wikitree.com/wiki/West-285

The Great Migration Begins, Immigrants to New England 1620-1633 Volume 3, P-W by Robert Charles Anderson, 1995. Boston, Massachusetts.

The Genealogical Dictionary of Rhode Island by John Osborne Austin, 1969 NEHGS Library 101 Newbury Street, Boston, Massachusetts. Reference Room Ref. F-78/AG 35.

The New England Marriages Prior to 1700 by Clarence Almon Torrey, Genealogical Publishing Co., Baltimore, Maryland. 4th Printing, 1992.

Genealogies of Mayflower Families by Gary Boyd Roberts, New England Historical & Genealogical Register, Volume II Reprinted for the Clearfield Company Inc. by the Genealogical Publishing Co., Baltimore, Maryland, 2000.

The "Silver Books" Mayflower Families Through Five Generations Volume III, George Soule, Published by the General Society of Mayflower Descendants, 1980.

The Kingston Rhode Island Court House Book of Taxes of the 1600 period, Kingston Rhode Island Court House Records.

George Soule: Mayflower Families In Progress, Revised Edition, by Robert S. Wakefield, FASG, Published by the General Society of Mayflower Descendants, Plymouth. Massachusetts , 1992.

Chapter 36: White

The White Family Line

John White "The Elder" 1450-1518	Alice Hungerford 1426-1471
Marcus White 1471-1530	Margaret ___ 1476-1530
John White Sr. 1572-1623	Margaret Gale 1590-1624
John Marcus White Jr. 1550-1618	Elizabeth Isabel Bawlie 1552-1601
Martha Susan White 1575-1648	Rev. William Cooke 1562-1615

WHITE FAMILY SHEILD

1. John White "The Elder"
John[1] White "The Elder"
- Born 1450 in Timsbury, Hampshire, England.
- Married circa 1470 Alice Hungerford (1426-1471). They were married in Hampshire Co., England.
- Died 1518 Winchester, Hampshire, England, age 68.

Child of JOHN[1] WHITE "The Elder "and ALICE HUNGERFORD was:

2.	I.	MARCUS WHITE b. 1471 in Timsbury, Hampshire, England. Marcus married Margaret _____ (1476-1530). They were married circa 1509 in Timsbury, Hampshire, England. They had 1 child during their marriage. Marcus died on 27 March 1530 in Timsbury, Hampshire, England at the age of 79.

2. Marcus "Mark" White

MARCUS[2] "MARK" WHITE (John[1])

- Born 1471 in Timsbury, Hampshire, England.
- Married circa 1509 Margaret _____ (1476-1530) in Timsbury, Hampshire, England.
- Died 27 March 1530 Timsbury, Hampshire, England at the age of 79.

Child of MARCUS[2] "MARK" WHITE and Margaret _____ was:

3.	I.	JOHN WHITE SR. b. 1510 in Timsbury, Hampshire, England. John married Mildred Weston (1528- ___). John Sr. and Mildred were married in 1549. They had 1 child During their marriage. John Sr. died 1 February 1579 in Timsbury, Hampshire, England at the age of 69.

3. John White Sr. of Timsbury

JOHN[3] WHITE SR. (Marcus[2], John[1])

- Born May 1510 in Timsbury, Hampshire, England.
- Married 1549 Mildred Weston (1528-___). John Jr. and Mildred were married in Timsbury, Hampshire, England.
- Died 1 February 1579 in Timsbury, Hampshire, England at the age of 69.

Child of JOHN[3] WHITE SR. of Timsbury and MARGARET GALE was:

4	I.	John Marcus White Jr. b.1550 Stanton, Oxfordshire, England. m. 1570 Elizabeth Isabel Bawle (1552-30 December 1601) in Staffordshire, England. John Jr. d. 1618 in Stanton, Oxfordshire, England.

4. John Marcus White Jr.

JOHN MARCUS[4] WHITE JR. (John Sr.[3], Marcus[2], John[1])

- Born 1550 Stanton, Oxfordshire, England.
- Married 1570 Elizabeth Isabel Bawlie (1552-30 December 1601) in Staffordshire, England.
- Died 1618 in Stanton, Oxfordshire, England at the age of 68.

Back in those days of the 1500s, the water was undrinkable in most towns and villages in England. They drank beer instead of the polluted water. The beer was sanitized. The first Mash of Beer, which was extraordinarily strong, was drunk by men. The second was drunk by women and the third, which was much weaker, was drunk by children.

Rev. John White "The Patriarch of Dorchester"

"The Patriarch of Dorchester"
Clergyman
Rev. John White
(1574/5-1648)

Rev. John White "The Patriarch of Dorchester" was born in 1575 in Stanton, Oxfordshire, England. **He was the son of John White (1550-1618) and wife Elizabeth "Isabel" Bawlie. (1552-1601).** He was born in the two-story house of Manor Farm which was situated across the street from the 13th-century Parish Church of St. John and only a few miles northeast of Oxford, England.

He was an older brother of our ancestor **Martha White Cooke (1589-1648), who was the wife of Rev. William Cooke.** Rev. John White married Anne Burgess in 1606, who was the daughter of John Burgess of Peterborough, England. Rev. John and Anne had four sons during their marriage.

Rev. John White's formal education & appointments consisted of the following:

New College BA Degree received on 12 April 1597.

New College MA Degree received on 16 January 1600.

Ordained at St. Peter's Church in East Oxford 7 March 1602.

Rector of Holy Trinity Church in Dorchester 11 November 1605.

Rev. John and Anne along with their family were settling into their home in Dorchester. Their church was growing and a few years later in 1613 a fire spread throughout the town and many places were severely burned. Their parish home was burned but not destroyed. The Great Fire of 1613 destroyed half the town. 170 homes including most of the public buildings were destroyed! Of the three main churches in Dorchester, only Holy Trinity, of which Rev. John White was the rector, was spared the devastating flames.

During the 17th century in England there was a great deal of religious persecution, resulting in the birth of the Puritan and the Separatists movements, both of which desperately sought greater freedom of worship. From as early as 1607 some escaped to Holland, but a new phase began when the *Mayflower* ship carrying the Pilgrim Fathers landed in Cape Cod, Bay State (later known as Massachusetts). They landed there on Christmas Day in 1620.

However, Rev. John White did not agree with either the Separatist or the Puritan movements. He believed that the church could be reformed from within. He did see and recognize the business and religious possibilities that the new colony in America represented. With his usual zeal, he set forth to start a movement of his own. He managed to raise up the Dorchester Company. Rev. John White felt that he could form the nucleus for a larger colony and a refuge for those who were persecuted for their religion, both from those wishing to leave the Separatist movement at Plymouth, Massachusetts and from those in England. License to search for a new plantation was granted to them (Rev. John White and his band of followers) on 18 February 1622 or 1623. They organized the "Dorchester Company" and formally organized their venture to the New World in the Bay State Colony. They soon raised funds with 119 stockholders. Many of his followers were merchants and investors from Dorset, Somerset, and the West Country. As news spread that the Puritans were being successful, more enthusiasm in England grew and they joined the followers of Rev. John White. He prepared his own ship called the *Mary and John* and they set sail for America on 20 March 1630.

The *Mary & John* -- 20 March 1630

The band of followers of Rev. John White settled in the area which is now known as Beverly, Massachusetts. It was called "The Cape Ann Enterprise." They settled on land near the Danvers, Massachusetts plantation of the ship *Abigail*. This plantation was under the leadership of John Endicott, who had arrived in 1628. By 1631 in this Danvers/Beverly area, they had a congregation of at least 2,000 souls.

In 1643 Rev. John White returned to Dorchester, England, and on 12 June 1643 he was called on the Assembly of Learned and Godly Divines to be consulted with Parliament to settle issues in the Government of the Church. The ordinance stated that all and every person named were to meet and assemble at Westminster in the King Henry VII's Chapel. This body became known as the Westminster Assembly of Divines. According to Anthony Wood, "Rev. John White was one of the most learned and moderate among them." He was obviously well respected as he was appointed chairman of one of the committees. Following this appointment, he then returned to the colony in America.

Three years later he again returned to Dorchester in 1646. He was now 71 years old and felt that he could no longer continue his pastoral duties properly. He was also burdened with financial concerns. Rev. John White died very suddenly on 21 July 1648. He was buried 3 days later under the south porch of the St. Peter's Church, where there is a plaque placed in his honor. He was financially destitute. The porch was hung in black for a full month following his funeral.

Children of John MARCUS[4] WHITE JR. and Elizabeth Isabel Bawlie were:

	i.	**MARY MARTHA WHITE** b. 1570 in Stanton, Oxfordshire, England. She married Rev. John Terry, rector of Stockton Church is Wiltshire, England. It is unknown if they had any children during their marriage. Mary Martha died 12 February 1637 in Dorchester, England at the age of 67.
	ii.	**REV. JOSIAH WHITE** b. 1572 in Stanton, Oxfordshire, England. He was a merchant in Dorchester, England. He married Margery Hallett of Bradpole. They had one son John. Rev. Josiah was made Dean and Priest of Queen's College Chapel in Oxford 3 June 1599. Josiah died in 1674 in Dorchester, England at the age of 102!
	iii.	**REV. JOHN WHITE "The Patriarch of Dorchester" Clergyman** b. 1574 in Stanton, Oxfordshire, England. He married Anne Burgess in 1606. She was the daughter of John Burgess of Peterborough, England. Rev. John and his wife had 4 sons during this marriage. Rev. John organized a political following, travelled to the Colonies, and returned to England. He died in 1648 back in Dorchester, England at the age of 74. (See picture above.)
	iv.	**STEPHEN WHITE** b. 1578 in Stanton, Oxfordshire, England. Stephen married Mary Waterhouse. They had 8 children during their marriage. It is unknown when and where Stephen died. His age at his death is unknown.
5.	v.	**MARTHA SUSAN WHITE** b.1589 in Stanton, Oxfordshire, England. Martha Susan married twice: Husband #1 Vicar Rev. William Cooke. They were married on 27 April 1597 in Stockton, Wiltshire, England. They had 11 children during their marriage. Husband #2 ____ Moore. There were no children born during this marriage. Martha Susan died 28 March 1648 in Stanton, Oxfordshire, England age 73.
	vi.	**ELIZABETH WHITE** b. 1590 married twice: Husband #1 Thomas Gardner. They had 7 children during their marriage. Husband #2 ___Allen. They had no children during this marriage. Elizabeth's death date and location at death are both unknown. Age at death is unknown.

5. Martha Susan White

MARTHA SUSAN[5] WHITE (John Marcus[4], John Sr.[3], Marcus[2], John[1])

- Born 1575 in Stanton, Oxfordshire, England.
- Married 27 April 1597 Husband #1 Vicar Rev. William Cooke in Stockton, Wiltshire, England.
- Married 1629 Husband #2____Moore. They were married in England.
- Died 28 March 1648 in Stanton, Oxfordshire, England at the age of 73.

Children of MARTHA[5] SUSAN WHITE and Vicar Rev. William Cooke are documented in the Cooke chapter.

There were no children born during the marriage of MARTHA SUSAN WHITE Moore and ___ Moore.

Source Citations for this Chapter

www.thehennesseefamily.com/getperson.php?personID=141174&tree=hennessee

www.thehennesseefamily.com/getperson.php?personID=141186&tree=hennessee

www.thehennesseefamily.com/getperson.php?personID=141187&tree=hennessee

www.thehennesseefamily.com/getperson.php?personID=143162&tree=hennessee

www.thehennesseefamily.com/getperson.php?personID=143164&tree=hennessee

Five Hennessee Family Pages includes the early White Family Genealogy.

https://freepages.rootweb.com/-fordingtondorset/genealogy/Files/DorchesterRevJohnWhite1575-1648.html Rev. John White MA (1574/5-1648) Patriarch of Dorchester and Founder of Massachusetts, Compiled by Michael Russell OPC for Fordington February 2009.

https://www.ancestry.com/family-tree/person/tree/4434176/person/422257754829/facts

https://www.wikitree.com/wiki/White-4322

The Great Migration Begins: Immigrants to New England, 1620-1633, by Robert Charles Anderson, New England Historical Genealogical Society, Boston, Massachusetts, 1995.

https://findagrave.com/memorial/116547944/martha-moore

Chapter 37: The Yorkes

The Yorke Family Line

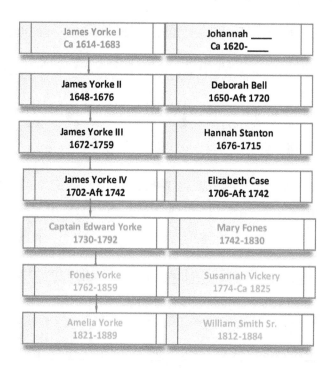

1. James Yorke Sr. (Immigrant)

JAMES[1] YORKE Sr.

- Born circa 1614 in Yorkshire, England.
- **Arrival circa 1630 in The Colony of Virginia on the sailing ship *Philip*.**
  James Sr. travelled up to the Bay State of Massachusetts and settled in the town of Braintree, Norfolk Co. where he met his bride-to-be Johannah ___.
- Married circa 1637 Johannah ____ (circa 1614 - ___). They were married in Braintree, Norfolk Co., Massachusetts.
- Died 1683 in Braintree, Norfolk, Massachusetts at the age of approx. 69 years.

Child of JAMES[1] YORKE SR. and JOHANNAH ____ was:

2.	i.	**JAMES YORKE JR.** b. 14 June 1648 in Braintree, Norfolk Co., Massachusetts. James Jr. married Deborah Bell (19 January 1669- after 1720). James Jr. and Deborah had 4 children during their marriage. Deborah remarried to Henry Eliot Sr. following James Yorke Jr.'s death and she had 8 additional children during that marriage. James Jr. died on 26 October 1676 in Stonington, New London Co., Connecticut at the age of 28.

2. James Yorke Jr.

JAMES^2 YORKE JR. (James Sr.[1])

- Born 14 June 1648 in Braintree, Norfolk Co., Massachusetts.
- Married 19 January 1669 Deborah Bell (1650-after 1720). She was the daughter of Thomas Bell Sr. and Anne _____. James Jr. and Deborah were married in Stonington, New London Co., Connecticut.
- Died 26 October 1676 in Stonington, New London Co., Connecticut, at the age of 28.

Children of JAMES² YORKE JR. and DEBORAH BELL were:

	i.	DEBORAH BELL YORKE b. 8 January 1670 in Stonington, New London Co., Connecticut. Deborah died on 21 February 1672 in Stonington, New London Co., Connecticut, at the age of 2.
3.	ii.	JAMES YORKE III b. 17 December 1672 in Stonington, (also called South Town), New London Co., Connecticut. James III married Hannah Stanton on 13 November 1695 in Stonington, New London Co., Connecticut. They had 9 children. James III died in 1759 in Stonington at the age of 87.
	iii.	WILLIAM YORKE b. 24 July 1674 in Stonington, New London Co., Connecticut. William married Mary Utley Alley on 18 December 1695 in Stonington, New London Co., Connecticut. It is unknown if they had any children during their marriage. William died in 1697 in Stonington, New London Co., Connecticut at the age of 23.
	iv.	THOMAS Yorke b. 14 October1676 in Stonington, New London Co., Connecticut. Thomas married Mary Brown on 9 January 1704. It is unknown if they had any children during their marriage. Thomas' death date and location at death are unknown. His age at his death is also unknown.

3. James Yorke III

JAMES[3] YORKE III (James Jr.[2], James Sr.[1])

- Born 17 December 1672 in Stonington, (also called South Town), New London Co., Connecticut.
- Married 13 November 1695 Hannah Stanton. Hannah (1676-1715) was the daughter of Joseph Stanton Sr. and Hannah Mead. James Yorke III and Hannah were married in Stonington, New London Co., Connecticut.
- Died 1759 in Stonington, New London Co., Connecticut, at the age of 87.

Children of JAMES^3 YORKE III and HANNAH STANTON were:

	i.	HANNAH YORKE b. 21 March 1697 in Stonington, New London Co., Connecticut. It is unknown if she ever married and if she had any children. Her death date and location at death are both unknown. Her age at death is also unknown.
	ii.	JOANNAH YORKE b. 31 December 1699 in Stonington, New London Co., Connecticut. Joanna married Joseph Larkin on 24 July 1730. It is unknown if Joannah and Joseph had any children during their marriage. Also unknown are her death date and her location at death. Her age at death is also unknown.

4.	iii.	**JAMES YORKE IV** b. 6 September 1702 in Stonington, New London, Connecticut. James IV married Elizabet Case on 11 June 1727 in South Kingston, Washington Co., Rhode Island. They had 6 children during their marriage. James IV died after 1742 at the age of approx. 40.
	iv.	**EDWARD YORKE** b. 14 March 1704 in Stonington, New London Co., Connecticut. It is unknown if he ever married and had any children. His death date and location at death are both unknown. His age at death is also unknown.
	v.	**STANTON YORKE** b. 14 March 1706 in Stonington, New London Co., Connecticut. It is unknown if he ever married and had any children. His death date and location at death are both unknown. His age at death is also unknown.
	vi.	**THANKFUL YORKE** 26 February 1711 in Stonington, New London Co., Connecticut. Thankful married Isaac Peckham circa 1730. It is unknown if they had any children during their marriage. Her death date and location at death are unknown. Her age at death is also unknown.
	vii.	**JOSEPH YORKE** b. circa 1713. It is unknown if he ever married and had any children. His death date and location at death are both unknown. His age at death is also unknown.
	viii.	**MARY YORKE** b. circa 1715. It is unknown if she ever married and had any children. Her death date and location at death are both unknown. Her age at death is also unknown.
	ix.	**PATIENCE YORKE** b. circa 1716. It is unknown if she ever married and had any children. Her death date and location at death are both unknown. Her age at death is also unknown.

4. James Yorke IV

JAMES[4] YORKE IV (James III[3], James Jr.[2], James Sr.[1])

- Born 6 September 1702 in Stonington, New London, Connecticut.
- Married 11 June 1727 Elizabeth Case (1706-after 1742). Elizabeth was the daughter of William Case and Elizabeth Stafford. James IV and Elizabeth were married in South Kingston, Washington Co., Rhode Island.
- Died after 1742 at age approx. 40 years.

Children of JAMES[4] YORKE IV and ELIZABETH CASE all born in Westerly, Washington Co., Rhode Island, were:

| 5. | i. | **CAPTAIN EDWARD YORKE** (Emigrated to Canada in 1760) b. 18 April 1730. Captain Edward married twice. Wife #1 Hannah Larkin, daughter of John Larkin of Charlestown, Rhode Island. There were no children born to Captain Edward and Hannah during their marriage. Wife #2 Mary Fones (1742-1820). Mary was the daughter of Captain Daniel Fones Sr. (1713-1790) and Mercy Remington (1715-1827). Captain Edward and Mary were married on 23 January 1755 in North Kingston, Washington Co., Rhode Island. Captain Edward and Mary had 9 children during their marriage. Captain Edward died on 14 March 1792 in Falmouth, Hants Co., Nova Scotia, at age 61 years. |

	ii.	**ELIZABETH YORKE** b. 11 February 1732. It is unknown if she ever married and had any children. Her death date and location at death are both unknown. Her age at death is also unknown.
	iii.	**STEPHEN YORKE** b. 24 May 1735. It is unknown if he ever married and had any children. His death date and location at death are both unknown. His age at death is also unknown.
	iv.	**HANNAH YORKE** b. 28 February 1738. It is unknown if she ever married and had any children. Her death date and location at death are both unknown. Her age at death is also unknown.
	v.	**JAMES V. YORKE** b. 20 November 1740. It is unknown if he ever married and had any children. His death date and location at death are both unknown. His age at death is also unknown.
	vi.	**WILLIAM YORKE** b. 20 January in 1742. William married Anne Peckham 15 November 1764 in Rhode Island. It is unknown if William and Anne had any children during their marriage. William's death date and location at death are both unknown. His age at death is also unknown.

5. Captain Edward Yorke (Emigrated to Canada)

CAPTAIN EDWARD[5] YORKE (James IV[4], James III[3], James Jr.[2], James Sr.[1])

- Born 18 April 1730 in Westerly, Washington Co., Rhode Island.
- Married circa 1750 Wife #1 Hannah Larkin. Hannah was the daughter of John Larkin of Charlestown, Rhode Island. They had no children during their marriage.
- Married 23 January 1755 Wife #2 Mary Fones (1742-1820). Mary was the daughter of Captain Daniel Fones Sr. (1713-1790) and Mercy Remington (1715-1827). Captain Edward and Mary were married in North Kingston, Washington Co., Rhode Island. They had 9 children during their marriage.
- Emigrated to Canada from Rhode Island in 1760.
- Died 14 March 1792 in Falmouth, Hants Co., Nova Scotia, at the age of 61.

Planters and Pioneers from New England and Yorkshire, England

The town of Falmouth, Nova Scotia was founded in 1760. Just before the Revolutionary War in America, some people left the New England colonies and came to the area known now as Falmouth, Nova Scotia. Land Grants were being granted to New Englanders as well as families from Yorkshire, England who were in search of a new life free of high taxes in England and fear of warning signs of a war in the colonies of America. These families were known as Planters and Pioneers. It is this time frame and area to which Captain Edward and his wife Mary (Fones) Yorke moved into and settled. This Yorke family eventually migrated to Parrsboro, Nova Scotia, which had been originally called Mill Town.

Captain Edward Yorke's name is found in the Newport Township of Nova Scotia's records dated 4 July 1760 as the Proprietors Clerk. He had been granted a Grantee at Falmouth Township: 750 acres Farm Lot #27. Captain Edward represented the Falmouth Township in the Legislature between 17 June 1771 and 20 July 1775. It was noted that Captain Edward Yorke was a man of considerable independence. However, he sometimes got into violent disputes with other Falmouth residents.

Here is an example of just that:

An incident which occurred in the home of Francis and his wife Elizabeth Layton's home in Falmouth, Nova Scotia on 28 March 1778 provides an interesting insight into the times of Captain Edward Yorke and a nearby neighbor named Francis Layton, who also was a relative of ours. Francis Layton and Captain Edward Yorke were preparing to go moose hunting together when a John Simpson came into the house. Simpson later took an oath that Yorke asked him if he and his host (Francis Layton) would have any luck that day with the moose hunting. When Simpson forecasted the contrary, Simpson claimed that Yorke called him names and threatened to beat him up. Simpson petitioned the justices to require Yorke to keep the peace. Francis Layton, however, disagreed with Simpson's account of the incident as did his wife Elizabeth. Here is Francis Layton's disposition:

".... Saveth that on the twenty-eighth day of March last the Complainant ... came into this Deponent's house and asked this Deponent if he was going a moose hunting upon which Edward Yorke ... says to said Simpson, Simpson do not you prophesy. The said Simpson then replied to said Yorke that he prophesied the said Yorke would kill No Moose – upon that the said Yorke damn would the said Simpson and said did I not give you a Caution beforehand, you might have said nothing. That afterwards he said Simpson began to sing and walk backwards and forwards on the floor where upon the said Yorke says to him, you are making a game of me .... And laid hold upon the said Simpson by the shoulder and pushed him backwards against a table and said he would give him a licking if he thought it worth his while or worth notice. This Deponent recollects that upon the said Yorke pushing the said Simpson backwards this Deponent said to the said Yorke – Captain Yorke don't strike him any further Deponent sayeth."

Elizabeth's account is like that of her husband's but adds that she thinks that John Simpson was a "little in Liquor."

Captain Edward Yorke appeared before the Justices on 10 April 1778 and posted a bond of eighty pounds to keep the peace. Yorke further undertook to attend the next General Sessions for the trial.

Captain Edward Yorke first married Hannah Larkin, daughter of John Larkin of Charlestown, Rhode Island, and then married his 2nd wife Mary Fones, daughter of Daniel Fones, Sr. They were married 12 January 1755 in Rhode Island. Mary Fones was from North Kingston, Rhode Island. Her father Daniel Fones, Sr. was the commander of the privateer ship *Defense* out of the seaport at Newport, Rhode Island in 1756 and of the privateer ship *Success*, also out of Newport, Rhode Island in 1760. When Captain

Edward and his wife Mary Fones Yorke were granted land in Newport, Nova Scotia in 1760, they moved and made their home there. They raised nine children (three of their children were born in Rhode Island and the remaining six children were all born in Falmouth, Nova Scotia). Captain Edward died there in Falmouth, Hants Co., Nova Scotia 14 March 1792 at the age of 61 years.

Captain Edward was a pilot aboard a British armed vessel which coasted along the Cobequid Bay to protect the coast and shipping from American privateers.

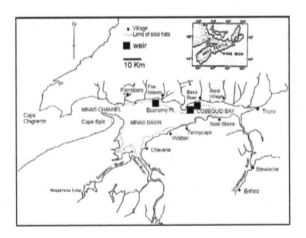

There were no children born to CAPTAIN EDWARD[5] YORKE and HANNAH LARKIN.

Children of CAPTAIN EDWARD[5] YORKE and MARY FONES were:

	i.	MARGARET YORKE b. 20 May 1756 in North Kingston, Washington Co., Rhode Island. It is unknown if she ever married and had any children. Her death date and location at death are both unknown. Her age at death is also unknown.
	ii.	BABY DAUGHTER YORKE b. 30 August 1758 in North Kingston, Washington Co., Rhode Island. She died on 30 August 1758 as a stillborn.
	iii.	JAMES YORKE b. 30 August 1759 in North Kingston, Washington Co., Rhode Island. It is unknown if he ever married and had any children. His death date and location at death are both unknown. His age at death is also unknown.

	iv.	**JOHN YORKE** b. 17 August 1761 in Falmouth, Hants Co., Nova Scotia. John died on 19 August 1761 in Falmouth, Hants Co., Nova Scotia at the age of 2 days old.
6.	v.	**FONES YORKE** b. 31 August 1762 in Falmouth, Hants Co., Nova Scotia. Fones married Susannah Vickery circa 1795. Susannah was the daughter of Jonathan Vickery IV and Jane Cunningham,. Fones and Susannah married in Falmouth, Hants Co., Nova Scotia. Fones and Susannah had 11 children during their marriage. Fones died in 1859 in Parrsboro, Cumberland Co., Nova Scotia at the age of 97.
	vi.	**STEPHEN YORKE** b. 2 February 1765 in Falmouth, Hants Co., Nova Scotia. It is unknown if he ever married and had any children. His death date and location at death are both unknown. His age at death is also unknown.
	vii.	**ELIZABETH YORKE** b. 11 June 1767 in Falmouth, Hants Co., Nova Scotia. Elizabeth married Christopher Armstrong Jr. circa 1787. It is unknown if Elizabeth and Christopher Jr. had any children during their marriage. Elizabeth died in 1836 at the age of 69 in Nova Scotia.
	viii.	**DANIEL YORKE** b. 25 July 1770 in Falmouth, Hants Co., Nova: Scotia. Daniel married Phoebe Church on 2 March 1796 in Nova Scotia. It is unknown if Daniel and Phoebe had any children during their marriage. His death date and his location at death are unknown. His age at death is also unknown.
	ix.	**SARAH YORKE** b. circa 1772 in Falmouth, Hants Co., Nova Scotia. Sarah married Henry Church on 18 January 1793 in Nova Scotia. It is unknown if Sarah and Henry had any children during their marriage. Also unknown are Sarah's death date and her location at death. Her age at death is also unknown.

6. Fones Yorke

FONES[6] YORKE (Captain Edward[5], James IV [4], James III[3], James Jr.[2], James Sr.[1])

- Born 31 August 1762 in Falmouth, Hants Co., Nova Scotia; Canada.
- Married circa 1795 Susannah Vickery, daughter of Jonathan Vickery IV and Jane Cunningham, in Falmouth, Hants Co., Nova Scotia. Susannah Vickery b. 1774-d. circa 1825.
- Died 1859 in Parrsboro, Cumberland Co., Nova Scotia at the age of 97.

Fones Yorke was born in Falmouth, Nova Scotia and married his bride Susannah (Vickery) who was the daughter of Jonathan Vickery IV and Jane Cunningham. They married in Falmouth, Nova Scotia and their first child was born there in Falmouth. However, they moved to Parrsboro where their next eight children were born. Fones Yorke became the attendant of the Block House which was a garrison which had been built to protect the town of Parrsboro from the privateers. The early settlers had built the Block House high upon a hill (or mount as it was referred to) as a watchtower where guns and ammunitions were stored. It was here where Fones was employed as the attendant to guard the Block House.

Picture here is the Blockade House. It is a big house on the top of the mounted hill. Fones Yorke was the attendant guarding all the militia weapons stored here circa 1836. The picture is hung on the 3rd floor of this author's home. The artist of the painting is B. E. Nutting.

The Blockage House

"Parrsboro, Nova Scotia seen from the Water"

Painting was done in 1836

Children of FONES[6] YORKE and SUSANNAH VICKERY were:

	i.	**MERCY YORKE** b. circa 1796 in Falmouth, Hants Co., Nova Scotia. Mercy married Nathaniel Holmes on 20 January 1813 in Parrsboro, Cumberland Co., Nova Scotia. It is unknown if they had any children during their marriage. Mercy's death date and location at death are both unknown, as is her age at death.
	ii.	**EDWARD YORKE** b. circa 1799 in Nova Scotia. Edward married Ann Nancy Hatfield on 25 July 1816 in Nova Scotia. It is unknown if Edward and Ann Nancy had any children during their marriage. Edward died March 1890 at the age of 91.
	iii.	**STEPHEN YORKE** b. circa 1802 in Nova Scotia. Stephen married Fanny Richards in December 1832 in Nova Scotia. It is unknown if they had any children during their marriage. Stephen's death date and location at death are both unknown. His age at death is also unknown.
	iv.	**DANIEL YORKE** b. circa 1805 in Nova Scotia. Daniel married Mary Salter. It is unknown if Daniel and Mary had any children during their marriage. It is unknown when Daniel died and his location at death. His age at death is also unknown.
	v.	**JAMES YORKE** b. circa 1808 in Parrsboro Shore, Cumberland Co., Nova Scotia. James married Rebecca Vickery. It is unknown if James and Rebecca had any children during their marriage. It is unknown when James died and his location at death. His age at death is unknown.

	vi.	**MARY YORKE** b. circa 1810 in Parrsboro Shore, Cumberland Co., Nova Scotia. It is unknown if Mary ever married and had any children. Her death date is also unknown as well as her location at her death. She died at an age unknown.
	vii.	**JANE YORKE** b. circa 1812 in Parrsboro, Cumberland Co., Nova Scotia. Jane married Johnathan Vickery on 17 December 1829 in Nova Scotia. It is unknown if Jane and Jonathan had any children during their marriage. Jane's death date and the location at her death are both unknown. Her age at death is unknown.
	viii.	**SARAH YORKE** b. circa 1814 in Parrsboro, Cumberland Co., Nova Scotia. Sarah married Vickery Davidson on 16 November 1844 in Nova Scotia. It is unknown if Sarah and Vickery ever had any children. Sarah's death date is also unknown as well as her location at her death. She died at an age unknown.
7.	ix.	**AMELIA YORKE** b. 26 November 1816 in Parrsboro, Cumberland Co., Nova Scotia. Amelia married William Smith Sr. (1812-1884). Amelia and William Smith Sr. were married circa 1837 in Diligent River, Cumberland Co., Nova Scotia, Canada. William Sr. was the son of John Smith Jr. and Mary Amelia Bowser. Amelia and William Sr. had 6 children during their marriage. Amelia died on 29 October 1889 at Diligent River, Cumberland Co., Nova Scotia, at the age of 68. She is buried in the Wharton Cemetery, in Wharton, Cumberland Co., Nova Scotia.
	x.	**ELIZA YORKE** b. circa 1818 in Parrsboro, Cumberland Co., Nova Scotia. It is unknown if Eliza ever married and had any children. Her death date is also unknown as well as her location at her death. She died at an age unknown.
	xi.	**ANN YORKE** b. circa 1820 in Parrsboro, Cumberland Co., Nova Scotia. It is unknown if Ann ever married and had any children. Her death date is also unknown as well as her location at her death. She died at an age unknown.

7. Amelia Yorke

AMELIA[7] YORKE (Fones[6], Captain Edward[5], James IV[4], James III[3], James Jr.[2], James Sr.[1])
- Born 26 November 1821 in Parrsboro, Cumberland Co., Nova Scotia, Canada.
- Married circa 1837 William Smith Sr. (1812-1884). William Sr. was the son of John Smith Jr. and Mary Amelia Bowser. Amelia Yorke and William Smith Sr. were married at Diligent River, Cumberland Co., Nova Scotia, Canada. They had 6 children during their marriage.
- Died 29 October 1889 at Diligent River, Cumberland Co., Nova Scotia, at the age of 68.
- Buried Wharton Cemetery, Wharton, Cumberland Co., Nova Scotia.

Children of AMELIA[7] YORKE and WILLIAM SMITH SR. are documented in the Smiths of Nova Scotia chapter.

Source Citations for this Chapter

The Heirs of Francis Layton – The Story of a Nova Scotia Family Compiled by Jack. Layton 1986.

Planters and Pioneers Nova Scotia, 1749-1775 by Esther Clark Wright Revised Edition 1982, Lancelot Press Limited, Hantsport, Nova Scotia, Canada.

Emigrants from England to the American Colonies (1773-1776) Port of Hull, England Records

https://www.ancestry.com/imageviewer/collections/49141/images/FLHG_EmigrantsEnglandtoAmericaColonies-0023?ssrc=pt&treeid=62293685&perso...

Township of Falmouth Nova Scotia by John Victor Duncanson, Mika Publishing Co., Belleville, Ontario, 1990.

1796-1800 A Number Came from Falmouth, Hants Co., to Parrsboro, Nova Scotia

by D. J. Taylor – "The Halifax Harold News," Halifax, Nova Scotia.

Verbal information from Marion Kyle, Genealogist from Parrsboro, Cumberland Co., Nova Scotia.

Yorkes United Newsletter Connecting the Yorke Family Near & Far, Issue #14 October 1995, Article "The Descendants of Captain Edward Yorke, A New England Planter in Nova Scotia" page 1.

Yorkes United Newsletter Connecting the Yorke Family Near & Far, Issue #60 Fall 2019, Article "Blockhouse Hill": page 16.

Yorkes United Newsletter Connecting the Yorke Family Near & Far, Issue #61 Fall 2019/Winter 2020, Article "Chance connection with Falmouth Kin": pages 1, 3. 4.

https://ancestry.com/family-tree/tree/62293685/story/bff9d316-881c-49be-b95a-4d3a3263ed2a?pid=&usePUBJs=true The Yorkes arrive in Parrsboro.

New England Genealogical Society Register Volume #63 January -April 1909 pgs. 28ff and 135ff. and

New England Genealogical Society Register Volume #65 April 1911 page 123 ff.

The Passenger Lists of the ships Albion, Jenny, and Two Friends with the Families sailing for Fort Cumberland in Nova Scotia.

Newport Township Land Records Book found at PANS (The Public Archives of Nov Scotia. Halifax, Nova Scotia).

Harris Jenks Journal by Jack Lawton. The Nova Scotia Articles at PANS in Halifax, Nova Scoti

Maternal Line

Chapter 38: The Beckers

The Becker Family Line

Martin Becker 1599-1684 — Liese Ratzloff 1603-1638

Michael Becker Sr. 1627-1714 — Maria Neumann 1633-1694

Martin Becker Sr. 1653-____ — Elisabeth Brunkow 1653-Aft. 1698

Martin Becker Jr. 1693-____ — Katharina Stolte 1691-Aft. 1620

Michael Becker Sr. 1720-1783 — Benigna Berndt 1723-1797

Benigna Becker 1760-1788 — Samuel Gottlieb Rades 1761-1829

1. Martin Becker

MARTIN[1] BECKER

- Born 1599 in Province of Pomerania, Kingdom of Prussia (which was part of the German Confederation).
- Married circa 1617 Liese Ratzlaff (1603-1838). They were married in Rehwinkel, Pomerania Province, and Kingdom of Prussia and in union with the Holy Roman Empire of the German Nation.
- Died 1684 in Rehwinkel, district of Saatzig, Pomerania, Kingdom of Prussia (which was a member of the German Confederation). Martin died at the age of 85.

Children of MARTIN[1] BECKER and LIESE RATZLAFF were:

	i.	HANS BECKER b. 1618 in Rehwinkel, district of Saatzig, Province of Pomerania, Kingdom of Prussia (which was part of the German Confederation). It is unknown if he married or had any children. He died in 1668.
2	ii.	MICHAEL BECKER. b. 1627 in Rehwinkel, district of Saatzig, Province of Pomerania, Kingdom of Prussia (which was part of the German Confederation). He married Maria Neumann, daughter of Jurgen Neumann and Liese Rawe on 27 June 1653 in Ball, Saatzig, Pomerania, Prussia. Michael and Maria had 9 children during their marriage. Michael died at the age of 87.

		iii.	**KASPAR BECKER.** b. 1629 in Rehwinkel, district of Saatzig, Province of Pomerania, Kingdom of Prussia (which was part of the German Confederation). It is unknown if he married and had any children. It is also unknown when and where he died.

2. Michael Becker Sr.

MICHAEL[2] BECKER SR. (Martin[1])

- Born 1627 in Province of Pomerania, Kingdom of Prussia (which was part of the German Confederation).
- Married 27 June 1653 Maria Neumann (1633-1694). They were married in Ball, Saatzig, Pomerania, and Kingdom of Prussia.
- Died 1714 in Rehwinkel, district of Saatzig, Pomerania, Kingdom of Prussia (which was a member of the German Confederation). Michael Sr. died at age of 87.

Children of MICHAEL[2] BECKER SR. and MARIA NEUMANN were:

		i.	**TWIN: BENIGNA MARIA BECKER** b. 1653 in Rehwinkel, district of Saatzig, Province of Pomerania, Kingdom of Prussia (which was part of the German Confederation). It is unknown if she married and had any children. It is also unknown when and where she died.
	3	ii.	**TWIN: MARTIN BECKER SR.** b. 1653 in Rehwinkel, district of Saatzig, Province of Pomerania, Kingdom of Prussia (which was part of the German Confederation). He was a fraternal twin of Benigna Maria Becker. Martin Sr. married Elizabeth Brunkow (1653-after 1698). They were married circa 1690. Martin Sr. and Elizabeth Brunkow had 5 children during their marriage. He died in Rehwinkel, district of Saatzig, Pomerania, Kingdom of Prussia. However, his death date is unknown.
		iii.	**DANIEL BECKER** b. 1656 in Rehwinkel, district of Saatzig, Province of Pomerania, Kingdom of Prussia (which was part of the German Confederation). It is unknown if he married and had any children. Also unknown is when and where he died.
		iv.	**ELISABETH BECKER** b. 1658 in Rehwinkel, district of Saatzig, Province of Pomerania, Kingdom of Prussia (which was part of the German Confederation). It is unknown if she married and had any children. Also unknown is when and where she died.
		v.	**MARIA BECKER** b. 1660 in Rehwinkel, district of Saatzig, Province of Pomerania, Kingdom of Prussia (which was part of the German Confederation). It is unknown if she married and had any children. Maria died in 1698. Her location at her death is unknown.
		vi.	**MICHAEL BECKER JR.** b. 1663 in Rehwinkel, district of Saatzig, Province of Pomerania, Kingdom of Prussia (which was part of the German Confederation). It is unknown if he married and had any children. Michael Jr. died in 1733. His location at his death is unknown.
		vii.	**KASPAR BECKER** b. 1666 in Rehwinkel, district of Saatzig, Province of Pomerania, Kingdom of Prussia (which was part of the German Confederation).

		It is unknown if he married and had any children. Kaspar died in 1753. His location at his death is unknown.
	viii.	**HANS BECKER** b. 1669 in Rehwinkel, district of Saatzig, Province of Pomerania, Kingdom of Prussia (which was part of the German Confederation). It is unknown if he married and had any children. Hans died in 1737 at the age of 68. His location at his death is unknown.
	ix.	**JACOB BECKER** b. 1672 in Rehwinkel, district of Saatzig, Province of Pomerania, Kingdom of Prussia (which was part of the German Confederation). It is unknown if he married and had any children. Jacob died in 1748. His location at his death is unknown.

3. Martin Becker Sr.

MARTIN[3] BECKER SR. (Michael[2] Sr., Martin[1])

- Born in 1653 in Rehwinkel, district of Saatzig, Province of Pomerania, Kingdom of Prussia. He was a fraternal twin and had a twin sister Benigna Maria Becker.
- Married circa 1690 Elisabeth Brunkow (1653-aft 1698). They had 5 children in their marriage.
- Died ___ in Rehwinkel, district of Saatzig, Pomerania, Kingdom of Prussia. Age at death is unknown.

Children of MARTIN[3] BECKER SR. and ELISABETH BRUNKOW were:

	i.	**KASPAR BECKER** b. 1691 in Rehwinkel, district of Saatzig, Province of Pomerania, Kingdom of Prussia. It is unknown if he married and had any children. He died in 1692. Kaspar's location at his death is unknown.
4.	ii.	**MARTIN BECKER JR.** b. 1693 in Rehwinkel, district of Saatzig, Province of Pomerania, Kingdom of Prussia. He married Katharina Stolte (1691-after 1720). They married circa 1712 in Rehwinkel, Pomerania, Kingdom of Prussia. They had 3 children during their marriage. Martin Jr.'s death date is unknown.
	iii.	**KATHARINA BECKER** b. 1694 in Rehwinkel, district of Saatzig, Province of Pomerania, Kingdom of Prussia. It is unknown if she married and had any children. Also, her death date and location are both unknown.
	iv.	**MARIA BECKER** b. 1695 in Rehwinkel, district of Saatzig, Province of Pomerania, Kingdom of Prussia. It is unknown if she married and had any children. Also, her death date and location are both unknown.
	v.	**BENIGNA MARIA BECKER** b. 1698 in Rehwinkel, district of Saatzig, Province of Pomerania, Kingdom of Prussia. It is unknown if she married and had any children. She died in 1779 at the age of 81.

3. Martin Becker Jr.

MARTIN[4] BECKER JR. (Martin[3] Sr., Michael[2] Sr., Martin[1])

- Born 1693 in Province of Pomerania, Kingdom of Prussia (which was part of the German Confederation
- Married circa 1712 Katharina Stolte (1691-aft 1720). They were married in Rehwinkel, Pomerania, and Kingdom of Prussia and in union with the Holy Roman Empire of the German Nation.
- Died ___ in Rehwinkel, district of Saatzig, Pomerania, Kingdom of Prussia (which was a member of the German Confederation. Martin Jr. died at age unknown.

Children of MARTIN[4] BECKER JR. and KATHARINA STOLTE were:

	i.	**ELISABETH BECKER** b. 1713 in Rehwinkel, district of Saatzig, Province of Pomerania, Kingdom of Prussia (which was part of the German Confederation). It is unknown if she married and had any children. She died in 1790 at age 77.
	ii.	**BARBARA JULIANA BECKER.** b. 1715 in Rehwinkel, district of Saatzig, Province of Pomerania, Kingdom of Prussia (which was part of the German Confederation). marriage. It is unknown if she married and had any children. She died in 1790 at the age of 75. Location at death is unknown.
5.	iii.	**MICHAEL BECKER SR.** b. 1720 in Rehwinkel, district of Saatzig, Province of Pomerania, Kingdom of Prussia (which was part of the German Confederation). He married Benigna Berndt (1723-1797) circa 1746. They had 6 children during their marriage. Michael died in 1783 at the age of 63 in Rehwinkel, district of Saatzig, Pomerania, Kingdom of Prussia.

4. Michael Becker Sr.

MICHAEL[5] BECKER SR. (Martin[4] Jr., Martin[3] Sr., Michael[2] Sr., Martin[1])

- Born 1720 in Province of Pomerania, Kingdom of Prussia (which was part of the German Confederation).
- Married circa 1746 Benigna Berndt (1723-1797) in Rehwinkel, district of Saatzig, Pomerania, Kingdom of Prussia.
- Died 1783 in Rehwinkel, district of Saatzig, Pomerania, Kingdom of Prussia (which was a member of the German Confederation. Michael Sr. died at the age of 63.

Children of MICHAEL[5] BECKER SR. and BENIGNA BERNDT were:

	i.	**MARIA BECKER** b. 1747 in Rehwinkel, district of Saatzig, Province of Pomerania, Kingdom of Prussia (which was part of the German Confederation). It is unknown if she married and had any children. She died in 1817.
	ii.	**DOROTHEA MARIE BECKER** b. 1749 in Rehwinkel, district of Saatzig, Province of Pomerania, Kingdom of Prussia (which was part of the German Confederation). It is unknown if she married and had any children. Her death date and location at death are both unknown.

	iii.	**MARTIN BECKER** b. 1751 in Rehwinkel, district of Saatzig, Province of Pomerania, Kingdom of Prussia (which was part of the German Confederation). It is unknown if he married and had any children. Death date and location at death are unknown.
	iv.	**EVA SOPHIE BECKER** b. 1756 in Rehwinkel, district of Saatzig, Province of Pomerania, Kingdom of Prussia (which was part of the German Confederation). It is unknown if she married and had any children. She died in 1820 location unknown.
	v.	**MICHAEL BECKER JR.** b. 1758 in Rehwinkel, district of Saatzig, Province of Pomerania, Kingdom of Prussia (which was part of the German Confederation). It is unknown if he married and had any children. Location at death unknown.
6.	vi.	**BENIGNA BECKER.** b. 1760 in Rehwinkel, district of Saatzig, Province of Pomerania, Kingdom of Prussia (which was part of the German Confederation). Benigna married Samuel Gottlieb Rades (1761-1829). They had 3 children during their marriage. Benigna died in 1788 at the age of 28 in the year of her third son, Gottlieb's birth.

6. Benigna Becker

BENIGNA[6] BECKER (Michael[5] Sr, Martin[4] Jr., Martin[3] Sr., Michael[2] Sr., Martin[1])

- Born 1760 in in Rehwinkel, district of Saatzig, Province of Pomerania, Kingdom of Prussia (which was part of the German Confederation).
- Married circa 1617 Samuel Gottlieb Rades (1761-1829) in Rehwinkel, Pomerania Kingdom of Prussia.
- Died 1684 in Rehwinkel, district of Saatzig, Pomerania, Kingdom of Prussia (which was a member of the German Confederation). Benigna died at the age of 28 in the year of her third son Gottlieb's birth.

Children of BENIGNA[6] BECKER and SAMUEL GOTTLIEB RADES are documented in the Rades chapter.

Source Citations for this Chapter

www.familysearch.org Becker family research

http://www.ancestry.com Becker family research

Allen Grasser Verbal and Email information on this Becker Family

Allen P. Grasser, "Becker Family Genealogy: Familial Data Abstracts," E-mail messages from <agrasser.msj3@gmail.com> at 1453 Vernon Ave.; Park Ridge, IL 60068-1563. From 20 September to 20 October 2021.

Chapter 39: The Dills

The Dill Family Line

Johann Dill Abt. 1695- 1762	Maria Bender Abt. 1700-____
Margaretha Dill Abt. 1716-1783	Johann Jacob Grasser Abt. 1700- 1763

1. JOHANN JACOB DILL

Johann[2] Jacob Dill

- Born circa 1695 in Sessenheim, France.
- Married 8 January 1748 Maria Bender (circa 1700-__). They were married in Sessenheim, France.
- Died 22 October 1762 in Auenheim, Bas-Rin, Alsace, France at the age of approx. 68.

The Dill Family was from Auenheim, Alsace, France. They were of the Roman Catholic faith.

Child of JOHANN JACOB[1] DILL and MARIA BENDER was:

2.	i.	MARGARETHA DILL b. circa 1716 in Elsenham, France. She married twice: Husband #1 Johann Jacob Grasser (ca 1725- after 1765). They were married on 8 January 1748 in The Blessed Virgin Mary of the Nativity Catholic Church in Sessenhelm, France. They had 2 children in their marriage including two sons. After Johann Jacob Grasser died in 1763. Margaretha remarried to Husband #2 Peter Bohn. They were married circa 1764 in Auenheim, Bas-Rhin, Alsace, France. Margaretha and Peter had a stillborn baby who died on 15 May 1765. Margaretha Dill died 13 October 1783 in Auenheim, Bas-Rhin, Alsace, France at the age of approx. 67.

2. MARGARETHA DILL

Margaretha[2] Dill (Johann Jacob[1])

- Born circa 1716 in Alsace-Lorraine, France.
- Married 8 January 1748 Husband #1 Johann Jacob Grasser in The Blessed Virgin Mary of the Nativity Catholic Church in Sessenhelm, France. Johann Jacob Grasser (circa 1700-after 1765).
- Married circa 1764 Husband #2 Peter Bohn in Auenheim, Bas-Rhin, Alsace, France.
- Died 13 October 1783 in Auenheim, Bas-Rhin, Alsace, France at the age of approx. 67.

Children of MARGARETHA[3] DILL and JOHANN JACOB GRASSER are documented in the Grasser chapter.

Child of Margaretha Dill and Peter Bohn was a stillborn who died on 15 May 1765.

Source Citations for this Chapter

www.familysearch.org Dill family research.

ancestry.com.

Allen P. Grasser Verbal and Email information on this Dill Family.

Allen P. Grasser, "Dill family Genealogy: Familial Data Abstracts," E-mail messages from <agrasser.msj3@gmail.com> at 1453 Vernon Ave.; Park Ridge, IL 60068-1563. From 20 September to 20 October 2021.

Chapter 40: The Fischbachs

The Fischbach Family Line

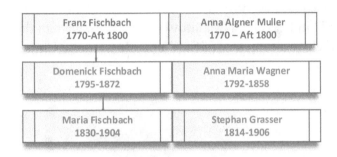

Franz Fischbach 1770-Aft 1800	Anna Algner Muller 1770 – Aft 1800
Domenick Fischbach 1795-1872	Anna Maria Wagner 1792-1858
Maria Fischbach 1830-1904	Stephan Grasser 1814-1906

The Fischbach Name

There is a town named Fischbach which is located about 15 miles north of the capital of Luxembourg. One of the royal castles is located there.
The German name "Bach" = stream or brook
The German name "Fisch" = fish
The town is in a valley with abundant fish in the brook. Verbal family story passed down states that the people living nearby were known as the Fischbachs.

1. FRANZ FISCHBACH
FRANZ[1] FISCHBACH

- Born 1770 Leudelange, Canton d'Esch-sur-Alzette, Luxembourg, Luxembourg.
- Married circa 1790 Anna Alger Muller in Luxembourg.
- Died after 1800 in Leudelange, Canton d'Esch-sur-Alzette, Luxembourg, Luxembourg at age 30+.

Franz[1] Fischbach and Anna had a large family, but this author does not know the names of all the children, except for the youngest child who was Dominicus "Domenick[2] Fischbach (1795-1872). See below.

2. DOMINICUS "DOMENICK" FISCHBACH (Immigrant)

DOMINICUS "DOMENICK" [2] FISCHBACH (Franz[1])

- Born 26 September 1793 Leudelange, Canton d'Esch-sur Alzette, Luxembourg, Luxembourg.
- Married 10 January 1822 Anna Maria Wagner, daughter of Heinrich "Harry" Wagner and Anna Maria Weber. Domenick and Anna Maria were married in the Grand Dutchy of Luxembourg.
- Departure from Antwerpen, Belgium 10 October 1852.
- Arrival in New York 1 December 1852 via the ship the *Lucia Field*.
- Died 21 April 1872 in Cleveland, Manitowoc Co., Wisconsin at the age of 79.
- Buried in the churchyard cemetery of St. Wendel's Catholic Church, Cleveland, Manitowoc Co., Wisconsin.

Domenick Fischbach
(Immigrant)
1793-1872

Domenick Fischbach was born in the country of Luxembourg. At that time, it was ruled by the Hapsburgs of Austria. Domenick was born during the end of the peaceful eighty-year Austrian rule. Luxembourg did not become officially a "Grand Duchy" until 9 June 1815. It was then given to King William I of the Netherlands to reign over as sovereign. He was given the title of Grand Duke.

King William I was the king of Holland and Belgium besides being the Grand Duke of the Grand Duchy of Luxembourg. This king tried to unite Holland and Belgium with Luxembourg, but the people revolted, wanting to keep their own separate identities. The countries went into a revolution about this issue in 1830, the very year that Maria Fischbach was born.

By 1840, Grand Duke William II took over the reign. Illiteracy was rampant, and the country of Luxembourg was impoverished by excessive taxes. Then came the Potato Famine of 1845-1846 which drove the country into further despair. Thousands of families, including the Fischbach family, decided to leave their homeland forever and set sail for America.

They departed on 10 October 1852 from Antwerpen port in Belgium and arrived in the New York City port of entry on 1 December 1852.

The Three-Masted Bark the *Lucia Field*
Departure from Antwerp, Belgium mid-November 1852
Arrival in port of entry: New York City, 1 December 1852

They made their way to Wisconsin where they settled in Centerville, Manitowoc Co., Wisconsin. Domenick purchased an 80-acre farm on 25 January 1853 for $203.46. They worked hard on the farm until they retired and then willed the farmland to their children.

Children of DOMINICK[2] FISCHBACH and ANNA MARIE WAGNER were:

	i.	**WILLIAM FISCHBACH** (Immigrant) b. 7 March 1823 in Leudelange, Canton d'Esch-sur Alzette, Luxembourg, Luxembourg. William married Anna Gertrude Hildenbrand (b. 1820). They were married in 1855. It is unknown if they had any children during their marriage. Wilhelm died on 10 June 1880 in St. Louis, Saint Louis Co., Missouri at the age of 57.
	ii.	**MARGARETHA FISCHBACH** (Immigrant) b.1825 in Leudelange, Canton d'Esch-sur Alzette, Luxembourg, Luxembourg. Margaretha married Nicholas Braun (1822-1880). They were married on 31 May 1853.in Sheboygan, Wisconsin. It is unknown if they had any children during their marriage. Margaretha died in 1862 in Centerville, Manitowoc Co., Wisconsin at the age of 37.
	iii.	**NICHOLAS FISCHBACH** (Immigrant) b. 4 March 1828 Leudelange, Canton d'Esch-sur Alzette, Luxembourg, Luxembourg. Nicholas never married. **He joined the Military 31 December 1863. He fought in the Civil War (Private in Company "E" 35th Regiment of Wisconsin.) He served for three years. Nicholas had a mental trauma (PTSD). He walked away from his service all the way home from Alabama to Wisconsin, still wearing his uniform.** Nicholas died 3 July 1900 in Manitowoc, Manitowoc Co., Wisconsin. He is buried in the Evergreen Cemetery in Manitowoc, Wisconsin at the age of 72.

	iv.	**CATHARINA FISCHBACH** (Immigrant) b. 8 September 1829 Leudelange, Canton d'Esch-sur Alzette, Luxembourg, Luxembourg. Catharina married John Nicholas Braun (1829-1911). Catharina and John Nicholas married in 1853. They travelled to America and settled in Wisconsin. It is unknown if they had any children during their marriage. Catharina died 15 November 1927 in Centerville, Manitowoc Co., Wisconsin. She and her husband are buried in the St. Wendel Cemetery in Cleveland, Wisconsin. Catharina died at the age of 98.
2.	v.	**MARIA FISCHBACH** (Immigrant) b. 14 September 1830 Leudelange, Canton d'Esch-sur Alzette, Luxembourg, Luxembourg. Maria married Stephen Grasser on 3 March 1853 in The Holy Name Catholic Church in Sheboygan, Sheboygan Co., Wisconsin. Maria and Stephen had 5 children. Maria died on 27 January 1904 at the age of 74. She and her husband, Domenick are buried in the Calvary Cemetery, Sheboygan, Sheboygan Co., Wisconsin.
	vi.	**SUSANNE FISCHBACH** (Immigrant) b. 11 April 1835. Leudelange, Canton d'Esch-sur Alzette, Luxembourg, Luxembourg. Susanne married Michael Wagner (1830-1900). They were married in 1858 in Centerville (Kiel), Manitowoc Co., Wisconsin. It is unknown if they had any children during their marriage. Family states that Susanne was a very creative woman, and she had a definite carefree spirit. Susanne died on 12 March 1916 in Cleveland, Manitowoc Co., Wisconsin at age 80. She and her husband are buried in Cleveland, Manitowoc Co., Wisconsin. Their tombstone (pictured here) is quite creative, and one can wonder if it had been designed by Susanne herself!  **Cemetery Monument for** **SUZANNA FISCHBACH WAGNER** **11 APRIL, 1835-12 MARCH 1916** **AND HER HUSBAND** **Michael Wagner** **1830-1900**

**Gravesite of
Domenick Fischbach (1783-1872)
and his wife
Anna Marie Wagner (1792-1858)**

This metal cross (above) is in the St. Wendel Catholic Church Cemetery, Cleveland, Manitowoc Co., Wisconsin, which marks the gravesite where Domenick Fischbach and his wife Anna Maria Wagner Fischbach were both laid to rest. They were parents of the above children of this Fischbach family.

3. Maria Fischbach (Immigrant)
MARIA[3] FISCHBACH (Domenick[2] Franz[1])
- Born 14 September 1830 in the Grand Dutchy of Luxembourg.
- Departure from Antwerpen, Belgium 10 October 1852.
- Arrival in New York 1 December 1852 via the ship *The Lucia Field*.
- Married 3 March 1853 Stephen Grasser (1814-1906) son of Joseph Grasser Sr. and Anne Mary Sali. Stephen and Maria were married in The Holy Name Catholic Church in Sheboygan, Sheboygan Co., Wisconsin.
- Died 27 January 1904 at the age of 74.
- Buried in the Calvary Cemetery, Sheboygan, Sheboygan Co., Wisconsin.

Stephen Grasser & Maria Fischbach Wedding Picture
3 March 1853
Sheboygan, Wisconsin

On 3 March 1903 Stephen and Maria celebrated their Golden 50th Wedding Anniversary with a huge family gala celebration in Sheboygan organized by their adult children.

Children of MARIA[3] FISCHBACH and STEPHEN GRASSER are documented in the Grasser chapter.

They had 13 children, all born on the St. Wendel Grasser farm in Manitowoc Co., Wisconsin.

Source Citations for this Chapter

Allen P. Grasser, "Grasser-Rades Family Genealogy: Familial Data Abstracts," E-mail messages from <agrasser.msj3@gmail.com> at 1453 Vernon Ave.; Park Ridge, IL 60068-1563. From 20 September to 20 October 2021.

1870 United States Federal Census.

New York Passenger and Crew Lists (including Castle Garden and Ellis Island from 1820-1957.

U. S. Find a Grave Index 1600's -> Current.

Wisconsin State Censuses, 1855-1905.

https://www.ancestry.com.

Chapter 41: The Grassers

The Grasser Family Line

Johann Jacob Grasser Abt. 1700-1763	Margaretha Dill 1716-1783
Simon Grasser 1749-1784	Anna Maria Schmitter 1755-Aft.1783
Joseph Grasser Sr. 1774-1846	Anna Maria Saali 1778-1840
Stephan Grasser 1814-1906	Maria Fischbach 1830-1904
Michael Grasser II 1874-1961	Wilhelmina Rades 1876-1947
Sylvia Mary-Louise Grasser 1903-1984	Albert Wintfield Kearney 1899-1989

1. JOHANN JACOB GRASSER

JOHANN JACOB[1] GRASSER

- Born circa 1700 in Alsace-Lorraine, France.
- Married circa 1732 1st wife Anna Maria Schaffer.
- Married 8 January 1748 2nd wife Margaretha Dill (1716-1783), daughter of Johann Dill and Maria Bender. Johann Jacob Grasser and Margaretha Dill were married in Sessenhelm, France. After Johann Jacob Grasser died in 1763, Margaretha remarried to Peter Bohn. They had a stillborn baby who died on 15 May 1765. Margaretha Dill died 13 October 1783 in Auenheim, Bas-Rhin, Alsace, France at the age of 67.
- Died 16 January 1763 in Rountzenheim at the age of approx. 63.

Rountzenheim, Alsace-Lorraine, France/Germany
Alsace-Lorraine
Germany or France?
It depends on the year!!

The area comprising the present French *départements* of Haut-Rhin, Bas-Rhin, and Moselle. Alsace-Lorraine was the name given to the 5,067 square miles (13,123 square km) of territory that was ceded by France to Germany in 1871 after the Franco-German War. This territory was retroceded to France in 1919 after World War I, was ceded again to Germany in 1940 during World War II and was again retroceded to France in 1945.

Historically, the area was at the center of Charlemagne's Frankish empire in the 9th century and later became part of the Germany of the Holy Roman Empire, remaining a German territory under various sovereignties up to the Thirty Years' War. The Peace of Westphalia (1648) concluding that war had given control of Alsace-Lorraine over to France.

Because of its ancient German associations and because of its large German-speaking population, Alsace-Lorraine was incorporated into the German Empire after France's defeat in the Franco-German War (1870–71). The loss of Alsace-Lorraine was a major cause of anti-German feeling in France in the period from 1871 to 1914. France also suffered economically from the loss of Alsace-Lorraine's valuable iron ore deposits, iron- and steelmaking plants, and other industries to Germany.

Auenheim Village, Germany

Children of JOHANN JACOB[1] GRASSER and MARGARETHA DILL were:

2.	i.	**SIMON GRASSER SR.** b. 21 January 1749 in north of Strasbourg, France, Rountzenheim, Alsace-Lorraine, France. Simon married Anna Maria Schmitter (18 August 1755-after 1783). Simon and Anna Maria were married in 1773. Anna Maria Schmitter was the daughter of Sebastian "Bastian" Schmitter and Maria Barbara Walck. Simon and Anna Maria had 5 children during their marriage. Simon Grasser Sr. died 26 February 1784 in Auenheim, France at the age of 35.
	ii.	**PETER GRASSER** b. 31 January 1751 in Auenheim, France. Peter died 5 December 1760 in Auenheim, France at the age of 9.

2. Simon Grasser Sr.

SIMON[2] GRASSER SR. (Johann Jacob[1])

- Born 21 January 1749 in north of Strasbourg, France, Rountzenheim, Alsace-Lorraine, France.
- Married 1773 Anna Maria Schmitter (1755-After 1783), daughter of Sebastian "Bastian" Schmitter and Maria Barbara Walck. Anna Maria Schmitter b. 18 August 1755 in Stollhofen, Germany. Her exact death date is unknown, but it was after 1783.
- Died 26 February 1784 at age 35 in Auenheim, France.

Children of SIMON[2] GRASSE SR. and ANNA MARIA SCHMITTER were:

3.	i.	**JOSEPH GRASSER SR.** b. 24 October 1774 in Auenheim, France. He married Anna Marie Saali on 13 October 1802 in Pountzenheim, Alsace-Lorraine, France. Anna Marie was the daughter of Johann Saali and Christina Losch. They had 10 children during their marriage. They settled together in France and raised their 10 children there. Joseph Sr. died 12 February 1846 in Auenheim, France at the age of 72.
	ii.	**SIMON GRASSER JR.** b. 7 January 1777 in Alsace-Lorraine, France. Simon Jr. died in 1780 in Alsace-Lorraine, France at the age of 3 years.
	iii.	**MARIA ANNA GRASSER** b. 10 August 1778 in Alsace Lorraine, France. Marie Anna died 3 March 1783 in Alsace-Lorraine, France at the age of 4½ years.

	iv.	**BARBARA GRASSER** b. 15 November 1781 in Alsace-Lorraine, France. Barbara died 22 April 1783 in Alsace-Lorraine, France at the age of 17 months.
	v.	**SEBASTIAN GRASSER** b. 30 January 1783 in Alsace-Lorraine, France. Sebastian died 6 March 1783 in Alsace-Lorraine, France at the age of 5 weeks.

3. Joseph Grasser Sr.

JOSEPH[3] GRASSER SR. (Simon Sr[2], Johann Jacob[1])

- Born 24 October 1774 in Auenheim, France.
- Married 13 October 1802 Anna Maria Saali (1778-1 July 1840), daughter of Johannes Saali and Maria Catharina Leger, were married in Rountzenheim, France. Anna Maria Saali b. 11 July 1778. She died on 1 July 1840.
- Died 12 February 1846 in Auenheim, France at the age of 72.

Joseph Grasser Sr., who was the firstborn child of his parents, Simon Grasser Sr. and Anna Maria Schmitter, was the only child who survived to adulthood. His other 4 siblings all died before they reached the age of 5 years.

Joseph Grasser Jr. and his wife Anna Maria Saali had 10 children during their marriage. Their 7th child was Stephan Grasser, who is our Grasser Immigrant who came to America.

Children of JOSEPH[3] GRASSER SR. and ANNA MARIA SAALI were:

	i.	**MARIA ANNA GRASSER** b. 20 June 1803 in Auenheim, France. She married Franz Joseph Oberle on 1 May 1830 in a Catholic church in Rountzenheim, France.
	ii.	**JOSEPH GRASSER JR.** b. 15 May 1805 in Auenheim, France. He married Catherina Halter 22 September 1835 in a Catholic church in Rountzenheim, France.
	iii.	**FRANZ ANTONI GRASSER I** b. 9 December 1807 in Auenheim, France. Franz died on 23 December 1807 in Auenheim, France at the age of 2 weeks.
	iv.	**MARIA MAGDALENA GRASSER** b. 16 January 1809 in Auenheim, France.
	v.	**ANNA MARIA GRASSER I** b. 11 November 1810 in Auenheim, France. Anna Maria died 27 November 1813 in Auenheim, France at the age of 3 years.
	vi.	**MARIA CATHERINA GRASSER** b. 8 December 1812 in Auenheim, France. She married Johannes Michael Halter on 12 January 1836 in a Catholic church in Rountzenheim, France.
4.	vii.	**STEPHAN GRASSER** (IMMIGRANT) b. 24 December 1814 in Auenheim, Alsace Lorraine, France. He was baptized on Christmas Day 25 December 1814. He married twice: Wife #1 Catherina ____ (Immigrant). Stephan married circa 1845 in Alsace-Lorraine. Catherina ____ (circa 1804-1852). They immigrated to America together on the sailing ship *Clarissa Andrews* of Boston, England. They debarked in New York City on 28 May 1846. Catherina died in Centerville, Manitowoc, Wisconsin. Stephan and Catherine had no children during their marriage. Wife #2 Maria Fischbach (Immigrant) married 3 March 1853 in

		Sheboygan, Wisconsin. Maria Fischbach (17 September 1830-1904). Maria was the daughter of Domenick Fischbach and Mary Wagner. Stephan and Maria had 13 children during their marriage. Stephan Grasser died 24 February 1906 in Sheboygan, Sheboygan Co., Wisconsin at the age of 91. He was buried with his wife Maria Fischbach in the Calvary Cemetery in Sheboygan, Wisconsin. <u>Note:</u> Stephan and his wife Catherina came to America one month after his father Joseph Grasser had died. He may have had an inheritance from his father's estate in France which supplied the finances for the trip to America.
	viii.	**ANNA MARIA GRASSER II** b. 28 November 1816 in Auenheim; France. Anna Maria II died 9 December 1816 in Auenheim, France at the age of 12 days.
	ix.	**FRANCOIS ANTOINE GRASSER II** b. 15 January 1818 in Auenheim, France. He married Madelaine Joerger on 11 January 1844 in a Catholic church in Wintzenbach, France.
	x.	**VERONIQUE GRASSER** (Immigrant) b. 4 February 1821 in Auenheim, France. She arrived in New York City 29 May 1843. The ship she sailed aboard was the ship named *Catharine*.

5. Stephan Grasser (Immigrant)

STEPHAN[4] GRASSER (Joseph Sr[3], Simon Sr[2], Johann Jacob[1])

- Born 24 December 1814 in Auenheim, Rountzenheim, Alsace-Lorraine, France.
- Married circa 1845 Wife #1: Catherina _____ in Rountzenheim, Alsace-Lorraine, France.
- Arrival in New York: 28 May 1846 on the sailing ship *Clarissa Andrews*. Emigrated from Le Havre, France.
- Married 3 March 1853 Wife #2: Maria Fischbach, (1830-1904), daughter of Domenick Fischbach and Mary Wagner. Stephan and Maria were married in The Holy Name Catholic Church, Sheboygan, Sheboygan Co., Wisconsin.
- Died 24 February 1906 in Sheboygan, Sheboygan Co., Wisconsin, at age 91 years.
- Buried in Calvary Cemetery, Sheboygan, Sheboygan Co., Wisconsin.

1st Marriage:

Note: Stephan and his wife Catherina came to America one month after his father Joseph Grasser died. He may have had an inheritance from his father's estate in France to make the trip to America.

Stephan and Catherina came to America and arrived in New York on 28 May 1846. They lived in New York state for 2 years until 1848 and then they travelled to Wisconsin where they settled and lived. Stephan and Catharina purchased 40 acres of land in Manitowoc County, Wisconsin on 4 May 1848. It was there in Wisconsin that Catherina died childless.

2nd Marriage:

Stephan later met Maria Fischbach and they married 3 March 1853 in The Holy Name Catholic Church, Sheboygan, Sheboygan Co., Wisconsin. They had 13 children during their marriage.

Children of Stephan[4] Grasser and Maria Fischbach were:

	i.	**MARY GRASSER** b. 15 March 1854 in St. Wendel, Manitowoc Co., Wisconsin. She was baptized Maria Katherina on 21 March 1854 at St. Mary's Magdalene (later called Holy Name) Catholic Church in Sheboygan, Sheboygan Co., Wisconsin. She married Nicholas Schram 26 February 1878 in St. Fidelis Catholic Church, Meeme, Manitowoc Co., Wisconsin. Mary and Nicholas had 5 children (4 girls and a 1 boy). The author of this book (Mary-Louise) was named for Mary Grasser Schram and her sister Louise Grasser Klessig (see child v.). Mary Grasser Schram died 21 February 1944 in Sheboygan, Sheboygan Co., Wisconsin, at the age of 89. She and her husband Nicholas are buried in St. Fidelis Catholic Cemetery, Meeme, Manitowoc Co., Wisconsin. Note: Nick Schram & Mary Grasser's marriage record is recorded at Holy Trinity Church in School Hill, Town of Meeme, Manitowoc Co., Wisconsin. It is possible at that time that St. Fidelis was being serviced by Holy Trinity. In 1883 and from then on, in the Schram children's baptismal records, the dates were recorded as at St. Fidelis Parish.
	ii.	**SIMON GRASSER** b. 18 February 1856 in St. Wendel, Manitowoc Co., Wisconsin. He married Margaret Schill 11 December 1879 in St. Mary's Catholic Church, Milwaukee, Milwaukee Co, Wisconsin. Simon and Margaret had 2 girls, Elizabeth & Anna, during their marriage. Simon died 9 July 1934 in Sheboygan, Sheboygan Co., Wisconsin at the age of 78. He and his wife Margaret are buried in the Calvary Cemetery, Sheboygan, Sheboygan Co., Wisconsin.
	iii.	**DOMINIC GRASSER** b. 1857 in St. Wendel, Manitowoc Co., Wisconsin. Dominic died in 1860 in St. Wendel, Manitowoc Co., Wisconsin at the age of 3 years.
	iv.	**SUSANN GRASSER** b. 1858 in St. Wendel, Manitowoc Co., Wisconsin. Susann died 1860 in St. Wendel, Manitowoc Co., Wisconsin at the age of 2 years.
	v.	**LOUISE GRASSER** b. 18 May 1860; in St. Wendel, Manitowoc Co., Wisconsin. Louise married Adolph Klessig 17 April 1883 in St. Wendel, Manitowoc Co., Wisconsin. They were married by a civil ceremony not a church wedding. They were not of the same faith. Louise was Catholic and Adolph was Lutheran. Louise and Adolph had 3 children, August, Erna, & Herbert, during their marriage. This author was named after Louise Grasser Klessig. See note in section (child i.). Louise Klessig died 19 April 1951 in Centerville, Manitowoc Co., Wisconsin, at the age of 90. She and her husband, Adolph are buried in the Evergreen Cemetery, Manitowoc Co., Wisconsin.
	vi.	**MAGDALENA GRASSER** b. February 1862 in St. Wendel, Manitowoc Co., Wisconsin. She died 12 April 1863 in St. Wendel, Manitowoc Co., Wisconsin at the age of 1 year and 2 months.
	vii.	**NICHOLAS GRASSER** b. 22 Nov 1863 at St. Wendel, Manitowoc Co., Wisconsin. Nicholas was baptized 11 February 1864 at St. Mary's Magdalene (later called Holy Name) Catholic Church in Sheboygan, Sheboygan Co., Wisconsin. He married Laura Krinn on 17 March 1920 in the St. Paul's United Church of Christ (Reformed Lutheran) in Chicago, Cook Co., Illinois. He owned and operated a paint store in Chicago. Nicholas is buried in the Forest Home (Waldheim Cemetery), in Forest Park, Cook Co., Illinois. The German translation of Waldheim is "Forest home" which is the name that is used today. Nicholas died at age 58 and never had any children. He and Laura Krinn only had been married 2 years when Nick died. Laura did remarry to Patrick John Cunningham circa 1926, There were no children born

		during that marriage either. Laura died on 9 December 1970 in Chicago, Illinois and is buried in the Forest Home Cemetery next to Patrick Cunningham, her 2nd husband.
	viii.	**HELEN "LENA" GRASSER** b. 25 July 1865 in St. Wendel, Manitowoc Co., Wisconsin. She was baptized on 30 July 1865 at the St. Wendel's Catholic Church in St. Wendel, Wisconsin. Helen "Lena" married Hermann Heinrichs Thiele on 14 October 1888 at St. Paul's German Evangelical Lutheran Church in Chicago, Cook Co., Illinois. Lena died 15 November 1937 in Sheboygan, Sheboygan Co., Wisconsin, at age 72. She and her husband were both buried in the Calvary Cemetery, Sheboygan, Sheboygan Co., Wisconsin. They had no biological children, but did raise 2 foster children. Also note: Erna Grasser did live with them for a while.
	ix.	**JOHN GRASSER** b. 14 February 1867 in St. Wendel, Wisconsin. He was baptized 24 February 1867 at St. Wendel's Catholic Church, in St. Wendel, Manitowoc Co., Wisconsin. He married Annie Covey on 24 December 1892 in Neillsville, Clark Co., Wisconsin by a Justice of the Peace. They had no children. He was a gold prospector. John searched for gold in Klondike-Yukon Territory in Alaska for 15 years. On the 1910 Census for the "Forty Mile River" of Alaska, John and Annie Grasser were enumerated together as "Placer Miners." In 1920 they were back living in California. John died 12 January 1939 in Porterville, Tulare Co., California, at the age of 71. John is buried in Crypt #4 – Hillcrest Memorial Park, Porterville, Tulare Co., California.
	x.	**CATHERINA "KATIE" GRASSER** b. 30 March 1869 in St. Wendel, Manitowoc Co., Wisconsin. She was baptized 4 April 1869 at St. Wendel's Catholic Church in St. Wendel, Manitowoc Co., Wisconsin. She married Frederick Carl Heyden 18 June 1893 in St. Paul's German Evangelical United Church in Chicago, Cook Co., Illinois. She and her husband "Fritz" were known as the "springboard off the farm" home for their nieces and nephews for 16 years. Catherine died on 21 September 1943 in Chicago, Cook Co., Illinois, at the age of 74. She and her husband Frederick Carl are buried in the Waldheim Cemetery, Forest Park, Cook Co., Illinois.
	xi.	**MARGARETHA "GRETCHEN "GRASSER** b. 15 March 1871 in St. Wendel, Manitowoc Co., Wisconsin. She was baptized 26 March 1871 at St. Wendel's Catholic Church in St. Wendel, Wisconsin. She married John Ludwig on 19 August 1894 in Holy Name Catholic Church, Sheboygan, Sheboygan Co., Wisconsin. They had 3 children, Ira John, Norma M., & Norbert, during their marriage. Gretchen died on 31 July 1961 in Wauwatosa, Milwaukee Co., Wisconsin, at age 90. She and her husband John are buried in the Calvary Cemetery in Sheboygan, Sheboygan Co., Wisconsin.
	xii.	**MICHAEL Grasser I** b. 28 January 1873 in St. Wendel, Manitowoc Co., Wisconsin. He was baptized on 30 January 1873 at St. Wendel's Catholic Church in St Wendel, Wisconsin. Michael, I died on 14 March 1873 in St. Wendel, Manitowoc Co., Wisconsin at the early age of 18 months.
5.	xiii.	**MICHAEL GRASSER II,** b. 26 February 1874 in St. Wendel, Manitowoc Co., Wisconsin. He was baptized on 20 February 1874 at St. Wendel's Catholic Church in St Wendel, Wisconsin. He married Wilhelmina Rades. daughter of Fridrich Wilhelm Rades Sr. and Margaretha Stahmer. Michael II and Wilhelmina were married on 20 February 1898 in Ss. Peter & Paul Catholic Church, Kiel, Manitowoc Co., Wisconsin. Michael and Wilhelmina had 12 children. 9 of whom lived to adulthood. They owned a large 80-acre farm in Porterfield, Wisconsin on Grasser

		Road which is still in operation today. It is now owned by their grandson, Allen Grasser. Michael II died 3 September 1961 in Sheboygan, Sheboygan Co., Wisconsin, at the age of 87. He and his wife Wilhelmina are buried in the Calvary Cemetery, Sheboygan, Sheboygan Co, Wisconsin.

6. Michael Grasser II

MICHAEL[5] GRASSER II (Stephan[4], Joseph Sr[3], Simon Sr[2], Johann Jacob[1])

- Born 26 February 1874 in St. Wendel, Manitowoc Co., Wisconsin.
- Married 20 February 1898 Wilhelmina Rades (1876-1947), daughter of Fridrich Wilhelm Rades Sr. and Margaretha Stahmer. Michael and Wilhelmina were married in Ss. Peter & Paul Catholic Church, Kiel, Manitowoc Co., Wisconsin. They had 12 children, 9 of whom grew to maturity. Their last two were twins who died as stillborn.
- Died 3 September 1961 in Sheboygan, Sheboygan Co., Wisconsin, at age 87.
- Buried in Calvary Cemetery, Sheboygan, Sheboygan Co., Wisconsin.

Michael Grasser II was the youngest of the large family of Stephan and Maria Fischbach Grasser, who were both immigrants. Michael II grew up in the St. Wendel area of Wisconsin on a farm in Manitowoc County. Michael's parents, Stephan and Maria, were getting older, and they retired in Sheboygan, Wisconsin when they sold their farm in St. Wendel, Wisconsin. Michael was then 16 years old, and he moved with them. Michael got a job making chairs for the Sheboygan Chair Company. A few years later, he left that job and went to Chicago working for his brother-in-law, Fred Heyden, who owned and operated a grain and feed store. Michael worked for Fred for a while and then later worked for a cement finisher laying sidewalks. Eventually, Mike returned to the land and the job he absolutely loved. He hired himself out as a farmhand.

It was during this period of his life that he met Wilhelmina Rades, known as Minnie. They met completely by chance or by the Lord's leading. They fell in love and were married 20 February 1898. They wound up on a farm where Michael worked as a farmhand. It was here that Mike started to work for Claus Wichmann. At that point, Mike and Minnie had two small children and not much money but Claus took a liking to Mike and his young family.

Let me pause here and tell you about how a major happening

affected our Mike and Minnie.

The date and time of major happenings on our planet often impact our own timeline. Allow me to share one of these true events which affected Michael and Wilhelmina's lives and the lives of their entire family.

The Devastating Peshtigo Fire

Many people know of the Great Chicago Fire of October 8, 1871, but few people know of the monumental natural disaster of the Peshtigo Fire which occurred on the very same day! It was far more costly in lives than the huge Chicago Fire. Why didn't people learn of this horrific fire and remember it? The answer: it was because of money and prestige! Peshtigo was a small lumber town in upper

Wisconsin and consisted of poor farmers and poor lumbermen. Chicago was a huge city with many wealthy people living there and had a huge newspaper, *The Chicago Tribune*. Chicago had a fire department. Peshtigo only had the river, which people threw themselves into to escape the burning, scorching flames. Peshtigo was completely wiped out. Very few people survived the flaming hell. However, there was one man who did survive and lived to write a book about it. He was the Catholic priest from Peshtigo and Marinette, the Reverend Father Peter Pernin. He wrote his account of the Peshtigo fire from Montreal, Canada to raise funds for the rebuilding of his church in Peshtigo. The Peshtigo Fire was by far the deadliest wildfire in American history. An estimated 2,500 people lost their lives that one day.

How did this disaster affect our Mike and Minnie Grasser, you might ask?

Thirty years after the fire, which had left acres of trees burnt and land barren, a young man named Michael Grasser rode up from Sheboygan, Wisconsin on his horse with his boss, Claus Wichmann, who was a well-to-do farmer in New Holstein, Wisconsin. Michael was married to Wilhelmina Rades, and they had two small children, Erna and Raymond, at that time. The day of the horseback ride into the Peshtigo area was 21 July 1902. His boss Claus told Michael as they rode side by side chatting, "You know, Mike, you have to purchase a piece of land to get ahead in this world, rather than keep on working for other people." They kept on riding through the Peshtigo area where the Peshtigo Lumber Company was then selling acres of land cheap because so much of it was burnt tree stumps. It was then that Mike became a visionary! Mike found a large piece of land in this area which he really liked a lot.

It was 80 acres of this burnt wasteland with the Peshtigo River running at the edge of the piece of land. Claus Wichmann agreed it was a good deal and Claus bought the land for Mike with the agreement that Mike would work the land and pay him back and then Mike and Minnie would own the land outright. Mike had little money and burnt land was all that he could afford. Claus was a good friend as well as his boss. Papers were drawn up and signed that very day. Mike and Claus both kept their agreement. Claus Wichmann paid $800 for the 80 acres of land on 21 July 1902. Mike and Minnie worked the land, and they built a home on it. Once Mike and Minnie were financially stable, they bought the title to the 80 acres from Claus Wichmann for $1,250 on 23 April 1914.

Mike was persistent and a diligent worker, as was his wife, Minnie. He and Minnie rented a house about a mile down the road from their new property. This rented house was where their third child, Sylvia Grasser, was born on 7 January 1903. Sylvia Grasser was this author's mother. Mike went on to build a home on their new land with his wife and they had 12 children altogether (9 of whom lived to maturity). Mike worked the land and dynamited all the 80 acres of tree stumps and took the burnt trees down. He built a log cabin from the trees, placing them vertically in the ground. He also built a log barn and dug a well nearby. It was a huge, arduous task! The only way of reaching the property was via an old logging supply trail that ran the whole southern length of the property along the Peshtigo River. Some of the trees had trunks six feet in diameter. Mike tried to plough the land around the massive and numerous tree stumps. He would also hire himself out with his team of horses and a sled to lumber camps during the winter months. During the spring, summer and fall he cleared about half the land himself by dynamiting the stumps. In 1915 Mike hired two German emigrants to finish clearing the growth and the stumps on the reminder of the property. They received $1 per day plus their room and board. It took them two years to complete the project.

Mike was a produce farmer, but in 1913 he also specialized in dairy farming. They grew potatoes, cabbages, and carrots and sold them locally. They also had chickens and sold the eggs. The livestock consisted of horses, cows, pigs, and sheep. They also had an apple orchard which produced 15 different varieties of apples. They also raised their own grain for the livestock and stored it in the silo next to the barn.

Mike was a large man with powerful physical strength. However, when in 1918 a 300-pound barrel of salt was being unloaded from the wagon, the horses moved unexpectedly and threw Mike off-balance. The barrel landed on Mike's leg, breaking his thigh bone. Cyrill, Mike and Minnie's eldest son, was living at home at that time as Cyrill's older brother Raymond had already left the farm. Cyrill, now 14 years old, rode bareback to the nearest phone to call for help. It took 2 years for Mike to recover and young Cyrill had to run the farm for them. Years later, it is Cyrill's son, Allen Grasser, who today owns the thriving working farm. There is a paved road now to the front of the property. The town of Porterfield has appropriately named this road "Grasser Road."

It wasn't just all work on the farm but there was a lot of work in those primitive days. However, there were joy and festivities also. Christmastime was always special. The Grasser family celebrated the German traditions. The boys would go out and find the perfect "Tannenbaum" (Christmas tree) which they set up in the parlor. The children would decorate it with streams of popcorn strings and paper chains as well as apples and candy canes. Mike played the accordion and always loved the German polkas! For a real treat one Christmas, Mike and Minnie saved up their money and surprised the kids with a modern-day Victrola with a huge horn for their family. The kids absolutely loved it!

When Cyrill Grasser celebrated his 90th birthday, the entire family had a huge reunion on the farm. There were about 200 family members who attend this reunion coming from all over the United States, sharing this special celebration. We had tents set up all over the farm, some camped out, others stayed in nearby bed and breakfast homes, still others in hotels in the city of Marinette, nearby. Great food! Great family meeting with cousins galore! We all danced in the barn that night. It was a joyous occasion for all. How the family has grown and how the land has improved from the burnt and barren state left by the devastating fire of years ago. The land that Mike had first seen and had a vision to improve is today a thriving farmland and produces abundant crops every year.

Children of MICHAEL[5] GRASSER II and WILHELMINA RADES were:

	i.	ERNA GRASSER b. 3 December 1898 in St. Nazianz, Manitowoc Co., Wisconsin. She married Gustav "Gus" Waldau 31 May 1927 in St. Joseph Catholic Church, Walsh, Marinette Co., Wisconsin. Erna and Gustav Waldau had 5 daughters and each daughter had at least 5 children each. Gus was a professional tailor. Erna died 25 December 1989 in Kaukauna, Outagamie Co., Wisconsin, at age 91. She and Gus are both buried in the Calvary Cemetery, Sheboygan, Sheboygan Co., Wisconsin.
	ii.	REV. RAYMOND GRASSER b. 21 December 1900 in New Holstein, Calumet Co., Wisconsin. He married Doris Goodrich 27 August 1923 in the Tremont Temple Baptist Church, Boston, Suffolk Co., Massachusetts. Rev. Raymond and Doris had no children. Raymond was a Minister of the Church of the Advent, Christian Faith. As a minister, Raymond married this author's parents, Albert and Sylvia Kearney, in 1938 in Portsmouth, New Hampshire. He also worked in the Portsmouth Navy Yard as a sheet metal worker and worked in assisting with the construction of the Kittery, Maine bridge. Raymond died 12 February 1975 of a massive CVA (stroke) in Vernon, Windham Co., Vermont, at the age of 74. Doris lived on until her 93rd year. He and his wife Doris are buried in the North Hampton Cemetery in North Hampton, Rockingham Co., in New Hampshire.
6.	iii.	SYLVIA MARY-LOUISE GRASSER b. 7 January 1903 in Porterfield, Marinette Co., Wisconsin. Sylvia left the farm and lived for a while at her aunt and uncle's "springboard home" and then got a job as a homemaker maid in Chicago. A few years later she took on a better-paying job working as a homemaker maid for a wealthy family in Baltimore, Maryland. She worked there for a few years until her

		brother was ordained a minister in Boston, Massachusetts. She went to the ceremony and her boss in Baltimore said she stayed too long, and she was fired! This ended up being a wonderful thing! Her sister Leona got her a new job working next door to where Leona was working in Newton (near Boston). The new family loved Sylvia and she thrived there working for them. Soon she met and fell in love with her future husband. She married Albert Wintfield Kearney on 11 September 1938 in Portsmouth, New Hampshire. However, their new home was in Cambridge, Middlesex Co., Massachusetts. They had two daughters, Mary-Louise Alberta (author of this book) and Diane Wilhelmina. Mary-Louise married Charles Albert McComas. They had 3 biological children and 2 adopted children during their 42-year marriage. The couple divorced in 2005. Diane married David Norman Gray. They had two children during their marriage. Sylvia died on 10 December 1984 at the age of 81. Her husband Albert W. Kearney lived on another 5 years. He died at the age of 90. They were both buried in the Mt. Hope Cemetery in Acton, Middlesex Co., and Massachusetts.
	iv.	**Cyrill Grasser b**. 3 December 1904 in Porterfield, Marinette Co., Wisconsin. Cyrill married three times. Wife #1 Rose "Rosely" DiMarco b. 23 May 1904 in Plaquemine, Iberville Parish, Louisiana from Sicilian parents. They married on 14 June 1927 in City Hall in Chicago, Cook Co., Illinois. There were no children born in this marriage. They divorced seven months later 9 February 1928 in Cook Co., Illinois. Wife #2 Viola Virginia Moore on 25 April 1931 in Ravenswood Methodist Church, Chicago, Cook Co., Illinois. They had 3 children during this marriage: Roland, Virginia, and Barbara. Cyrill and Viola Moore were divorced 1 April 1943 in Chicago, Cook Co., Illinois. Wife #3 Marjorie Schwering married on 20 May 1947 in St. Joseph Catholic Church, Duncombe, Webster Co., Iowa. Cyrill and his third wife Marjorie Schwering had 2 sons: Norman & Allen. Cyrill was an electrician and worked on elevators throughout the city of Chicago. Cyrill died at the age of 96 on 10 March 2001 at the Lakeview Living Center in Pineville, Mecklenburg Co., North Carolina and he is buried with his third wife Marjorie in the All-Saints Cemetery, in Des Plaines, Cooke Co., Illinois.
	v.	**Myron Grasser** b. 26 September 1907 in Porterfield, Marinette Co., Wisconsin. Myron married twice: Wife #1 Gertrude Mills. They were married on 18 June 1934 in Chicago City Hall, Chicago, Cook Co., Illinois. Myron and Gertrude had 3 children: Walter and twin girls Vivian & Velma. Velma was born with the disability of cerebral palsy. Myron was a shipfitter hand and worked for a long time in Portsmouth, New Hampshire in the Navy Yard in Portsmouth. After WWII was over, he and his family relocated to Waltham, Middlesex Co., Massachusetts. Gertrude died suddenly after a gallbladder surgery and Myron remarried to her sister. Wife #2 Dorothy Mills Chernoff (who was Gertrude Mills' sister). They were married on 21 November 1964 in the First Baptist Church, Waltham, Middlesex Co., Massachusetts. They had no children during this marriage. Myron died 15 March 1979 in Raynham, Bristol Co., Massachusetts, at age of 71. Myron is buried in the Mount Peake Cemetery, Waltham, Middlesex Co., Massachusetts.
	vi.	**Elmyra Grasser** b. 12 July 1909 in Porterfield, Marinette Co., Wisconsin. Elmyra married Sigvald Johnson 20 June 1942 in St. Joseph Catholic Church, Walsh, Marinette Co., Wisconsin. They had two sons, Leonard and Christopher, during their marriage. Elmyra died 10 March 1972 in Chicago, Cook Co., Illinois, at age 62. She

		and her husband Sigvald are buried in the Irving Park Cemetery, Chicago, Cook Co., Illinois.
	vii.	**LEONA GRASSER** b. 2 August 1911 in Porterfield, Marinette Co., Wisconsin. Leona worked as a homemaker maid until she met and married her husband. She married Joseph Pouliot on 8 August 1937 in St. Joseph French Catholic Church, Waltham, Middlesex Co., Massachusetts. Joseph owned and operated his own moving company. Leona and Joe had 2 daughters: Leona "Lee," known to us as "Cookie," and her sister Nellie. Leona died 24 April 1992 in Marlborough, Middlesex Co., Massachusetts, at age 80. She and her Joe were buried in the Calvary Cemetery Waltham, Middlesex Co., Massachusetts.
	viii.	**FIRST LIEUTENANT SYLVANUS GRASSER** b. 21 July 1913 in Porterfield, Marinette Co., Wisconsin. He married Ursula Huls on 11 April 1942 in Harmony Church, at the Army Base Chapel Cantonment of Fort Benning in Columbus, Muscogee Co., Georgia. Sylvanus was in the United States Army in World War II. He was a First Lieutenant in the 63rd Infantry Regiment of the 6th Division. Sylvanus and Ursula had 1 child, a son named William who was born after Sylvanus went overseas on active duty. He knew of William's birth but never was able to see his son, William, known as "Billy." Sylvanus was on a mission in the military during WWII, in the waters near Australia when his PT boat hit a hidden bomb and was blown up. Sylvanus was killed in action, dying at sea in Milne Bay near Hihilai Plantation, Territory of Papua, New Guinea on 24 April 1944 at the age of 30.
	ix.	**BABY GRASSER** b. 1915 in Porterfield, Marinette Co., Wisconsin. Died in 1915.
	x.	**EVERIST GRASSER** b. 1 March 1917 in Porterfield, Marinette Co., Wisconsin. He married Nina Schmidt on 10 April 1942 in Calvary Lutheran, Antigo, Langlade Co., Wisconsin. Everist and Nina had no children during their marriage. Everist took over the Grasser family farm after his parents retired in 1942. Everest was a dairy farmer for 25 years and a farm machinery salesman and an AMC car dealership owner in Porterfield, Wisconsin. His wife Nina managed a hair salon in the front of their home on the farm. Later in life, Everest went into automobile repair and sales. Everist died 17 January 1984 in Menominee, Menominee Co., Michigan, at the age of 66. Everist and Nina are buried together in the Glenwood Memorial Gardens, Marinette, Marinette Co., Wisconsin.
	xi.	**TWIN GRASSER I** b. 1919 in Porterfield, Marinette Co., Wisconsin. Died at birth 1919.
	xii.	**TWIN GRASSER II** b. 1919 in Porterfield, Marinette Co., Wisconsin. Died at birth 1919.

6. Sylvia Mary-Louise Grasser

SYLVIA MARY-LOUISE[6] GRASSER (Michael II[5], Stephan[4], Joseph Sr[3], Simon Sr[2], Johann Jacob[1])

- Born. 7 January 1903 in Porterfield, Marinette Co., Wisconsin.
- Married 11 September 1938 Albert Wintfield Kearney (6 November 1899-29 December 1989), son of James Wintfield Kearney and Alberta Buchannan Atkinson. Sylvia and Albert were married in Portsmouth, Rockingham Co., New Hampshire. The minister who married them was Sylvia's brother, the Reverend Raymond Grasser.
- Died 10 December 1984 Cambridge, Middlesex Co., Massachusetts at the age of 81.
- Buried Mount Hope Cemetery, Acton, Middlesex Co., Massachusetts.

Sylvia Grasser, growing up on the farm, was quite a sickly child. But being one of the older children, she had to take care of the younger siblings. Life on the farm was hard. Sylvia told her younger daughter, Diane, years later that her feet always hurt her when she was growing up. The reason for this was that she never had shoes that fit her correctly. She always had to wear "hand-me-downs." Sylvia's older sister Erna's shoes never fit her, but there was really no choice! Erna's hand-me-down shoes or go barefoot, and in the cold winter days in Wisconsin, walking to school in the snow was a real challenge! Her hand-me-down shoes always pinched her toes! Ouch! Sylvia left the family farm when she had reached maturity and went to Chicago to her paternal aunt in Chicago. Aunt Catherine Heyden's home was a "springboard" off the farm, helping the Grasser kids one by one find their own identity. Sylvia stayed with Aunt Catherine for a while until she found a local homemaker job and later, she found a better job in Baltimore, Maryland where she worked for several years as a nanny and cook for a wealthy family.

Her brother Raymond Grasser was being ordained as a Protestant minister in Boston, Massachusetts, so Sylvia travelled to see him and celebrate his ordination. She stayed longer than her Baltimore boss had wanted her to, and she got fired. However, she immediately found an excellent job next door to where her sister Leona was working in Newton, Massachusetts. This was the home of Dr. and Mrs. Thorne. It was a wonderful job and for Sylvia, living right next door to her sister Leona was a real treat. It was here she met and became great friends with Elsie. Elsie became Sylvia's best friend. Then Elsie fell in love with Ken Bell and Elsie asked Sylvia to be her maid of honor in her wedding. Sylvia was delighted. Wedding plans turned into quite a celebration. Ken's best man was a guy named Albert Kearney. With all the wedding preparations, Sylvia and Albert met. They fell in love and shortly thereafter there was another wedding! Sylvia and Albert became this author's parents. Raymond, now an ordained minister, married them. They were married on 11 September 1938 in Portsmouth, New Hampshire. A joyous wedding it was. They had a wonderful honeymoon in upstate New York and travelled by car through the Berkshire mountains in western Massachusetts. When they returned home, there was a huge hurricane, known now as the Hurricane of '38! Trees were down and the city of Cambridge, where their apartment was, looked like a war zone! It was quite a disaster they came home to. Sylvia, now married, left her job with the Thorne family with their blessings. She went to work as her new husband's right hand in the printing office which he now owned and operated as of 1936. They ran the Weston Printing Company for close to 50 years.

They had two daughters, Mary-Louise and Diane. Sylvia was never able to attend school further than the eighth grade. She had always dreamed of becoming a nurse or a schoolteacher. She fulfilled these dreams through her two daughters. One became a registered nurse and the other a special needs elementary school teacher. Sylvia was a wonderful mother and a patient, hardworking helpmate for her husband. Sylvia was a wonderful cook and made the most delicious homemade Sunday meals that you might ever imagine! She ran the office at the printing company and had unique business skills. In the evenings she enjoyed gardening with her husband. Both she and Albert were raised on farms. As the saying goes, *"Although they both left the farm, the farm never left them!"* They raised vegetables and flowers. Sylvia, like her mother. did enjoy making delicious piccalilli and did canning and made "Heavenly Delight Jelly" which her older daughter, this author, continued making at Christmastime for family and friends. Sylvia also enjoyed classical music and especially the Strauss waltzes like the "Blue Danube."

She was continually active in her church and in the Eastern Star Lodge. Her husband was also into Lodge work, being a member of the Masonic Order and the Royal Arcanum. They loved having parties at their home. Laughter always flowed from these parties and could be heard all over the entire house. Fond memories of a wonderful woman who was my special mother and a very dear friend.

Children of SYLVIA MARY-LOUISE[6] GRASSER and ALBERT WINTFIELD KEARNEY are documented in the Kearney chapter.

Source Citations for this Chapter

Allen P. Grasser, "Grasser-Rades Family Genealogy: Familial Data Abstracts," E-mail messages from <agrasser.msj3@gmail.com> at 1453 Vernon Ave.; Park Ridge, IL 60068-1563. From 20 September to 20 October 2021.

1860 United States Federal Census.

1870 United States Federal Census.

New York Passenger and Crew Lists (including Castle Garden and Ellis Island from 1820-1957.

Firestorm at Peshtigo, A Town, It's People and the Deadliest Fire in American History by Denice Gess & William Lutz, Henry Holt & Co., Publishers, New York, 2002.

U. S. Find a Grave Index 1600's -> Current.

Wisconsin State Censuses, 1855-1905.

https://www.ancestry.com.

Chapter 42: The Neumannes

The Neumann Family Line

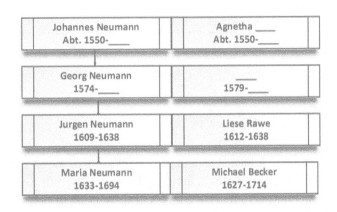

1. Johannes Neumann
JOHANNES [1] NEUMANN
- Born circa 1550 in Province of Pomerania, Kingdom of Prussia (which was part of the German Confederation).
- Married circa 1573 Agatha ___ (circa 1550-___). Johannes and Agatha were married in Rehwinkel, Pomerania Province, Kingdom of Prussia and in union with the Holy Roman Empire of the German Nation.
- Died ___ in Rehwinkel, district of Saatzig, Pomerania, Kingdom of Prussia (which was a member of the German Confederation). Johannes died at age unknown.

Child of JOHANNES [1] NEUMANN and AGATHA ___ was:

2.	i.	GEORG NEUMANN b. 1574 in Rehwinkel, district of Saatzig, Province of Pomerania, Kingdom of Prussia (which was part of the German Confederation). Age at death is unknown.

2. Georg Neumann
GEORG [2] NEUMANN. (Johannes[1])
- Born 1574 in Province of Pomerania, Kingdom of Prussia (which was part of the German Confederation).
- Married circa 1608 _____ (1579-___). Georg and ___ were married in Saatzig, Pomerania, Kingdom of Prussia.
- Died ___ in Rehwinkel, district of Saatzig, Pomerania, Kingdom of Prussia (which was a member of the German Confederation. Georg died at age unknown.

Child of GEORG ^{2}-NEUMANN and _____ was:

3.	i.	**JURGEN NEUMANN** b. 1609 in Rehwinkel, district of Saatzig, Province of Pomerania, Kingdom of Prussia (which was part of the German Confederation). He married Liese Rawe 20 October 1628 in Rehwinkel, Saatzig, Province of Pomerania, Kingdom of Prussia. They had one child, a daughter named Maria. Jurgen died in 1638 when his daughter was 5 years old.

3. Jurgen Neumann

JURGEN ^{3} NEUMANN (Georg^2, Johannes^1)

- Born in 1609 in Rehwinkel, district of Saatzig, Province of Pomerania, Kingdom of Prussia.
- Married 20 October 1628 Liese Rawe (1612-1638). Jurgen and Liese were married in Rehwinkel, Pomerania, Prussia. Liese Rawe was the daughter of Heinrich Rawe (b. 1586 and Ursula Grapentin b. 1584). Jürgen and Liese had 1 child (Maria) in their marriage. Maria was only 5 years old when both her parents (Jurgen & Liese) died in the same year of 1638.
- Died 1638 in Rehwinkel, district of Saatzig, Pomerania, Kingdom of Prussia at the age of 29.

Child of JURGEN ^{3} NEUMANN and LIESE RAWE was:

4.	i.	**MARIA NEUMANN** b. 1633 in Rehwinkel, district of Saatzig, Province of Pomerania, Kingdom of Prussia. Maria married Michael Becker on 27 June 1653 in Ball, Saatzig. Pomerania, Prussia. They had 9 children during their marriage. Maria died in 1694 at the age of 61.

4. Maria Neumann

MARIA ^{4} NEUMANN (Jurgen^3, Georg^2, Johannes^1)

- Born 1633 in Rehwinkel, Province of Pomerania, Kingdom of Prussia.
- Married 27 June 1653 Michael Becker (1637-1714). Maria and Michael were married in Ball, Pomerania, Kingdom of Prussia. They had 9 children during their marriage.
- Died 1694 in Rehwinkel, district of Saatzig, Pomerania, Kingdom of Prussia. Maria died at age 61.

Children of MARIA ^{4} NEUMANN and MICHAEL BECKER are documented in the Becker chapter.

Source Citations for this Chapter

www.familysearch.org Neumann family research

http://www.ancestry.com   Neumann & Becker family research

Allen Grasser Verbal and Email information on the Becker & Neumann Families

Allen P. Grasser, "Becker Family Genealogy: Familial Data Abstracts," E-mail messages from
<agrasser.msj3@gmail.com> at 1453 Vernon Ave.; Park Ridge, IL 60068-1563. From 20
September to 20 October 2021.

Chapter 43: The Radeses

The Rades Family Line

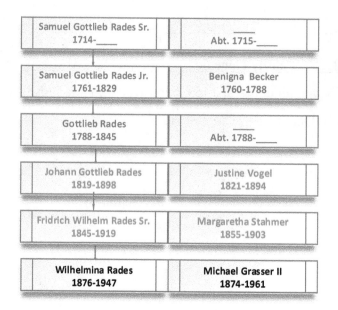

Samuel Gottlieb Rades Sr.
1714-____

_____ Abt. 1715-____

Samuel Gottlieb Rades Jr.
1761-1829

Benigna Becker
1760-1788

Gottlieb Rades
1788-1845

_____ Abt. 1788-____

Johann Gottlieb Rades
1819-1898

Justine Vogel
1821-1894

Fridrich Wilhelm Rades Sr.
1845-1919

Margaretha Stahmer
1855-1903

Wilhelmina Rades
1876-1947

Michael Grasser II
1874-1961

1. Samuel "Gottlieb" Rades Sr.

SAMUEL[1] "GOTTLIEB" RADES SR.

- Born circa 1714 in Province of Pomerania, Kingdom of Prussia (which was part of the German Confederation).
- Married 1751 _____. Samuel and ___ were married in Pomerania. Kingdom of Prussia and in union with the Holy Roman Empire of the German Nation.
- Died ____ in Rehwinkel, district of Saatzig, Pomerania, Kingdom of Prussia (which was a member of the German Confederation). Samuel Gottlieb Sr. died at age unknown.

Children of SAMUEL GOTTLIEB[1] RADES SR. and _____ were:

	i.	**ANNA REGINA RADES** b. 1759 in Rehwinkel, district of Saatzig, Province of Pomerania, Kingdom of Prussia (which was part of the German Confederation). It is unknown if Anna ever married and unknown if she ever had any children. She died in 1834 age 75.
2	ii.	**SAMUEL GOTTLIEB RADES JR.** b. 1761 in Rehwinkel, district of Saatzig, Province of Pomerania, Kingdom of Prussia (which was part of the German Confederation). He married Benigna Becker, daughter of Michael Becker and Benigna Berndt on 14 January 1785 in the Evangelical church in Rehwinkel. District of Stargard, Pomerania, Kingdom of Prussia and in union with the Holy Roman Empire of the German Nation. They had one known child; a son named Gottleib Rades. Samuel Gottlieb Jr. died on 15 October 1829 in Rehwinkel, district of Saatzig, Pomerania,

		Kingdom of Prussia (which was a member of the German Confederation). He died about the age of 68.

The Rades family for many generations was from the German "Dorf" (Village) of Rehwinkel, District of Saatzig, Province of Pomerania, Kingdom of Prussia, where northern Poland is today.

NOTE:

- The orange marker shows where the village of REHWINKEL, district of Saatzig, Province of Pomerania, Kingdom of Prussia (which was part of the German Confederation) is located.
- Prommern (Pomerania) is the province or State where Rehwinkel is located.
- Saatzig is where the government district of Rehwinkel is located, like the USA county system inside each state.
- Ball is where the Civil Registration of Rehwinkel is located.
- Stargard is where the District Military Command of Rehwinkel is located.
- Rehwinkel has an Evangelical Protestant Parish Church which is where the Rades family worshiped.

During the Napoleonic Wars (1803-1815) the national boundaries in Europe kept changing and were quite fluid. The Rades family was German. However, the boundaries of where they resided kept changing over the years, sometimes in Germany and other times in Poland.

2. Samuel "Gottlieb" Rades Jr.

SAMUEL "GOTTLIEB"[2] RADES JR. (Samuel Gottlieb Sr.[1])

- Born circa 1761 in Rehwinkel, district of Saatzig, Province of Pomerania, Kingdom of Prussia (which was part of the German Confederation).
- Married 14 January 1785 Benigna Becker (1760-1788). She was the daughter of Michael Becker and Benigna Berndt. Samuel Jr. and Benigna were married in the Evangelical church in Rehwinkel, District of Stargard, Pomerania, Kingdom of Prussia - in union with the Holy Roman Empire of the German Nation.
- Died 15 October 1829 in Rehwinkel, district of Saatzig, Pomerania, Kingdom of Prussia (which was a member of the German Confederation). Samuel died about the age of 68.

Samuel "Gottlieb" Rades Jr.'s wife Benigna Becker (1760-1788) was born 13 February 1760 in Ball, and she died 30 November 1788 in Rehwinkel. Source for these dates is www.familysearch.org.

For more information, please see the Becker chapter.

Children of SAMUEL GOTTLIEB[2] RADES JR. and BENIGNA BECKER were:

	i.	**CHRISTIAN FRIEDRICH RADES** circa 1790 in the village of Kremmin. Province of Pomerania, Kingdom of Prussia (which was part of the German Confederation). It is unknown if he ever married and had any children. His death date and location at death are both unknown.
	ii.	**WILHELM FRIEDRICH RADES** circa 1792 in the village of Kremmin. Province of Pomerania, Kingdom of Prussia (which was part of the German Confederation). It is unknown if he ever married and had any children. His death date and location at death are both unknown.
3.	iii.	**GOTTLIEB RADES** b. 1788 in the village of Kremmin. Province of Pomerania, Kingdom of Prussia (which was part of the German Confederation). Married twice. 1st wife ___. 2nd wife Maria Kohn married on 17 August 1835 in the Evangelical church in Altheide, Parish of Ravenstein, district of Saatzig, Pomerania, Kingdom of Prussia. **Gottlieb served in the Prussian Army**. Also, he served as postmaster in Jacobshagen, Kreis Saatzig, Pomerania for a time. He was also the Stadthalter (the Governor of the Province of Lobitz). Gottlieb died in 1845 at age 57 in Neu Lobitz, district of Dramburg, Province of Pomerania, Kingdom of Prussia (which was part of the German Confederation).

3. Gottlieb Rades (A Stadthalter = Governor) of the province Lobitz
He was also a Veteran of the Prussia Army

GOTTLIEB[3] RADES (Samuel Gottlieb Jr[2], Samuel Gottlieb Sr[1])

- Born 1788 in the village of Kremmin, Province of Pomerania, Kingdom of Prussia (which was part of the German Confederation).
- Married circa 1818 Wife #1 ___ Gottlieb and ___ were married in Pomerania, Kingdom of Prussia.
- Married 17 August 1835 Wife #2 Maria Kohn. Gottlieb and Maria were married in the Evangelical church in Altheide, Parish of Ravenstein, district of Saatzig, Pomerania, Kingdom of Prussia.
- Died 1845 in Neu Lobitz, district of Dramburg. Province of Pomerania, Kingdom of Prussia (which was part of the German Confederation). Gottlieb died at the age of 57.

Gottlieb served in the Prussian Army and was a veteran. There is a death plaque at the church in Jacobshagen noting he was a veteran in the Prussian Army. Also, he was a Postmaster at Jacobshagen, Kreis Saatzig, Pomerania for a time.

Child of GOTTLIEB[3] RADES and 1ST WIFE _____ was:

4.	i.	**JOHANN GOTTLIEB RADES** (Immigrant) b. 9 May 1819 in Neu Lobitz, district of Dramburg, Province of Pomerania, Kingdom of Prussia (which was part of the German Confederation). He married Justine Vogel, daughter of Friedrich Wilhelm Vogel and Maria Elisabeth Becker. Johann Gottlieb and Justine married circa 1844 in Saataig, Jakoboshagen, Pomerania, Prussia. Johann Gottlieb and Justine Vogel immigrated to America. Johann Gottlieb and Justine had 6 children during their marriage. Johann Gottlieb died 3 October 1898 in Schleswig, Manitowoc Co., Wisconsin, at the age of 79. He and his wife Justine Vogel are buried in the Schleswig Cemetery, Rockville, Manitowoc Co., Wisconsin.

There are no known children of GOTTLIEB[1] RADES and 2ND WIFE MARIA KOHN.

4. Johann Gottlieb Rades (Immigrant)

JOHANN GOTTLIEB[4] RADES (Gottlieb[3], Samuel Gottlieb Jr[2], Samuel Gottlieb Sr[1])

- Born 9 May 1819 in Neu Lobitz, district of Dramburg, Province of Pomerania, Kingdom of Prussia (which was part of the German Confederation).
- Married circa 1844 Justine Vogel. She was the daughter of Friedrich Wilhelm Vogel and Maria "Elisabeth" Becker. Johann Gottlieb and Justine were married in Saatzig, Jakoboshagen, Pomerania, Prussia.
- Immigration: 20 July 1867. Johann and Justine left Hamburg, Deutschland (Germany) with their family aboard the ship *Cimbria*. They arrived at the New York harbour Castle Garden, in Manhattan, New York several weeks later.
- Died 3 October 1898 in Schleswig, Manitowoc Co., Wisconsin, at the age of 79.
- Buried in Schleswig Cemetery, Rockville, Manitowoc Co., Wisconsin.

Johann Gottlieb Rades' wife Justine Vogel's family of Origin:

Justine Vogel's father Friedrich Wilhelm Vogel was a shepherd and cotter from Saatzig.

Her mother was Maria Elisabeth Becker who died 22 February 1867 in Marienflieb, district of Saatzig, Pomerania, Kingdom of Prussia and this area was a member of the North German Confederation.

Justine had three brothers

1. Christian Vogel (his wife Maria Zuhike)
2. Johann "David" Vogel (his wife Johanna "Hannah" Louise Becker)
3. August Wilhelm Vogel (his wife Ottilie Emillie Schroder)

Note: All Justine's brothers and their wives came to America except for August's wife Ottilie. who chose to stay in Pomerania.

Note:
The district of **SAATZIG** in **Prussia** is now today known as the district of **SZADZKO** in **Poland**.

Johann Gottlieb Rades
(1819-1898)

Map of **Pomerania, Prussia**:

**For a wider view of where Pomerania, Prussia is located,
here is a map with the countries' names.**

Quite like in other countries in Europe, there were many reasons for people wanting to flee the oppression: there was lack of food, poor living conditions, higher rents, plus the opportunities in America that these ancestors had heard about advertising that they needed to take advantage of the opportunities available for them. They risked their lives for the change of life plus freedom of religion which they sought. They left their homeland. One of the main reasons they left was that our great grandfather Friedrich Wilhelm Rades' decision to leave was based on avoiding being conscripted into the Prussian army! The Rades family, like the Grasser family, sought a climate like the one they were leaving. They chose Wisconsin. It was also where a member of the family Wilhelm Rades had led the way in 1865, ten years earlier. He had gone before them. They first sailed to New York via a steamship and had entrance to America at Castle Garden in New York which was the point of entry prior to Ellis Island. This area is now known as Castle Clinton in Lower Manhattan. From there they made their way to upstate Wisconsin, circa 1875.

Note: Ellis Island was not established until 1892 and Castle Garden operated from 1855 to 1890. The Rades and Stahmer families were processed through the Immigrant Landing Depot at Castle Garden located in Manhattan. Castle Garden was originally a fort located on Castle Island which was later filled in with dirt to connect it all to Manhattan.

Children of JOHANN GOTTLIEB[4] RADES and JUSTINE VOGEL were:

| 5. | i. | **FRIDRICH WILHELM RADES SR. (IMMIGRANT)** b. 11 March 1845 in the village of Saatzig, district of Saatzig, Province of Pomerania, Parish of Jakobshagen, married Margaretha Stahmer on 15 April 1874 in the town of Schleswig, Manitowoc Co. Wisconsin. Margaretha Stahmer b. 16 May 1855 in the village of Schleswig, Friedrichsberg, district of Schleswig, Danish Duchy of Schleswig. Margaretha died 14 September 1903 in the town of Schleswig, Manitowoc Co., Wisconsin. She was the daughter of Johann "Carl" Christian Stahmer. Fridrich Wilhelm and Margaretha had |

		8 children in their marriage. They were of the Lutheran faith. Fridrich Wilhelm Sr. died 31 May 1919 in Kiel, Wisconsin. He and his wife Margaretha are buried together in the Schleswig Cemetery near Rockville, Town of Schleswig, Manitowoc Co., Wisconsin.
	ii.	**FRIEDERIKE WILHELMINA RADES** (IMMIGRANT) b. 18 December 1847 in the village of Saatzig, Province of Pomerania, Parish of Jakobshagen, Prussia. She married Johann Joachim Heinrich "John" Boje 17 November 1869 in Sheboygan Co., Wisconsin. Friederike and John Boje had 4 children during their marriage. Friederike Wilhelmina died 23 May 1915 in the village of Howards Grove, Sheboygan Co., Wisconsin, at the age of 67. She is buried in the Siemers Union Cemetery, Howards Grove, Sheboygan Co., Wisconsin.
	iii.	**AUGUSTA RADES** (IMMIGRANT) b. 4 September 1853 in the village of Saatzig, Province of Pomerania, Parish of Jakobshagen, Prussia. She married Henry H. Peters on 10 December 1871 in the town of Schleswig, Manitowoc Co., Wisconsin. Augusta and Henry H. Peters had 2 children during their marriage. Augusta died 18 January 1938 in Black Creek, Outagamie Co., Wisconsin, at the age of 84. Augusta is buried in the Sassman Cemetery in Black Creek, Outagamie Co., Wisconsin.
	iv.	**FRANZ "FRANK" RADES** (IMMIGRANT) 14 May 1857 in the village of Saatzig, Province of Pomerania, Parish of Jakobshagen, Prussia. He married Wilhelmina Goedeke on 27 August 1877 by the Justice of the Peace in the town of Schleswig, Manitowoc Co., Wisconsin. Franz and Wilhelmina had 9 children during their marriage. Franz died 30 March 1933 near Louis Corners, Manitowoc Co., Wisconsin. They are both buried in the Union Cemetery in Louis Corners, Wisconsin.
	v.	**MARIE RADES** (IMMIGRANT) b. 9 July 1858 in the village of Saatzig, Province of Pomerania, Parish of Jakobshagen, Prussia. She married Wilhelm Friedrich Bleek (anglicized name to William F. Blake) on 23 December 1875 in Outagamie Co., Wisconsin. Marie and William F. Blake had 6 children during their marriage. Marie died. 2 November 1919 in the town of Cicero, Outagamie Co., Wisconsin, at the age of 61. She was buried in Sassman Cemetery, Outagamie Co., Wisconsin.
	vi.	**ALBERTINE RADES** (IMMIGRANT) b. 14 March 1862 in the village of Marienfliess, district of Saatzig, Province of Pomerania, Kingdom of Prussia. She married Joseph Buchholz on 16 March 1880 in the town of Schleswig, Manitowoc Co., Wisconsin. Albertine and Joseph Buchholz had 8 children during their marriage. Albertine died on 21 March 1927 in Milwaukee, Milwaukee Co., Wisconsin, at the age of 65. She was buried in the Schleswig Cemetery, near Rockville, town of Schleswig, Manitowoc Co., Wisconsin.

Two Families Headed to New York

Johann Gottlieb Rades and his wife Justine Vogel left Hamburg, Deutschland, (Germany) with their family aboard the ship *Cimbria* on 20 July 1867. They arrived in the New York harbour 16 days later. They stayed in New York a brief time, living in the Palisades area (a small hamlet in Rockland County in upstate New York). After a short stay of a few months there, they continued onward to the town of Schleswig, Manitowoc, Wisconsin where they purchased 80 acres of land on 30 September 1867.

Johann "Carl" Christian Stammer and his wife Anna Christine Krohn, along with their family, are on the Hamburg Passenger List. They left the port of Hamburg, Deutschland (Germany) on 21 October 1874 and arrived in New York on 6 November 1874.

Son of Johann Gottlieb Rades **Fridrich Wilhelm Rades** met the daughter of Johann Carl Christian Stahmer **Margaretha Stahmer**, Margaretha immigrated with her family on 20 March 1873, and it was one year later that she fell in love with her future husband Fridrich Wilhelm. They were married on 15 April 1874 in the town of Schleswig, Manitowoc Co., Wisconsin by the Justice of the Peace. They had 8 children during their marriage.

The Johann Gottlieb Rades Family was already in the town of Schleswig, Manitowoc Co., Wisconsin by 1867 where he had purchased 80 acres of land there on 30 September 1867.

5. Fridrich Wilhelm Rades (Immigrant)

FRIDRICH WILHELM[5] RADES SR. (Johann Gottlieb[4], Gottlieb[3], Samuel Gottlieb Jr[2], Samuel Gottlieb Sr[1])

- Born 11 March 1845 in the village of Saatzig, district of Saatzig, Province of Pomerania, Kingdom of Prussia.
- Married 15 April 1875 Margaretha Stahmer. She was the daughter of Johann "Carl" Christian Stahmer and Anna "Christine" Krohn. Margaretha and Fridrich Wilhelm were married by the Justice of the Peace in the town of Schleswig, Manitowoc Co., Wisconsin.
- Died 31 May 1919 in Kiel, Manitowoc Co., Wisconsin, at the age of 74.
- Buried in Schleswig Cemetery, near Rockville, town of Schleswig, Manitowoc Co., Wisconsin.

His name is pronounced "FREED-rick VEEL-helm" "RAW - Des"

Fridrich Wilhelm (William) Rades Sr.

(1845-1919)

Children of FRIDRICH WILHELM[5] RADES SR. and MARGARETHA STAHMER were:

6.	i.	**WILHELMINA RADES** b. 1 November 1876 near Rockville, town of Schleswig, Manitowoc Co., Wisconsin. She married Michael Grasser II on 20 February 1898 in the St. Peter and St. Paul Catholic Church in Kiel, Wisconsin. Michael Grasser II (b. 26 February 1874 and died 01 September 1961). He was the son of Stephan Grasser and Maria Fischbach. Wilhelmina and Michael II Grasser had 12 children 9 of which reached adulthood. Wilhelmina died 17 September 1947. She was buried in Calvary Cemetery in Sheboygan, Wisconsin.
	ii.	**BERTHA RADES** b. 26 August 1882 in the town of Schleswig, Manitowoc Co., Wisconsin. She married William "Otto" Louis Paul 3 July 1900 in St. Peter German Congregational Church in Kiel, town of Schleswig, Manitowoc Co., Wisconsin. Bertha and William Paul had 11 children during their marriage. Bertha died 17 November 1932 in the town of Meeme, Manitowoc Co, Wisconsin, at the age of 50. They are both buried in the Ucker Cemetery, Kiel, Manitowoc Co., Wisconsin.
	iii.	**HERMAN RADES** b. 26 August 1884 in the town of Schleswig, Manitowoc Co., Wisconsin. Herman died 3 March 1886 in the town of Schleswig, Manitowoc Co., Wisconsin, as a small child at age 1½ years.
	iv.	**FRIEDRICH WILHELM RADES JR.** b. 26 March 1887 in the town of Schleswig, Manitowoc Co., Wisconsin. He married Elsa Roesch 11 April 1908 in Wisconsin. Friedrich Wilhelm Jr., known in the family as "Uncle Bill Rades," and his wife Elsa had one child, a daughter named Elva Rades Peterson. Frederick William Jr. died 29 February 1968 in Chilton, Calumet Co., Wisconsin, at the age of 80. On his death record as well as his newspaper obituary his name is spelled "Frederick William."
	v.	**EMMA MARIE RADES** b. 22 September 1889 in the town of Schleswig, Manitowoc Co., Wisconsin. She married twice. Husband #1 Edgar Sievert. who was a farmer and a lumber company worker. They were married on 10 December 1907 in the Zion Evangelical-Lutheran Church at Louis Corners in the town of Schleswig, Manitowoc Co., Wisconsin. Husband #2 George Neuman. George was a cheese maker. They were married on 15 April 1925 in Wisconsin. Emma had no children in either marriage. Emma Marie died 6 August 1927 in St. Nicholas Hospital in Sheboygan, Sheboygan Co., Wisconsin, at the age of 37. She was buried with her 1st husband Edgar Sievert in the Ucker Cemetery, town of Schleswig, Manitowoc Co., Wisconsin.
	vi.	**ELSIE MARGARETHA RADES** b. 24 July 1892 in the town of Schleswig, Manitowoc Co., Wisconsin. She married Carl Koeser 10 April 1909 in Wisconsin. Elsie and Carl Koeser had 9 children during their marriage. Elsie Margaretha died 27 August 1953 in her home, town of Herman, Sheboygan Co., Wisconsin, at the age of 61years. She was buried next to her husband, Carl Koeser in the Union Cemetery, Schleswig, Manitowoc Co., Wisconsin.
	vii.	**TWIN: ERNA RADES** b. 4 July 1897 in the town of Schleswig, Manitowoc Co., Wisconsin. Erna died 14 December 1897 at the age of 4 months old in the town of Schleswig, Manitowoc Co., Wisconsin. Erna was buried in the Schleswig Cemetery, near Rockville, Manitowoc Co., Wisconsin.
	viii.	**TWIN: ERWIN RADES** b. 4 July 1897 in the town of Schleswig, Manitowoc Co., Wisconsin. Erwin died 23 December 1897 at the age of 4 months old in the town

		of Schleswig, Manitowoc Co., Wisconsin. Erwin was buried in the Schleswig Cemetery, near Rockville, Manitowoc Co., Wisconsin.

Fridrich Wilhelm Rades Sr. & Margaretha Stahmer with family

Wilhelmina (author's maternal grandmother) is in the center.

6. Wilhelmina Rades

WILHELMINA[6] RADES (Fridrich Wilhelm[5], Johann Gottlieb[4], Gottlieb[3], Samuel Gottlieb Jr[2], Samuel Gottlieb Sr[1])

- Born 1 November 1876 near Rockville, town of Schleswig, Manitowoc Co., Wisconsin.
- Married 20 February 1898 Michael II Grasser. He was the son of Stephan Grasser and Maria Fischbach. Wilhelmina and Michael II were married in the St. Peter and St. Paul Catholic Church, in Kiel, Manitowoc Co., Wisconsin.
- Died 17 September 1947 in St. Nicholas Hospital, in Sheboygan, Sheboygan Co., Wisconsin, at the age of 70. She died of an insulin coma as she adamantly refused insulin injections for her late-onset diabetes mellitus.
- Buried in the Calvary Cemetery, Sheboygan, Sheboygan Co., Wisconsin.

Pioneer Days – A Black Wedding Dress was the Custom

Back in pioneer days, the bride would wear a nice dress – the only fancy dress she owned. It would be a dress that she could wear again at another big festival. My grandmother wore a beautiful dress with lace, but it was black with white lace. The reason for the black was that it did not show any dirt and mud was less noticed. These were pioneer women, and they had a rough life. It was their best dress, but they also were very practical and after hiking to the church or riding on horseback to the church their beautiful black dress was the custom of the day.

Pictured below are the author's maternal grandparents Michael Grasser and Wilhelmina Rades, married February 20th, 1898, Kiel, Wisconsin. Although 50 years after the tradition change in England, in which Queen Victoria introduced the white wedding dress, the poor but practical pioneer women of the Unite States continued wearing the black wedding dress until well after the change into the next century of the 1900s .

Wilhelmina Rades and Michael Grasser II

Wedding Day 20 February 1898

Children of WILHELMINA RADES [6] and MICHAEL GRASSER II are documented in the Grasser chapter.

Author's Reflections about her Maternal Grandmother

Wilhelmina Rades Grasser known as "Minnie Grasser."

Unfortunately, I did not know Grandma Minnie as well as my older cousins knew her. I lived in the Boston area, and she lived in Chicago as well as in northern Wisconsin. When I first met her, I was 2 years old. On my second visit with her I was 5 years old. In my third, and unfortunately, final meeting with her, I was 7 years old. The last time I saw her, I was at camp when she came to see me, and it was a brief visit. However, I absolutely loved her dearly. She was born on November 1st (All Saint's Day), and I think of her every time that date rolls around. She was truly a saint!

I know her mostly through my mother's eyes as well as through my older cousins.

She was loving but also stern! This may be where I get my spunky backbone! She raised 9 children to adulthood as a pioneer woman. When they bought the land in Porterfield, Wisconsin, they built a home upon it. However, while waiting for the house building to be completed, they rented a house down the road to live in. It was on the Kington family farm. It had a dirt floor. This was the home where my mother was born in January 1903. My mother was Minnie's third-born. It was in northern Wisconsin which had very COLD winters. One day a large snake appeared inside the house. Grandma Minnie grabbled the shotgun and did away with the threatening snake! You do not mess with Grandma Minnie! She had three small children in the house at that time. She became very defensive!

Like my Grandma Minnie, I always am running late. They told Grandma Minnie when she attended the school play. "Well, we can begin now as Minnie Grasser has arrived. No one arrives later than she does!"

I think of her as I am making her delicious recipe "Heavenly Delight" Jam which I share with family, friends, and neighbors every Christmas and have done so for years. It is a large recipe and cannot be made smaller. Grandma Minnie never did anything small. When she made a pie, she made 8 pies at one time. She was always working and in primitive conditions. Diapers were always being washed and hung on the clothesline. There was no dryer. There was no bathroom, only an "outhouse." There was no running water – she had to pump the water from the well. Every morning Grandma Minnie was collecting eggs which the chickens had laid, feeding them, and milking the cows. She weeded the garden and was cooking and baking in the kitchen, plus raising and teaching her children. She spoke German as well as English. Before she and Michael married, she left the Lutheran faith and became a Roman Catholic, so that their children would be raised in one faith. Church was three miles down the road and they all faithfully attended Mass as a family every Sunday.

Nothing alarmed her. Even when one of her little ones (who later became a minister) was playing with matches in the barn near the hay pile. Well, the hay caught fire, and little Raymond ran and hid in his mom's (Minnie's) laundry basket. He covered himself with the dirty clothes thinking no one would ever find him. Well, the barn completely burned down, despite neighbors from near and far, trying to assist with buckets of water. There was no fire department to be called. Within weeks the barn was rebuilt by these friendly and kind neighbors. Raymond was found and forgiven but he learned a hard lesson that difficult day!

A tragic happening which caused Grandma Minnie to be heartbroken was the day her son Sylvanus Grasser was killed in World War II in the Pacific Ocean. There is more about his death in the Grasser section of this book.

In Minnie's last years, she was diagnosed as being a diabetic. The family in Chicago advised her to go to Boston, Massachusetts to seek treatment. She and Grandpa Mike made the trip (when I was 7 years old) and she went to the Joslin Clinic at the New England Deaconess Hospital, known worldwide for their expertise in diabetes. They told her she needed insulin by injection. She exclaimed, "You're not putting that new stuff in MY body!" She and Grandpa returned to Chicago where they had retired. Three weeks later she went into a diabetic coma and died. I was personally heartbroken!

Years later, wanting to be a nurse, I chose that hospital (New England Deaconess Hospital School of Nursing) for my schooling where I received my RN training mainly because of Grandma Minnie. I met and worked with Dr. Joslin, one of the founders of our modern-day insulin treatment. He was still alive and working there at the hospital 10 years later after seeing my Grandma Minnie. My first cousin Vivian Grasser became a pharmacist and became a teacher in insulin therapy. Grandma Minnie has influenced so many in our family in so many ways. She was a true treasure and a real saint to behold. I only wish I had known her a little longer!

Source Citations for this Chapter

Allen P. Grasser, "Grasser-Rades Family Genealogy: Familial Data Abstracts," E-mail messages from <agrasser.msj3@gmail.com> at 1453 Vernon Ave.; Park Ridge, IL 60068-1563. From 20 September to 20 October 2021.

1860 United States Federal Census.

1870 United States Federal Census.

New York Passenger and Crew Lists (including Castle Garden and Ellis Island from 1820-1957.

MLM Author's Personal Recollections

Wisconsin State Censuses, 1855-1905.

https://www.ancestry.com.

https://www.findagrave.com/memorial/49592286/johann-gottlieb-rades

https://www.findagrave.com/memorial/49592288/friedrich-wilhelm-rades

Chapter 44: The Retzloffs

The Retzloff Family Line

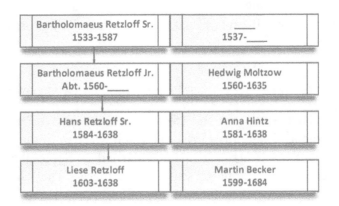

Bartholomaeus Retzloff Sr. 1533-1587	_____ 1537-____
Bartholomaeus Retzloff Jr. Abt. 1560-____	Hedwig Moltzow 1560-1635
Hans Retzloff Sr. 1584-1638	Anna Hintz 1581-1638
Liese Retzloff 1603-1638	Martin Becker 1599-1684

1. Bartholomaeus Retzloff Sr.

BARTHOLOMAEUS [1] RETZLOFF SR.

- Born 1533 in Province of Pomerania, Kingdom of Prussia (which was part of the German Confederation).
- Married 1558 female's name unknown (circa 1533-____). The couple was married in Ball, Pomerania Province, Kingdom of Prussia, Germany.
- Died 1587 in Rehwinkel, district of Saatzig, Pomerania, Kingdom of Prussia (which was a member of the German Confederation). Bartholomaeus Sr. died at age 54.

Children of BARTHOLOMAEUS[1] RETZLOFF and _____ were:

	i.	**GEORG RETZLOFF** b. 1564 in Rehwinkel, district of Saatzig, Province of Pomerania, Kingdom of Prussia (which was part of the German Confederation). Age at death is unknown.
	ii.	**PERPETUA RETZLOFF** b. 1565 in Rehwinkel, district of Saatzig, Province of Pomerania, Kingdom of Prussia (which was part of the German Confederation). Age at death is unknown.
2.	iii.	**BARTHOLOMAEUS JR.** b. circa 1566 in Rehwinkel, district of Saatzig, Province of Pomerania, Kingdom of Prussia. He married Hedwig Moltzow (1560-1635). They had 3 children. Bartholomaeus Jr.'s age at death is unknown.

2. Bartholomaeus Retzloff Jr.

BARTHOLOMAEUS² RETZLOFF JR. (Bartholomaeus¹ Sr.)

- Born 1574 in Province of Pomerania, Kingdom of Prussia (which was part of the German Confederation).
- Married 1583 Hedwig Moltzow (1560-1635). Bartholomaeus Jr. and Hedwig were married in Rehwinkel, Pomerania, Kingdom of Prussia.
- Died ____ in Rehwinkel, district of Saatzig, Pomerania, Kingdom of Prussia. He died at age unknown.

Children of BARTHOLOMAEUS² RETZLOFF JR. and HEDWIG MOLTZOW were:

3.	i.	**HANS RETZLOFF SR.** b. 1584 in Rehwinkel, district of Saatzig, Province of Pomerania, Kingdom of Prussia (which was part of the German Confederation). He married Anna Hintz (1581-1638) married 20 September 1602 in Ball, Province of Pomerania, Kingdom of Prussia, Germany. They had 5 children during their marriage. Hans Sr. died at the age of 54.
	ii.	**ANNA RETZLOFF** b. 1586 in Rehwinkel, district of Saatzig, Province of Pomerania, Kingdom of Prussia (which was part of the German Confederation). Her death date is unknown.
	iii.	**BARTHOLOMAEUS RETZLOFF III** b. 1595 in Rehwinkel, district of Saatzig, Province of Pomerania, Kingdom of Prussia (which was part of the German Confederation). His age at death is unknown.

3. Hans Retzloff Sr.

HANS³ RETZLOFF SR. (Bartholomaeus² Jr., Bartholomaeus¹ Sr.)

- Born in 1584 in Rehwinkel, district of Saatzig, Province of Pomerania, Kingdom of Prussia.
- Married 20 September 1602 Anna Hintz (1581-1638). Hans and Anna were married in Ball, Pomerania, Prussia, Germany. Anna Hintz was the daughter of Martin Hintz (b. 1556 and Sara Classia b. 1560). Hans and Anna had 5 children during their marriage.
- Died 1638 in Rehwinkel, district of Saatzig, Pomerania, Kingdom of Prussia. Hans Sr. died at the age of 54.

Both Hans and Anna died in the same year 1638.

Children of HANS³ RETZLOFF SR. and ANNA HINTZ were:

4.	i.	**LIESE RETZLOFF** b. 1603 in Rehwinkel, district of Saatzig, Province of Pomerania, Kingdom of Prussia. Liese married Michael Becker circa 1617 in Rehwinkel, Pomerania, Prussia. They had 3 children during their marriage. Liese died in 1638 at the age of 35.
	ii.	**ANDREAS RETZLOFF** b. 1613 in Rehwinkel, district of Saatzig, Province of Pomerania, Kingdom of Prussia. Andreas died in 1678 at the age of 65.
	iii.	**JOACHIM RETZLOFF** b. 1618 in Rehwinkel, district of Saatzig, Province of Pomerania, Kingdom of Prussia. Joachim died at age unknown.

	iv.	**TRINA RETZLOFF** b. 1622 in Rehwinkel, district of Saatzig, Province of Pomerania, Kingdom of Prussia. Trina died at age unknown.
	v.	**HANS RETZLOFF JR.** b. 1624 in Rehwinkel, district of Saatzig, Province of Pomerania, Kingdom of Prussia. Hans Jr. died at age unknown.

4. Liese Retzloff

LIESE[4] RETZLOFF (Hans[3] Sr., Bartholomaeus[2] Jr., Bartholomaeus[1] Sr.)

- Born 1603 in Rehwinkel, Province of Pomerania, Kingdom of Prussia.
- Married circa 1617 Martin Becker (1599-1684). Liese and Martin were married in Rehwinkel, Pomerania, Kingdom of Prussia. They had 3 children during their marriage.
- Died 1638 in Rehwinkel, district of Saatzig, Pomerania, Kingdom of Prussia. Liese died at age 35.

Children of LIESE[4] RETZLOFF and MARTIN BECKER are documented in the Becker chapter.

Source Citations for this Chapter

Allen P. Grasser, "Grasser-Rades Family Genealogy: Familial Data Abstracts," E-mail messages from <agrasser.msj3@gmail.com> at 1453 Vernon Ave.; Park Ridge, IL 60068-1563. From 20 September to 20 October 2021.

https://www.ancestry.com.

www.familysearch.org Becker family research

http://www.ancestry.com   Becker family research

Chapter 45: The Wagners

The Wagner Family Line

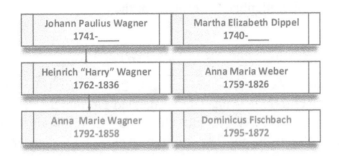

Johann Paulius Wagner 1741-____	Martha Elizabeth Dippel 1740-____
Heinrich "Harry" Wagner 1762-1836	**Anna Maria Weber 1759-1826**
Anna Marie Wagner 1792-1858	Dominicus Fischbach 1795-1872

1. JOHANN PAULIUS WAGNER

JOHANN PAULIUS [1] WAGNER

- Born 1741 Oberellenbach, Germany.
- Married circa 1762 Martha Elizabeth Dippel.
- Died date and place unknown. Age at death is unknown.

Child of JOHANN PAULIUS [1] WAGNER and MARTHA ELIZABETH DIPPEL was:

2.	i.	**HEINRICH "HARRY" WAGNER** b. circa 1825 27 December 1762 Heffingen, Mersch, Luxembourg, Luxembourg. Harry married Anna Maria Weber (1759-18260). Anna Maria was the daughter of Margaretha Thomas. Harry and Anna Maria married in 1778 in Heffingen, Mersch, Luxembourg. Harry and Anna Maria had one child during their marriage. Harry died on 21 February 1836 in Oberellenbach, Germany at the age of 74.

Old Oberellenbach (Bavaria) Germany

2. HEINRICH "HARRY" WAGNER

HEINRICH "HARRY"[2] WAGNER (Johann Paulius[1])

- Born 27 December 1762 Heffingen, Mersch, Luxembourg.
- Married 1778 Anna Maria Weber (1759-1826). Anna Maria was the daughter of Margaretha Thomas. Harry and Anna Maria married in Heffingen, Mersch, Luxembourg.
- Died 21 February 1836 in Oberellenbach, Germany at the age of 74.

Child of HENRICH "HARRY"[2] WAGNER and ANNA MARIE WEBER was:

3.	i.	ANNA MARIE WAGNER (Immigrant) b. 20 October 1792 Hunsdorf, Canton de Mersch, Luxembourg. Anna Marie married Dominicus "Domenick" Fischbach on 10 January 1822 in Grand Duchy of Luxembourg. She immigrated to America with her husband & children. Anna Marie died in 1858 in Cleveland, Manitowoc Co., Wisconsin at age 66.

3. ANNA MARIA WAGNER (IMMIGRANT)

ANNA MARIE[3] WAGNER (Heinrich "Harry"[2] Johann Paulius[1])

- Born 20 October 1792 Hunsdorf, Canton de Mersch, Luxembourg.
- Married 10 January 1822 Dominicus "Domenick" Fischbach in the Grand Duchy of Luxembourg.
- Departure from Antwerpen, Belgium 10 October 1852.
- Arrival in New York 1 December 1852 via the ship the *Lucia Field*.
- Died in 1858 in Cleveland, Manitowoc Co., Wisconsin at the age of 66.

Children of ANNA MARIA[3] WAGNER and DOMINICUS FISCHBACH are documented in the Fischbach chapter.

Source Citations for this Chapter

Allen P. Grasser, "Grasser-Rades Family Genealogy: Familial Data Abstracts," E-mail messages from <agrasser.msj3@gmail.com> at 1453 Vernon Ave.; Park Ridge, IL 60068-1563. From 20 September to 20 October 2021.

New York Passenger and Crew Lists (including Castle Garden and Ellis Island from 1820-1957.

U. S. Find a Grave Index 1600's -> Current.

Wisconsin State Censuses, 1855-1905.

https://www.ancestry.com.

Author's Note

In the kitchen of Abigail Adams, wife of President John Adams, you will find a tiled floor with one tile not in the correct place. Abigail noticed the error and chose to leave it there, stating that it represented her being human and that life is not perfect.

This book has been a labor of love but within these pages you may find a few mistakes, errors in spelling or in punctuation. I have done my best to proofread it but like Abigail, I am truly human.

I hope you have enjoyed this book and will pass it on to future generations and hopefully they will add to the research and add also to the family pages.

Three quotes I leave you from Abigail Adams"

"Great difficulties may be surmounted by patience and perseverance."

***

"No one is without difficulties where in high or low life, and every person knows best where their own shoe pinches."

***

"I desire you would remember the ladies and be more generous and favorable to them than your ancestors."

Quotes of Abigail Adams (1744-1818) who was the wife of

John Adams

2nd President of the United States of America

Printed in the USA
CPSIA information can be obtained
at www.ICGtesting.com
LVHW050831051023
760132LV00008B/151